Jordan

Jordan

Politics in An Accidental Crucible

SEAN YOM

OXFORD
UNIVERSITY PRESS

Oxford University Press is a department of the University of Oxford. It furthers the University's objective of excellence in research, scholarship, and education by publishing worldwide. Oxford is a registered trademark of Oxford University Press in the UK and in certain other countries.

Published in the United States of America by Oxford University Press
198 Madison Avenue, New York, NY 10016, United States of America.

CIP data is on file at the Library of Congress.

ISBN 9780190097264

DOI: 10.1093/oso/9780190097264.001.0001

Printed by Marquis Book Printing, Canada

The manufacturer's authorized representative in the EU for product safety is Oxford University Press España S.A., Parque Empresarial San Fernando de Henares, Avenida de Castilla, 2 – 28830 Madrid (www.oup.es/en or product.safety@oup.com). OUP España S.A. also acts as importer into Spain of products made by the manufacturer.

For Zeynep and Ada, my perpetual present,

And my dearest friends and colleagues in Jordan, for their boundless future.

CONTENTS

PREFACE

This book is a roadmap for understanding the people and politics of the Hashemite Kingdom of Jordan. It is a work of scholarship, but it is not only for scholars. It also informs journalists, policymakers, pundits, diplomats, and other readers generally interested in the Middle East. It takes the style and form of synthesis, balancing depth with accessibility. The goal is to convey useful knowledge about this oft-misunderstood Arab country, beginning first by dispelling the contrived misunderstandings that swirl around it. There are many, including Jordan's own apocryphal creation.

Legend holds that Jordan was conceived by Winston Churchill with the stroke of a pen on a lazy Sunday afternoon in Cairo in 1921. At the height of their imperial power, the British were busily carving up the shattered remnants of the Ottoman Empire. Churchill, then–colonial secretary of the United Kingdom, took it upon himself, after lunch during a stopover in Egypt, to sketch a map of a new Arab country. He did the task, but his drunken, unsteady hand also drew the bizarre zigzag on the Jordanian-Saudi border, now affectionately known as "Winston's Hiccup." That was that: Jordan was all the work of a Western imperial baron sipping brandy under the Egyptian sun.

Repeated obsequiously in popular discussions of Middle East politics, this amusing myth encapsulates why Jordan occupies such a peculiar place in the Western imagination—an Arab country that beckons tourists and travelers with fabled lore, yet its true politics and knotty history hidden from view. British officials indeed convened in Cairo during March 1921 to ruminate over their territorial loot from the Great War. But only in Jerusalem weeks later did Churchill engage the future (and first) monarch of Jordan, Abdullah bin Hussein, as part of a frenetic campaign of postwar diplomacy. Through halting and frustrating discussions, the summitry agreed that Abdullah—son of Britain's wartime Arab ally, Sharif Hussein of Mecca—would not invade French Syria as he intended and would instead accept a six-month experiment of ruling a rural hinterland on the east bank of the Jordan River. Adjacent to historic Palestine, this was an unmarked area that had never before known statehood. No great cities or famed Islamic centers dotted its dusty terrain. Neither the incoming monarchy nor the many communities already living there, each of which carried their own unique identity and history, had much idea of the other. The future was tinged as much by doubt and fear as ambition and hope.

The Emirate of Transjordan thus flickered into existence through not a Cairene fountain pen, its whimsical destiny foretold by the historical gods, but rather an uneasy bargain forged between hesitant politicians in the heat of Palestine. Nobody could have imagined the political order that would eventually coalesce on these desert steppes. Following World War II, this fledgling state gained formal independence from Britain to become the Hashemite Kingdom of Jordan. Not long after, it would treble in population by absorbing many of the Palestinian refugees from the 1948 Arab-Israeli War. In the succeeding decades, Jordan rapidly modernized, its cities and populace growing as fast as the power of its kingship and military. It gave rise to democratic struggles, authoritarian impulses, and regional aspirations. Its monarchical regime would retrench, reorganize, and rule; its people would tussle, mobilize, and work. Their shared political dramas and economic traumas would shake the country's fabric but leave behind a remarkable feat: to this day, Jordan is the rare Arab state that has never seen mass revolution, institutional collapse, or regime change, unlike some of its neighbors and much of the Middle East.

Such basic facts are little appreciated by the outside world, except for a hardy band of academic experts who have devoted their careers studying Jordan. But beyond correcting antiquated parables, why should anyone outside the Middle East care about Jordan today? To be sure, this is a diminutive country. Three dozen cities around the world each have more people than Jordan's entire population, and its economy is among the smallest in the Middle East. What it lacks in size, though, Jordan makes up in relevance. Wedged between Israel, Syria, Iraq, and Saudi Arabia, and almost touching Lebanon and Egypt at their closest points, Jordan lies proximate to the epic events that continue to sculpt the Middle East and fill Westerners with anxiety—the Israeli-Palestinian conflict, wars in Syria and Iraq, senseless terrorism, revolutionary uprisings like the Arab Spring, the waxing and waning of Islamist ideology, and other headline-grabbing trends. Jordan, by itself, does not create crises. Yet it is always touched by them, and so will always matter whenever global powers like the United States seek to influence, control, and define this region.

For another, peek underneath the Hashemite Kingdom's docile exterior nowadays, where a seemingly placid public ruled by a proud Muslim dynasty welcomes visitors with open arms. Jordanian politics are not so placid, because how this outwardly stable place coheres together raises tantalizing puzzles that should interest all aficionados of modern politics and international affairs. How does an authoritarian monarchy that never needs to win elections exercise its power and claim popular legitimacy? When does a population obey, or resist, a government that demands obedience behind phalanxes of soldiers and police? How do courageous democratic movements representing workers, women, youths, and other marginalized voices protest for greater rights? Why does an economy infused by massive foreign aid and guided by enterprising capitalist reforms always flounder? How does a weak country with indefensible borders interact with bigger neighbors, hostile rivals, regional conflicts, and a daunting world?

The answers to these questions are complicated. This is for good reason: in the Middle East, the only thing worse than simple questions are simple answers, because just a little bit of knowledge can be a dangerous thing. Jordan gives complex, but provocative, answers to these timeless questions. Indeed, it has a fractal-like quality. The more one peers into its state and society, the more elaborate and mesmerizing the picture becomes. Hence the title of this book: however accidental its historical genesis might have been, Jordan has become a crucible of knowledge about how autocratic governance, democratic opposition, economic institutions, and geopolitical intrigue operate in the Middle East and, more broadly, the modern world.

In penning this book, I drew upon a variety of sources. These include written works, such as English and Arabic-language books, journal articles, policy briefings, media clippings, and government reports. Political science theories, historical evidence, and empirical data all figure into the following pages. More important, however, has been the personal knowledge gleaned from many trips to Jordan since 2006. Much of what I have learned of this country has come from the numerous Jordanian reporters, officials, activists, students, teachers, professionals, humanitarians, diplomats, scholars, and above all friends who lent me their time and expertise. Our interviews and discussions, a small spattering of which are referenced in this book, took place in copious locales that made Jordan feel like a second home across two decades of my life—houses, cafes, offices, restaurants, taxis, markets, bookstores, rooftops, lobbies, and streets.

This book conveys this accumulated knowledge while illustrating a singular point. Jordan cannot be reduced to the banalities of orientalist folklore, much less the other tropes that have long garbled how the Western media describe the kingdom: a resilient state survivor that should be happy it merely exists, an oasis of moderation and stability in a sea of Middle East extremism, or the last redoubt of a fabled Islamic kingship. Only by thoughtfully peeling back these layers, with patience and open eyes, can we appreciate what politics truly entails in this fascinating corner of the world.

ACKNOWLEDGMENTS

Penning this volume was a labor of love. I am indebted, firstly, to countless Jordanian friends who over the years have lent inexhaustible time and knowledge during my stays in their country. Among these magnanimous souls are Mohammad al-Momani, Wael al-Khatib, Marwan Kardoosh, and Katrina Sammour. I will never forget their wisdom, or their willingness to entertain even my silliest questions over the past decades. I have also benefited from the fathomless generosity of many other Jordanians since my first days traversing the Hashemite Kingdom in 2005, who are too countless to name. This is a complicated country, but it is also a most hospitable and gracious one.

My senior academic colleagues, who like me constitute the small canon of Jordan specialists, have long inspired my scholarship—and more importantly served as role models on how to conduct patient fieldwork and write rigorous analysis in the Middle East when I began studying Jordan. Among them are Curtis Ryan, Jillian Schwedler, Marc Lynch, Pete Moore, Janine Clark, and Laurie Brand. Astute readers will note that their works make gratuitous appearances in the following pages, alongside those of many other brilliant researchers and writers, especially from Jordan. Some of these innumerable colleagues courteously provided comments to early drafts of my book, consummating the sense of community that has long bound the field of Jordanian studies.

Temple University has been my institutional home since 2010, and it has always sustained my scholarship. I am grateful for the research support and sabbatical given in recent years that enabled me to finish this volume, especially during and after the Covid-19 pandemic.

I owe David McBride, formerly at Oxford University Press, endless thanks for encouraging this project from the start. David's enthusiasm was matched only by his patience and commitment, not to mention his golden advice to think beyond the bricks we fashion to build our walls of knowledge and instead to rethink the purpose of those walls themselves. No author could ask for more from an editor. His crack editorial team and production staff at the press also handled this book superbly, while external reviewers furnished decisive feedback along the way.

Finally, I give my wife, Zeynep, infinite credit for tolerating my inanities with endless love and compassion while sharing the radiant joy of welcoming our daughter, Ada Maryam, to the world as I wrote this book. Authoring books is hard; authoring new life is cosmic. I am blessed to have experienced both.

NOTES ON TRANSLITERATION

Transliterating Arabic into English is always a perilous process. While many academic conventions exist, this book follows a quotidian approach. Common names, places, and terms in Arabic are written as how they most frequently appear in other popular works in English, so as to ensure easy recognition. Little-known words and phrases, such as titles of Arabic books and articles cited as references, are transliterated according to the technical system used by the *International Journal of Middle East Studies,* absent most diacritics excepting hamzation and ʿayn.

1

Myth-Busting over the River Jordan

Why Should We Care about the Hashemite Kingdom?

In 2021, the Hashemite Kingdom of Jordan celebrated its centennial. Most of the world did not notice, and for good reason. Since its colonial birth, Jordan has been defined by what it is *not*—not big, not rich, and not powerful. In its early years, few expected such a meager kingdom in the heart of the Arab world to outlast the British Empire that spawned it. Fewer still thought Jordan would withstand the upheavals that befell the Middle East and North Africa (MENA) after European colonialism gave way to an era of independence. For generations following World War II, kings fell, armies marched, nations seethed, rebellions exploded, markets crumbled, and oil flowed across the region. Wars came and went; terrorism came and stayed. Democratic dreams shattered against the misery of unyielding dictatorships, which surrendered power only when overwhelmed by endless protests or besieging armies. Small, poor, and weak states like Jordan were not supposed to withstand this terrible gauntlet.

Yet it has. Jordan has stood for more than a century, having experienced none of the revolutions or regime changes that have roiled the geographic crescent around it. Its current leader, King Abdullah II, was enthroned in February 1999; this makes him the longest-serving national ruler in the MENA region. These facts alone would seem incredibly illogical to many who observed this small kingdom over the past 100 years. Beyond its longevity, though, are two more tangible facts about this country. First, the West needs Jordan. It is an open country whose Hashemite monarchy has long supported the interests of the United States and its European allies in the Middle East—for better or for worse—such as waging war, containing Iran, countering terrorism, and protecting Israel. As its global patron, the United States especially values the kingdom's cooperation given its unpredictable neighborhood. Jordan is jammed between Israel,

Palestine, Lebanon, Syria, Iraq, and Saudi Arabia. This area has generated numerous crises since the mid-twentieth century; the Arab-Israeli wars, several Palestinian intifadas, the 2003 Iraq War, the Syrian Civil War, and the Gaza War that began in 2023 are among the most wrenching. The kingdom was swept up in the wave of popular uprisings known as the Arab Spring during 2011–2012, which brought a new era of people power and political conflict to the Middle East. Lying close to such dangers but never upended by them, Jordan is a perplexing case of stability and steadfastness under the awnings of American hegemony.

Second, more salient than its strategic repute in Western capitals, Jordan has intrinsic importance as a contemporary state in the Global South that has sprouted ever-evolving political dramas despite its contrived origins. It houses a system of government and vocal society that encapsulate the most endearing topics within the study of comparative politics and international affairs. It brims with paradoxes that buck common theories about what modern countries should look like. Here is one of the world's last true ruling monarchies, an authoritarian regime that flaunts its dynastic regalia and exercises power through an eclectic mix of targeted repression and public outreach. A sluggish national economy produces little of value and flirts with insolvency, but somehow meanders onward. Elections occur, citizens vote, and opposition groups utter sharp dissent because few citizens live in absolute fear of tyranny. Yet this is still no democracy, because ordinary people cannot choose who makes the rules that dictate their lives, and social forces like the Muslim Brotherhood and teachers' union suffer crackdowns when they become too critical. Citizens protest over all sorts of issues—political restrictions, Palestinian injustice, women's rights, high unemployment, widespread corruption—though seldom to the point of revolutionary violence. Foreign policy likewise stumbles through boundless contradictions. Jordan is a small state, more a follower than leader in regional affairs; but its royal leadership cycles through war, peace, alliances, and rivalries like a mercenary, while absorbing as much foreign aid as the West and other donors give. The majority of citizens in this kingdom have Palestinian heritage, but Jordan is not Palestine, and its monarchy and society alike are deeply affected by every violent spasm from the neighboring Israeli-Palestinian conflict.

There are few countries where all these beating pulses of twenty-first century politics—aspirations for democracy, the durability of despotism, the rawness of people power, the misery of economic torpor, a creative foreign policy, a clouded peace process—collide together in the same cramped territorial space. And none are what Jordan is: a not-big, not-rich, and not-powerful place that happens to be a peace partner of Israel that is also awash with American dollars and Western guns.

A Practical Framework

This book unpacks the complicated layers of this paramount Arab state. This is not an instant read about current events in Jordan, which tend to become dated quickly. Neither is this a traditional academic study, even though it draws upon a heap of Middle East scholarship and theoretical works to make its conclusions. Nor is this a standard history, a chronology that puts all the people and dates of Jordan's past in linear order—not least because impressive histories of Jordan already exist.[1] This volume, rather, does something more elusive: it provides a roadmap to the kingdom's state and society. Politics is about rule-making—how power is structured, exercised, and contested across governing institutions, the economy, society, and foreign relations. In that spirit, this book clarifies *who* rules Jordan, *who* are asked to follow those rules, *what* happens when they refuse, and *how* those rules configure the domestic economy and foreign relations.

This commonsense approach is needed more than ever, given what we might call the conventional wisdom on the Hashemite Kingdom. Within academic circles, a hardy bunch of social scientists spanning political science, history, sociology, anthropology, and adjacent disciplines have produced a small but magnificent literature about Jordanian affairs for decades. But like much scholarship, such specialized expertise seldom seeps into the public sphere. Instead, when audiences of interested readers, curious listeners, and social media perusers seek stories and news about Jordan, they have few places to turn. They become captive instead to narrow stereotypes peddled by pundits, policymakers, and other interlocutors who have little real knowledge of the country. Such conventional wisdom functions as the pithy answer to a quick Google search or a ChatGPT query asking, "What is Jordan?"

For instance, Jordan is often described as a triumphant story of stability amid crisis, the dogged Arab survivor that always resides on the brink of disaster due to economic or social strife. Somehow, though, it refuses to collapse while living on the edge, which shows an astonishing knack for persistence. In this sense, Jordan is an island of stability and resilience. For foreign policy wonks, Jordan is something else—a sanctuary of pro-Western moderation and a strategic ally from which Western powers can temper the Middle East. Its monarchy and people appear an affable bunch, willing to host American troops and endorse US interests across the region. The West must admire the kingdom and even defend it from the bitter bloods of its surrounding environs. Jordan is an oasis of geopolitical calm. For still others, Jordan is the stomping ground of its ruling Hashemite monarchy, whose dynastic lineage beckons to a more celebrated time of Islamic grandeur. Jordanian politics hence expresses the heroism of its larger-than-life rulers, who flirt with danger and dabble in diplomacy. In stoically defending their nation, these gutsy leaders prove that kings still have a place in the world. Jordan therefore embodies the grit and glitz of modern royalism.

Consider these three tropes: the obstinate survivor, the geopolitical stronghold, the Arabian stockade of royal glory. In the United States, ceaseless news articles and foreign policy discussions of Jordan traffic in these clichés. They appear in congressional speeches, classroom lectures, public seminars, and think tank reports. But such typecasting reflects more of what Jordan is *supposed* to be to outsiders rather than what it actually *is* on its own terms. Truly understanding its politics requires debunking this misguided lore and taking an honest look across the panorama of the country's government, society, economy, and foreign policy.

To that end, the chapters proceed as follows. The remainder of this first chapter situates Jordan against its historical and regional milieu. It explains why this kingdom has drawn more Western attention over the past two decades: what was once known as a "boring" Arab country has become a more visible—and *visitable*—destination for outsiders unfamiliar with the Middle East. It examines the stereotypical motifs that blur knowledge of the country's politics, in particular colorless images of Jordan as the perennial survivor, a geopolitical oasis, or embodiment of royalism. It finally ends with a few useful conclusions that guide the next chapters regarding the legacies of the past, the fluidity of the present, and the unexpected nature of change.

Chapter 2 paints an overview of Jordan's people. For such a small society, the Hashemite Kingdom has astonishing pluralism. With every furrow of diversity, though, comes a political implication. Its extremely urbanized and youthful population pulses with energy and creativity—including demands for more economic opportunities and democratic rights, which authorities cannot provide. Most Jordanians are Sunni Muslim, but the government approaches this predominant faith with an eye toward regulating and controlling Islam. Many religious and social minorities exist, yet each has fared differently: compare the political comfort of many Arab Christians and Circassian Muslims, for instance, against the marginalized status of refugees. And above all, citizens of all stripes struggle to find a common national identity that involves something other than hailing Hashemite rule. A major reason why no coherent sense of "Jordan-ness" exists is the historical divide between the Palestinian-origin majority and the tribal (i.e., Transjordanian) minority. This remains the most salient, if fading, social wrinkle in modern Jordan and continues to influence political relationships.

Chapter 3 pivots from society to the state and fastidiously peels back the curtains onto the political institutions that govern Jordan. The Hashemite Kingdom is not a democracy, despite its officials dowsing Western audiences with liberal rhetoric. The monarchy heads an authoritarian regime, where the rules that shape people's lives are determined not by electoral results but by an opaque set of unelected decision-makers. Those powerful figures include the king and his palace; a coercive apparatus comprising the military, police, and intelligence services; the cabinet government, headed by a royally-ordained Prime Minister; and a vast public bureaucracy that operates the state itself. Within this political elite class of royals, advisers, ministers, generals, and functionaries are certain pathologies often found in other autocracies, such as endemic favoritism and ingrained corruption. High politics essentially operates like a closed circle, giving ordinary people trivial influence with their state. The elected lower house of parliament has little say in controlling the most important national affairs, from setting foreign policy to formulating the budget; likewise, local governments—even when elected—do relatively little.

Chapter 4 delves into this framework of government to answer a burning question: how does this bluntly nondemocratic system stay in power? Two mechanisms fuel Jordanian autocracy: coercion and coalitions. This regime commands many men with guns through the military, police, and intelligence directorate—organs of violence that specialize in quashing not just terrorism and extremism but also peaceful dissent. Manipulative laws and softer tactics of intimidation further encage political critics. Despite this repressive carapace, though, the monarchy does not rule from a bunker. Historically, it has drawn loyalty and support from mostly Transjordanian communities, in particular East Bank tribes. Whereas many Palestinian-Jordanians suffer political marginalization, many tribal groups have long received special benefits in return for endorsing royal authority. They almost exclusively staff the army and police and represent the regime's social base. Since King Abdullah assumed power in 1999, economic and political frustrations have upset many Transjordanians and eroded this tribal-state bargain. Still, enough East Bank tribes wearily stick by the monarchy to ensure its power remains secure.

Chapter 5 considers the fiery issue of why Jordan has not democratized. It sets aside Western assumptions that Arab culture and despotism go hand in hand: when it comes to democracy, Jordanians are no quiet bunch. They have always criticized their government and demanded more political participation. Indeed, Jordan's history is marked by several epic "near-miss" moments of *potential* democratization, in which popular uprisings seriously challenged royal power. The Transjordanian National Congresses of the early 1930s, the Jordanian National Movement of the 1950s, and the efflorescence of civil society in the 1990s all embodied voices of collective dissidence insisting that the monarchy share power and change its ways. Through violence and co-optation, the ruling autocracy managed to outlast them all. Still, these clashes seriously disrupted national politics and represented episodes of democratic hope. They also forced the Hashemite regime to adapt. Today, it has learned to exercise power through a shrewd set of strategies known as liberalized autocracy, mixing soft democratic elements with hard authoritarian practices. Officials tolerate some dissent but crush the loudest critics, whether online or on the street; they champion parliamentary elections, but only after hobbling opposition parties and rendering the legislature powerless; and they issue never-ending promises of superficial democratic reform designed to fail.

Chapter 6 zooms into the dynamic of the streets, which have witnessed swells of contentious mobilization during the quarter-century reign of King Abdullah. Jordanians protest frequently over grievances such as economic hardship, autocratic repression, widespread corruption, and the peace treaty with Israel. The 2011–2012 Arab Spring gave rise to thousands of demonstrations and rallies, but these were not the only years where the indomitable enthusiasm of popular opposition spilled into public life. For decades, an assortment of peaceful groups—civil society organizations, trade unions, Islamists, tribal networks, grassroots movements, and more—have pioneered daring confrontations with the government. These activists are not revolutionary. They do not want to overthrow the monarchy, but they do want a better economy, more political rights, less corruption, and a more independent foreign policy that is less reliant upon the United States and its Western allies. They have espoused creative strategies of mobilization, which compel authorities to fight back with legal tools, coercive weaponry, and tribal support to resist these tides of contestation. Nonetheless, their perpetual mobilization highlights an ebullient truth: Jordanians are loud, proud, and hungry for change.

Chapter 7 analyzes the Jordanian economy, whose stunted development hangs over national politics. It is small, does not grow consistently, has limited wealth, and nurtures few competitive industries. High unemployment, poverty, and inequality pervade the lives of many. Such a sorry outcome stems from many sources. One is the surrounding region, as frequent conflicts and geopolitical pressures often disrupt Jordan's trade and commerce. Another is the natural environment: the resource-poor country has little water and must import most of its energy and food at considerable cost. Atop this, however, political imperatives from the authoritarian regime have subverted the best-laid economic plans. The monarchy embraced neoliberal, or market-oriented, capitalist reforms after the 1990s following a dreadful financial crisis. Yet reflecting past habits, officials have also continued overspending on the military and security, privileging a rich business elite, maintaining an inefficient and costly public sector, and devouring foreign aid from key donors such as the United States and World Bank. In the end, such measures skew development toward narrow goals and ensure the economy barely grows.

Chapter 8 shifts from the domestic to the international, catapulting foreign relations into the forefront. Viewed from the outside, Jordan is a small, poor, and weak state. Still, the Hashemite Kingdom's foreign policy—led by its monarchy, with little room for public contribution—delivers a captivating window into how a country that cannot buy or bully its way through the Middle East navigates a hazardous world. Historically, this royal autocracy has calibrated its external strategies to neutralize whatever palpable threat appears most imminent, such as hostile states, radical ideologies, and domestic pressures. It frequently cycles through alliances and rivalries to maximize its security. There are two constants, though. One is Jordan's avowedly pro-Western stance anchored by a tight alliance with America. The United States has furnished vital lifelines of diplomatic support, economic aid, and military assistance to Amman since the 1950s; in effect, Jordan has become an American client state. Yet this has not helped resolve the existential predicament of the neighboring Israeli-Palestinian conflict, the other foreign policy constant. No other Arab country has as great of a stake in crafting a permanent peace settlement that would allow for a sovereign Palestinian state independent of Israel. As this tragedy grows more violent and unsettled, fears of instability stalk the kingdom.

The final chapter provides lasting reflections. It delivers the core insights of the book, accentuates the usable conclusions, and anticipates the untrodden future of this vibrant Middle East country.

From the Margins to the Limelight

A few facts acclimate strangers to the Hashemite Kingdom of Jordan (Map 1.1). This is a small country. The area enclosed by its kinked borders occupies a tad under 35,000 square miles, the same size as Portugal or the US state of Indiana. Geologically, this expanse of land straddles the northern stretches of the Arabian plateau. From west to east, it encompasses three environmental zones.[2] First, along Jordan's western borders with Israel and the West Bank runs the fertile Jordan Valley. Within this temperate band runs the famous Jordan River (from which the kingdom derives its Arabic name, *Al-Urdun*), the kingdom's major perennial river. Second, to the east of the Jordan Valley slopes the central highlands. Most of Jordan's inhabitants reside on these steppes, mostly within or close to the three core cities: the sprawling capital of Amman, followed distantly in size by Irbid and Zarqa. The rest live in towns and rural villages, the number and size shrinking as one moves away from these urbanized centers. Third, to the east and south of this central strip juts out the rest of Jordan, comprising a *baadia* (desert) interspersed by dunes and mountains. The breathtaking red canyons of Wadi Rum are here; so too is the kingdom's tiny coastline, a 16-mile southern shore along the Red Sea around the port city of Aqaba.

Map 1.1 Jordan and the Mashriq. Source: Reproduced with permission from iStock.

Geographically, Jordan resides in the center of the Levant (in Arabic, *Mashriq*), the chunk of the MENA adjoining North Africa, Anatolia, and the Arabian Peninsula. Its borders touch Israel, Palestine, Syria, Iraq, and Saudi Arabia, with Lebanon and Egypt not far off (Map 1.2). Historically, Western cartographers termed this territorial area as Transjordan, with the Latin prefix "trans" meaning across—as in, literally, the eastern lands across the Jordan River. In Arabic, Transjordan is spoken as *Sharq al-Urdun* (in English, the East Bank).

Those Jordanians today considered "Transjordanian" or "East Banker" have old ties to this land. Most descend from the mostly tribal Arab communities that lived here before British imperialism turned the area into an emirate in 1921. Some migrated to Transjordan during previous centuries, when this expanse fell under the sway of the Ottoman Empire. By contrast, another key social force—the Palestinians—came in great numbers after the 1948 and 1967 Arab-Israeli wars. Most of these refugees gained Jordanian nationality early on but never carried the political influence of the East Bank tribes. As the next chapter discusses, the resulting rift between Transjordanians and Palestinian-Jordanians

Map 1.2 Jordan. Major towns and cities marked. Source: Reproduced with permission from iStock.

is a convoluted issue that cuts through the state, economy, and society. It partly explains why many citizens struggle to define who is Jordanian and what Jordanian identity means.

Over time, Jordan's population has grown tremendously. When the British created the country in 1921, it held well under a quarter-million Transjordanians. By 2025, it boasted over 11.5 million people—more than neighboring Israel, Palestine, or Lebanon. Of this total, approximately 70 percent are citizens, and of the citizenry, the majority are of Palestinian origin. Among noncitizens are around a million foreign workers (although only one-third are officially documented by the government). Refugees compose most of the remaining non-citizen population. Among Jordan's sizable refugee communities are Palestinians who arrived after the 1967 Arab-Israeli War and were never granted Jordanian nationality (Palestinians who came earlier, for the most part, became Jordanian citizens), Iraqis who fled to Jordan after the 2003 Iraq War, and the nearly million Syrians who came during the Syrian Civil War after 2011.

Despite this diverse social tapestry, Jordan is the canonical definition of a small state. Such smallness has concrete implications. Forget great power status: Jordan has never been even a regional power in strategic terms, one capable of waging war alone or dominating Middle East affairs. As Chapter 7 discusses, the lightly industrialized economy is no world-beater. Gross domestic product (GDP) per capita measures about $4,600—not quite impoverished, but closer to poor than rich. This puts the country's social depth into perspective. Jordan is one of the most educated countries in the MENA, with over 99 percent literacy. Yet overall unemployment is well over 20 percent, with youth joblessness at least double that. Few people starve, but rising inequality and job shortages expose the limits of what this wispy economy can sustain.

From a Marginal State . . .

For all its marginal size, though, Jordan's past is a cultural treasure. The country is renowned among scholars of antiquity, given its location as the crossroads of different ancient civilizations. It boasts a half-dozen UNESCO World Heritage sites. The East Bank has biblical relevance; it gave rise to the Kingdom of Moab, while Mount Nebo, the Dead Sea, the Jordan River, and other locales are evoked in Abrahamic scripture. John the Baptist baptized Jesus Christ here, and that holy site on the Jordan River (Bethany Beyond the Jordan, or in Arabic *Al-Maghtas*) attracts Christian pilgrims. From the third century BC, the Nabataean Kingdom flourished from its capital city of Petra—now a major attraction in southern Jordan, whose exquisitely preserved buildings still jut out from red sandstone hills and canyons. The Romans conquered Transjordan in the first century AD, and their ruins scatter the town of Jerash and elsewhere across the central highlands. Then came the Byzantines, who also left behind impressive edifices such as Christian churches and giant mosaic maps, of which the best examples exist in Madaba. Islam arrived in the seventh century AD, and soon the entire Mashriq became subsumed into successive caliphates. An old Umayyad palace still stands in downtown Amman, alongside older Roman ruins. The area then hosted fierce battles during the Crusades, which left behind formidable citadels and castles, such as in the towns of Karak and Ajloun.

Yet while archaeologists know Jordan by its ancient past, most other Westerners had little reason to notice the area until the twentieth century. By World War I, Transjordan was "one of the blank spots on the globe" for most foreigners, for good reason.[3] Transjordan did not give rise to any coherent political state after antiquity. The Islamic caliphates ruled this hinterland but never assigned it much importance; the cities of Cairo, Damascus, and Baghdad were the true centers of Muslim civilization. The Ottoman Empire came in the sixteenth century, but only saw the East Bank as an unproductive expanse filled with resistant Arab tribes, mainly peasant farmers and nomads (i.e., Bedouin). Merchant caravans and Muslim pilgrims transiting to Mecca plied their way through this peripheral wilderness, stopping only at a few major towns like Ma'an. Amman, the future capital, was little more than a large village as late as the 1900s.

War changed this. World War I saw not just the disintegration of the Ottoman Empire but also a chain of imperial events culminating in Jordan's creation. The Great Arab Revolt began in 1916, when the British collaborated with the Islamic steward of Mecca, Sharif Hussein bin Ali, whose Hashemite dynasty ruled much of the Hijaz region in what is now Saudi Arabia. Their insurrection passed north across the East Bank until it reached Damascus. Today, that Arab moment still pervades the symbolism of Jordan's state and monarchy; even the national flag—with its white-starred red triangle transposed upon black, white, and green stripes—is mostly borrowed from the banner of Sharif Hussein's forces during the Great Arab Revolt.

Sharif Hussein hoped the British would grant him a unified Arab state covering much of the Mashriq after the war. The 1916 Sykes-Picot Agreement and 1920 San Remo Conference dashed that revery. Instead, Britain and France chiseled colonial protectorates from these former Ottoman lands. Jordan emerged from this postwar shuffle. The game of thrones began in 1920, when French dominion over Syria ejected Faisal, Sharif Hussein's third son, from his proclaimed rulership in Damascus. The British transferred the disappointed Hashemite to Baghdad and thereby created Iraq, although revolution would end this monarchy decades later. In 1921, they likewise crafted another protectorate—the Emirate of Transjordan—and convinced another son of Sharif Hussein, Abdullah, to rule over it.

From these unpropitious circumstances crystallized a new state on the East Bank. Yet, the fledgling kingdom was still an afterthought: it was smaller than Iraq, and it was poorer than the British Mandate of Palestine and French Syria as well. During the 1920s through World War II, the British saw Jordan as a dull stop along the military basing and trade networks that kept their empire together. A bit more international relevance came after World War II. Jordan became an independent sovereign state in 1946, but besides offering allyship, the kingdom had little that interested the West. It had no oil to pump and no large military to mobilize. Despite its hallowed religious credentials of descending from the Prophet Muhammad, which in centuries prior had served as the foundational identity for the Hashemite dynasty when it ruled over Mecca, the monarchy had no transcendent ideology that electrified the masses of an Arab world entering an era of post-colonial sovereignty, unlike Egypt's Nasserist regime with its Arab Nationalist creed.

Throughout the Cold War, intellectual trends tracked closely with this marginal status, with Jordan near the bottom of the regional pecking order. Few Western envoys from academia, think tanks, and government circles flocked to the country. As one doyen of Jordanian studies conceded after the 1990s, "Let's face it: works on Jordan have rarely gained the kind of recognition among Middle East scholars as those about Egypt, Palestine, and Syria. . . . [Jordan's] size and influence have rarely matched up against the main power brokers in the region."[4] For decades, bookshelves about Middle East politics and history were filled with volumes on these other states, but rare was the monograph on Jordan.

Through the late twentieth century, likewise, Western journalists covering regional affairs based their operations not in Amman, capital of what many derided as the "Hashemite Kingdom of Boredom," but instead from more adventurous destinations like Casablanca, Jerusalem, and Cairo. Beirut, for instance, was the "Paris of the East," garnering poetic rhapsodies by a generation of Western expatriates based there.[5] By contrast, Jordan looked staid and dull. In sleepy Amman, there were few terrorists and conspirers to interview; but in more exciting places like Lebanon or Algeria, one need only "wait for the front to visit you."[6]

. . . To a Popular Place

This has all changed in the twenty-first century. Jordan has become among the most inviting destinations for foreign researchers, travelers, and tourists seeking a slice of the Middle East—or what one sardonic Jordanian observer calls "Arabia for beginners."[7] Its heightened prominence has come at the convergence of two trends. First, Jordan has been closely tied to the militarized footprint of American hegemony in the post–Cold War era. Having signed a peace treaty with Israel in 1994, the Hashemite monarchy became integral to subsequent US projects to reshape the Arab world, such as the 2003 invasion of Iraq and the War on Terror after 9/11. Those in Amman during the Iraq War recall the many Western contractors, humanitarians, and soldiers who crowded its bars and hotels on account of its convenient proximity and perceived safety. As Jordan created stronger diplomatic and cultural linkages with the West, it also gained more favorable exposure.

The second trend came from a bit of irony. Crises elsewhere in the MENA made Jordan's relative calm, once an unflattering quality, a positive attribute. This became apparent during the 2000s, when the country seemed surrounded by anarchy. The Al-Aqsa Intifada in Palestine raged across the Jordan River to the west, and to the east, America invaded and occupied Iraq, triggering internecine violence. In the summer of 2006, Hezbollah and Israel also fought a bloody war in southern Lebanon. The ominous threat of Salafi-jihadist terrorism, personified by Al-Qaeda, loomed large over the entire region. Yet apart from the 2005 Amman hotel bombings—a tragic but fortunately rare terrorist strike—political order seemed secure on the East Bank. There were no invasions or insurgencies, no carnage or revolution in this ambit of the Middle East.

The 2011–2012 Arab Spring magnified this sense of serenity. Jordan experienced thousands of protests during those years. However, there was hardly any violence. Bystanders could not help but contrast this with unnerving events elsewhere. Pessimists compared the Middle East during the Arab Spring to Europe prior to World War I, warning that its "chain reactions" of uprisings, counterrevolutions, and terrorism would obliterate the region.[8] Yet Jordan did not suffer civil war, like Syria and Iraq did. Its state institutions did not crumple, as they did in Libya and Yemen. Neither did it experience a military coup like Egypt in 2013 or ruthless crackdowns as occurred in Saudi Arabia and Bahrain. It did absorb many Syrian refugees and endure ugly attacks by the Islamic State of Iraq and Syria (ISIS), but these did not cause any institutions to collapse. In essence, Jordan resided safely outside the foreboding Western lexicon used to describe the MENA—failed states, revolutionary rage, sectarian slaughter, and radicalized extremism. The flotilla of Western humanitarian groups that came to the kingdom during the 2010s, some drawn to its Syrian refugee communities and others seeking a secure base for their entire Middle East operations, would agree.

That Jordan enjoys elevated standing under Western eyes shows in several respects. One is the spurt of intellectual traffic that now winds through the kingdom. What was previously a small but hardy troupe of social scientists studying the country broadened by the mid-2000s as a younger generation of scholars flocked to the kingdom. As one metric, between 1960 and 1999, the *International Journal of Middle East Studies* and the *Middle East Journal*, two leading English-language scholarly outlets about Middle East affairs, published fewer than twenty full-length articles dedicated to the country. In the next two decades, well over forty research essays on Jordan graced their pages (i.e., more than twice the coverage in half the time).[9] The number of scholarly books devoted to Jordan's politics, economics, and society has also sharply risen since the 1990s, signaling how the country's openness has attracted social scientists and humanists hoping to undertake ethnographies, surveys, and other research projects. By contrast, formerly popular destinations in the MENA such as Egypt,

Syria, and most of the Gulf kingdoms became less enticing locales for research after the Arab Spring due to either ongoing violence or government repression.

Jordan's repute as a tranquil locale in the Middle East in recent decades has also helped elevate its global profile. The government has invested heavily in marketing its cultural heritage and antiquities to international audiences, framing the kingdom as the rare Arab sanctuary that dutifully maintains its ancient lineage for all of humanity.[10] Archaeological sites like Petra frequently make touristic bucket lists and *Condé Nast* travelogues, drawing their fair share of celebrity visitors like Oprah Winfrey. Tourists have come to the kingdom in ever-increasing numbers: in 2023, Jordan recorded 6.4 million tourists, shattering its pre–Covid 19 pandemic record. This glowing impression has been amplified by newsworthy moments that cast Jordan onto the world stage, like the papal visits of 2009 and 2014. Hollywood blockbusters such as *Aladdin, The Martian,* and *Dune* were filmed in the picturesque Wadi Rum area in the southern desert, which makes for a convenient stand-in for alien landscapes.[11] The acclaimed 2014 Jordanian movie *Theeb,* an Academy Award finalist in the international film category, also thrust attention onto Jordan's bustling arts scene.

Yet the Jordan greeting casual visitors is a manicured image, designed to impress those hungry for a slice of orientalist modernity. It is not a place of politics, but a land of ancient wonders, Bedouin coffee, and gleaming hotels. In Amman, Westerners are often astonished by the capital's energetic spaces and social practices that seem strangely ordinary. One American writer gushed about the sushi restaurants and nightclubs adorning Jordan's metropole, concluding that it was "pretty wild" to find Arab women drinking with such abandon.[12] The presumptive tone aside (in fact, Amstel established its first beer brewery outside the Netherlands in Jordan in 1958), the point is clear enough. As foreign guests like freelance writers, Arabic students, and American soldiers have discovered, Jordan offers legendary hospitality for adventurers of the Arab world. There are rock concerts, biblical sites, Crusader castles, Dead Sea resorts, Red Sea beaches, "glamping" in the desert, and scrumptious food paired with local wines. Only the melodious *adhan,* the Muslim call to prayer periodically broadcast from the nearest mosque, and the rapid strums of Jordan's several Arabic dialects remind them that this is a Middle East country.

All this has not been lost on Jordanian officials, who fondly speak of a "Jordanian model" to the diplomats, investors, celebrities, and reporters. King Abdullah II and other national voices have championed the kingdom as a beacon of peace, security, reform, and innovation in international venues, from the halls of the United Nations and World Economic Forum to anglophone broadcast programs such as *60 Minutes* and *BBC News*. As one American editorial crooned, this is the "little kingdom that could."[13] But could do what? Words such as "moderate," "stable," and "progressive" carry the risk of replacing critical reproach with anodyne positivity. After all, it is not difficult for Jordan to look good when the surrounding neighborhood looks so *bad*—witness the abattoir of civil war in Syria, the sectarian jumble of postwar Iraq, Lebanon's shocking economic freefall, or the wrenching cycles of violence in neighboring Palestine involving Israel. These create depressingly low barometers of success. To appreciate Jordan's political life, we must discard these rhetorical pirouettes and instead emphasize what the country *is* rather than what it is not.

Beyond Tropes: How Not to Study Jordan

Herein lies the real gauntlet. When newcomers to Jordan seek information about its politics, they often draw upon a conventional wisdom. By this, I mean three basic tropes, or assumptions, that flavor how Western interlocutors see Jordan's state and society: the survival-collapse binary, geopolitical theater, and royal romanticism. They represent the most popular ways of seeing Jordan, peddled by pundits and policymakers whenever the country breaks into the international news cycle. Like all stereotypes, though, they replace the complex realities of politics with facile generalizations. Serious knowledge requires discarding them.

Is Jordan about to Collapse?

For Western governments, no other question shapes perceptions about Jordan more than whether the country will survive or collapse. In quiet times, the country seems to have humdrum stability; the Hashemite Kingdom of Boredom indeed. However, whenever a major crisis—say, a neighboring war, terrorist attack, refugee flow, public protest, or financial dip—transpires, analysts forecast its impending fall. In policy commentaries and media headlines, Jordan is described as standing at the edge or brink of disaster, and its stability is framed as delicate or precarious due to the economic turmoil or regional chaos engulfing its people.[14] When the foretold calamity passes, the alarm bells are snoozed. Jordan is commended for its uncanny resilience, as a gritty survivor that refuses to fold—until the next crisis. After generations of such hand-wringing, it seems the only thing more predictable than the kingdom's existence is the Western tendency to agonize over that existence.

This infatuation with Jordanian stability begins from an unvarnished premise: Jordan has no business being a country. This colonial invention began its statehood with indefensible borders, an impecunious economy, and a foreign Arabian dynasty implanted into a desert hinterland populated by defiant tribes with little conception of nationhood. Observers quipped that without Britain's imperial muscle there was "no possible reason for Jordan's survival."[15] During Jordan's early post-independence years, Westerners continued bemoaning its future prospects. British reporters saw this as a "shaky and impotent" state lost in "dark and terrifying" times, not least because the country had just absorbed almost a million Palestinians after the 1948 Arab-Israeli War.[16] A young King Hussein enthroned in 1953 was considered a political novice, hopelessly overmatched against magnetic Arab rulers like Gamal 'Abdul Nasser of Egypt. US policymakers, nervous about its newest anti-Communist ally as the MENA underwent decades of upheaval, entertained contingency plans. "We have little confidence," the Central Intelligence Agency concluded in 1959, "in the viability of Jordan . . . dangers are inherent in the essential political instability of this weak and heterogeneous state."[17]

Jordan did not collapse then, but the parlor game of projecting disaster continued. Western analysts penned premature obituaries after Jordan lost the West Bank in the 1967 Arab-Israeli War and again following the 1970 Black September civil conflict against Palestinian militant organizations. "For most nations," one American researcher rued, "various events in Jordan in almost any particular year would represent crises."[18] Even into the 1990s, experts continued wondering whether Jordan was doomed, thanks to its economic decay and social tensions between Transjordanians and the Palestinian majority.[19] Such musings continued after King Abdullah's 1999 succession. "Look at a map to hear the clock ticking on the monarchy," whispered one reporter in 2004 after Jordan found itself caught between the Al-Aqsa Intifada in Palestine to the west and the Iraq War to the east.[20] An American news article published not long after compared King Abdullah to the Mohammad Reza Shah Pahlavi prior to his ignominious deposal in the Iranian Revolution, warning that Jordan was about to suffer similar rebellious mayhem on account of the corruption, inequality, and repression that stoked opposition against monarchy.[21] The Arab Spring years raised more dread despite the peaceful nature of Jordan's protests: "It would not be surprising," one assessment declared in 2016, "to see the country succumb" to revolution.[22]

How does one make sense of this paradox—a seemingly stable country in constant danger of ruination? To be sure, Jordan has plenty of troubles. But such scaremongering has become a crafty tool of authoritarianism. For decades, Jordanian officials have dangled the perils of *fitna,* or strife, destroying their country to justify more support from the United States and other global donors. They blame the violent conflicts of the Middle East, their weak economic institutions, and sometimes their own protesting citizens to rationalize why democratic reforms must wait. And it works, at least in Washington. Whenever political trembles like popular demonstrations occur, American observers predictably propose increasing Jordan's already-large foreign aid and military assistance to "save" it and thus ensure that this peace partner of Israel does not implode into revolutionary bedlam. Doomsday prophesying, in essence, helps to perpetuate autocratic rule.[23]

This broaches a second critique: imagery about Jordan teetering on the precipice of disintegration conflates *state* with *regime*. In the postcolonial era, few states understood as sovereign territorial entities have disappeared. Not even wholesale invasions by hostile neighbors have managed to erase independent countries from existence—think South Korea (1950), Lebanon (1982), Kuwait (1990), or Ukraine (2022)—because, for the most part, international powers refuse to write them off. In recent decades, even so-called failed states like Yemen, Somalia, and Haiti, not to mention war-torn ones like Kosovo, Bosnia, and East Timor, are deemed worth rescuing through humanitarian interventions and international trusteeships.[24] In general, the international system blanches at the burden of redrawing established maps. For Western stakeholders like the United States, talk of stability and survival therefore has less to do with Jordan's physical statehood and more to do with the existence of its friendly ruling monarchy. If the Hashemite dynasty loses power due to, say, a mass uprising, Jordan would still exist as a country—but with a very different government, one that may question whether it would still pursue a pro-Western foreign policy.

Finally, the language of emergency cannot be the only way to talk about the kingdom, as if the sole query worth posing concerns its overall stability, much less whether its royal autocracy will exist tomorrow. Crying wolf incessantly fuels befuddling leaps of logic. During the Arab Spring, for instance, early dispatches from *The Economist* proclaimed the country "surprisingly stable," with the monarchy at the "zenith" of its power given the quick downfall of dictatorships in Tunisia, Egypt, and elsewhere. However, just a few years later, it returned to calling the country "wobbling" and "struggling" despite that everyday life for most Jordanians was still the same as ever: economically arduous and politically closed, but hardly revolutionary.[25] In this way, the survivalist trope glosses over the human face of politics. Jordanians do not live out every hour contemplating national stability. Every day is not a crisis, and not every crisis is a brush with annihilation.

Geopolitical Theater

If the survival-collapse binary abbreviates Jordanian politics into the slender question of stability, then the second trope eclipses Jordan altogether within the strategic morass of the Middle East. Call this geopolitical theater, in which the country carries importance only because of its pro-Western stance. To repeat the oldest mantra in real estate, one of the Hashemite Kingdom's most identifiable assets is location, location, location. Prince Hassan bin Talal, a former crown prince and uncle to King Abdullah, memorably described Jordan as the "terra media" of the Middle East, the shatter belt linking the eastern Mediterranean to the Fertile Crescent and, beyond, the Arabian Peninsula.[26] That description aptly captures how the country's borders literally touch on regional problems that have preoccupied the United States and its allies for many decades, such as Israel's security, the Palestinian conflict, Iraqi sovereignty, the Syrian Civil War, Arabian oil production, nuclear proliferation, and radical Islamist terrorism, among others. Jordan, so to speak, lives in the "crossfire" of regional maelstrom.[27]

The geopolitical tendency to see Jordan only through its importance for Western strategic interests became entrenched during the Cold War, when the US-Soviet rivalry embroiled the Middle East. When Washington replaced the fading British as Jordan's foreign protector in the late 1950s, American think tanks scrambled to decipher this pint-sized state. In the context of the global struggle between the West and Soviet Communism, Jordan presented little innate value: it had no large military, no oil resources, and not even a usable coastline beyond a sliver of land abutting the Red Sea. Instead, these strategists saw the kingdom's "salvation" in serving as a quintessential firebreak against the nefariously radical forces swirling all around it, from the Arab Nationalist regimes of Egypt and Syria to the ideological enticement of Soviet Communism. It would be a hardy outpost of moderation that rebuffed these dark enemies under the protective cover of Western hegemony. The Hashemite leadership directed its foreign policy accordingly by cooperating with the United States and its allies in return for significant foreign aid and military arms, as Chapter 8 explains in detail. Western governments were grateful. When the Cold War ended, American and European onlookers had become used to valorizing Jordan as one of the Arab world's good guys—a courageous bastion to be commended for its partnership despite being "squeezed uncomfortably . . . between the political extremes of the Arab world," or more colloquially stuck "between Iraq and a hard place."[28]

Israel contributed to this tendency to instrumentalize Jordan. The kingdom fought in the 1948 and 1967 Arab-Israeli Wars, and it controlled the West Bank and East Jerusalem between the two conflicts—a territorial claim not relinquished until King Hussein's 1988 decision to administratively disengage from this Palestinian territory. Yet even when the two countries were locked in formal hostility, many Israeli analysts considered Jordan not as a hated foe but as a "pivotal state."[29] Because it had absorbed the most Palestinian refugees in the Middle East, the country was integral to resolving the Palestinian question. The two also grudgingly shared interdependent interests as avowedly pro-Western states, such as resisting Arab Nationalism and rejecting Communism; these ideologies denigrated both Israel and Jordan as byproducts of Western imperialism. For Israel, Jordan was the ideal "buffer" state, a frenemy that shielded its eastern flank from more dangerous Arab foes like Iraq and Syria.[30] It was the lesser of all Arab evils.

Once Jordan made peace with Israel in 1994, it garnered even more Western diplomatic acclaim, economic support, and military assistance. In the first post–Cold War decade, the kingdom was "respected, admired, and esteemed" as an island of peace amid a region bursting with violence, such as civil wars in Algeria and Yemen, the rise of radical Islamism, and a recalcitrant Iraqi state under Saddam Hussein.[31] Despite the demise of Soviet Communism and Arab Nationalism ideology, Jordan still looked like a stalwart pro-Western fortress resisting the vortex of Middle East crises. As Prince Charles of Great Britain waxed when commemorating King Hussein's passing in 1999, Jordan was "an oasis of moderation . . . in a harsh desert of extremes." In the twenty-first century, American commentators have celebrated Jordan even more as a faithful Arab comrade playing the part of dutiful cog in the US war-making machine. They applauded as King Abdullah maneuvered the kingdom to back the post-9/11 War on Terror, the 2003 Iraq War, the campaign against ISIS in Syria, and defending Israel against Iranian air strikes after the outbreak of the October 2023 Gaza War. The sudden collapse of Syria's Assad regime in December 2024 hammered home the point: as the Middle East grew more unruly, the kingdom refused to buckle. In the laconic words of Western diplomats and officials, Jordan remains the "backbone of stability" for the entire MENA—making it easier to justify the ever-growing armada of US and European military forces based in the country.[32]

Seeing Jordan through the prism of geopolitical payoffs prevails within the expedient vocabulary of Western policymakers. However, it is stunningly myopic. For one, it imposes woefully flimsy benchmarks for assessing the political importance of countries. The MENA is indeed an unpredictable place, and the Hashemite monarchy has played its "game of nations" well in terms of deploying an opportunistic foreign policy to defuse the constant thrum of regional crises.[33] But then, most sovereign states do as a matter of course, including even the smallest and weakest ones. Across a century of history, Jordan still exists despite being buffeted by a seemingly never-ending stream of regional shocks and external pressures. Yet simply *existing* cannot be its immutable feature.

For another, this approach glosses over the internal failings of Jordan's authoritarian politics. Take, for example, the kingdom's repute as the Middle East's oasis of moderation that advances a kinder, gentler sort of Arab order. What do such hazy terms mean? For the United States and its European allies, these are coded terms for allegiance: the Hashemite monarchy reliably supports Western strategic interests against its vaunted foes, such as an ambitious Iran and terrorist movements. Domestically, though, many Jordanians see nothing moderate or peaceful about the repressive tendencies of their autocracy—about how martial law squelched all dissent during the 1970s and 1980s, for instance, or how those who publicly criticize Jordanian foreign policy or complain about royal corruption today still wind up in court or prison, even if they did nothing more than post criticism on Facebook. Obligatory talk about the kingdom's strategic magnitude for outsiders ignores homebound issues like democracy and human rights.

Finally, such geopolitical views commit a classic orientalist sin. They frame the Middle East as a giant chessboard, and countries like Jordan are nothing more than disposable pieces to be moved around, their significance defined purely by how useful they are to foreign puppeteers. Such a perspective holds the fate of all local states as "dictated by bigger forces and decided at a higher level."[34] Needless to say, Jordanians strive for something greater than serving as pawns for global actors. More poignantly, this also disregards the divide between rulers and the ruled. The Hashemite monarchy forged its pro-Western foreign policy many decades ago for logical reasons, but many citizens have always spurned this controversial alignment, wondering why their country has become synonymous with American hegemony. Indeed, Jordan's close ties with the West have ironically put it within the crosshairs of Salafi-jihadist terrorists seeking to destroy those whom they deem apostates (Muslims who have betrayed Islam by, for example, hosting US military forces or making peace with Israel). The 2005 Amman hotel bombings orchestrated by Al-Qaeda and the 2016 ISIS shootings in Karak were dreadful examples of this.

Royal Romanticism

The final narrative is royal romanticism. This mistakenly holds that all Jordanian political affairs are outgrowths of its intrepid Hashemite kings: to truly know Jordan, one need only study its handful of rulers. The first was Abdullah bin Hussein, who served as emir-*cum*-king from 1921 to 1951. After the brief interlude of his mentally ill son, Talal, came his grandson, Hussein bin Talal, who ruled from 1952 and 1999. Then came his own son, Abdullah II bin Hussein, who still rules today. The next ruler will likely be King Abdullah's son and crown prince, Hussein bin Abdullah, who turned 18 in 2012.

Fixating on kings in a land ruled by them does not initially seem bizarre. After all, the metaphorical idea of royal embodiment—that all of a nation's people and politics live inside the sacred body of the king—is common to many monarchies. In Jordan, the Hashemites proudly broadcast this principle. Official media, national holidays, and public textbooks praise the House of Hashem as among the noblest in Islam. Jordanians learn that the Hashemites descend from the Prophet Muhammad, served as stewards over the holy city of Mecca for centuries, played a crucial role in modern Middle East history by leading the 1916 Great Arab Revolt, and now bravely personify all of Jordan itself.[35] Such lofty talk not only legitimates the monarchy's right to rule but also infuses Jordanian kings with an aura of virtue and justice. The paternalistic language used by Hashemite leaders when dealing with the Transjordanian tribes that represent their historical base of public support similarly invokes these ideals. In its view, the monarchy sees Jordan as a giant tribal family in which the king stands as the fatherly *shaykh al-mashaayikh* (the sheikh of sheikhs, or paramount chieftain), and all the rest of society are his loyal kin and children.[36]

Some Western writers have taken such adoration to the extreme, imbuing the Hashemite kings with mystical admiration through hagiographical treatment. It began with Emir Abdullah, the founding ruler. John Bagot Glubb, the British commander of Jordan's colonial army, the Arab Legion, mythologized Abdullah after his 1951 assassination like an avatar from the *Arabian Nights*: "So immense [was] the power and influence of one man," he waxed, that when standing in the same room, Abdullah's steely will alone could make other leaders quake.[37] For the next half-century, King Hussein harvested a more Shakespearean sense of awe. For the legions of American and European journalists who followed him, Hussein was among the bravest and most charismatic Arab leaders—a Machiavellian "master of self-preservation" who, in between dodging foreign conspiracies or dashing to diplomatic summits, could be seen racing cars, chasing glamorous women, training with his troops, and sipping coffee with the Bedouin tribes of the Jordanian desert.[38] Indeed, a biographical genre that might be dubbed "Husseinism" has flourished by burrowing into the late Hussein's sangfroid, retelling the life story of this plucky dynast as a microcosm about the triumphs and travails of Jordanians themselves.[39]

The same glorification fell upon Hussein's son, King Abdullah II. Shortly after his 1999 enthronement, Abdullah won praise among global admirers as the Arab world's young, liberal, and Georgetown-educated "can-do" leader who would usher in a new era of democracy and prosperity.[40] Decades later, the reverence persists despite neither democracy nor prosperity having come to Jordan. Western leaders commend him as the Middle East's most enlightened Muslim voice, one "evangelizing for liberal, secular, democratic rule"—a welcome contrast to the horrific civil wars in Syria and Yemen and political disorder in Egypt and Libya since the Arab Spring.[41] At times, such imaginings produced the spectacle of Abdullah as a Spartan gladiator, valiantly defending Jordan against the dark hordes of violent extremism and revolutionary chaos spreading across the region. In February 2015, a photograph of Abdullah in paratrooper fatigues on a combat plane instigated erroneous buzz that he would personally lead air strikes against ISIS in Syria to avenge its murder of captured Jordanian air force pilot Mu'ath al-Kasasbeh. Not long after, Crown Prince Hussein began gathering his own parade of positive attention and was quickly regarded as an even more promising leader whose future rule would be characterized by stability, moderation, and democracy.[42]

To be sure, kings will always matter in Jordan, where the monarchy reigns and rules—unlike the constitutional monarchies that abide by parliamentary democracy elsewhere in the world, from Japan to Belgium. In ruling monarchies, by contrast, birth into a royal bloodline singularly determines who commands supreme power. Understandably, no discussion of Jordanian politics can transpire without mentioning its kings. Yet at the same time, one cannot *only* focus on these kings. We cannot know Jordan through riveting encomiums of its Hashemite leaders alone, who should be conceived as not timeless sovereigns of an ancient dynasty but rather as very human politicians. They are autocrats. They lord over a nondemocratic political system in which the masses do not elect who rules them or determines the laws that shape their lives. In doing so, Jordanian kings have done much good for their country. However, they have also made plenty of mistakes in appointing the wrong governments, enacting misguided policies, and suppressing public opposition.

Moreover, by misconstruing the Hashemite throne as the only relevant political force within Jordan, royalist preoccupations conflate Jordan's national identity with its kingship, suggesting that the essence of "Jordan-ness" means venerating the crown. However, Jordanians have many conflicting, divergent ideas about their identity. Assorted peoples flesh out this society: individuals and groups, movements and organizations, citizens and refugees, Transjordanians and Palestinians, Muslims and Christians. They are not mere reflections of their kings, and their political struggles demand attention. More than a few have opposed the monarchy and sought to curtail its superlative authority through protests and mobilization. Today, a Jordan without the Hashemites would be a very different place, but a country nonetheless; the Hashemites without Jordan, however, would be little—another deposed dynasty relegated to the footnotes of history.

Finally, royalist perspectives ignore why ruling monarchies have become an endangered species in the world, most of which are still found in the MENA.[43] In truth, royal autocracies are a brittle type of authoritarian regime; if not, then most would still be around. They tend to last only as long as the genetic lottery allows. Kings can be visionary leaders, but they can also be bumbling and corrupt despots who plant the seeds of their own overthrow. What qualifies them for the job is not merit or competence but the biological luck of being born into a bloodline. Especially in the Middle East, plenty of ineffectual absolutists clothed in dynastic garb have been overthrown since the 1950s, and even a related Hashemite branch of Jordan's monarchy in Iraq was toppled by a revolutionary coup in 1958. This puts the Hashemites of Jordan in sobering perspective. The kingdom's future will not be determined by the personalities and foibles of a few men, but instead by how these powerful rulers engage everyone else who toils, dreams, and resides here.

Beyond the Tropes

In sum, these three tropes distill the richness of Jordan into futile questions that presuppose their own answers: Will Jordan collapse or survive? How can Jordan better serve the West? How are the Hashemites doing? These are relevant inquiries, if only because they continually permeate how Jordan is interpreted, invoked, and understood. But they reflect a grim Western bias that ignores how the kingdom's people themselves envisage the future. Upon the 2021 centennial, Jordanians asked not these useless questions, but instead a weightier one infused with the same mix of uncertainty and optimism that accompanied their country's birth a century earlier: "where do we want to be at the end of the *next* coming century?"[44]

The answer cannot merely be to exist as a sovereign state, to serve as a pro-Western oasis of moderation and peace, or even to be content with having a proud Hashemite dynast in power. Many Jordanians would instead suggest that their country should be more democratic, less corrupt, more prosperous, and less dependent on the West. Such an outlook means that the extant *rules* of Jordan's politics and economy must change. Rules, here, are the stuff of political order: they mean the institutions and laws that shape how power is rendered, people are treated, the economy is structured, and the country maneuvers in its foreign relations.[45] In autocracies like Jordan, unelected regimes and leaders make the rules; everyone else in society is supposed to follow them. What those rules are, and how people have worked to change them over time, constitutes much of the upcoming chapters.

Memorable Themes

Deep dives best commence with modest wading. A few core ideas run throughout the past and present of Jordan, and they help us appreciate its political complexity.

First, history matters. History matters everywhere, but this adage has special sway in postcolonial states like Jordan, where many of the physical touches of its statehood—the monarchy, military, national borders, and other structures—were inscribed by British colonialism in the 1920s. In turn, unintended consequences echo throughout Jordan's historical development. British authorities did not envision a great country arising on the steppes of the East Bank. Rather, carving out a protectorate here simply helped achieve other regional goals, such as defending their more lucrative holding in Palestine, preventing conflict with French Syria, and pacifying the soon-to-be Emir Abdullah, the second-eldest son of wartime ally Sharif Hussein. The British gave little thought to whether the kingdom could someday thrive or what its future government, economic markets, and social life might look like.

Unlike other Arab countries, Jordan did not gain independence through nationalist revolution, because there was not much of a nation to begin with. In the 1920s and 1930s, the British-backed Emir Abdullah imposed new authoritarian institutions and economic routines on a Transjordanian populace that had seldom experienced direct rule before. It was a messy process that provoked equal parts resistance and compliance. Eventually, major social groups like tribal communities, merchant families, and minorities such as Circassians became incorporated into this new royal autocracy, supporting Hashemite rule in return for various inducements and compromises. The social foundations of the Jordanian state today harken back to these early decades. However, so do its most destructive political habits, such as extreme reliance on Western support, a distaste for democratic participation, and a penchant for military overspending. These are interminable features of Jordanian rule-making today, and they originate from the past.

Second, Jordanian society is not monolithic. The kingdom is often described as a Muslim Arab country, but this obscures a fluid social tapestry in constant flux. Jordanians are a diverse people: they do not practice their faiths in lockstep, and differences in economic wealth, political privilege, generational age, and other status markers greatly influence their views. War and migration have frequently reshaped this social terrain. That the country gained most of its Palestinian populace through two wars with Israel is a testament to this, and the arrival of so many Syrian and Iraqi refugees over the past two decades further illustrates this point. As a result, thorny questions about loyalty and belonging—including who counts as a truly *authentic* Jordanian—still play out in public discussion. Cultural change, new technologies, and a booming youth population mean that social life continues to redefine itself over time.

In particular, the Palestinian-Transjordanian divide represents a hotly debated issue. The 1970 Black September civil conflict against Palestinian guerillas, discussed in detail in the next chapter, sowed tensions between these social forces, sabotaging the quest for an inclusive national identity. An informal division of ethnocratic labor still exists: the Transjordanian tribes continue to staff the government and military, while many Palestinian-Jordanians feel like second-class citizens despite largely driving the commercial economy. Even so, both Palestinians and Transjordanians have sprouted powerful historical resistance against Hashemite rule, driven by a mutual desire to have a greater say in politics. Over time, social assimilation and intermarriage have also eroded the sharpness of this demographic cleavage. But it still exists, and no discussion of Jordanian politics can avoid it.

Third, political change in Jordan often comes from critical junctures—sudden events that trigger new pathways of development. They defy the best theoretical predictions of academic specialists. Foreign relations offer a case in point. The 1990–1991 Gulf War not only ended the last vestiges of pan-Arab unity in the Middle East but also compelled the Jordanian monarchy under King Hussein to unexpectedly challenge the West and back Iraq's invasion of Kuwait. While the move was popular with Jordanians, it economically and diplomatically isolated the country. Clawing back from this predicament required a game-changing event: the 1994 peace treaty with Israel, which ended two generations of formal hostility. This did more than end the temporary chilliness in the US-Jordanian relationship; the accord raised it to an unprecedented high. Since then, the kingdom's dependence on American aid and arms has come to resemble the colonial era, when British economic and military support kept it alive. That Jordan has also become, since the early 2010s, a regional hub for Western military forces as they wage new wars across the MENA is something few Jordanians could have fathomed in the twentieth century.

Unexpected change also defines domestic politics. The prime exhibit is Jordan's financial tailspin of the late 1980s. That meltdown instigated riots in some tribal communities, prompting two monumental turns. Economically, officials began implementing neoliberal reforms, replacing the old model of state-led development with market-driven capitalist policies like privatization and free trade. Politically, the Hashemite regime experimented with liberalizing reforms that relaxed some repression and promised more political rights. Thus, crisis forced the national leadership to deliver extraordinary promises of bread and democracy to its people. By the 2000s, Jordanians had neither, which inaugurated a new era of mobilization and opposition under King Abdullah. The protests of the Arab Spring, and many demonstrations since then, centered on issues of worsening corruption, unemployment, and political restrictions, along with rising anger against Israel for its actions in the Palestinian territories. Authoring such contentiousness has been a vast spectrum of society, including civic activists, tribal movements, students, workers, Islamists, and other groups who demand that the regime hears their grievances. The Covid-19 pandemic only briefly interrupted this trend, which highlights a quixotic lesson that will be revisited in this book's concluding chapter: Jordanians have come to expect the unexpected; after more than a century of political time, however, nothing is unexpected anymore.

Conclusion

Jordanians know well how poorly construed their kingdom has become in the West. As historian Tariq Tell laments, while Jordan "is amongst the most accessible of the countries of the Arab East, it is also one of the least understood."[46] This denotes the great riddle of the country. This is a Middle East state that welcomes visitors and travelers and poses few barriers to those wishing to learn more about its history and politics. Yet, despite its prominence as a peaceful Arab country garnering copious global acclaim in the twenty-first century, hackneyed mythologizing still obscures Jordan's politics and people from outside eyes. The survival-collapse dichotomy dangles the specter of doom over the kingdom; the theater of geopolitics filters Jordan through the essentializing arc of Western strategic interests; and the monarchical mirage conflates king with country, scrying into the deeds of a few powerful men.

Undoing such typecasting is work for the rest of this book, which addresses the authoritarian institutions, popular forces, economic dilemmas, and foreign relations that animate the Hashemite Kingdom. For such a small country, Jordan holds a great many puzzles worth pondering. The first step is to explore the base of the country—its people. Politics in Jordan is built upon social forces and historical legacies often subsumed by flippant stereotypes. To this end, the kingdom's human setting, including matters of demography, religion, and identity, forms the subject of the next chapter.

2

The Breadth and Depth of Jordanian Society

Who Are Jordanians?

In Jordan, government authorities and the official press often hail their people as the kingdom's single greatest resource. Yet the typical explanation why—that this mostly Muslim Arab people, guided by an intrepid monarch, has overcome innumerable crises amid the tides of geopolitical chaos—will not do. As Jordanian journalist Rana Sweis eloquently opines, only by looking beyond the "tragic news headlines" of the Middle East can we grasp that in this lively country "most personal stories are not marked by the kind of violent drama that punctuates international coverage of the region."[1] Jordan's population is creased with furrows, and in them reside the political concerns, economic struggles, and social dilemmas that quietly shape public life.

Consider the most basic question: what does being *Jordanian* mean? In 1921, the British counted 225,000 mostly tribal residents in their new Transjordanian protectorate; more than a century later in 2025, the government counted over 11.5 million residents, most of them crowded in urban centers never meant to accommodate this many people. However, nearly a third of this population comprise noncitizens—mainly foreign workers and refugees, the latter of which includes Palestinians, Iraqis, and Syrians, some of whom have stayed for decades and others of whom yearn to return home. Within the citizenry itself, disagreement surrounds conceptions of "Jordan-ness," not least because the majority is of Palestinian origin but feel like lesser citizens compared to those hailing from Transjordanian tribal backgrounds. This matters little to the ruling monarchy, which under King Abdullah has insisted that to be Jordanian is to celebrate the order and stability proffered by Hashemite rule; it means unbending loyalty and national unity centered on royal mottos like *Kulluna al-Urdun* (We Are All Jordan). There is neither conflict nor discontent here, only an enduring pride of place that transcends all social divides and personifies the irreducible essence of Jordan.

Such an innocuous interpretation conceals a more confounding reality. Modern Jordanian society refracts innumerable images through its layered patchwork of individuals and groups. This chapter digs through this rich tapestry, going beyond superficial revelry of Jordan's openness or stability to instead highlight the nuances of its human terrain, which casual visitors may not necessarily see in their curated sojourns to Petra or the Dead Sea. It first accentuates the country's most obvious structural feature, namely an extreme degree of urbanization. The frenzied expansion of Amman and other cities over the past generation has changed daily social routines, but it has also aggravated underlying problems of overcrowding and inequality. Second comes the populace that lives within this urbanized topography, defined by the striking demographic trend of youthfulness. Jordanian society is younger than most others in the Middle East and North Africa (MENA). Many of its young residents crave what the authoritarian state cannot provide, such as greater political participation, more economic opportunities, and information untethered from repressive control.

The third layer of society entails religion. Islam is the state religion, but the Muslim faith carries divergent meanings for the kingdom's people. While the monarchy promotes its own official version of Islam, Muslims in Jordan espouse their own spectrum of piety, some quite liberal or even secular and others abiding by conservative norms and practices. Fourth, the chapter burrows deeper into Jordanian society to assess its sizable range of religious, ethnic, and political minorities. These groups have vastly different experiences based on their importance to the Hashemite state. Compare the political advantages of Christian (and thus non-Muslim) and Circassian (and hence non-Arab) Jordanians, for example, with the peripheral status of foreign workers and refugee communities.

The fifth layer is the prickly issue of national identity. Deceptively simple questions of what Jordan-ness means—about what binds people together in Jordan and what they think their country should be—elicit no easy answers. The Hashemite monarchy has its own vision, but its idioms about nationhood and patriotism often fly far over the heads of how ordinary Jordanians define their sense of place and belonging. Finally, the chapter settles on the Transjordanian-Palestinian divide, the most common reference point in understanding Jordan's society and identity. This communal cleavage shapes much of the kingdom's contemporary politics. Yet, it remains poorly understood. Palestinian-Jordanians and East Bank tribal Jordanians carry different political roles and economic standing and have sometimes been at historical odds. However, they are not immutable groups defined solely by mutual opposition. They also include disparate branches and smaller communities that wield their own narratives about who belongs in Jordan and what their kingdom should strive to become.

This is a necessarily truncated catalog of Jordan's society, which has many other social layers. A book wholly devoted to these human dimensions would more deeply probe issues of gender, sexuality, rural life, education, the arts, and its refugees' lives. The focus on politics requires, regrettably, sidestepping these fertile pastures in order to capture, in the most useful way, broad social structures for those unfamiliar with the country.

An Urbanized Populace

Despite the slick impressions of remote desert wonders and quaint Bedouin tribes that fill its tourist brochures, Jordan is one of the most urbanized countries in the Middle East. Over 92 percent of its residents live in urban areas, the result of a long process of citification that began during the 1950s. Refugee flows, local migration from rural areas, and natural family growth have all contributed to the steady expansion of urban communities. The urban populace is not evenly distributed over the kingdom, however. Jordan has twelve governorates, or provinces (Map 2.1). Most have an eponymously named city or township serving as their largest population center. The majority of Jordanian society lives in an extremely dense conurbation between just three central cities and governorates. Imagine a triangle linking the capital of Amman to Irbid in the north and Zarqa to its northeast; the resulting area has less than 2 percent of the national territory but contains more than two-thirds of its people.

Table 2.1, which lists Jordan's population by governorate for 2024, further illustrates the scale of this urban concentration. Consider Amman. Combining the city proper with its sprawling metropolitan area, this capital governorate contains 42 percent of the national populace, or more than 4.8 million residents—more than Tel Aviv in Israel and nearly equaling Lebanon's capital of Beirut and Syria's capital of Damascus *combined*. Another third of Jordan's populace live in the governorates of Irbid and Zarqa, anchored by their respective cities. The other nine governorates have far smaller cities and towns and a higher proportion of people living in rural areas: Ajloun and Jerash in the north; Mafraq in the east; Karak, Tafileh, Ma'an, and Aqaba in the south; and Balqa and Madaba to the west of Amman.

Extremely concentrated urbanization thrusts Jordan into theoretical conversations about what anthropologists and sociologists call the "urban question"—how built environments have reconfigured the social practices and cultural meanings of daily life.[2] For instance, Jordanian cities exhibit similar themes reflecting how the authoritarian state sees its subjects. There are few public parks

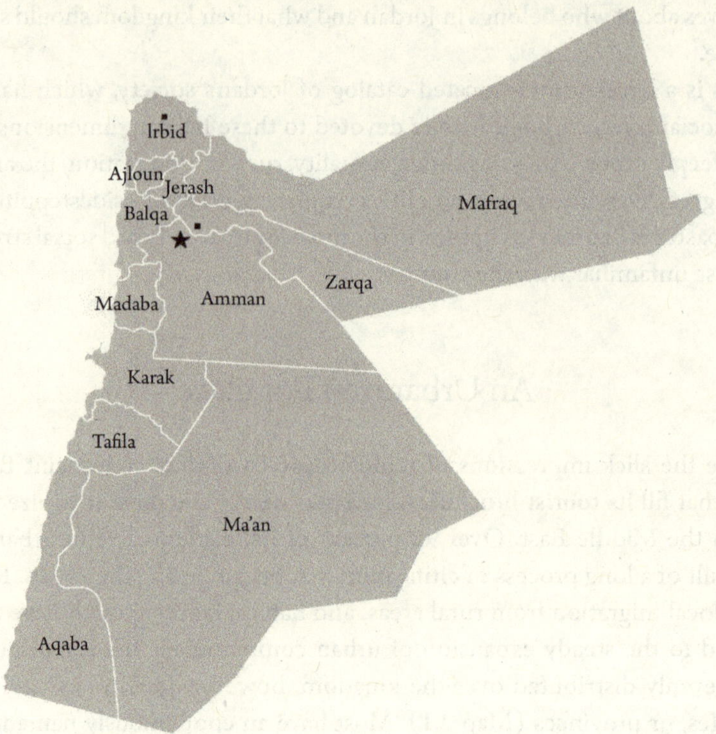

Map 2.1 Jordan's 12 Governorates. Jordan's three largest cities (Amman, Irbid, and Zarqa) are marked in their eponymously named governorates. Source: Reproduced with permission from iStock.

because what little water exists is reserved for thirsty industries and private households. Neither are there many free-flowing public squares because authorities know that wide open spaces can become hotspots of mass protests. There is no functional railway or mass transit system, so transportation requires joining the ever-growing parade of cars and buses that pack streets and highways—physical channels of movement that the government can monitor, regulate, and close if necessary. Urban planning entails a "tyranny of decision-making" by officials, whose architectural choices and commercial priorities often favor privileged stakeholders like foreign investors and wealthy elites rather than local communities.[3] Many of the richest residents live in protective bubbles of affluent neighborhoods for a simple reason: they can afford it, even if such class-based segregation serves to reproduce rather than reduce the wider economic inequality seen across Jordan.

Obversely, rural areas suffer absolute neglect when compared to the government funds and attention assigned to developing urban zones. Thus, the farther one moves away from the Amman-Irbid-Zarqa conurbation, the greater

Table 2.1 **Jordan's National Population by Governorate, 2024**

Governorate	*Number of Residents*	*Percentage of National Population*
Amman	4,834,500	42.0
Irbid	2,135,400	18.5
Zarqa	1,646,600	14.3
Mafraq	663,400	5.7
Balqa	593,200	5.2
Karak	381,900	3.3
Jerash	286,000	2.5
Madaba	228,200	2.0
Aqaba	227,000	2.0
Ajloun	212,500	1.8
Ma'an	191,100	1.7
Tafileh	116,200	1.0
Total	11,516,000	100

Source: Department of Statistics, *Jordan Statistical Yearbook* (DOS, 2024).

the hardship.[4] Southern rural towns such as Karak, Tafileh, and Ma'an have long felt economically abandoned, given their shoddy infrastructure and social services; many of their tribal communities remain dependent on public employment and military service as financial lifelines. Elsewhere, many agrarian settlements—from small farming villages in the Jordan Valley to Bedouin communities in eastern Mafraq—languish in relative poverty, the result of market forces and domestic investment passing them by. For the technocratic visionaries of King Abdullah's governments in recent decades, Jordan's future connotes images not of bucolic farms and tribal nomads but of gleaming skyscraper-filled metropolises in the mold of Dubai and other ultra-modern cities.

To see the riptides of urbanization most vividly, live in Amman. Historically, this was never a grand city. Known as Philadelphia in Greek and Roman times, Amman was largely abandoned after the seventh century. In the era of the Islamic caliphates, the modest town was an afterthought compared to great imperial capitals like Cairo, Baghdad, and Damascus. Only in 1878 did the settlement come alive again, when the Ottomans filled its hilly plateau with thousands of Circassian migrants seeking refuge from the Caucasus. While some local Arab families and traders followed, Amman still had just 5,000 inhabitants when the

British created Transjordan in 1921. Even within the fledgling emirate, the upstart seat of Hashemite power had less prestige than Irbid and Salt to the north or Karak and Ma'an to the south—more established towns that had served as administrative hubs under Ottoman rule or as trading centers for local merchants.[5] Ironically, this made Amman the perfect capital for the new monarchy and its British minders. They needed an isolated town they could control first before flexing their authority to subdue more distant parts of the Transjordanian expanse.

In turn, anointing Amman as Jordan's urban nucleus radically reversed the political geography of the East Bank. As Jillian Schwedler notes, what was once a tangential settlement became the locus of authoritarian power, while older commercial hubs or administrative townships like Ma'an and Salt were shunted to the periphery of the burgeoning state.[6] From the 1920s onward, officials doubled down on their choice of capital by building new roads, houses, markets, schools, and government edifices to expand Amman. More change came with the 1948 Arab-Israeli War, which brought Palestinians to Jordan. Not only did Amman host several large refugee camps, but Palestinian migrants also energized civil society and local commerce. As social life blossomed, so too did real estate, commerce, and education. Jordan University, the kingdom's flagship university, was founded here in 1962. New neighborhoods developed outward in starburst fashion, attracting not only other Palestinians but Transjordanians from rural areas as well.

The numbers reveal Amman's brisk postwar enlargement. On the eve of the 1948 war, the capital had 60,000 people; it then jumped to 330,000 by the 1967 Arab-Israeli War, 624,000 by 1979, and nearly 900,000 by 1990.[7] In addition to hosting royal palaces and government ministries, Amman also gave rise to the biggest banks, hotels, companies, and markets that underwrote the developing economy. The next two decades brought more rapid expansion due to high birth rates and the return of hundreds of thousands of Palestinian-Jordanians expelled from the Gulf kingdoms amid the 1990–1991 Gulf War. By 2004, greater Amman counted 2.4 million people. Since then, the capital has gained on average over 140,000 people per year. Amman's population these days is more than what *all* of Jordan had in 1995.

There are good and bad sides to life in such a frenetic metropole. Amman's noisy thrum has regularly birthed epic political moments for the past century. Since the 1950s, many of the largest protest movements and contentious disturbances in Jordan have either begun in the capital or spread quickly to it. The energy pulsating through its streets has given rise to a radiant artistic scene as well. The city was a natural setting for renowned Jordanian literary works such as Abdulrahman Munif's memoir-driven *Story of a City* (1996), in addition to jolting novels like Elias Farkouh's *Land of Purgatory* (2007) and Jamal Naji's *When the Wolves Grow Old* (2009).

However, Amman's hectic urban fabric has also bred severe difficulties. For one, its layout can confuse even longtime inhabitants. The hilly city is a mishmash of centrally planned areas and labyrinthian neighborhoods connected by packed streets, traffic circles, and highway overpasses. Residents regularly complain about grinding congestion, which a rapid bus transit system inaugurated in 2021 has barely alleviated. Government proposals to reduce overcrowding by building a new master-planned city twenty-five miles east have elicited understandable cynicism: Jordan has enough people for it, but authorities do not yet have the money.

For another, Amman has come to embody the deeper inequities that prowl the kingdom. In its older eastern quarter of traditional low-rise structures, tourist-heavy areas like downtown (*wasat al-balad*) and Lweibdeh burst with quaint cafes, hip restaurants, and nostalgic charm. These are the well-kept areas that Western visitors romanticize when they describe Amman as a "beautiful blend of tradition and more liberal cosmopolitanism."[8] Not far away, though, underserved neighborhoods like Hay al-Tafaileh and Jofeh are filled with dilapidated buildings and starker poverty. Similarly, the wealthier parts of western Amman have given rise to lavish commercial and residential megaprojects built since the 2000s through government-backed schemes to modernize the city.[9] Expensive neighborhoods like Abdoun and Dabouq, as well as luxury complexes like Taj Mall, Abdali Boulevard, and the Jordan Gate towers, stand as monuments to globalization and capitalism. But most families cannot afford them; they instead cater to elite businesspersons, foreign investors, and wealthy expatriates. Such opulent development partly explains why, in 2018, the Economist Intelligence Unit ranked Amman as the most expensive Arab city and twenty-eighth worldwide, ahead of London and Rome—this, in a country where poverty afflicts at least a quarter of the populace.

Youthfulness

Besides its urbanized concentration, Jordan's society is also young. Nearly two-thirds of Jordanians are under age thirty, almost evenly split between those who are zero to fourteen years old and those who are fifteen to twenty-nine. As of 2024, the median age is twenty-four years old. In the Arab world, of course, Jordan is not alone in its youthfulness. The kingdom is part of the MENA's wider "youth bulge"—that is, the many millions of teenagers and millennials who hanker for more political freedom and economic opportunities, with the 2011–2012 Arab Spring serving as a stern warning to autocratic governments who insist on stymying their aspirations.[10]

Youthfulness has long typified the Jordanian people. Figure 2.1 tracks the proportion of the population under thirty years old from 1950 to 2020, as compared

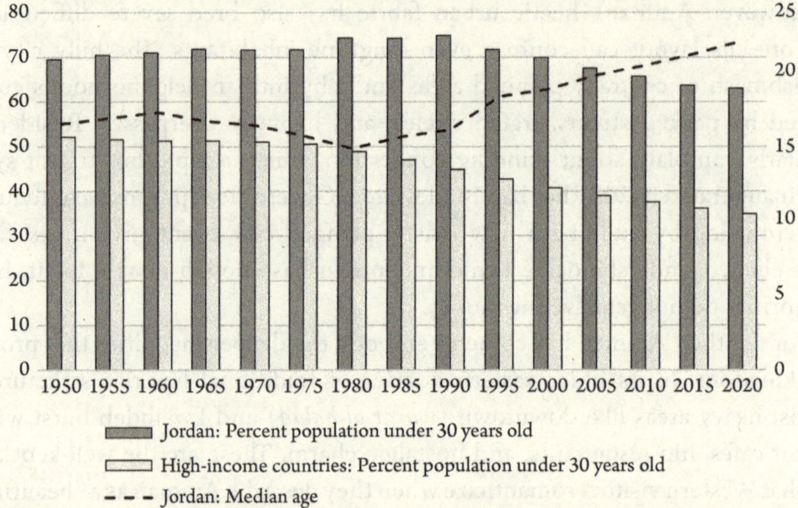

Figure 2.1 Jordan's Population under 30 and Median Age, 1950–2020. The left vertical axis measures the percentage of population under 30 years old, and the right vertical axis measures Jordan's median age. Sources: Jordanian Department of Statistics, *Population and Housing Census* (Amman, DOS: various years), and United Nations, Population Division, *World Population Prospects 2022*, https://population.un.org/dataportal/

to all high-income countries in the world (i.e., those with a per capita gross domestic product, GDP, of at least $12,000). Also shown is Jordan's median age. In wealthy countries, the percentage of young people has lessened over time as diminishing fertility rates—driven by economic development and access to contraception—have flattened the age distribution. In 2020, those zero to twenty-nine years old represented just a third of the population in high-income countries. By contrast, Jordan's larger youth base has only marginally shrunk from its high in 1980, when a whopping 75 percent of the populace were under thirty years old and the median age was barely sixteen.

Crucially, while most Arab countries have youthful populations, the Hashemite Kingdom is among the youngest. Only a few poorer regional countries such as Sudan and Yemen have lower median ages. One reason is that Jordanian fertility rates have only marginally declined over time, partly due to the slow spread of family planning and reproductive rights. As of 2020, Jordanian women were expected to have, on average, about 2.6 children over their lifetimes—higher than most other MENA states and higher than two-thirds of other global countries such as India (2.18), Brazil (1.71), and the United States (1.64). This presents a double challenge for the country. Today, an enormous cohort of millennials desires political and economic change; and tomorrow, another swell—today's children and teenagers—will follow suit.

The voices of the youth (in Arabic, *al-shabaab*) rumble everywhere. Younger Jordanians are slowly transmuting social life by questioning staid patriarchal norms and sexual attitudes. Rebuffing threats of repression, they find quiet spaces in homes and cafes to partake in defiant discussions about the political troubles and economic stagnation that choke them. They have also helped renew Jordan's rich local heritage of poetry, storytelling, music, and dance. In literature, fresh authors like Hisham Bustani have garnered international accolades for their genre-bending writing, mirroring the pioneering work of new filmmakers and other artists. Jordanian young people have likewise led the way for digital technology and social media adoption. In a country with a nearly 93 percent Internet penetration rate, young citizens are avidly plugged into online trends.[11] Most own a smartphone and access the Internet daily. Facebook ranks as the top social media platform in Jordan, followed by Snapchat, X (formerly Twitter), Telegram, YouTube, and Instagram; WhatsApp stands as the most popular messaging application.

Online spaces have given Jordanian youth ways to circumvent the traditional press and media, which officials heavily control in order to sway what information reaches society. Daily newspapers are dreary: some, such as *Al-Dustour* and *Al-Ra'i*, are partly government owned, while others, such as *Al-Ghad* and the now-defunct *Al-Arab Al-Yawm*, once claimed independence but were eventually pressured into toeing the line of authorities. Journalists self-censor themselves lest they attract the wrong kind of attention. Government-affiliated broadcasters dominate the mainstream television and radio sectors, as well. And when in doubt, the monarchy can gag all press coverage of controversial stories—like the April 2021 detention of Prince Hamzah after his alleged coup-mongering—while the authorities arbitrarily arrest or prosecute writers who dare to opine on sensitive topics like royal corruption and foreign relations.[12]

In the 2000s, Jordanians tried to sidestep such autocratic domineering by tuning into newer satellite channels free of state control like Al-Jazeera. By the 2010s, young people went a step further by pioneering a wave of online news portals, whose mix of clickbait gossip and guerilla reporting embarrassed officials. The regime fought back with censorship, issuing a Cybercrimes Law in 2013 to block access to hundreds of critical websites. In response, tech-savvy Jordanians turned to tools such as virtual private networks and Tor browsers, as well as social media platforms and podcasts, to preserve their digital freedom. Authorities responded with more online restrictions. In recent years, they have blocked a litany of online platforms, from beloved satirical websites like *Al-Hudood* and liberal Arabic media sources like *Raseef22* to social media apps like Clubhouse and TikTok. The 2023 Cybercrimes Law went furthest by criminalizing nearly all online content and activities that authorities could freely interpret as being too critical of the government.

This cat-and-mouse game nurtures a deeper problem. There is a generational chasm between young people and their elders, an almost psychological disconnect that flavors political opinions and social action.[13] Young Jordanians today have little memory of King Hussein, whose half-century reign helped define Jordan's postcolonial statehood and politics, or the martial law that characterized much of his rule. Some critics see his son, King Abdullah, not as an awe-inspiring figure but as an aloof autocrat who has ignored the toils of ordinary people for decades. Under his reign, the monarchy's broken promises of democratic reform have magnified their cavernous pessimism. Indeed, most young Jordanians do not bother voting. They see general elections as authoritarian farces and the resulting parliament as hopelessly impotent under the powerful royal autocracy—a correct presumption, as the next chapter explains.

Economically, the situation is no better. As Chapter 7 expounds, high unemployment leaves many young people stuck in what sociologists call "waithood," because without steady work and salaries they cannot marry, start families, and begin their adult lives. Unfortunately, joblessness among the youth (those aged sixteen to twenty-four seeking work) has tracked at double the overall unemployment rate; in 2023, it peaked at nearly 50 percent, one of the worst figures in the world.[14] Royal authorities regularly issue stately projects to educate and inspire young citizens, whom they worry will turn to protests and opposition—or worse, radical extremism—given their immobility. Government organs such as the Ministry of Youth and Crown Prince Foundation, often flush with Western aid and technical support, preach the importance of entrepreneurship and harnessing Jordan's demographic dividend.[15] Yet, such efforts have had little impact. Many disenchanted young people wish to leave Jordan altogether, believing there is no place for them given the slumbering economy and closed political system. The Arab Barometer's 2021–2022 Wave VII survey revealed that two-thirds of citizens under thirty wished to emigrate, higher than even war-torn Libya and Sudan.[16] Some of those who stay represent the target audience for narcotic usage, which has caused local media to increasingly fret about the ever-rising use of Captagon tablets and other illicit drugs smuggled from Lebanon and Syria, as criminal networks use Jordan as an overland route to supply other Middle East markets.

Islam

Religion gives another aperture into how social life coheres. Jordan's state religion is Islam, as declared by the constitution. Islam thus influences many areas of society. Over 97 percent of Jordanians identify as Muslim—almost all Sunni, with the few Shi'a accounted by migrants or refugees from Iraq and Syria. Government offices and much commerce shut down on Friday, Islam's holy day (although savvy political activists often choose this day to hold protests). Muslim holidays, such as Ramadan and Eid al-Adha, are celebrated widely. Many legal strictures favor Islam. For instance, the criminal code penalizes insulting the Prophet Muhammad and Islam in general. Muslim men may marry non-Muslim women, but not the other way around unless the man converts to Islam. Proponents of socially conservative positions, such as veiling women or penalizing homosexuality, also predicate their arguments upon religious understandings of what Islam, in their view, is supposed to condone or ban.

However, Jordanian Muslims are not equally devout in their beliefs and practices. A closer look exposes considerable pluralism—and conflict—within the religious arena, with the Hashemite state playing a huge role in influencing how Islam is interpreted across society.

Religiosity in Society

Piety is not a binary concept in Islam, as if Muslims are either besotted proponents of theological doctrine or else completely secular beings. As with all religions, piety for Muslims manifests as a social spectrum of behavior that reflects not just personal commitment but also public pressures, family structure, economic class, and other external factors that influence how liberally or conservatively they conceive their faith.

Hard data speak to this complexity. The Arab Barometer's 2021–2022 Wave VII survey showed that a majority of Jordanians (61.4 percent) identified as *somewhat* religious as opposed to simply religious (35.3 percent), while few claimed to be not religious (2.9 percent). The Arab Barometer's earlier 2018–2019 Wave V survey likewise showed that as many Jordanians never attended Friday prayers (40.8 percent) as did those who always attended (39.5 percent); they also were split almost fifty-fifty on whether women should wear the hijab (veil). A reasonable generalization from these findings is that most Jordanian Muslims probably do not want a Western-style civil state that relegates faith purely to private life in the name of secularism. Yet, neither do they yearn for a theocracy, where religious figures prescribe the politics and laws of the land. Most also reject the extremist versions of Islam advanced by violent Salafi-jihadist groups like Al-Qaeda and the Islamic State of Iraq and Syria (ISIS) and tolerate Jordan's Christians and other non-Muslim faiths.

Generational change has also shifted the boundaries of religiosity and piety. For instance, in 2016, state educational reforms removed some Islamic content, such as Qur'anic references from school textbooks. Jordan's Muslim public fractured on the issue; older conservatives decried the move, while younger, more liberal proponents celebrated this pedagogical revamp. Others find creative ways to accommodate their personal Muslim identity with the exigencies of modern life. As Sarah Tobin's ethnography reveals, humble acts like depositing money into Islamic banks (which operate on different financial principles than mainstream ones) and veiling oneself as a woman mean different things to Muslim adherents.[17] These actions can be signs of spiritual devoutness or merely practical conveniences; it varies for every believer.

Still, one bigger trend within Jordanian society is undeniable: the rise of Islamism. In the early twentieth century, Islamist movements emerged across the MENA as a reaction to the perceived decline of Muslim civilization in the face of Western imperialism. Its advocates and preachers saw faith as not only the crux of their identity but also a mode of political resistance. For them, the restoration of Islamic greatness required rejecting foreign influences, restoring conservative religious values within society, and aligning the state itself with a traditional interpretation of *shari'a* (Islamic law)—ideally by securing political power and thereafter using modern government to inculcate religious guidance in every aspect of public life.

As Jordanian specialists like Muhammad Abu Rumman have shown, Islamism in the kingdom is a microcosm of Islamist mobilization across the globe.[18] As in many other Muslim countries, Islamism gained a significant following in Jordan in the late twentieth century by appealing to the urban middle class, which felt the acutest brunt of economic decline and authoritarian bungling. Islamists proselytized and preached; they promised a less-corrupt political future and in many areas provided much-needed services such as education, healthcare, and financial assistance. As Chapter 6 discusses, Jordan's most prominent Islamist group is the Muslim Brotherhood, founded in 1945 but banned in 2025 by the government in a final political crackdown. Its tens of thousands of members have historically promoted a religious orthodoxy that more liberal Muslims in Jordan reject, and until the recent prohibition they energetically mobilized for social and political changes despite repeated government efforts to muzzle them. The Brotherhood's Islamic Center Charity Society, for instance, became the kingdom's largest charitable organization after its 1963 establishment.[19] Its political party, the Islamic Action Front, evolved into a leading opposition force in the 1990s. Another strand of Jordanian Islamism comprises the more conservative Salafists, who promote literalist readings of Islamic doctrine. An extreme branch of Salafism, the Salafi-jihadists, includes terrorist actors like Al-Qaeda and ISIS who promise salvation through violence (including, to the horror of other Islamists, terrorism against fellow Muslims).

Islam through the State

The Jordanian state commands its own religious footprint. But it is subtle. Like most other Muslim countries, high politics in Jordan is—for lack of a better term—secular. While the king must be Muslim, Islam does not form the basis of government; neither does the state mandate Islam as a condition of citizenship, as the constitution forbids religious discrimination. As Chapters 3 and 4 explain, there is nothing inherently religious in the model of authoritarian rule that the Hashemite regime has embraced or in how it wields power, controls opposition, and surveils society. Neither is there any clearly Islamic content in its matter-of-fact daily policies, such as conducting diplomacy, subsidizing gasoline, and paying bureaucrats. Indeed, the only obvious sign of the state legally exercising religious authority comes from the national judiciary: Jordan has both civil and criminal courts, but it also has shari'a courts with jurisdiction over family and personal status matters such as marriage, divorce, and inheritance. (These only apply to Muslims, as most Christian communities have their own ecclesiastical councils.) Shari'a courts carry a well-earned reputation for conservatism, and many women's rights advocates decry their rulings as grossly privileging men and thus perpetuating gender inequality.[20]

More broadly, however, Jordan's powerholders understand the importance of influencing how their Muslim believers interpret and practice their faith in everyday life.[21] They know religion can be a tool of resistance and protest. Some regard the clarion call of Islamism, and its promise of emancipating society through religious rekindling, as coded language for toppling the monarchy. Jordan's leadership has thus long disseminated an "official Islam," a government-sanctioned version of the Muslim faith.[22] Official Islam includes all the ways that the Hashemite regime tries to monopolize and standardize Islamic beliefs and practices within society. Despite that Sunni Islam's egalitarian nature frowns upon religious hierarchy, Jordan's royal autocracy nonetheless exploits its superlative powers to promote certain religious viewpoints. The most prevalent is that Jordanian Muslims should be "moderate." In the official Islam expounded by authorities, to be moderate is to eschew Islamism and Salafism, observe the autocratic writ of the monarchy, and reject social protest and opposition in favor of political quiet.

Many examples exist of this. The government's Ministry of Awqaf and Religious Affairs supervises the kingdom's roughly 6,000 mosques and oversees which *imams* (preachers) are hired, and what Friday sermons they deliver.[23] Such regulation keeps Islamists and other unsanctioned religious voices out of these sacred spaces. The General Iftaa Department likewise employs Islamic jurists to decree a *fatwa* (a ruling predicated on Islamic law). Every year, they issue thousands of fatwas that emit the government's formal opinion on matters both mundane (like the wickedness of social media) and serious (such as that too much protest can incite anarchy), with hopes that some Jordanians will heed them. Educational officials likewise keep a close watch over the religious content propagated through public institutions, from primary schools to university faculties specializing in Islamic law, to ensure that all interpretations of faith abide by their guidance.

Outside these government bodies, the monarchy also promotes official Islam. Despite its descent from the Prophet Muhammad, the Hashemite dynasty does not brandish spiritual authority in a doctrinal sense. Unlike the Moroccan kingship, which also shares genealogical heritage from the Prophet, monarchs here do not don sacred titles reserved for the caliphs and sultans of past Islamic empires, such as *amir al-muminin* (commander of the faithful). Jordanian kings frame themselves not as theological authorities, but rather as religious stewards who wish to gently guide all Muslims toward proper Islamic behavior. But they do so also as autocratic political rulers, which has great consequence for those believers in Jordan: it means that royal pronouncements about matters of faith carry the full weight of the Jordanian state behind them. For instance, in 2004, King Abdullah famously delivered a religious declaration called the Amman Message, which argued that true Islam represented unity, tolerance, and pluralism rather than the extremism of Al-Qaeda or the nastiness of sectarian conflict.[24] Such verbiage not only sent a message of peace but also justified Jordan's stern crackdowns on Islamist radicalism in close concert with the United States and its post-9/11 War on Terror. This plea for progressive values also comported with what the United States and other Western donors wanted to see: a liberal interpretation of Islam issued by a friendly Muslim Arab kingship.

Minorities, Citizenship, and Refugees

The fifth way to understand Jordan is through the lens of minority groups in society. At first glance, this may seem like a peculiar optic. After all, Western governments see Jordan as being far more homogenous than fractious neighbors such as Iraq, Syria, and Lebanon, where deep religious and ethnic divisions are associated with sectarian conflict. Nonetheless, remarkable diversity exists in Jordan—and with no less political impact but without the violence. Here, not everyone is Muslim; not everyone is Arab; there are non-Muslim Arabs (e.g., Christians) and Muslim non-Arabs (e.g., Circassians); and nearly a third of the population are not even Jordanian citizens at all.

This multiplicity furnishes a stark lesson in how identity is malleable. As many political scientists and sociologists argue, observed differences like religion or race that set minority groups apart from a societal majority are not primordial givens that predestine conflict.[25] Both governments and social groups alike can manipulate and reconstruct their identities, creating new forms of inclusion or exclusion over time. As even Western countries would concede, for example, whether refugees are welcomed or demonized has less to do with their humanitarian plight or identity as displaced people and more to do with the political views of their hosting communities. In Jordan, such malleability explains the very disparate treatments afforded to religious minorities, ethnic minorities, and refugees. Some are an indelible part of the Jordanian panorama, while others reside on the outskirts of the nation.

First, religion. The roughly 3 percent non-Muslim portion of Jordan breaks down into mostly Christians, with very small communities of Druze, Bahai, Buddhists, and others. Christianity has ancient roots in Jordan. Archaeological excavations have uncovered churches dating back to biblical times, and sacred locales like Mount Nebo are often included in "Holy Land" tours marketed to foreign tourists. The Greek Orthodox and Roman Catholic traditions claim the most followers, although nearly a dozen other smaller churches abound, including Armenian, Coptic, and Maronite denominations. Christianity in Jordan is also cross-cutting, as it includes several hundred thousand people of both Transjordanian and Palestinian origin.

Politics has made Christians a protected, and sometimes privileged, social category. During the British colonial decades of the 1920s and 1930s, the Hashemite monarchy struck an implicit bargain. Christians in Transjordan could have a "communal sphere" of autonomy—they could worship openly, create civic organizations, and practice their own family and personal status laws—in return for supporting the monarchy.[26] Today, the same Jordanian state that broadcasts official Islam also features a king who attends Christmas services and sponsors interfaith tolerance and Christian-Muslim dialogues.

Partly due to such royal benefaction, many Christian Jordanians have done well across politics and the economy. Within the regime and state, they have served as ministers, advisers, and generals. Only the highest positions—such as the office of prime minister and top military command staff—remain informally off limits to them. Christians are also found among the storied class of elite business families tied to Hashemite patronage. The Mu'asher clan, for instance, helped found Ahli Bank in 1955, the kingdom's first local bank and now a major financial institution. It owns many other commercial holdings, and has also produced famed politicians who have ably served the crown. Moreover, every version of Jordan's legislature since the colonial era has reserved a special quota for Christian deputies. As of 2025, the lower house of parliament allocates 9 of its 138 seats to Christians, overweighting their demographic size. That said, Christians are also well represented in the historical ranks of political opposition, particularly among leftist parties, civil society groups, and Palestinian organizations.

Ethnicity is another axis of politics. About 2 percent of the Jordanian citizenry is not Arab, defined in the narrowest racial sense. Some non-Arabs suffer crude racism and ostracism, such as the Ghawarna—a small community of Black Jordanians living in the Jordan Valley—as well as the itinerant Romani community. Others have integrated far better, such as the 3,000-strong Armenian community. The most numerous non-Arab minorities, however, are the 100,000 Circassians and Chechens. These Sunni Muslims peoples were displaced by Russian occupation across the northern Caucasus in the late nineteenth century and relocated by Ottoman authorities to the region. By the 1900s, Circassian settlers had revived the derelict town of Amman; Chechens did likewise to Zarqa. From the colonial era onward, Hashemite patronage ensured that both groups enjoyed a sheltered status similar to Christians. For instance, the monarchy encouraged Circassian associations to preserve their cultural traditions and create local solidarity networks.[27] Chechens had similar experiences. They remain tight-knit communities today, with a dual self-conception as both Caucasian diasporas and integral members of an Arab society.

As with Christians, Hashemite recognition yielded significant benefits to these minorities. It made Circassians and Chechens feel secure not as Ottoman-era holdovers but as East Bankers second only to Transjordanian tribes so long as they endorsed monarchical rule. Consequently, Circassians and Chechens have served the monarchy at the highest rungs. A famed prime minister in the 1950s, Sa'id Mufti, was Circassian; since then, so too have been other high-ranking ministers, intelligence chiefs, and military generals. Indeed, Circassians and Chechens are overrepresented in the military, with the former even staffing a symbolic royal bodyguard. The legislature has likewise retained special quotas guaranteeing their representation, and as of 2025 a 3-seat ethnic quota out of 138 lower house seats are reserved for Circassian and Chechen members of parliament (MPs). Like Christian Jordanians, however, more than a few Circassians have also figured into political opposition movements. Among the most renowned is former MP Toujan al-Faisal, who became the first woman elected to parliament in 1993, only to see her career destroyed by relentless threats and prosecutions after her repeated criticism of the monarchy and its government.

The final aspect of Jordan's minority politics is nationality. Nearly a third of its residents are not citizens. This is a critical statistic, because the government's convoluted criteria for who counts as a citizen exposes not just legal pedanticism but also the potency of authoritarian interests in determining who "belongs" to the country.[28] Most Jordanians today claim citizenship on basis of two laws: the 1928 Nationality Law, which conferred citizenship upon all those Transjordanians residing on the East Bank then, and the 1954 Nationality Law, which bestowed the same on the new Palestinian majority produced by the 1948 Arab-Israeli War, including both refugees on the East Bank and those in the Jordanian-controlled West Bank.

Since those sunbursts of enfranchisement, however, citizenship laws have contracted the boundaries of the nation. Royal authorities have refused to incorporate new waves of Palestinians into Jordan. After the 1967 Arab-Israeli

War, for instance, officials did not provide citizenship to Palestinian refugees who came to the East Bank from the Israeli-occupied Gaza Strip. These Gazan Palestinians now number nearly 200,000, and most remain stateless despite their generations-long presence in Jordan. Furthermore, in 1988, King Hussein dissolved Jordan's administrative ties and economic responsibility over the Israeli-occupied West Bank, which the kingdom had maintained under Israeli agreement since 1967. This withdrew Jordanian nationality from its nearly 800,000 Palestinians, giving them only border-crossing permits to enter Jordan and other symbolic licenses.

In other respects, Jordanian nationality—including the right to hold a passport—remains an inscrutably closed shop. Palestinians in the West Bank and Jerusalem, for instance, can request Jordanian passports, but not citizenship. In Jordan itself, officials can revoke citizenship arbitrarily, which thousands of Palestinian-Jordanians have experienced for mostly political reasons.[29] Citizenship is also gendered, being patrilineal: it extends to children of Jordanian fathers regardless of the mother or place of birth, but not so for those born to Jordanian mothers and foreign fathers. Non-Jordanians can apply for citizenship, but only after having long-term residency, proving Arabic proficiency, showing good political conduct, and many other requirements. Money provides one shortcut for a lucky few, as foreign investors can obtain Jordanian nationality if they sink millions of dollars into the economy.

Membership in the Jordanian nation is therefore exclusionary. This is not a state that encourages migrants and expatriates to assimilate into its society. Foreign workers present one example. As Chapter 7 describes, the Jordanian economy is quirky, as the reluctance of some Jordanians to accept unskilled or semiskilled jobs (e.g., construction, agriculture, and restaurants) has resulted in foreign labor filling those positions. They include Egyptians, Syrians, Iraqis, Yemenis, and Asians, the latter mostly from Bangladesh, the Philippines, Sri Lanka, and India. Many work without legal documentation, thanks to lax enforcement and employer demand. For instance, the Labor Ministry formally allows around 300,000 foreigners to hold licensed employment permits, but undocumented workers (excluding Syrian refugees) number about double that.[30] Jordan's nearly million foreign workers can face harrowing conditions, including illegally low wages and unsafe workplaces. They have virtually no pathway to citizenship. Yet much like other countries, including the United States, their is mostly tolerated because labor-intensive industries such as construction, food services, and hospitality need a viable workforce, and businesses profit from their employment. Deporting unlicensed foreign employees is seldom high on the national priority list.

Refugees also occupy a disadvantaged position in terms of political treatment. Jordan has one of the world's highest rates of refugees per capita, and international agencies estimate the kingdom had over 3 million refugees in 2025. Of course, as with many things in Jordan, such a seemingly naked fact is misleading. At least 2.4 million of the refugee populace are Palestinians registered with the United Nations Relief and Works Agency (UNRWA), of whom most also hold Jordanian citizenship (but conversely, not all Palestinian-Jordanians are classified as refugees by the government or international agencies).[31] A fair estimate, then, is that Jordan has well over about 1 million mostly Arab, noncitizen refugees. They include sizable numbers of Gazan Palestinians, as discussed earlier. A half-million Iraqis arrived after the 2003 Iraq War; however, most have since returned. Perhaps 750,000 Syrians entered during the Syrian Civil War, but some have begun returning home after the December 2024 toppling of Bashar Assad's regime. Small refugee communities also originate from Sudan, Yemen, and Somalia.

Collectively, the stories of refugees in Jordan are heart-rending. Most of these displaced peoples find themselves stuck in an "immobility chessboard"—displaced from their homelands and traumatized by conflict, yet still suffering legal precarity as noncitizens.[32] Jordan has never granted citizenship en masse to any refugee group since the 1954 Nationality Law extended that right to Palestinians. Because it never signed the 1951 UN Refugee Convention and its 1967 Protocol, Jordanian authorities also internally classify many refugees (excepting Palestinians with Jordanian nationality) as "guests," a hazy legal category that forecloses future citizenship and prevents many from obtaining legal documents and formal work.

However, Jordan also accepts the international principle of *nonrefoulement*—the right of refugees not to be forcibly returned to the very conditions that endangered their lives. Such neighborly positioning has long helped this authoritarian state procure massive foreign assistance to underwrite and outsource its humanitarian obligations. In the 1950s, UNRWA took charge in providing education, healthcare, and other services to Palestinian refugee camps. These camps now number nearly a dozen, although most of Jordan's Palestinians no longer live in them; Jordanian citizens of Palestinian origins, generally, live in Amman and other cities. In the mid-2000s, Jordan reaped US and EU aid to accommodate displaced Iraqis, although critics suspected the government was inflating their refugee numbers to garner more funding.[33] When displaced Syrians began arriving in 2012, the UN High Commissioner for Refugees (UNHCR) took the lead to monitor, administer, and house this new influx. Even so, the country required mammoth humanitarian aid to expand services like education and healthcare and bolster public goods in short supply like food and electricity. In 2019, at the cusp of the Covid-19 pandemic, the cost of refugee accommodation peaked at $2.4 billion annually, or over 5 percent of the GDP. To ensure ever-higher aid payments through international agreements like the 2016

Jordan Compact, officials played on the fears of Western donors: if they could not help Jordan, then its miserable Syrians might bolt elsewhere—to European lands, for instance, or perhaps into the hands of the Islamic State terrorist movement.[34]

Global generosity has not prevented frictions from flaring between refugees and local communities. To be a refugee in Jordan these days is to knock on the door of nativist resentment while bearing a political identity assigned by the state—a forever foreigner whose time in Jordan should be hospitable but also fleeting. The Syrian Civil War provides the latest example. As Syria's conflict worsened in the mid-2010s, officials did little to dissuade many Jordanians from blaming Syrian refugees for their economic woes, such as high unemployment and rising living costs.[35] In reality, such problems far predated the war, having resulted from prior decades of government mismanagement and scarce resources. Nonetheless, Jordanian authorities piled on blame after the Covid-19 pandemic, and some even called for local Syrians to return home given the kingdom's financial troubles. Only after the Assad regime collapsed in December 2024 did many refugees feel safe enough to do so.

National Identity and Hashemitism

Within its exclusionary boundaries, the Jordanian nation is more a muddled mosaic than monolith. Citizens still search for a coherent sense of national identity, meaning one's cultural and historical self-conception as part of a larger national body of people. When nations have robust identities, they can resemble "imagined communities" that evoke a powerful sense of belonging among its members that springs from collective understandings about the origins, struggles, and greatness that make them whole.[36] Like all identities, as well, a national identity is malleable. It can be manipulated in many ways. It changes over time, and it intersects with more parochial identity components that some people hold closely, such as ethnicity, gender, tribe, class, and religion. Nonetheless, some national identities are more coherent than others; that is to say, it is easier to answer the loaded question, "Who are we—and whom should we become?" in some countries than in others.

In Jordan, few other questions are more elusive to answer. Many citizens still search for a sense of Jordan-ness, or a common understanding of what being Jordanian *means* beyond obeying laws, paying taxes, fluttering the national flag, or carrying the national passport. Local sociologists, historians, and scholars struggle with this topic, often describing Jordan's national identity has having "compound," "multiple," or even "hybrid" qualities.[37] Such terms capture the ambiguity of Jordan's national imagination, further corroborated by survey

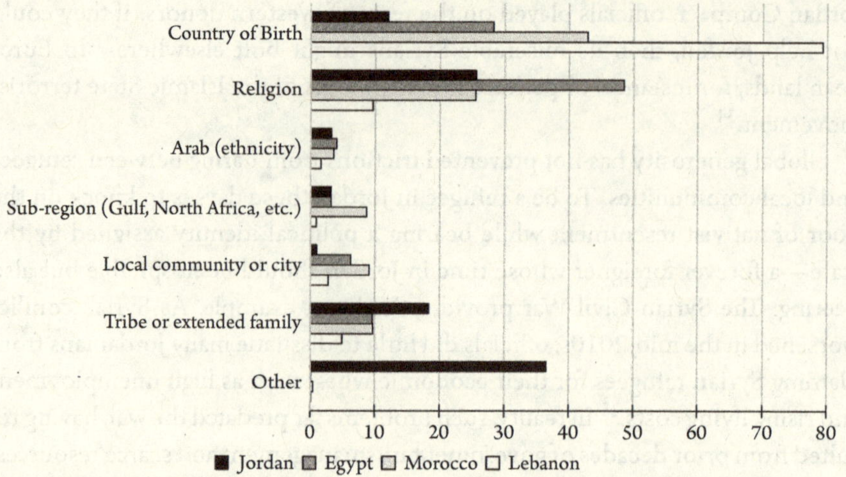

Figure 2.2 National Identity in Jordan and Selected Arab Countries, 2016–17.
The data show responses to the survey question, "If you have been asked to identify yourself, with which of the following do you most closely identify yourself?" Source: Arab Barometer, https://www.arabbarometer.org/

evidence exposing the weakness of many Jordanian citizens' attachment to their nation versus more parochial affinities to tribe, family, or religion. During its 2016–2017 Wave IV surveys, the Arab Barometer asked respondents across the Arab world to choose how they would most closely identify themselves. As Figure 2.2 shows, under 12 percent of Jordanians chose their country, whereas 18.3 percent picked tribe or family, 25.6 percent picked religion, and nearly 36.5 percent selected "other." This ranked, by far, as the lowest rate of national identification in the region. For example, Egyptians identified with Egypt by 28.2 percent, while the Lebanese—renowned for their confessional divides and sectarian conflict—selected Lebanon by a whopping 79.3 percent.

Why is finding an overarching national identity so confounding in Jordan? A major reason today is the historical fissure between the kingdom's Palestinian-origin majority and its mostly tribal Transjordanian communities, which the next section of the chapter engages. Ask Jordanians about their *wataniyyah* (patriotism), national pride, or emotional attachments to the kingdom, and their answers may reflect not just other identity components like gender or religion but also this communal backdrop. For a long time, the primal question "*Min wayn inta*?" (Where are you from?) was the most relevant but also most provocative thing to ask locals. These knotty dilemmas underscore the equivocality of Jordanian national identity, contested by three different forces: the monarchy, Transjordanian tribes, and the Palestinians.

Hashemitism

The Jordanian monarchy has an unfussy framework for national identity. Call it Hashemitism, in which Jordan-ness entails patriotically cherishing the resilience, moderation, and benevolence of the ruling dynasty.[38] It means reminding everyone that as Sharifian descendants of the Prophet, the Hashemites stand for justice and sovereignty for all Arab peoples, embodied by the family's role in the 1916 Great Arab Revolt against Ottoman rule. The day the revolt began, June 10, remains a national holiday (Army Day) for this reason, much as the Jordanian flag borrows its design from the banner flown by the revolt. By venerating both Hashemite greatness and the military that protects it, remembrance of the wartime episode gives the monarchy a founding myth more convenient than British imperialism. Hashemitism also signifies that monarchical rule is fair and prosperous and that Jordanians should embrace national unity (*al-wahdah al-wataniyyah*) over anything that divides them, such as religious differences, economic grievances, or political dissent.

The Jordanian government has promoted Hashemitism like a civic faith through official venues, including royal speeches, public ceremonies, military events, national museums, media programs, and public education.[39] It does not take long to recognize that its theme of royal togetherness hides a political intention. Hashemitism poses as a national identity but aims also to instill an indissoluble sense of obedience to autocratic rule. Even seemingly innocuous metaphors, such as how Jordanian kings speak of their nation as a household or family, reflect this. King Hussein perpetually beseeched Jordanians as fellow brothers or kin living in the same giant family, summoning familial imagery in his affective role as sheikh of all sheikhs (*shaykh al-mashaayikh*). Yet this distorts history, for many Transjordanian tribes rejected the British-backed Hashemites in the 1920s as their figurative fathers. Loyalty came after their political suppression and economic incorporation into the colonial state. Along the way, imperial officials invented many cultural symbols for the nation they hoped to conjure, including even mansaf—the rice-and-lamb dish now famed for being Jordan's "national" dish.[40]

Moreover, Hashemitism's own understanding of national unity has evolved over time. It changed after the 1948 Arab-Israeli War, when Jordan controlled the West Bank and Palestinians became the demographic majority. Confronting sudden social change, the monarchy chose to enfranchise Palestinians as citizens and proclaim itself as guardian of the Palestinian cause. Hashemitism, at least in theory, saw Transjordanians and Palestinians as equal members of its family. However, such hybridity diminished after the 1967 loss of the West Bank and the 1970 Black September civil conflict, as discussed in the next section. That rupture drove Hashemitism back to its East Bank tribal linchpins, whose more zealous nativists painted Palestinian-Jordanians as perfidious vassals. The monarchy continued projecting its advocacy of the Palestinian cause as part of Jordan's national identity, but more meekly.

When King Abdullah came to power in 1999, Hashemitism stood at a new juncture. King Abdullah has reproduced the organic overtones of his late father. After his enthronement, he observed that his family of four had now become a family of millions and that he loved every one of his new brothers and sisters.[41] The palace also initiated public relations campaigns emphasizing national unity over all internal frictions. Catchy slogans abounded with royal fervor, from Jordan First (*al-Urdun Awallan*) in 2002 and We Are All Jordan (*Kulluna al-Urdun*) in 2006 to Raise Your Head, You Are Jordanian (*Irfa' Ra'sak Inta Urduni*) in 2015. Endless public conferences and optimistic royal speeches have since instructed citizens—and especially the youth—to work hard and take pride in Jordan's stability and leadership.

As many astute critics note, though, such political sloganeering has failed to catch on. It is hard to exude naked patriotism in the way Hashemitism demands when the economy does not create jobs and promised democratic reforms never materialize. And it is impossible when different groups still see their place in the nation as fundamentally unequal.[42] Still, the royal state soldiers onward, insisting that it knows what Jordan-ness entails for the masses.

The Transjordanian-Palestinian Divide

For all its bombast, Hashemitism strains to reconcile the Transjordanian-Palestinian divide. There are no official data about the total number of Jordanians of Palestinian origin, as the national census does not report this. However, a reasonable assumption is that Palestinian-Jordanians represent the majority of the roughly 8 million–strong citizenry, with popular figures varying from 55 to 70 percent.[43] Most no longer live in UNRWA camps, although over 2.4 million still have UNRWA-designated refugee status given by the agency after the 1948 Arab-Israeli War. In the global Palestinian diaspora of nearly 15 million, the only place with more Palestinians than Jordan is the state of Palestine itself, counting the West Bank and Gaza Strip.

In Jordan, the communal dynamic between the Palestinian majority and Transjordanian minority has become a simplistic descriptor that outsiders use to characterize these two Arab groups inhabiting the country. Crude binaries guide them through this social wrinkle. For example, there are East Bankers (Transjordanians) and West Bankers (Palestinians); those who claim to *be* Jordan (i.e., Transjordanian tribes) versus those who *built* Jordan (Palestinians) after 1948; the rural tribal sons who work for the government and army, and the Palestinian urbanites who fuel the commercial economy; the tribal sheikhs who embrace the king versus troublesome Palestinian dissidents; the East Bank patriots who wear red *kufiyah* headdresses and the Palestinian activists who wear black ones; and so forth.

These are caricatures. Yet, they do hint at a real wedge within Jordan's national identity: these social forces have different histories and political statuses. For instance, despite growing complaints against King Abdullah, Transjordanian tribes still form the Hashemite monarchy's core base of support, and rural areas remain its political heartland even if they stand on the economic periphery. By contrast, Palestinian-Jordanians continue to suffer political discrimination, despite their economic productivity and predominance in the urban centers that hold most of the populace. The state and its institutions, including the coercive apparatus discussed in Chapter 4, remains staffed almost exclusively by East Bank Jordanians, while relatively few Palestinian-Jordanians have ever reached high government positions, with only one (Taher Masri) serving as prime minister in the last half-century.

At the same time, Transjordanians and Palestinians are not immutable forces. Authorities discourage researchers from fielding public surveys that touch on this sensitive topic, such as by asking Palestinian-Jordanian respondents about their views on Transjordanians and vice versa. However, some elementary facts suggest that the Transjordanian-Palestinian divide is less a razor-sharp rift and more a blurred marker that obscures the finer graduations in how members of each category see themselves and each other.

Transjordanians and Tribalism

Most Transjordanians trace their heritage to the tribal residents who lived on the East Bank before 1921. As a concept, tribalism eludes easy definitions. Orientalist work depicted Arab tribesmen as camel-riding warriors ululating in the desert, whereas many Westerners now see tribal persons as rural bumpkins walking in solemn deference to their sheikh and king—the antithesis of enlightened citizens. Such views need updating. Classically, a tribe (*'ashira*) means a network of kinship based on common patrilineal descent. Tribes hence manifest as social communities that impress a flexible, localized identity upon their members, even if they have long departed rural settings—as most Transjordanians have—for towns and cities. Tribal identities prize solidarity, the notion that members constitute a tribal "we" as transmitted through oral histories, unwritten codes, family bonds, and shared memories.[44] Another constant is the *sheikh* (chieftain), who in many tribal settings wields the customary respect and authority to regulate local conflicts, lead communal affairs, and influence local opinions.

When Jordanians speak of tribes, they can mean anything from sprawling confederations linking dozens of clans and hundreds of extended families together—like the Bani Hassan and Huwaytat—to tiny groupings clustered around ancestral villages and towns. In total, the East Bank has hundreds of tribes defined by verifiable genealogical lineage.[45] Prior to Transjordan's colonial birth, they pursued diverse livelihoods. Contrary to popular belief, most were not Bedouin nomads. Most were peasant farmers (*fellahin*), and the remainder either nomadic (*badawi*, from which Bedouin is Anglicized) or semi-nomadic (*hadhari*). Some were Christian, but most were Muslim. They farmed, herded, migrated, traded, raided, feuded, and negotiated. There was violence and contestation, but there was also an indigenous social order within an expanse that had never experienced statehood.[46]

Within that order swirled tribal claims to land stretching back for centuries. Whereas Western chronicles of Transjordan during the 1920s and 1930s depict the British-guided monarchy taming a lawless wasteland, tribal narratives tell a different tale. These internal histories describe the Hashemite project (and Ottoman rule decades prior) as foreign occupations, whose administrative rules disrupted the self-governance and economic autonomy that had long defined Transjordanian life.[47] As Chapters 5 and 6 discuss, such fecund memories have inspired tribal oppositionists whenever they dissented against the royal autocracy, from the Transjordanian National Congress groups of the late 1920s to the grassroots activist movements, or *hirak*, of the Arab Spring a century later. They emit the thunderous idea that Transjordanians are the East Bank's original inhabitants, far predating any Hashemite interlopers. If anyone can righteously beseech the king, the sheikh of sheikhs, it is the tribes themselves. King Abdullah has faced such heat for decades, as a growing number of tribal critics associate his reign with prolific corruption and economic calamity.

Such independence coexists with the fact that most tribal communities have also backed Hashemite rule since the colonial era, due to their economic and political incorporation into the state. Moreover, as Chapter 4 discusses, the monarchy's ethnocratic strategy after the 1960s favored Transjordanians within public institutions like the government and military, thereby fusing tribalism with a bigoted version of Jordanian nationalism. It stoked a conservative strain of East Bank nativist identity that juxtaposed Palestinians as a megalithic "other" who were, at best, glorified guests. By contrast, Transjordanian tribespersons were the truest sons of the state (*abna' al-dawla*), who, as soldiers and politicians, watered the East Bank's parched soil with their blood.

Such chauvinism is not the only Transjordanian view, though. Many East Bankers today care little for this communal distinction, for both they and Palestinian-Jordanians share many common grievances over the terrible economy and their regime's autocratic excesses. During the 2011–2012 Arab Spring, tribal activists filled many streets with protesters who walked alongside dissenting Palestinian-Jordanians as they demanded democratic reform. The same Transjordanian nativists that vilify King Abdullah's wife, Queen Rania, for her Palestinian background care little that the late King Hussein's third wife, Alia, was also Palestinian, or that her name adorns Jordan's international airport outside of Amman. Indeed, on a daily basis, most tribal happenings have little to do with Palestinians at all. When conflicts emerge between tribal followers on account of perceived insults or dishonor, from university student brawls to tit-for-tat blood crimes, the focus of both sheikhs and local authorities falls upon maintaining social balance and order—not on finding a Palestinian bogeyman.

The Transjordanian-Palestinian dynamic becomes politically tricky, nonetheless, whenever the neighboring Israeli-Palestinian conflict comes into view. Like the Hashemite monarchy and Palestinian-Jordanians, tribal Jordanians disparage Israel for its withering assaults on the West Bank and Gaza Strip; anti-Israel protests and allies always attract East Bankers. They believe that Palestine must have independent statehood, but for different reasons. Some embrace the Palestinian cause as a matter of Arab solidarity or basic human rights. Others want a Palestinian state so that Palestinian-Jordanians would leave the kingdom to go there.

Above all, though, most fear that the Israeli state intends to annex parts or all of the Palestinian territories, thereby expelling millions more Palestinian refugees onto Jordan. This reckless idea of "Jordan is Palestine" (*al-watan al-badil*, or alternative homeland), has been espoused by many right-wing Zionists for decades.[48] In recent years, powerful American voices have also stoked this fire. For instance, President Donald Trump proposed in early 2025 to relocate all Palestinians from Gaza, ravaged from the latest war with Israel which began in October 2023, onto Egypt and Jordan, and afterwards redevelop the depopulated strip with Israeli support into a touristic wonderland. However, Jordanians universally reject such venomous ideas. For not just Transjordanian conservatives but also Palestinian-Jordanians and the monarchy, the alternative homeland project represents an existential threat.[49] It would replace the promise of Palestinian statehood with ethnic cleansing. Moreover, if Jordan becomes the new homeland for all Palestinians, then East Bank tribes would become an even smaller minority in the country, ratcheting up communal strains and calling into question what Jordan is supposed to be as a political entity.

That tribal identity in Jordan is "fuzzy," to cite one anthropological treatise, is thus an understatement.[50] There is no neat way to capture what being Transjordanian means. It certainly does not connote instinctive hostility against Palestinian-Jordanians or undying adoration of the monarchy. Indeed, some tribal activists see little contradiction between decrying the economic dominance or corruption of wealthy Palestinian-Jordanians, a very common complaint, and more liberally demanding greater democracy and political rights from their monarchy. Some Transjordanians complain just as loudly about tribal inequalities, in that larger or more prestigious East Bank tribes like the Tarawneh, ʿAbbadi, and Bani Sakhr enjoy far more political influence than smaller and poorer clans, whose favored sons are seldom picked by the king as government ministers and army generals. Internally, as well, the patriarchal structure of tribal communities is changing. In many communities, the traditional authority of gerontocratic sheikhs has faded, as youthful tribal influencers have learned to secure their own followers through social media to opine on controversial issues and question old political habits.[51]

All this suggests that Transjordanian tribes do not comprise a single, ossified body. Their historical memories and social imaginations map onto identity politics in unexpected ways. Such pluralism also applies to Palestinians, whose segmentation similarly shows that identity politics in Jordan are far more intricate than often assumed.

Palestinian-Jordanians

Jordan and Palestine have long been intertwined due to their geographic contiguity. Under Ottoman rule, regular trade linked East Bank towns such as Salt and Karak with West Bank counterparts such as Nablus and Hebron.[52] Transjordanian and Palestinian peasants and workers crisscrossed the Jordan River in search of seasonal jobs, as did sheikhs, merchants, and other notables seeking new markets and partners. These were socially distinctive lands, but not defined by rigid state boundaries until British imperialism cleaved them into separate administrative units.

The Palestinian transformation of Jordan came through war and migration. The 1948 Arab-Israeli War infused the kingdom with nearly 900,000 Palestinians atop a preexisting mostly Transjordanian populace of 400,000. Among the newcomers were farmers, workers, teachers, administrators, engineers, and merchants. Overall, Palestinians were better educated and more urbanized than Transjordanians, and they quickly diversified the economy and culture of the amalgamated kingdom.[53]

Yet they did not come under Hashemite rule by choice. Many resided in the West Bank and East Jerusalem, which Jordan annexed after the war. Others were displaced onto the East Bank, settling in refugee camps or migrating to cities like Amman. Most from this 1948 generation became Jordanian citizens thanks to the 1954 Nationality Law. Some Palestinian businessmen and bureaucrats also integrated quickly into their new state, thanks to their resources and connections. However, the promise of national unity eventually crumbled, not least because of King Abdullah's 1951 assassination in Jerusalem by a local Palestinian militant. Tensions simmered through the 1950s, as Palestinian activists joined with Transjordanian dissidents in mobilizing democratic opposition against Hashemite rule, as Chapter 5 describes. Early on, some East Bank officials worried the Palestinian masses would overwhelm the tribal-oriented political structure cultivated since the colonial period. Conversely, many Palestinians grew suspicious that they were not political equals; they were "subject to the state but not psychologically members of the nation."[54]

Such communal stress worsened as regional conflict unleashed more change. The 1967 Arab-Israeli War expelled 250,000 more Palestinians to the East Bank due to the Israeli occupation of the Gaza Strip and the West Bank. The Gazans, as mentioned earlier, never received Jordanian citizenship. West Bankers, still citizens, came to UNRWA-run refugee camps or maturing urban centers like Amman. To add further complication, by now a Palestinian bourgeois elite thrived in Jordan; the most prosperous families, like the Masri and Nuqul clans, developed lucrative commercial enterprises with government support. At the same time, the regime also confronted a new challenge: the Palestine Liberation Organization (PLO). Founded in 1964, the PLO proclaimed itself as the rightful representative of all Palestinian people, including those in Jordan. The monarchy saw the organization, therefore, as undermining not just its regional stature but also its domestic authority.

The Palestinian experience in Jordan would rupture once again through war. Most Palestinians in Jordan supported the PLO's armed campaign to liberate Palestine from Israel. However, many questioned King Hussein's decision to allow the PLO and its various commando groups (*fida'iyin*) to operate from the East Bank in launching guerilla strikes into Israel, which in the late 1960s produced ugly border skirmishes with the Israeli military. Escalating hostility between the regime and these Palestinian militant organizations exploded in the Black September war of 1970. That civil conflict was brief but costly, as the Jordanian army suppressed insurgent PLO forces seeking to depose the monarchy and repelled a half-hearted Syrian intervention supporting them.

Black September remains a delicate topic in Jordan. Few public institutions and school textbooks discuss it. Having produced thousands of casualties, the conflict ranks as Jordan's second-bloodiest conflict after the 1967 Arab-Israeli War. Yet the Jordanian government does not regard it as a civil war, even though it meets the literal definition: organized combat between adversaries over control of a contested territory.[55] Rather, the royal perspective—shared by Transjordanian nativists—frames Black September as political *restoration*. In using the East Bank as their political and military base in their struggles against Israel, nearly a dozen PLO-affiliated commando groups had amalgamated too much power. By 1970, they had usurped Hashemite authority by controlling significant chunks of Amman and other areas, creating their own "state within a state" replete with local conscription and taxes. Even so, only after surviving several assassination attempts from PLO elements did King Hussein order the liquidation of these guerilla groups. As heroically retold in this version, the king and his steadfast tribal army—with a little help from the United States, which supplied emergency aid and arms—vanquished thousands of treasonous Palestinians yearning to install a pro-Soviet revolutionary regime in Amman.

Palestinians in Jordan have a different take: the 1970 Black September war revealed the revolting side of Transjordanian xenophobia. By the time of the conflict, most Palestinian-Jordanians embraced the notion of Palestinian nationalism (*al-qawmiyyah al-filistiniyyah*)—an independent and sovereign Palestine, a dream shared by the global Palestinian diaspora. However, this did not mean instigating revolution in Amman. In fact, most *fida'iyin* organizations had struggled to recruit local fighters and volunteers after relocating to Jordan following the 1967 Arab-Israeli War.[56] One reason stemmed from their poor internal discipline and squabbling leadership, which turned off many Palestinian-Jordanians. Another was a moral disconnect in goals. The cause of militant struggle against Israel to liberate the occupied West Bank, which most locals backed, was quite different than a homegrown insurgency against King Hussein, which meant bringing conflict and violence to the home front.

Nonetheless, Jordanian elites did not make this distinction, and treated many Palestinian-Jordanians as potential combatants during Black September. The army rounded up thousands on trumped-up charges of sedition and shelled several large Palestinian refugee camps.[57] Complicating matters further, the PLO's *fida'iyin* also attracted thousands of Transjordanian supporters. Memoirs from former guerillas reveal that East Bank students, activists, and even army defectors joined their units, on basis of sharing their leftist ideology or else because they too wished to fight against their autocratic monarchy.[58] In the end, as older Palestinian-Jordanians recall, Black September laid an ugly legacy. As soon as the crisis ended, reactionary officials began conveying a nasty strain of East Bank nativism that portrayed all Palestinian-Jordanians as disloyal rebels. Many of the politicians and officials who led Jordan under King Hussein for decades after the conflict treated Palestinians as second-class citizens, preventing them from entering military service or obtaining government jobs. Urban Palestinian neighborhoods bore the brunt of heavy-handed repression during these martial law years, despite being engines of economic productivity.

In this tense climate, many Palestinian-Jordanians left the country. Their journey embodies the multiplicity of Jordan's Palestinian experience. In the 1970s and 1980s, several hundred thousand Palestinian-Jordanians departed to work elsewhere, particularly the oil-rich Gulf kingdoms. They did well there, and the remittances they sent back contributed to Jordan's economic boom. However, their forced relocation back to the kingdom during and after the 1990–1991 Gulf

War prompted more castigation by Transjordanian conservatives, who worried that these "outsiders" would finish the job of conquering Jordan that the PLO started two decades earlier.[59] In truth, given their long time away, this segment of Palestinians had the weakest attachment to Jordan, and many struggled to readjust.

Crucially, the stories of these returnees diverge from those Palestinian-Jordanians who stayed. Today, many Palestinian refugees in UNRWA camps, including stateless Gazans, reside on Jordan's economic and institutional fringes, their political interests ignored by the government.[60] Other Palestinian-Jordanians who have better assimilated into society have branched into different directions. The elites, from wealthy business families to posh technocrats, often rally around Hashemitism because they reap privileges and favors from the monarchy. Middle-class and poorer Palestinian households have a more complicated status.[61] Many retain close family ties to the West Bank and still experience social or political discrimination in Jordan. However, being citizens, they also see Jordan as their home. Few Palestinian-Jordanians resisted the monarchy's 1988 disengagement from the West Bank, which Chapter 8 discusses further, revealing their agreement that any future Palestinian state across the Jordan River must be legally separate from the kingdom. That view still holds today.

The richness of this Palestinian-Jordanian experience gets lost in festering stereotypes that frame Palestinians in Jordan as being fundamentally different from Transjordanians. Fortunately, this communal rupture is becoming less rigid over time. As Chapters 5 and 6 show, Palestinians in Jordan are hardly the only source of political opposition. While they have historically mobilized many protests, so too have tribal activists and rural dissidents. This makes it harder for East Bank nativists to broadcast facile narratives framing Palestinians as untrustworthy guests and Transjordanians as loyal denizens. Furthermore, over the past several decades, many Palestinian-Jordanians have come to work for the government as public school teachers and medical staff in public hospitals, although informal rules still exclude them from making inroads into more sensitive state institutions like the military and security forces. Socially, the constant hum of education, work, and Transjordanian-Palestinian intermarriage—plus the fading memories of Black September—make questions of personal origin less salient than before. For many young Jordanians today, the question of where a fellow citizen may be from originally has little purpose, for such information has little utility when both tribal and Palestinian communities face serious economic challenges and political problems.

As a result of these constructive shifts, Jordanians in the twenty-first century have been able to nurture more honest debates about the status and treatment of Palestinians in the kingdom. They have interrogated the interwoven meanings of their vexing nationhood in ways that were once taboo. Daring cultural documentaries like Khalil Qamouk's 2011 *Filistiniyu al-Urdun: Illa Ayna?* (*The Palestinians of Jordan: To Where?*) attest to this.[62] To be sure, the Transjordanian-Palestinian fault line still matters. Transjordanian conservatives still hold sway within the Hashemite state and its institutions of power, as Chapter 3 dissects. Anti-Palestinian discrimination persists in many political and social settings, especially against those who still reside in UNRWA-administered refugee camps. Nonetheless, the discourse of Jordanian identity is changing with the march of time, and this means so too will the values and interests of its residents evolve.

Conclusion

There are many Jordans, depending on the vantage point. From the West, the Hashemite Kingdom is the consummate political survivor and geopolitical island of stability, demarcated more by its strategic value and friendly Hashemite dynasty than anything else. From within, Jordan is a kaleidoscope of overlapping layers, the picture changing as one switches optics.

Each of those layers shown here illustrates this diversity while also highlighting how politics saturates public life. Jordan is highly urbanized, but with its citification comes distinctive challenges such as social change, unrestrained growth, and deepening inequality that disconnect residents from their built environment. The population is also quite young. Young Jordanians have given rise to restive yearnings for freer information and creative expression, often through online spaces that nervous authorities can only partially control. Most of Jordan is Muslim, but Islam means divergent things to those who practice the faith. The rise of Islamism has introduced more conservative religious norms into civil society and politics, while state institutions and the monarchy impose their own sanitized version of official Islam.

How religious and ethnic groups, as well as non-nationals, fare is likewise tinged with political consequences. Contrast the deliberate accommodation of Christians and Circassians into the state and economy, for example, with the exclusion of foreign workers and refugee communities from any talk of gaining citizenship. However, Jordanian citizens themselves do not have a consensual model of national identity, one that can pinpoint what being Jordanian means beyond attachments to family, tribe, religion, and other parochial identities. The Hashemite monarchy sponsors its own vision of belonging, suffused with patriotism and obeisance to its autocratic writ; needless to say, this does not satisfy many people. Finally, the communal divide between Jordan's Palestinian-origin majority and Transjordanian, or tribal, minority shows how political conceptions of nationhood and belonging have changed. Mutual relations carry lingering tension and uncertainty, and the royal autocracy still treats many tribes with political favor. Yet, not only has this social cleavage softened over time, but each of these groups also includes many different voices and contradictory views—including healthy doses of political opposition.

Having depicted these ambits of society, the next step to explore is political power. Ruling over Jordan's social landscape is an authoritarian regime headed by the ruling Hashemite monarchy. It cloaks itself in democratic rhetoric but exercises vast unelected authority. Its inner workings appear murky for good reason: autocracies close to the West gain little by admitting to their excesses. It is therefore vital to reveal how power and authority operate within the Jordanian state, which harbors unexpectedly curious paradoxes borne out of royal imperatives and institutional design. The next chapter investigates this.

3

The Hashemite Regime and State Institutions

Who Makes the Rules in Jordan?

In March 2011, as the Arab Spring uprisings tore throughout the Middle East, Jordan's leadership sprang into action. As popular protests spread throughout the streets, the Hashemite monarchy announced a new era of political reform, promising to democratize the kingdom to satisfy the dreams of its citizens. Jordanian commentators demurred, not least because past pledges for democracy proved so illusory. Yet they minced their words. They did not question the intentions of parliament (*majlis al-ummah*) or even the prime minister's government (*al-hukumah*), for those institutions had little authority to order such hefty changes. Instead, they gingerly spoke about this ambitious offering from the "decision-making circles" (*dawaa'ir san'a al-qiraar*) and wondered it would satisfy a frustrated society.[1]

In the end, their cynicism was justified: nothing happened. But consider the verbiage. Whenever Jordanians openly mention the powerholders who oversee their domestic politics and foreign policy, they use obfuscating terms such as "decision-making circles"—or another popular locution, the "political kitchen" (*al-matbakh al-siyaasi*). These euphemistic phrases refer to the monarchical regime that wields untrammeled political power over the country: the king and his royal court, military and security chiefs, and other senior officials. Many do not publicly call out these mighty figures, because it is a costly move. It would puncture the illusion that Jordan is a moderate and progressive state rather than an autocracy and thus draw the unwanted attention of the police or intelligence services looking to arrest troublemakers.

Citizens, of course, can still say political things. They can complain about some government policies; they can join opposition parties and participate in protests. Yet, this is an authoritarian system all the same: a small number of unelected elites makes the rules that everyone else in society must follow, and the latter do not have a choice in the matter. That is the theme of this chapter. Across the world, authoritarian regimes can often look like black boxes, their interior workings shrouded behind impenetrable walls of repression or fear. This chapter lifts that veil in Jordan. It demystifies its political structure, revealing the actors and institutions that govern this nondemocratic state. It includes four sections.

First, it introduces the theoretical concepts of regimes, democracy, and authoritarianism by lightly drawing upon political science scholarship. It identifies Jordan as a rare subtype of authoritarianism: ruling monarchism, an endangered species in global politics. Second, it reveals the internal workings of Jordan's political system under its ruling monarchy. Most democracies distribute power horizontally across various branches of government held together by checks and balances. By contrast, power within this royal autocracy is concentrated within the Hashemite kingship, and from this royal cynosure flows through other state organs like the royal court, coercive apparatus, and appointed government. The monarchy stands along at the top, being the most important political actor. It is not absolutist, because the king needs other institutions to carry out national governance and a vocal public can push back against unpopular decisions. Still, Jordanians lack an irreducible right inherent to democracies: they cannot choose those who govern them, and they have no electoral means to replace them.

Third, this chapter outlines the role of the government and parliament, which compose the most observable faces of Jordanian politics. Headed by the prime minister, the royally appointed government administers state functions and undertakes the daily task of running the country. It is beholden to the monarchy and its repressive institutions, being the product not of elections but royal decree. The bicameral parliament, meanwhile, is a weak legislature. It neither forms the government nor does much actual legislating, while being hamstrung by legal restrictions and internal squabbles. Nonetheless, its lower house remains Jordan's sole nationally elected institution and helps preserve Jordan's democratic veneer to the world. Finally, the chapter dissects the hidden patterns governing political relationships within this system. It accentuates the ubiquity of clientelism, which allows a small class of elites to dominate politics by trading favors and peddling influence. It also reviews how the state and its bureaucracy operate, which entail a great deal of inefficiency and corruption. It finally touches upon the centralized nature of national governance, with local municipalities and provincial governorates having little independence from the national center of power based in Amman.

Democracy and Authoritarianism in Comparative Perspective

The term "political regimes" refers to the ensemble of institutions and routines within countries that regulate access to power and determine how that power is exercised.[2] In plain terms, it denotes how leaders come to office and claim authority over society. In turn, regimes inhabit the larger space of a state, which encompasses many public institutions, bureaucratic organizations, and administrative livery. Regimes come in a dizzying variety. Some types of regimes no longer exist, such as fascism and totalitarianism; others are antiquated, such as oligarchies and plutocracies. The simplest modern conceptualization distinguishes between two regime types: democracy and authoritarianism. Both are crucial in understanding Jordanian politics.

Democracies and Autocracies

Democracies spring from the inimical wellspring of political contestation. Those who make rules—such as social programs, economic initiatives, public laws, and foreign policies—are elected by the much bigger mass of people who must follow those rules. In democratic regimes, rulers and legislators must be chosen through regular, competitive elections that allow adult citizens to freely vote, campaign for office, and oppose the incumbent. Democratic elections enshrine fair and peaceful competition that require the alternation of power between rival parties and politicians: "those in power lose when a majority of voters so wish."[3]

Of course, democracy should involve more than this. That citizens cast ballots every few years for a president or parliamentary parties says little about the extent of their rights between elections. Comparative political scientists have long argued that beyond the "minimalist" criterion of holding elections, truly liberal or high-quality democracies must also honor thicker principles grounded in philosophical commitments to liberty, even if they disagree on how to measure them.[4] Generally, however, most specialists hold that full-fledged democracies should feature elected governments that respect freedoms of speech, belief, assembly, faith, and publication, which in turn promote pluralism and diversity; an independent judiciary enforcing laws fairly and transparently; horizontal accountability, in which legislative and constitutional checks prevent executives from abusing power; the rule of law, to inhibit corruption and abuses of power; civilian oversight over the military; protections for minority rights; and gender equality, among other principles.[5]

Jordan fails the litmus test for not just this ideal model of liberal democracy but also the minimalist version of electoral democracy. Authoritarianism (i.e., autocracy or dictatorship) typifies its political regime. Under authoritarian rule, free, fair, and competitive elections do not determine who holds power. Instead, autocratic leaders usually seize or inherit their executive office and then stay in power for as long as possible. In Jordan, hence, citizens cannot vote their ruling monarchy out of office; indeed, local and parliamentary elections have little bearing on government policies at all. Moreover, those living under authoritarianism face serious restrictions on their civil liberties and political rights. Most dictators pay lip service to ideals like representation, accountability, and pluralism. In practice, however, they brandish great powers to attenuate and punish opposition groups, suppress popular expressions like public protests and independent media, and impose their preferred social policies, economic programs, and foreign relationships upon the populace.[6] Again, this description matches Jordan; as Chapters 4 and 5 explain, citizens have frequently risked suffering repression and other harms whenever they have sought to oppose their monarchical regime and call for radical democratic changes.

Ruling Monarchism

In the post–World War II era, political scientists have recognized that contemporary authoritarian regimes come in four varieties: militaristic, personalistic, party-based, and monarchical.[7] In military dictatorships, the armed forces take the reins of power through coups and exercise their control over the state either directly or indirectly behind a civilian façade. South America during the middle decades of the Cold War had an abundance of such regimes, as praetorian generals ran much of the show. In personalistic autocracies, a single individual ruler can wield absolutist power and resources. He may style himself as a grandiose visionary, father of the nation, or cultish savior of the people. In extreme cases, like that of Ferdinand Marcos of the Philippines or Idi Amin of Uganda, all of government turns upon the whims of this one strongman. By contrast, party-based authoritarianism orients around a dominant ruling party. Such parties control the state, convey ideological messages, and link the national leader to a large membership base.[8] These have been widespread over the past century; the longest-lasting examples include the Soviet Union, the seventy-one-year-long grip of El Partido Revolucionario Institucional in Mexico, and contemporary China under its Communist Party.

Most of the world's nearly ninety autocracies fall under these three categories of militaristic, personalistic, and party-based regimes. Jordan does not.

It embodies a fourth, much rarer type of authoritarianism: *ruling monarchies*. In ruling monarchies, a hereditary sovereign serves as both head of state and chief executive. In constitutional monarchies (a subtype of democracy), royal heads reign but do not rule; they are heads of state but concede executive power to democratic governments formed by elected parliaments. In ruling monarchies, by contrast, kings represent the immovable heart of all politics. They hold office until death or abdication, which naturally induces some personalistic flourishes. In Jordan, thus, portraits of King Abdullah—and often his father, King Hussein, as well as his son, Crown Prince Hussein—adorn public venues as an omnipresent sign of Hashemite leadership. More importantly, monarchical rulers have much flexibility in crafting the institutions that transmit their authority and influence, such as royal courts, governing cabinets, public bureaucracies, and militaries. They have little need for political parties. Power is inherited and justified as a matter of dynastic right, not engineered through complex ideologies or mobilizing organizations.

Ruling monarchies receive little academic attention today given their rarity. After World War II, social scientists declared the era of powerful kingships over, seeing their archaic symbolism and traditions as incompatible with modernity. They famously argued that such antediluvian regimes suffered a "king's dilemma," in which either mass pressures for democratic reform or else violent revolutions would extinguish these dynastic relics.[9] This prediction played out through the collapse of royal autocracies across the world over the past century. Many countries—including Russia, Ethiopia, and Afghanistan—saw their familial monarchies dislodged by revolution or coup; the Middle East and North Africa (MENA) also saw its fair share of toppled kingships from the 1950s through 1970s, such as in Egypt, Iraq, Libya, and Iran. Others, such as Japan and Bhutan, saw their imperial dynasties shrink into constitutional monarchies that allowed for parliamentary democracy, much like European countries such as the United Kingdom, Belgium, and Denmark.

Today, ruling monarchism persists in just ten countries around the globe, of which eight reside in the Arab world. Apart from Jordan, this includes Morocco and the six Arabian Gulf kingdoms of Saudi Arabia, Kuwait, Bahrain, Qatar, the United Arab Emirates, and Oman. Elsewhere, only tiny Eswatini in Southern Africa and Brunei in Southeast Asia qualify. Crucially, most of these monarchies have written constitutions, replete with hollow praise for political rights and liberal freedoms. However, this does not make them democratic, for these constitutions also either inscribe mammoth executive power into their monarchs or else are so regularly violated by political practices as to be meaningless. Moreover, their defining trait of hereditary succession is anathema to democracy, for it institutionalizes the deepest political inequality of all: the idea that *blood* always trumps ballots.[10] The logic of hereditary succession holds that kings, emirs, and sultans need never subject their power to popular consent through electoral competition. The most well-qualified commoner has zero chance to rule, whereas the most incompetent royals can claim power thanks to the blood coursing through their veins. It is a genetic lottery of the most unpredictable sort.

Ruling monarchism is a dying species of authoritarianism, which makes Jordan's political system unique. However, it is not immune to the same challenge that all dictatorships face: how to preserve power by both controlling opposition and cultivating public support.[11] While the next chapter addresses this fundamental dilemma, understanding Jordanian politics now requires diving deeper to show its innards of power.

The Rule-Makers

To casual observers these days, Jordan's brand of ruling monarchism shows many twinkles of democratic life. This is a "politely run" autocracy, as one shrewd observer coined it.[12] Citizens periodically cast ballots for parliamentary legislators and municipal councils in open elections. The kingdom has a long constitutional history, with both the 1928 Basic Law and 1952 constitution brimming with buoyant language about participation and equality. Opposition parties exist, and public protests are common. Unlike the most violent Arab autocracies like Syria under its former Assad regime or Iraq under Saddam Hussein, no bloody massacres ravage crowds of dissidents. Government officials are not completely wrong when they give a familiar refrain to visiting researchers: "Jordan is no police state; it is not Iran or North Korea. People here can breathe, they can travel, they can talk. The only ones who can't are extremists."[13]

Beyond this affable imagery, however, exists an underlying reality. This is an authoritarian regime where elections have little importance, the monarchy and its institutions enjoy immense power, and hardened rules still penalize people—just not brutally, for the most part—should their criticisms of this system become too brazen.

Dispelling the Democratic Delusion

When important international delegations like diplomatic convoys, foreign investors, sporting teams, and so on come to Jordan for the first time, their local counterparts often provide a rosy picture of domestic politics to acclimate their visitors. In this mirage, as Figure 3.1 shows, Jordan's political structure is portrayed as containing multiple branches of power instantly recognizable to anyone familiar with democracies. The bicameral parliament exemplifies popular will, with its lower house elected by the citizenry. As per the constitution,

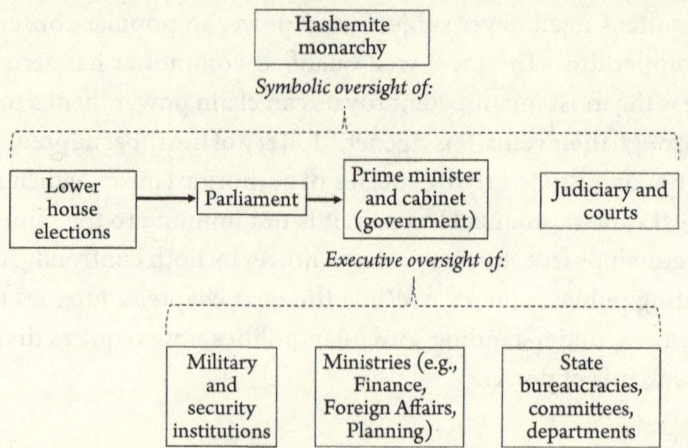

Figure 3.1 The Democratic Illusion of Jordanian Politics. Source: Author's illustration.

this legislature passes laws and works with the prime minister and cabinet, who represent the executive. Within this executive branch, the prime minister serves as head of government; he appoints other ministers, and together they supervise all state institutions. Finally, an independent judicial branch comprises the courts, jurists, and prosecutors overseeing civil laws, criminal cases, and Islamic law. In this imagined framework, the Hashemite palace appears benign. It stays far above the fray of politics, content to only deliver cheerful speeches, call for productive policies, and unite the nation around its calls for stability and patriotism.

Discard this fantasy. The Hashemite monarchy is not above the fray; it *is* the fray. Rather than horizontal branches, the more appropriate metaphor for Jordanian politics is one of concentric circles, in which power flows outward from the paramount royal center. Figure 3.2 depicts this configuration. In Jordan, political authority radiates from the king. Flanking the king is the Royal Hashemite Court, the coercive apparatus, and the leading figures of the cabinet-based government that the king appoints, namely the prime minister and other senior ministers. Herein lies the regime, whose power is beholden to neither electoral competition nor popular oversight. It goes by many names. Today, it is the decision-making circles; in the past, it was called the wise men (*al-rijaal al-hukamaa'*), the palace group, or even "patriarchal oligarchy," as political scientist Nasser Aruri coined a half-century ago.[14] No matter the appellation, these rule-makers represent the autocratic locus of power. They are the answer to the question, "Who matters the most in Jordanian politics?" They do.

The closer one stands to the royal epicenter, the more influence one carries with the regime and its internal deliberations. As Figure 3.2 shows, the outer layer includes secondary political actors that are entrusted with substantial

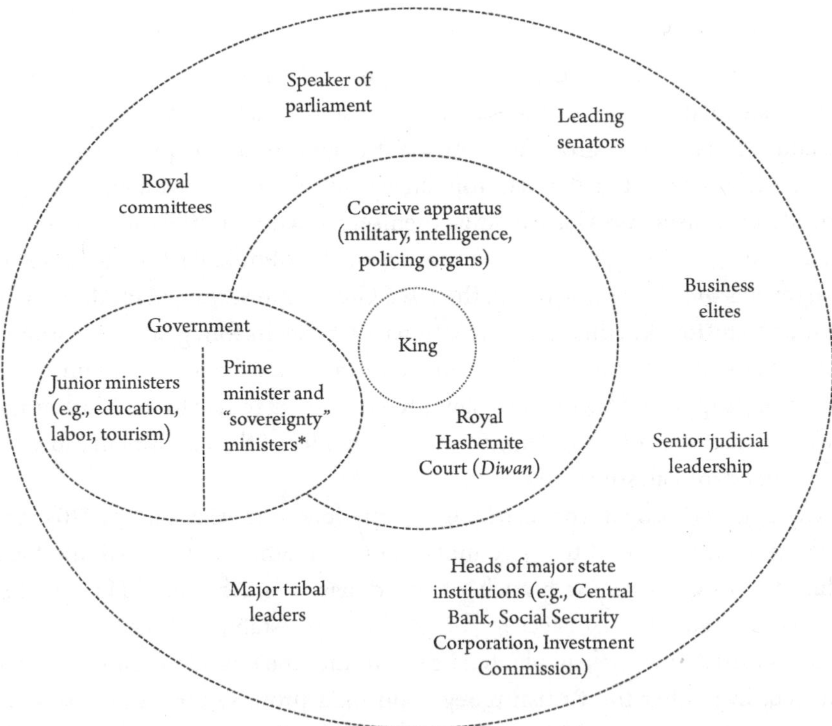

Figure 3.2 Real (Authoritarian) Structure of Jordanian Political Power. * Sovereignty ministers refer to those leading portfolios that implicate national security issues and require close coordination with the monarchy, such as the Ministries of Foreign Affairs, Finance, and Interior. Source: Author's illustration. Inspired by André Bank and Oliver Schlumberger, "Jordan: Between Regime Survival and Economic Reform," in *Arab Elites: Negotiating the Politics of Change*, ed. Volker Perthes (Lynne Rienner, 2004), 35–60.

authority. For instance, leading tribal sheikhs have sway when supplicating the king for attention, given the historical centrality of Transjordanian support for Hashemite rule. Money always talks, and so do wealthy businesspersons and merchants—a historically important constituency for the regime, as Chapter 7 explains. Senior judges presiding over high courts figure into political calculations, as they are royal appointees and are expected to heed the monarchy's direction on crucial cases. The bosses of major state institutions, like the Central Bank, Investment Commission, and Social Security Corporation (the national work-related insurance provider), have natural clout given the vital policies they oversee. The speaker of parliament, selected by the lower house, enjoys visibility as the titular head of the legislature and is sometimes involved within the regime's political consultations; so too are leading members of the royally appointed Senate, the upper chamber of parliament.

The King

The Hashemite monarchy is the nucleus of political power in Jordan. It sports an identity steeped in religious and historical lore and broadcast to society through the educational system and official media. Religiously, as Chapter 2 described, it claims Islamic prestige derived from lineage to the Prophet Muhammad. Historically, the Hashemites have defined themselves as not just the rulers of Jordan but also the guiding light for Arab unity across the Middle East. While such an ideal reflects the Hashemite role in the 1916 Great Arab Revolt, in modern times the monarchy invokes this self-conception to validate its foreign policy commitments. For instance, the notion of being an Arab voice for peace and unity has historically supported Hashemite claims to serve as custodian to the Muslim and Christian holy sites of Jerusalem, as well as defender of the Palestinian cause for an independent Palestinian state.

Tragedy, too, tinges the Hashemite experience. In the early 1920s, the Hashemites were one of the preeminent political families of the Middle East. While the original senior branch of the dynasty under Sharif Hussein bin Ali served as guardian of Mecca—a regal position established many centuries earlier—British imperialism planted its scions into the new kingdoms of Jordan and Iraq. Even after the British reneged on their promise for an independent pan-Arab state after World War I, a pledge made to convince Sharif Hussein to help orchestrate the Great Arab Revolt in 1916, the clan still aspired to the leadership of all Arabs (and perhaps all Muslims, too). Yet Saudi conquest drove the Hashemites from Mecca in 1924, while the Iraqi kingship under King Faisal II, the great-grandson of Sharif Hussein, was extirpated by revolution in 1958. Jordan is the last Hashemite citadel.

Despite this regal, symbolic past, monarchical rule in Jordan is neither mysterious nor unknowable. It entails routine practices that would be familiar to any student of authoritarianism. Plainly, the Jordanian kingship has tentacular powers. The king is both the head of state and chief executive. He appoints prime ministers (and thus governments), the crown prince (and thus his successor), senators, military commanders, security chiefs, senior judges, and other figures within high officialdom. He also monopolizes certain reserved domains of policymaking. As Chapter 8 notes, foreign policy is one such area: the Hashemite king cartelizes foreign relations, having the primal role in declaring war, making peace, inking treaties, and overall deciding how Jordan should behave externally. The king also steers all high-level domestic matters that impact on political stability, such as internal security, military concerns, tribal relations, and financial priorities. Indeed, the coercive apparatus, mentioned later in this chapter and fully explained in Chapter 4, reports to him—not to the prime minister or parliament. In times of emergency, he can also rule by decree without the token presence of parliament. In relational terms, the king is the supreme veto player, in that no major domestic or foreign policies can occur without his participation and approval.

The Hashemite monarchy is technically a "constitutional" one, insofar that Jordan's 1952 constitution—which incorporates some elements of the 1928 Basic Law, the first constitution-like document in the kingdom's history—ensconces royal power within a broader framework of institutions and laws. Some sections of the constitution read like a democratic manifesto, making admirable mention of parliamentary government, regular elections, labor unions, and political parties. Yet as Jordanian legal experts like Sufian Obeidat have argued, constitutions are only as good as the politicians who obey them.[15] The monarchy has long overstepped the guidelines of the original constitution or else pushed through amendments—as it did during 2015–2016 and 2022—to vest even more executive authority into the king.

Indirectly, the monarchy controls the national political agenda because royal preferences guide the overall direction of national policymaking. All political figures abide by an implicit standard: what the king *wants* dictates what the rest of the government and state should *do*.[16] For example, as Chapter 7 discusses, the pursuit of neoliberal economic policies after the 1990s, which heralded a new era of privatization and fiscal austerity, was King Abdullah's personal priority. The king can also reach into society himself to personally touch the lives of citizens. For instance, the monarchy has long provided special dispensations to grateful Jordanians, from educational scholarships to humble families to economic allowances for tribal communities. The king can further summon those who intrigue or irk him—such as business magnates, tribal sheikhs, civil society leaders, and even opposition activists—for carefully shepherded meetings.

Bolstering this primacy are three further qualities. First, the Hashemite monarchy tightly directs public reporting about its affairs. Unofficial media coverage of royal matters is prohibited, from internal family dramas to the king's private life and personal wealth. The latter came under scrutiny during the 2021 investigative documents leak known as the Pandora Papers, which showed that King Abdullah possessed overseas real estate and financial accounts worth more than $100 million—a revelation that the national press was forbidden from covering, but which some Jordanians privately complained hinted at either corruption or, at best, indefensible inequality.

Second, Jordan's royal family is small. Unlike some Gulf ruling families, such as Kuwait's Sabah dynasty or the House of Saud, Jordan does not have thousands of royals spread across its state and society. King Abdullah has eleven siblings and half-siblings—fellow children of his late father, King Hussein, who was married four successive times—alongside ten cousins through Hussein's two brothers, Prince Hassan and Prince Muhammad, and sister Princess Basma.

More distant relatives float around, including the descendants of the deposed Hashemite branch that once ruled Iraq, but they seldom figure into political matters. As Jordanian kings also serve as heads of the family, it is far easier to manage the affairs of small dynasties rather than large ones; there fewer relatives to monitor and appease.

Finally, Jordanian kings are creative. Given their substantial presence and personal influence, they can weave whatever public image suits them best depending on the context. In 2013, for instance, Abdullah gave a frank interview with *The Atlantic*, portraying himself to Western audiences as a proudly liberal visionary using his majestic powers to modernize Jordan by implementing long-overdue and wildly popular reforms. At home, however, local journalists with the rare opportunity to speak with the king came away with a different image: he was a beleaguered royal boxed in by regional pressures and swamped at home with the conservative demands of tribal sheikhs and security chiefs.[17] Perhaps both depictions are true; perhaps neither is. That few Jordanians truly know is testament to how pliable that royal likenesses can be.

The Politics of Succession

Most Hashemite kings have reigned until their death, providing continuity atop the regime. Such long-lived dynastic leadership is a common feature of most other Arab monarchies today.[18] Emir Abdullah ruled from 1921 until his assassination in 1951, adopting the new title of king after Jordan's independence in 1946. As the lone exception, Abdullah's son, King Talal, ruled for just over a year until August 1952, his term cut short by mental illness. From that point on, Talal's son, King Hussein, ruled until 1999. That half-century royal tenure has been the longest in Jordan's short history. Since 1999, King Hussein's eldest son, Abdullah II—the great-grandson of the founding Emir Abdullah—has occupied the throne. As of 2025, he remains the longest-ruling national head of state in the Arab world. It is a fair bet that King Abdullah, born in 1962, will hold forth for some time longer and that afterward his eldest son, Crown Prince Hussein, will bear the crown. Such a pattern of hereditary succession is called agnatic primogeniture: the eldest male offspring takes over.

Historically, handovers of power within the Hashemite dynasty have been peaceful. This is blessing to autocracies, Jordan included. Competition over succession is the weak underbelly for many dictatorships, for the prize of lifelong power can spur a vicious game of thrones between violent competitors that can consume all of politics.[19] Yet while the Hashemites have never known true succession crises, tensions have lurked. After Emir Abdullah was murdered in 1951 in Jerusalem, Talal was nearly prevented from returning to Amman from his Swiss sanitarium by his half-brother, Prince Nayif, whom some British officials preferred to take the throne.[20] Nayif ruled for a few months as regent before giving way. Another minor succession hiccup came under King Hussein. In 1965, King Hussein appointed his brother, the venerable Prince Hassan, as crown prince. This was a logical choice given their similar age and close relationship, and because his only son then was a three-year-old Abdullah. In 1999, shortly before his death, a cancer-stricken King Hussein transferred the crown prince title from Hassan to Abdullah. The move shocked many. Some commentators suggested brotherly strains between Hassan and Hussein in their later years, while others suggested the ill king had intended for Abdullah, as his eldest son, to succeed him all along.[21]

Likewise, King Abdullah's 2004 decision to divest the crown prince title from one of his four half-brothers, Prince Hamzah, elicited much social chatter. Hamzah is the oldest son of Queen Noor, King Hussein's fourth and final wife, and he accompanied the ailing king during his cancer treatments in America in the late 1990s. One popular account holds that Hussein intended Hamzah to be the eventual king and wanted Abdullah to serve only as caretaker of the throne until the much younger Hamzah, born in 1980, gained more experience—an expectation that caused friction between the newly enthroned Abdullah and Queen Noor's side. In one leaked cable at the time, the US Embassy noted "frosty" relations between King Abdullah and Queen Noor, giving some credence to this theory.[22] Whatever the case, in 2009 Abdullah formally anointed his own eldest son, Hussein, as the crown prince and heir apparent.

There have been other familial intrigues under King Abdullah's reign. In December 2017, he dismissed two siblings and a cousin from the military's senior echelons, stirring rumors of an internal shakeup. A more scandalous wrangling came in April 2021, when Prince Hamzah and a dozen of his political associates were detained on accusations of plotting a coup against the king, replete with alleged Saudi knowledge. The roundup sparked innuendo about worsening rifts inside the royal family; Abdullah's defenders saw Hamzah as a cagey pretender to the throne, while Hamzah's backers accused the king of jealousy over his half-brother's popularity among some tribal communities, who shared his complaints about Jordan's worsening corruption and economic crisis.[23] In April 2022, Hamzah—never formally charged with any crime—publicly renounced his title as royal prince. Abdullah responded by keeping him under house arrest.

For all these missteps, though, these controversies ended as they began: with the monarchy intact and King Abdullah's power unperturbed. As the king explained in a CNN interview after Prince Hamzah's 2021 detention, "Politics at the end of the day is a purview of the monarch," and there was no doubt who Jordan's true monarch was.[24] The next summer, no doubt remained regarding who the next monarch would be, as the family held a glamorous wedding— which Prince Hamzah, still under house arrest, did not attend—for the marriage of Crown Prince Hussein to Rajwa al-Saif, who hails from a wealthy Saudi business family with close ties to the Saudi monarchy. This hints at another curious pattern. Despite the historical importance of Transjordanian tribes to the monarchy (as Chapter 4 discusses), Hashemite kings do not marry their women. King Abdullah's mother is King Hussein's second wife, the British-born Princess Muna. Abdullah's wife, Queen Rania, is Palestinian, a fact that still incenses some conservative East Bank nativists. And now, the next queen of Jordan will be Saudi-born.

The Diwan

While the prime minister and his cabinet comprise the official government, the king floats ideas and formulates decisions through an equally important institution: the Royal Hashemite Court, or *Diwan.*[25] The Diwan is largely invisible to outsiders, but it serves as a parallel government to the one that the prime minister leads. In this protected circle, discussions are held, ministers chastised, summits convened, civil society leaders summoned, ambassadors credentialed, tribal sheikhs received, gifts presented, and laws deliberated upon.

In the British colonial years, the Diwan was a gathering place for the covey of personal courtiers and officers serving Emir Abdullah. During King Hussein's long tenure, it grew into a cocooned bureaucracy where royal advisers and high officials could work directly for the king. It also served as a reservoir for political elites, as favored politicians would cycle in and out of its ranks in between their appointments to the government. Over time, the Diwan morphed into an executive organ in its own right, the palace counterpart to the prime minister's government. The chief of the Diwan was especially potent, serving as not only the king's closest adviser but also the gatekeeper charged with coordinating political traffic with other state bodies. Under King Abdullah, the Diwan's role as a shadow government has become even more evident given the addition of new departments devoted to economic affairs, foreign relations, strategic studies, public opinion, and other areas. Acclaimed journalist Randa Habib described the remade royal court in the 2000s as "swarming with technocrats" who worked behind the scenes to set national policy priorities and support the king's agenda.[26]

Because it remains insulated from public scrutiny, the Diwan can undertake sensitive tasks that the official prime minister–led government cannot. For example, among the Diwan's oldest charges since the days of Emir Abdullah has been maintaining the monarchy's social ties with tribal communities, by acting as liaison to leading sheikhs and Transjordanian notables who come to air grievances, share ideas, or request help. Moreover, given its large discretionary budget, the Diwan can ply popular sympathy by selectively funding civil society organizations, charitable foundations, and social initiatives on behalf of the king. Unofficially, the royal court can also dispense money and private gifts as rewards to ministers and officials who please the monarch. While some Jordanians welcome such munificence, others see it as unadorned corruption. Such patronage can sow political servitude, for its beneficiaries have little reason to ever turn against the palace that gave it.

The Coercive Apparatus

Alongside the king and the royal court stands the coercive apparatus. As political scientists know well, a coercive apparatus refers to institutions like the military, police, and intelligence services endowed with the capacity to wage violence on behalf of its state. Coercion is integral to all governance: a regime cannot enforce laws, protect borders, extract taxes, and achieve other political tasks without also brandishing the credible threat to punish those who disobey. What distinguishes authoritarianism from democracy is how the coercive apparatus spends considerable time controlling domestic society, thereby repressing, intimidating, and cajoling opposition—activists, protesters, critics, writers, artists, ideologues, and others—into silence.

While Chapter 4 discusses Jordan's coercive apparatus in close detail, a few aspects suffice here. Jordan's coercive apparatus is a tripod of three institutions. The Jordanian Armed Forces (JAF) is the national military, led by the chairman of the joint chiefs of staff. Second, the General Intelligence Directorate (GID, or *mukhabarat*) is a combination of spy agency and secret police, charged with monitoring all threats against the monarchy and state. Third, the Interior Ministry controls the civil police and gendarmerie forces, which enforce laws and regulate everyday public behavior.[27] In total, these institutions devour a colossal portion of Jordan's financial resources, employ over 200,000 people, and help the regime oversee what Jordanians say, write, and think about politics. They are stakeholders to, and defenders of, Hashemite rule.

Signaling its towering importance, the coercive apparatus is impervious to popular pressure. Laws prohibit Jordanians from overtly discussing most military matters, while the GID and police are quick to pounce on those who denigrate the monarchy. Behind this curtain of impunity, they weigh heavily on royal decisions affecting national stability. This includes not just problems like terrorism and border security, but also domestic issues such as how to deal with popular protests, limit the reach of opposition groups, control refugee movements, conduct upcoming elections, and other matters.

On the spectrum of civil-military relations, Jordan's coercive institutions remain firmly under royal direction.[28] Military and intelligence chiefs report directly to the king. Because their very appointment requires securing the king's confidence, they stand within the regime's inner circle. There is little friction with the prime minister's government because it has no oversight in matters of national security; that is the prerogative of the king. Sacrosanct issues like the JAF's budget, the GID's covert operations, and counterterrorism strategies are adjudicated not by government ministers or parliament but instead by the monarchy at a higher level. Indeed, Jordan does not have a functional Defense Ministry. Since the 1970 Black September civil conflict, the prime minister has symbolically also served as defense minister, although that secondary title is simply a placeholder. There is no real Defense Minister because civilian control over the Jordanian military emanates from the palace, not the government.

Government and Parliament

As the preceding discussion expounded, Jordan's political system vests prodigious power around the Hashemite monarchy and its coercive apparatus. They anchor its autocratic regime, forming the innermost circle of power. However, Jordan also has a government and parliament, which represent the visible side of national politics. The former oversees much of the state's bureaucratic machinery, and its senior officials are rule-makers too—just not as important as royal ones. Parliament allows for popular participation in politics but has little authority. Among its most important functions is to burnish the kingdom's façade of democracy for both Jordanians and the outside world.

Prime Ministers and the Government

Jordan has a cabinet-based government led by the prime minister. The king alone appoints prime ministers from a small pool of politicians, advisers, and luminaries who have won his trust and favor. They almost never come from parliament, and so few have ever won—or even competed within—an election. From the Mandatory years through the 1950s, Jordanian premiers were often forceful leaders who approached the esteem of the king as they implemented new policies, engaged British officials, and cracked the whip against democratic opposition. The iron fist of Tawfiq Abul-Huda, whose fourth and final premiership featured his single-handed manipulation of the 1954 parliamentary elections to gash leftist and Arab Nationalist parties, is a case in point. From the 1960s onward, though, the position of prime ministers slowly became more subordinate under the royal thumb. Premiers with close personal ties with the king could still experiment with new economic policies and political strategies; among the more famed ones were Wasfi Tal and Bahjat Talhuni. Overall, however, their roles became less about sharing national leadership with the king and more about carrying out his faithful delegate.

The appointments of prime ministers are major events in Jordan's political calendar, sparking gossip and predictions among commentators. Historically, all Jordanian prime ministers have been men, and almost all Transjordanian rather than Palestinian; the latter reflects the Hashemite regime's deliberate political bias toward East Bankers, as Chapter 4 describes. Beyond this, the personalities and backgrounds of prime ministers reveal much about the monarchy's behind-the-scenes thinking. For instance, selecting a conservative politician from a renowned tribe suggests the palace and its coercive apparatus are prioritizing order and security during uncertain times. It was no coincidence that King Abdullah appointed Ma'rouf Bakhit—a retired army general from the respected 'Abbadi tribe—as prime minister after two hectic crises: the November 2005 Amman terrorist attacks and the January 2011 outburst of national protests at the dawn of the Arab Spring. A more liberal, popular figure can gesticulate royal willingness to entertain economic or political reforms desired by the public, however hollow they turn out to be. This was the case when the king installed the Harvard-trained 'Omar Razzaz following the June 2018 anti-tax demonstrations, which roiled the country for weeks. His advocacy for battling corruption and leftist background won applause from irate citizens desiring fresher faces in politics.[29]

Yet, this is not an easy job. To be prime minister means bearing the Sisyphean weight of managing the messiness of insider politics. Once appointed, the first task is assembling a cabinet to lead over the government's two dozen ministries—but with one hand tied behind the back. Rarely can Jordanian premiers invite potential ministers from parliament or political parties much less those from oppositionist backgrounds, as the palace and its security chiefs can scrap any appointment they find questionable. Neither can prime ministers consider all candidates on merit alone, for they must also balance different political forces that seek representation. By tradition, an informal quota system exists. The largest, most prestigious East Bank tribes and clans regularly garner ministerial appointments. Circassians and Christians, being favored minorities, also receive occasional positions. Palestinian-Jordanians are underrepresented, although those from wealthier business backgrounds and, under King Abdullah, a newer generation of technocratic elites have managed to secure some government posts.

Critically, the monarchy casts a long silhouette over this process. The king, for instance, can instruct the prime minister to fill the most important positions with his handpicked choices. This is often true with the so-called sovereignty ministries (*wizaaraat al-siyaadah*), namely Foreign Affairs, Interior, and Finance, because their portfolios involve matters of national security and thus require close coordination with the palace.[30] Junior portfolios (say, Agriculture or Tourism) hold far less significance, as do other appointees down the totem pole like ministerial deputies and general secretaries. Figure 2.2 illustrates this imbalance. The prime minister and sovereignty ministers can have frequent contact with the king or the Diwan, whereas lesser ministers may only engage royal actors occasionally.

Once formed, these cabinet-based governments have three tasks. First, they govern, but not wholly. They manage the state's vast bureaucracy and services for the populace but leave sensitive issues like foreign policy and national security to the monarchy and coercive apparatus. Second, they uphold "the king's directives," meaning the royal agenda of policy objectives and goals issued to the incoming prime minister.[31] In essence, they must fill in the details for the monarchy's broad mandate. At times, this is straightforward. During the Covid-19 pandemic, the government had strict orders to implement national lockdowns and other public health campaigns to minimize the spread of the disease. At other times, palace missives are so hopelessly nebulous as to invite failure. For instance, King Abdullah has repeatedly admonished his governments to improve Jordan's economic performance; but as Chapter 7 explains, this is an impossible task, given the deep structural barriers to equitable development and financial growth. It does not help that because so many high-level matters are royal prerogatives, official cabinet meetings can have little to discuss. Some come off as droning talk-shops, where ministers and their deputies air out technical minutia rather than mull over national priorities, such as foreign relations or reducing public spending.[32]

Third, by serving at the pleasure of the monarchy, the government acts as its shock absorber for crises. Whenever economic problems or political setbacks spark mass discontent, prime ministers take the blame. Popular demonstrations, for example, initiate a well-rehearsed theater of contrition in which the king orders the cabinet to be reshuffled, in hopes of quieting the street, or else sacks it altogether and appoints a new prime minister and government. As one former prime minister demurred, "The job is to make sure that when the public mood explodes, the heat never reaches the political kitchen. Every government knows it is one bad protest away from being fired."[33] Every political generation across Jordanian history has seen this happen. For example, in December 1955, urban riots against the Baghdad Pact, a British attempt to loop Jordan into an anti-Soviet defense treaty, tore down Hazza' al-Majali's premiership. In April 1989, rural rioting caused by a devastating financial downturn forced Zeid al-Rifa'i, in his second stint as prime minister, to resign. In June 2018, widespread protests against steeper tax laws imposed under International Monetary Fund guidelines toppled Hani Mulki's government.

Such uncertainty creates an oddity that has become a proprietary feature of Jordanian authoritarianism. Bound so closely to monarchical instruction, governments suffer an extremely high level of turnover. From its 1946 independence through 2025, Jordan had over sixty cabinets; on average, a prime minister's tenure lasts less than eighteen months. King Abdullah alone has appointed over a dozen prime ministers since 1999. In true parliamentary democracies, governments change whenever elections bring different parties to power or when parliaments withhold confidence from a flailing premier. None of these mechanisms apply to Jordan, where the royal sacrifice of governments is a time-honored strategy of regime survival. It does not always pacify popular opposition, but nonetheless it gives the monarchy the advantage of deflecting blame onto its delegated political elites.[34]

The Parliament

As the centerpiece of the kingdom's democratic mirage, the Jordanian parliament has a long history. Originating in the small Legislative Council that served Emir Abdullah in the British Mandatory years, parliament in its modern guise coalesced after the 1952 constitution. It hardly convened during the martial law period spanning from the late 1950s through 1980s, as Chapter 5 notes. Since the political liberalization following economic crisis in the late 1980s, it has become an enduring feature of public discourse.[35] It comprises an elected lower house, or House of Representatives (*majlis al-nuwaab*), and a royally appointed Senate (*majlis al-'ayaan*). Both of their members serve four-year terms. As the elected chamber, the lower house chooses the position of its speaker, who in turn carries some influence with the regime. The Senate, by contrast, is more of an advisory body that serves as a sinecure for political veterans—that is, a retirement prize for aging ministers, ambassadors, and other elites whom the king wishes to indulge.[36] In terms of seats, the Senate is half the size of the lower house, a rule set by the constitution.

On paper, the Jordanian parliament looks capable enough. It meets under an impressively domed hall in Amman's bourgeois Abdali neighborhood. The lower house even has a usable website filled with legislative studies, bills under review, and committee records.[37] In practice, however, it does not do many parliamentary things normally found in democracies. For instance, members of parliament (MPs) do not form the government, which the king appoints; and while in theory they can withhold confidence or grill ministers to show their displeasure, this happens only rarely. Lower house sessions can feature lively discussions about bills, and more than a dozen parliamentary committees convene regular hearings on issues like foreign affairs, agriculture, and education. However, despite its elected and popular basis, the lower house has little way of influencing how the monarchy, its coercive apparatus, and government deliberate on major policies.[38] MPs cannot recall the prime minister or audit the government, and their committees have little way of convincing officials to answer even basic requests. By law or tradition, neither can the lower house check the monarchy by probing royal spending, rejecting palace decrees, or reversing the king's appointments into state bodies like the Central Bank, the judiciary, and other institutions. Indeed, the king can even suspend the legislature at will whenever its nominal presence proves to be a nuisance. For example, King Abdullah dissolved parliament from June 2001 to June 2003, during which period the government decreed into existence over 100 new laws.

Above all, this legislature does not *legislate*. In democracies, legislation is a public affair: elected representatives propose bills, interest groups weigh in, and government officials haggle over wording against the backdrop of public opinion. In Jordan, by contrast, parliament is usually the last stop in the policymaking circuit. In theory, the constitution grants the Jordanian parliament significant weight: any bloc of ten MPs or senators can draft potential legislation and reverse royal vetoes of laws with a two-thirds majority vote. In practice, however, lawmaking follows a far more linear, controlled process that gives parliament only minor input. The government or other state bodies writes most major bills; the Legislation and Opinion Bureau, one of the Prime Ministry's many internal units, ensures proposed laws conform to the wishes of all regime stakeholders. The ideas behind proposed laws can originate from many sources—a royal committee, a government ministry, the Diwan, or even the GID. The drafted bills are then submitted to parliament, where various committees review them. Both the lower house and Senate pick over their wording, and parliament as a whole must ratify laws with a majority vote, at which point the king may promulgate them into law. Some bills undergo considerable debate, and on rare occasions parliament can push back on submitted legislation.

However, in the end, ratification is mostly perfunctory. For controversial laws like those curtailing press freedoms, a combination of royal pressures and implied threats inveigles all but the most principled MPs who oppose the legislation. Few parliamentarians wish to be caught in the regime's crosshairs. Moreover, many would-be laws are structured in a way that prevents legislative oversight. Public spending provides a pertinent example. Each year's national budget originates not from technical work of parliamentary committees but from opaque internal discussions within the regime and administrative institutions, such as the Finance Ministry and Central Bank. After the government submits that budget to parliament, legislators can marginally revise a few line items, but by tradition they cannot veto the biggest and most sensitive articles, such as public salaries and military spending. Neither can they propose their own counter-budget. In this way, elected representatives in Jordan technically review and ratify how their government spends money, but without having much actual say in the process.

To be sure, interesting things do happen within parliament. In the lower house, winning elections carries cachet, if nothing else because being an MP brings a political title and financial perks. Knowing they are public figures, many parliamentarians do take their jobs seriously. Some MPs, like those from independent parties like the Muslim Brotherhood's Islamic Action Front, play the role of democratic opposition by, for instance, querying the government for information and criticizing proposed laws.[39] Others work with civil society groups, lending their voice to popular campaigns for reform. Overall, however, the pressures to conform with the regime can be relentless. As one MP conferred, "Once you get a reputation as opposition or troublemaker, the doors close. The government ignores you, and the official media attacks you. It is like you are fighting the whole state, even though we are supposed to be part of the state."[40]

Without the mandate to form the government or write most laws, many MPs spend their time doing other things. Some ingratiate themselves with the regime, promising to support government legislation or share political information to elevate their careers. Others work as "service deputies" (*nuwaab al-khadamaat*) by funneling goods and services back to their voters.[41] Many MPs have accumulated influence in this way—by distributing the resources that come with their legislative office, such as civil service jobs, bureaucratic exemptions, and financial grants, to constituents in their home districts. However, such intermediary politics can be destructive. It means that many aspiring MPs fill their election campaigns not with policy proposals but with rather feckless promises to deliver personal benefits to voters; and once in office, they spend far more time haggling over patronage than dealing with political issues. This explains why many detractors of parliament (and there are many) in Jordan call it the national *dukaaneh*—local Arabic for convenience store, the place where MPs and citizens come together to buy and sell favors.

It is little surprise that parliament, and the lower house in particular, thus carries a pitiable reputation among the public. A 2021 poll by the Center for Strategic Studies at Jordan University showed that just 38 percent of Jordanians trusted their elected representative, and 70 percent ignored parliamentary debates and affairs altogether.[42] Widespread cynicism has kept voter turnout low for most elections, which in turn ensures that the lower house is filled with a familiar chorus of tribal notables and other independent, generally conservative figures. To be sure, many MPs make such apathy easy. On the floor of the lower house, the cadence of daily business is sometimes punctuated by performative politics, driven by personal feuds or grandstanding speeches by legislators competing for public attention. Hostile floor disputes have occasionally turned violent, replete with fisticuffs and Kalashnikovs. Female parliamentarians are woefully sidelined through paternalistic gestures.

Such enfeeblement is by design. As Chapter 5 elucidates, autocratic manipulations such as electoral malapportionment and selective repression since the 1990s have crippled Jordanian opposition parties, making it impossible for them to win legislative majorities. That would be the only way that the lower house could make a principled stand for democracy, for an opposition-led parliament could outrightly refuse to ratify laws, withhold confidence from the government, or even demand the monarchy downsize its powers. At the same time, however, the monarchy needs parliament. The existence of an elected legislature symbolically keeps alive the dim promise of democracy, for the king's democratic reform talk has no credibility unless there is also an electoral conduit for popular participation.[43] It further gives the regime a novel institution by which to reward loyal political supporters, whether by royal appointment into the Senate or through gerrymandered elections into the lower house. Finally, it serves an external purpose. As the lower house goes through the motions of elections, the monarchy can flaunt its liberal pretense for international audiences: *see, Saudi Arabia has no elected parliament—but Jordan does*. The United States and its allies have played along with this charade for decades, financing democracy promotion programs that have trained and supported MPs despite that their legislative work matters little for national decision-making.[44]

Political Dynamics

The political configuration of autocratic power in Jordan rests on a small set of authoritative actors, beginning firstly with the Hashemite monarchy. However, the monarchy does not reign from a bunker, the security around its historic Amman compound (*Al-Maqar*) notwithstanding. A few other essential facts flesh out this picture of Jordanian politics. A small political elite dominates this system, thanks to clientelistic practices of favoritism and cronyism. They operate the administrative state itself, weighed down by a bloated bureaucracy that propagates considerable corruption. In turn, this state maintains an extremely centralized system of national administration, with scant room for local and provincial autonomy.

Clientelism's Closed House

In 2019, a stinging editorial in *Al-Quds Al-Arabi*, a regional Arabic daily newspaper, joked that Jordan might be better off if it imported ministers from China.[45] The jab was meant not to valorize the Chinese, but to bemoan that while governments often changed in the kingdom, they remained ineffectual all the same—so perhaps Jordanians should buy more competent politicians from abroad. The witticism did not go over well with authorities, not least because it plucked an awkward chord: for all the royal talk of enhancing popular participation and fostering democracy over the past few decades, political life still ran through a small class of privileged elites, knit together by personal networks of clientelist relationships that recycled the same stale faces.

Also called "neopatrimonialism" by sociologists, clientelism describes political arenas shot through by a transactional logic, in which clients rise and fall based on how well they curry favor with more powerful patrons, who reward them for their services.[46] As clients scale the ladder of success, they become new patrons, using the lucrative bounty of their office to enlist new clients. In such environs, ideological commitments and policy ideas mean little; neither do electoral competition and popular accountability. Instead, the most important qualities are loyalty and subservience to one's superior—ranging all the way up to the monarchy—for all politics requires an exchange of benefits.

Not all Jordanian politicians play this game. More than a few engineers, lawyers, professors, businesspersons, and other professionals only want to enter government to contribute their talent in the service of their country. Principled MPs from opposition backgrounds also see parliamentary service as a useful way to call attention to Jordan's economic and political problems rather than exploit their legislative offices to enrich themselves. However, for those officials and politicians with more naked ambitions—say, a ministerial position in government, a prestigious appointment within the Diwan, or a cushy leadership post for another state body—mastering the nepotistic pulse of clientelism is a must.

This has four implications. First, clientelism in Jordan makes not competence but *connections*—who you know and what you can offer in return for support—as a decisive arbiter of political careers. This saturates many political relationships with cronyism, which is why the most scornful Jordanian citizens have come to see all of national politics as a den of crooked officials who got their jobs (and, in turn, hire others) through the corrupt swapping of favors and gifts. Indeed, there is a denigrating Arabic word in Jordan, *mustawzirin*, for scheming politicos trying to become government ministers by any means necessary. Such characterizations are not completely unfounded. In her study of over 300 government ministers who served during 2006–2016, Sa'eda Al-Kilani estimated that only one-fifth attained their appointment without using personal, tribal, or business connections, and that an astonishing one-quarter had no qualifications or training at all that matched their assigned ministerial portfolio.[47]

Second, clientelistic politics weakens parties. Most party organizations in Jordan are weak and small, reflecting the legacy of historical repression as well as the corrosive effects of electoral engineering since the 1990s, as Chapter 5 explains. The Hashemite monarchy also needs no ruling party by virtue of its dynastic power. Even so, few aspiring politicians in Jordan desire to join or create their own parties for a simple reason: they do not need them. While dominant ruling parties in other autocracies like Zimbabwe, Türkiye, and Malaysia have given rise to their own internal clientelistic politicking and corruption, in Jordan political figures prefer to work directly through personal connections and face-to-face dealings. They seldom ever need to compete for elected office, since climbing the institutional rungs of the regime and state seldom requires winning a lower house seat as MP. As a result, few Jordanian officials have ever had the democratic experience of party life—of stumping for votes, learning organizational platforms, or running public campaigns.

Third, clientelism gives the Hashemite regime a useful tool to enlist political subordinates. Acting as patron, the monarchy can dangle appointments into the government or other state institutions as a powerful lure to make even critics and detractors indebted to its amity. For instance, the late King Hussein was renowned for offering many oppositionists, once released from jail or allowed to return from exile, plum positions as ministers, ambassadors, or even senators in return for never raising dissent again. Such co-optation works to the advantage of those who already have power, making it even harder for truly honest political aspirants to succeed.

Fourth, clientelism has allowed a narrow stratum of elites to dominate Jordanian politics, taking turns serving as ministers, functionaries, administrators, directors, and advisors across the government, Diwan, and public institutions.[48] Each vies for a slice of the political pie; the closer one gets to the king, the richer the prize in terms of influence, profit, and stature. Almost all are male, which mirrors another unfortunate outcome of clientelistic politics: gender bias, as patriarchal networks of elite men ensure their spoils do not leak to outsiders. The most masterful personalities enjoy decades-long careers, banking on their perceived value and reliability to the regime to stay relevant. They never stray far from the monarchy, being one phone call away from a new political stint. One prominent example is the late Fayez Tarawneh, who from the 1980s onward served as royal adviser, minister of various portfolios, ambassador, senator, prime minister twice (1999, 2012), and chief of the Diwan twice (1999, 2013). A younger instantiation is Nasser Judeh, who served as foreign minister for nearly a decade (2009–2017). Prior to that, Judeh served in the Diwan and was director of Jordan Radio and Television Corporation, minister of information, and an official government spokesperson. As is often the case with clientelism, personal backgrounds shed light onto their staying power. Fayez Tarawneh originated from a powerful Transjordanian tribe based in Karak that has contributed many members to the military and state institutions. Judeh's father was a long-serving minister and senator. Judeh is also maternal nephew to the late Zeid al-Rifa'i, another stalwart East Bank politician with a long and storied career involving multiple stints as prime minister and Diwan chief; Zeid's son, Samir, himself served as prime minister during 2009–2011.

These personal connections underscore another byproduct of clientelism. To glean the "who's who" of Jordanian politics for the past few generations, focus on surnames. Royal connections and loyal service have allowed a small pool of Transjordanian families to crowd the highest ranks of the courtiers, ministers, and officials that have figured eminently into national political life for many years; a sampling includes Mulki, Rifa'i, Tarawneh, Majali, Fayez, Lawzi, and Tal. Some even claim a progenitor who served Emir Abdullah during the colonial era, a local pedigree that grants them an almost aristocratic status within political salons.[49]

At the same time, clientelism does not mean that political life is quiet. Personal rivalries regularly erupt among the elites who serve the crown and state, a byproduct of their own competing ambitions and temperamental disagreements. One common divide pits security-minded traditionalists against more open-minded reformists, who all support Hashemite rule but disagree about which domestic and foreign policies require attention. For example, in the late 1970s, when martial law afforded the regime some breathing room after the Black September civil war, King Hussein caused a stir by appointing the reformist 'Abdel Hamid Sharaf as prime minister, much to the consternation of his two conservative predecessors, Zeid al-Rifa'i and Mudar Badran. Their bruising fights over corruption and tribalism were legendary, and one conspiracy theory today murmured by Jordanian historians insists that Sharaf's premature death by heart attack was not accidental.

Under King Abdullah, this intra-elite squabbling has veered into a new direction. In the 2000s, Abdullah began promoting a new wave of young, Western-educated elites into high positions. Controversially, they included some from Palestinian backgrounds. Personalities like Bassem Awadallah, Suhair Ali, and Imad Fakhoury rose to prominence as they implemented the king's neoliberal economic policies and restructured government institutions. Such "digital ministers," as political analyst Wael Al-Khatib called them, bristled against the political establishment—the "old guard" (*al-haras al-qadim*) of Transjordanian politicians, who recoiled from these fresh-faced newcomers.[50] However, this change did not transform the political system so much as introduce newer forms of cronyism, as a younger cohort of technocrats and investors became the beneficiaries of royal appointments, business contracts, and other benefits. The fortunes of some of these new elites fell as dramatically as they peaked once they fell out of royal favor. For instance, Awadallah was one of the two former officials imprisoned after being found guilty of conspiring against the monarchy during the April 2021 events that entangled Prince Hamzah. It was an improbable demise for the former Diwan chief once regarded as the king's right-hand man.

Bureaucracy and Corruption

While Hashemite powerholders lead the regime, they do not constitute the state. Jordan's state is the broader administrative entity charged with implementing the laws and services that govern the populace. For such a small country, the Jordanian state is sprawling, with 100 different public organizations and official agencies. They include cabinet-level ministries; the judiciary and legal system; financial institutions, such as the Central Bank and Social Security Corporation; infrastructural organs like the National Electricity Company and postal service; public media outlets, such as the Jordan News Agency and the Jordan Radio and Television Corporation; the expansive educational system; and a flotilla of other bureaus. Before King Abdullah began his push for economic privatization after 1999, the state also included dozens of government-controlled firms and companies. Manning these bureaucratic ramparts are hundreds of thousands of civil servants, who—like most in the regime and coercive apparatus—are predominantly Transjordanian rather than Palestinian. As Chapter 4 explains, such overstaffing serves a political purpose, as public employment has long given East Bank Jordanians an institutional stake in Hashemite rule.

Jordanians see this bureaucratic state through contrasting lenses. On the one hand, it is *sturdy*. Unlike the conflict-ridden Arab states nearby, such as Lebanon, Syria, and Iraq, few citizens see their public institutions jeopardized by violence or collapse.[51] Indeed, for the most war-stricken countries in the MENA—like Yemen, Libya, and Sudan—the absence of centralized state structures deprives inhabitants of basic security and infrastructure.

On the other hand, the Jordanian state also labors under ineptitude. For many citizens, the national bureaucracy appears like an "inefficient, inhuman, and an inaccessible system" centered on "hierarchy, status, secrecy, specialization, rules, and unflinching obedience."[52] Many Jordanians recall dreadful stories of dealing with incompetent bureaucratic factotums unwilling to process paperwork for the most basic tasks, such as obtaining passports or correcting invoices. Even state ministries can harbor bizarre inadequacy in undertaking the most basic work. The Finance Ministry struggles to collect income taxes, the Education Ministry lords over an obsolete national curriculum, and the

Ministry of Industry and Trade drags its feet in granting permits and licenses to entrepreneurs. More broadly, the archives of government ministries are littered with half-finished initiatives and national projects abandoned midway due to unforeseen costs or bungled mismanagement.

Such inefficiency partly stems from a baffling love of institutional redundancy. After generations of relentless expansion, Jordan's state encompasses a gargantuan labyrinth of bureaucratic organs that waste hefty public resources. There are nearly thirty government ministries, but just as many other special committees and governing bodies with overlapping authority, each enjoying its own leadership, staff, budget, and offices. For instance, there is a Ministry of Health, but also a Higher Council of Health; there is a Ministry of Youth, but also the Crown Prince Foundation, which specializes in youth-oriented educational and civic programming. The Jordanian state is a machine, but a squeaky one laden with unnecessary parts.

To top it off, at times the monarchy also sometimes creates royal councils with the executive mandate to create new laws, thus making its own appointed government feel unnecessary at times. One historical example is King Hussein's Economic Security Committee, which after the 1967 Arab-Israeli War came to control Jordan's trade and industrial policies independently of the prime minister.[53] King Abdullah's own brain trust was the Economic Consultative Council, which in the early 2000s spearheaded the drive toward neoliberal policies like privatization and free trade. Another example from those years was the Aqaba Special Economic Zone Authority, founded to help Aqaba become a commercial and touristic hub on the Red Sea—but which ultimately functioned like a "state within a state" in commandeering financial and logistical control over the entire port city.[54] The various democratic reform schemes that have amounted to little over the past several decades have likewise come from high royal committees assigned by the king to renovate national politics but with the understanding that monarchical power would always be the institutional backbone for the political system.

With such turgid governance comes corruption. Bribery, embezzlement, graft, and other abuses of office happen everywhere, but they especially flourish under autocracies that rely on personal networks and oversized institutions: the bigger and opaquer the state, the more likely politicians will find some way to squeeze money and benefits from it. Jordan is no exception. As Chapter 6 notes, under King Abdullah's reign, public anger over systemic corruption has stimulated frequent protests. Despite ombudsman bodies like the Jordanian Integrity and Anti-Corruption Commission, many citizens see corruption polluting every level of politics and development—from the ministers who pocket mysterious gifts and administrative cronies who siphon public funds to the lavish commercial projects financed by unknown deals and shadowy investors.

The most common corruption is the pettiest and so hardest to eliminate: *wasta*. In everyday life, wasta refers to the personal favoritism granted to those requesting public services, but whose family ties, tribal pressures, political brokers, or some other intermediary give an unfair advantage.[55] Any casual discussion with Jordanians will reveal plenty of examples where knowing the right person who can be reached a quick phone call—for instance, a government official, tribal sheikh, discerning bureaucrat, or even influential MP—helped someone gain entrance to a university, receive better medical care, obtain a contract, or secure a job. A 2014 public survey conceded that 83 percent of Jordanians saw wasta as corruption, but conversely 65 percent conceded they wanted *more* of it.[56] Wasta is so prevalent that it has become a go-to word for any seemingly unfair economic or political event. An unqualified person becoming a minister, a chummy businessperson profiting handsomely, a local neighborhood suddenly receiving a fulsome development project: for many citizens, such outcomes suggest that someone leveraged their clientelistic connections unjustly, leaving their hapless peers in the dust.

Whether or not this is true, the perception of all political life being infected by such corruption has caustic effects. Many Jordanians have come to see politics as a degenerate coliseum where consummate insiders incestuously benefit one another. This deepens perceptions of inequality and reinforces corrosive social divides in which one side appears to have more privilege than others: Transjordanians versus Palestinians, for instance, or wealthy urbanites versus poorer rural dwellers. Above all, it underpins popular mistrust by making many Jordanians feel as if their voices will never matter under their encrusted political elites. A 2018 survey by the International Republican Institute showed that most Jordanians believed that they had absolutely no influence over national decisions.[57]

Hyper-Centralization

The final dynamic of Jordanian politics concerns space. In modern states, rulers must transmit their power across a national territory and figuratively "see" the spaces and communities they putatively control.[58] Some countries, like Germany, are highly decentralized, with leaders allowing communities and provinces to make their own policies. Other states, like the United States and India, have federal systems that balance local government with national power structures. Jordan's political geography is the extreme opposite of both. This is a unitary state with little tolerance for subnational autonomy. While the country has twelve governorates (*muhaafazaat*) and nearly 100 municipalities (*baladiyyaat*), power remains concentrated in the central capital of Amman.

Governorate and municipal officials do not make laws, but instead administer some basic services and monitor local affairs. Indeed, as Janine Clarke has argued in her fastidious study, Jordan exemplifies "hyper-centralization," with an extreme degree of authority distilled in the spatial core of Amman.[59]

This centripetal structure dates back to the colonial period. The first task of the British-backed monarchy in the 1920s was subduing East Bank towns and tribes, first by violence and later through the coalitional enmeshment described in Chapter 4.[60] Since then, the Hashemite regime has seldom entrusted its provinces or municipalities to govern themselves. For instance, after the 1948 Arab-Israeli War, the government's ironclad control over economic resources enabled it to channel development funding away from the Palestinian West Bank and toward supportive tribes on the East Bank. Moreover, because municipal and provincial authorities had little power to govern themselves, local politics historically revolved around jockeying for jobs, contracts, and services provided by the monarchy and its royal government in Amman.

Despite repeated promises to decentralize the country, Jordan's political space under King Abdullah has remained highly unitary. For instance, the 2015 Decentralization Law promised to install democracy by promoting more local elections across the kingdom, but in actuality did little.[61] Jordan now features elections for mayors and municipal councils (excepting Amman, whose mayoralty is still a government appointment). Yet, such elections—which feature extremely low turnout—produce local bodies with little governing authority. Without the involvement of a relevant state body or government ministry, municipal officials cannot undertake basic services such as auditing the police, reviewing school performance, rerouting electricity lines, or even changing bus routes. They collect garbage and levy property taxes, but lack budgetary autonomy. This is how Jordan's rule-makers make their national political geography legible: the regime in Amman constitutes the hub of the nation, and everyone else revolves around it.

Conclusion

The internal politics of Jordan's authoritarian order can seem arcane to the uninitiated. When fully revealed, they look even odder—even contradictory. A ruling monarchy downplays the fact that it rules, even as its executive writ palpably manifests through an unelected king, a powerful royal court, and a coercive apparatus staffed by hundreds of thousands of armed men. A prime minister–led government and bicameral parliament draw substantial attention, but the former is an appendage of palace authority that conveniently tumbles when national crises demand, while the elected legislature does little legislating. A slender class of elite figures dominates this autocratic system, their careers measured not by electoral victories but by clientelist connections that stretch on for decades. An enormous administrative state rambles onward, despite the corruption and redundancy that swells within its bureaucratic recesses. There are plenty of provincial and local governments across the kingdom; like parliament, though, they do not have the authority to do much of anything, as political resources are extremely centralized in Amman.

These are the patterns and institutions that sustain Jordanian rule-makers and gird their political order. It is neither democratic nor efficient, but it is constant. It is also among the most stable in the Middle East. Jordan's royal autocracy has bent but never broken throughout the various crises and conflicts interposed across the past century, exhibiting an admittedly impressive streak of durability.

Such authoritarian stability is the next conundrum about Jordanian politics that demands explanation. The longevity and resilience of autocracy here do not stem from the mystique of Hashemite royalism or from any cultural value or religious norm. Rather, it results from the adroit use of strategic tools found in many modern dictatorships: securing aid and arms from international allies, maintaining a huge coercive apparatus, and rallying a coalition of public support. While Chapter 8 explores the critical aspect of the kingdom's positive relations with the West and the outside world, Chapter 4 investigates these last two domestic strategies by illumining how selective repression and coalitional ties with Transjordanian tribes have kept democracy at bay in Jordan.

4

How Coercion and Coalitions Create Stable Authoritarianism

What Keeps Authoritarianism So Durable in Jordan?

Jordan's brand of royal authoritarianism has evolved with each passing generation, but it has never given way to democracy or revolution. It is tempting to ascribe such puzzling stability to monarchism itself. After all, recent events have treated the Arab world's kingships well. The 2011-2012 Arab Spring uprisings shook republican dictatorships in Tunisia, Egypt, Libya, Yemen, and Syria; its aftershocks in 2018–2019 roiled the generals, presidents, and prime ministers ruling Sudan, Algeria, Lebanon, Palestine, and Iraq. The Assad regime in Syria finally collapsed in December 2024 after a long civil war, removing the last of the Arab presidents-for-life who had held power since the 1990s. During this time, Jordan saw plenty of protests, but they did not reach any riotous crescendo. Among the kingdoms of the Middle East, only in Bahrain did public unrest nearly topple a monarchy, in March 2011, if not for a Saudi-led military intervention that saved the day.

Based on this admirable record, many Western observers have supposed that Middle East monarchies like Jordan are exceptionally durable. Their palaces and kings are immune to the winds of change for a simple reason: unlike the "fake republics" run by corrupt political parties and praetorian tinpots, Arab monarchies are culturally appropriate forms of government for their mostly Muslim peoples.[1] According to this view, Arabs lust for the primeval air of royal dictatorships. They hanker for the regalia of dynastic rule draped in the majesty of Islamic tradition and tribal despotism. They crave the quiet stability and "predictable governance" issued from the absolutist hands of kings and emirs over the unruliness of mass participation and democratic politics.[2]

Such orientalist logic flops against a longer view of history, however. In proper perspective, the track record of monarchical perseverance in the Middle East and North Africa (MENA) is actually quite poor.[3] No grandeur of royalism prevented coups or revolutions from extinguishing the autocratic monarchies of Egypt in 1952, Iraq in 1958, North Yemen in 1962, Libya in 1969, and Iran in 1979. No culture of Arab docility or Islamic code of obedience has foreclosed public opposition under the Arab kingships that survive today—including Jordan, which has experienced popular uprisings for as long as the Hashemites have ruled. In truth, the resilience of the Hashemite monarchy stems not from any surreptitious cultural essence, but from its use of pragmatic tools of governance that are little different from those wielded by other successful modern autocracies. Durable authoritarianism in Jordan here rests on three pillars: first, repressing and regulating opposition; second, drawing a supportive coalition of Transjordanian tribes; and third, leaning on the United States and other international allies for aid, arms, and legitimacy.

As Chapter 8 covers Jordanian foreign policy and its Western backstop, this chapter deals with the first two strategies: political repression and coalitional politicking. It proceeds in several sections. First, to set the theoretical stage, it raises seminal insights from the comparative study of authoritarian regimes. All dictatorships repress. They deploy violence, or the threat of it, to punish and deter undesirable behavior, such as dissent and demonstrations. However, autocrats cannot repress everyone, and neither can they rule alone. They must also rally their own base of support to help them rule. This means convincing at least some group of citizens to become stakeholders in their survival, typically by providing social, economic, or political benefits in return for conditional allegiance. These two tactics hence go hand in hand. Long-lasting dictators convene what loyalties they can muster from society, and their police and armies subjugate the rest.

Second, the chapter applies these two precepts to Jordan. It unpacks Jordan's coercive apparatus, mentioned in Chapter 3 but fully distilled here, as comprising three institutions serving the monarchical regime: the armed forces, the intelligence directorate, and the police. It reviews their historical function and changing tactics in regulating, and when necessary quashing, public protests, critical speech, and other expressions of public resistance. Third, it investigates coalitional politics. Jordan's autocratic regime has historically rallied support from Transjordanians rather than Palestinians. East Bank tribes represent its staple constituency, and since the colonial decades these communities and clans have received considerable economic benefits and political privileges under Hashemite rule. This tribal-state compact has frayed under King Abdullah, as financial difficulties and changing policies have sparked dissension from some Transjordanians. Nonetheless, this coalition endures today, with the well-being of many tribes—and smaller groups like Circassians, Christians, and wealthy business elites—still wedded to the monarchy.

As political scientists know well, persistent authoritarianism depends on many factors beyond coercion and coalitions. In many dictatorships around the world, gender inequities, economic structures, and ideological appeals all help reinforce the privileges of ruling elites while undermining democratic opposition in society. Foreign policy matters too, and Jordan's rulership excels in neutralizing regional threats and attracting Western support to buttress its power at home. Nonetheless, coercion and coalitions are the central strategies in domestic politics here; without them, autocratic rule would not last long.

The Dictator's Dilemma

Whether monarchies or republics, all autocracies face a fundamental problem of knowledge. In the absence of competitive and regular elections, they never know how much their society truly reveres or loathes them.[4] Revolutions, coups, and civil wars are spectacular events that deliver mass repudiation against dictatorships, but they are rare. In most nondemocratic states, public life is strikingly normal, as most citizens go about their day in a humdrum manner. Authoritarian rulers hence have little idea whether people secretly despise them and are conspiring to revolt or if they obey the law out of genuine respect or loyalty. They do not field public polls that allow respondents to give their true opinions about the leadership. In Jordan, for instance, academic surveys (which must be approved by the authorities) can ask citizens about their confidence in parliament, the prime minister, and even the army—but never the monarchy, whose all-mighty status is sacrosanct. This is the dictator's dilemma: not even the absence of unrest on the streets tells autocrats much about the true preferences of their society. In democracies, by contrast, politicians always know their popularity thanks to channels of mass participation that expose them to constant pressures. They must endure competitive elections, deal with opposing parties, engage the independent media, face the results of approval polls, and interact with civic groups lobbying for their interests.

The expansive literature on authoritarianism in comparative political science offers a rational solution to this problem. Given their inability to capture the true feelings of their populace, autocrats must hedge their bets. They should craft an equilibrium of power that minimizes their vulnerability of being overthrown, restraining their enemies while rewarding their allies.[5] Survival requires balance. They must efficiently repress their societies, so as to quell those individuals and groups that dare to criticize or oppose them. Simultaneously, they must reach out to other parts of the populace and win their support. They coerce some and make coalitions with others.

First, repression occurs when governments inflict violent sanctions against individuals and groups to discourage or penalize actions that challenge their power.[6] To some extent, all modern states do this. They command violence over the bodies and liberties of their citizens. Indeed, they monopolize it; only legitimate governments can, for instance, lawfully imprison individuals, raise a military trained to kill, and regularly extract wealth (i.e., taxes) from its subjects under threat of punishment. Authoritarian rule, however, greatly expands the scope of everyday behavior subject to coercive regulation. Dictators leverage repression against not only individual dissenters who question their authority but also against public protests, critical speech, uncooperative minorities, independent organizations, and other groups who do not publicly conform to their demands. The goal is to not only punish oppositionists but also to deter bystanders from joining them, thereby lowering the risk of collective action such as popular revolts or even coup attempts.[7]

Repression requires specialized institutions proficient in the use of violence. Herein stands the coercive apparatus, which for autocratic regimes typically consists of the national military, intelligence services, uniformed police, and paramilitary troops. A loyal and unified coercive apparatus that monitors society and muzzles critics can give recalcitrant autocrats very long tenures.[8] Long-lasting dictators therefore take great pains to dollop generous funding and prestige on their soldiers and policemen so that they enjoy high morale and obey orders. They also maintain iron-fisted control over these repressive organs to ensure that ambitious generals and security chiefs do not plot to usurp power for themselves.[9] Finally, their techniques of control also adapt with changing times—for instance, by exploiting new digital tools of subversion like hacking to combat online critics or tactically relaxing repression in order to deflect Western human rights pressures.

However, coercion alone is never enough to immunize autocracies from being ousted. Not even the most repugnant tyrants can repress everyone all the time: it is prohibitively expensive, can spur international backlash, and above all can alienate too many people and paradoxically raise the likelihood of a coup or revolution.[10] Successful authoritarian rulers, hence, not only deploy repressive sticks but also coalitional carrots. They mobilize a social foundation, a willing coalition of individuals and groups within society who believe in the rightness of their government to lead them. In democracies, the winning coalition is fixed as the minimum number of votes needed to win elections: those who win fair elections have, by definition, a popular base. Dictatorships, however, must themselves determine how "much" loyalty they need to capture from the populace, because there are no competitive elections that reveal their precise level of backing.[11] For citizens, supporting a dictatorship does not connote that they agree with every policy and law. But it engenders a sense of legitimacy: all else being equal, they prefer their autocracy stay in power when compared to other alternatives, such as a newer dictatorship or even democracy.

Authoritarian regimes, thus, have latitude to pick winners and losers in society in assembling their coalitions. They have many ways to procure the fealty of winners (i.e., supporters). In some republics, for instance, dominant parties attract a following by providing political access and resolving conflicts.[12] Other leaders exploit ideologies or religion to create a cultural connection with their base. Most commonly, rulers extract loyalty by distributing material patronage, such as jobs, subsidies, and services, to their constituents and fellow politicians. They can further entice them with pledges of symbolic protection and privileges that deliver a seductive message: *if I am not around to look out for you, who else will?* When done effectively, such outreach allows a dictatorship to "enmesh" targeted citizens, wedding their well-being with their own survival.[13] Should their regime collapse, so too will the fates of supporters. The result is a stout ruling coalition, one that centers on a perverse social contract that exchanges loyalty for benefaction. But it also requires that leaders honor their end of the deal, no matter what—even during financial crises that sap their ability to deliver benefits.

Both coercing opposition and mobilizing coalitional support explain how Hashemite rule in Jordan has endured for more than a century. As the next section shows, so central are these stratagems that they consume much of the regime's domestic resources. As Chapter 7 notes, they also partly account for why the economy is so stagnant: it is hard to foster economic growth and development when the lion's share of national financing is trussed to the political obligations of paying soldiers and servicing Transjordanian tribes. Nonetheless, they remain indelible aspects of authoritarianism in Jordan.

Coercion and Its Practices in Jordan

Since the early 1990s, when political reforms ended several bleak decades of martial law, Jordan has sported a veneer of liberal moderation to the world. As one buoyant Western commentary reasoned, "Compared to its Arab neighbors, Jordan is a relatively benign police state."[14] This is true. Leaders here do not inhumanely massacre domestic opposition, unlike Syria under the Assad regime or Iraq under Saddam Hussein. Neither do most ordinary folk live in abject fear of being disappeared and tortured on a daily basis. But for many activists and critics, the kingdom can still feel like a police state all the same. An enormous coercive apparatus stands at the center of the political system, accountable only to the king and committed to preserving Hashemite rule. This apparatus is best visualized as a tripod consisting of the military (or Jordanian Armed Forces (JAF), the General Intelligence Directorate (GID), and civil policing, undertaken by the Ministry of Interior's two core agencies, namely the Public Security Directorate (PSD) and the General Directorate of Gendarmerie Forces (in Arabic, *darak*).

This coercive apparatus is intertwined with Jordanian authoritarianism in decisive ways. First, it gobbles economic resources. As Table 4.1 illustrates through

Table 4.1 **The Costs of Coercion in Jordan, 1965–2024 (in millions, current Jordanian dinars)**

Year	*Military and Security Spending*	*Total Current Spending*	*Military and Security Spending as Percent of Total Current Spending*
1965	22.2	35.8	62
1970	38.1	59	64.6
1975	58	125.7	46.1
1980	140	336.1	41.7
1985	229.5	542.5	42.3
1990	263.2	841.4	31.3
1995	400.9	1225.2	32.7
2000	631.8	1627.2	38.8
2005	973.4	2469.8	39.4
2010	2162.8	4499.1	48.1
2015	2489.3	6701.8	37.1
2020	2633.2	8333.9	31.6
2024	3141.4	10,641.9	29.5

Note: Military and security spending includes the official budgets for the Jordanian Armed Forces and policing line items of the Interior Ministry. Figures for the General Intelligence Directorate are excluded, as they are not publicly reported.

Sources: General Budget Department, *Summary of General Budget* (GBD, various years), and Central Bank of Jordan, *Yearly Statistical Series* (CBJ, various years).

five-year increments since 1965, Jordan's military and security spending has consumed, on average, more than 40 percent of all official current spending for the past sixty years. In effect, more than two out of every five dinars expended by the government have flowed to institutions that specialize in violence—a crippling total for such a small developing economy. In 2024, the JAF and Interior Ministry together received more public funding than every other government ministry *combined* save for the Finance Ministry. These figures make Jordan one of the most militarized and securitized countries in the world, despite not fighting a full-scale war since the 1970 Black September civil conflict.[15] Jordan no longer fights wars, but it *spends* like it does.

These armed organs also drain Jordan's human resources by employing a giant chunk of the national workforce. In 2024, out of kingdom's over 1.5 million citizens with registered formal jobs, around 220,000 drew salaries from the JAF,

GID, PSD, and darak.[16] More Jordanians work for the coercive apparatus than in manufacturing, tourism, and agriculture—three important civilian economic sectors—combined. Indeed, in global perspective, few other countries feature such mammoth proportions of productive labor working for their military and security forces, particularly in the absence of conscription. Consider as well that almost all these Jordanian personnel are males, which produces another startling statistic given than less than 20 percent of Jordan's employed workforce is female: today, one in six employed Jordanian men makes a living by soldiering, policing, or spying for the state.[17]

Beyond these numbers, a few other trends jump out. First, most who work in the coercive apparatus are Transjordanians rather than Palestinian-Jordanians. This is no coincidence. Political scientists call this "stacking," whereby an autocracy allows its preferred ethnic or communal groups to dominate and lead its vaunted agencies of violence.[18] This keeps its repressive guardians close and subservient to the regime leadership. Jordan's coercive apparatus has long been stacked with members of East Bank tribes, as part of the social pact tying Transjordanian interests to Hashemite rule as this chapter later discusses. Hence, while some military and police retirees have protested about rising living costs and corruption under King Abdullah for the past two decades, there is little chance their brethren still in the state's employ would move against the monarchy. Indeed, Jordan's only experience with a military coup that nearly came to fruition occurred during the infamous strife of April 1957, when a handful of army officers who sympathized with democratic opposition clumsily confronted King Hussein.

Second, these repressive institutions are secretive. For many decades, strict laws have prevented public reporting about their operations. Conventional information normally available in democracies—such as what military arms are purchased, what policing tactics are used, or how much the intelligence directorate spends—are considered classified matters of national security. It is thus difficult to gauge how Jordanians *feel* about their coercive apparatus. For instance, a 2018 survey by the Jordan Strategy Forum, an Amman-based think tank, heralded that over 90 percent of citizens trusted the military and security forces, as opposed to 54 percent for the royally appointed government and 21 percent for parliament.[19] Undoubtedly, many Jordanians are grateful when the GID prevents terrorist attacks or the army interdicts drug smugglers from Syria or Iraq. But they also complain—privately, of course—when intelligence officers browbeat journalists or when the police harangue teenagers for protesting. Citizens have little recourse when suffering corporeal harm like arbitrary detentions and abusive interrogations, because these coercive institutions operate with legal impunity. Complaints to the National Centre for Human Rights, a government entity created in 2006 to track alleged human rights abuses, usually lead nowhere, because like all official bodies, its authority extends only as far as the regime allows.

Finally, the intensity of repression has evolved over time, a crucial lesson in the importance of authoritarian learning and adaptability. During the martial law period of the late 1950s through the 1980s, Jordan's coercive apparatus meted out "high-intensity" repression, meaning public and physical acts of violence.[20] Old activists from those dark years recount harrowing tales of the army arresting and beating protesting crowds, activists and organizers suffering torture at the hands of the GID, and critical publications being shuttered under unflinching censorship laws. Fierce crackdowns against opposition occurred regularly, much like other dictatorships during the Cold War. In the post–Cold War era, though, Western norms of liberal democracy and human rights became the new girding principles for a rules-based global order. Jordan's monarchy took heed of this. As Chapter 5 recounts, King Hussein undertook liberalizing reforms following a devastating economic crisis in 1989. Officials ended martial law, legalized political opposition, and promised more democratic freedom during the 1990s.

Since then, repression in the Hashemite Kingdom has transmogrified into low-intensity form: less violent than before and disguised with measured tolerance. Under King Abdullah, officials have trumpeted this approach as *al-amn al-naa'im* (soft security).[21] This does not mean complete leniency as befitting democracy. The regime always stands by certain "red lines" that citizens cannot cross, such as impugning the military, insulting Islam, and above all questioning the monarchy's legitimacy. The absolute scope of *lèse-majesté* laws also means that even innocuous criticism of the king or royal family is forbidden. Rather, soft security means that short of these boundaries, the regime exercises a lighter touch in dealing with opposition. As Chapter 5 discusses, since the 1990s authorities have learned to stomach moderate dissent given the end of martial law. For instance, they allow many spontaneous protests to transpire, even though laws require organizers to garner forty-eight-hour advance approval. The regime does not disappear thousands of activists into torturous interrogation rooms, and decrepit prisons are not overflowing with trodden dissidents. It knows that such callousness has become unacceptable in an era where the West sees Jordan as a kinder, gentler Arab autocracy—one whose monarchical state appears far more enlightened and progressive than other dictatorships in the Middle East given its allowance for an active civil society and legal opposition.

However, repression has not disappeared so much as become nimbler. In the current ecology of soft security, the Jordanian regime treats public life as a vast gray zone governed by vague laws, which technically criminalize so much speech and behavior that anyone can be capriciously targeted depending on its subjective whims. For instance, officials do permit many street protests, but they surround them with police and riot troops while always singling out some participants for arrest. Activists do not face lethal punishment, but the most opinionated still suffer egregious abuses and trumped-up legal charges that ruin their lives. The government does not ban most civic organizations, but they sabotage many by sowing division, harassing members, and occasionally imprisoning leaders. Opposition parties like the Muslim Brotherhood's Islamic Action Front (IAF) can run in parliamentary and municipal elections, but restrictive electoral rules prevent them from winning too many seats. Artists, writers, reporters, and filmmakers do not answer to a towering censorship office that requires them to disseminate propaganda. However, should their political discourse be deemed too anti-government or controversial, prosecutors can creatively interpret ambiguous statutes—like the Press and Publications Law or the Cybercrimes Law—to bury them with steep financial penalties or even criminal cases, thereby ensuring they self-censor their opinions.

This preference for soft repression shows the Jordanian state's ability to adapt over time. From insouciant students to street vendors, plenty of citizens still suffer arrest and imprisonment for voicing too critical an opinion.[22] But officials know they cannot punish everyone. For one, it is too costly, especially with global monitors like Human Rights Watch and Amnesty International tracking the latest happenings in Jordan. In the twenty-first century, a regime cannot credibly claim to promote democratic values while committing mass human rights violations. For another, in purely tactical terms, selective coercion can be just as effective as blanket violence. It allows authorities to keep oppositionists in a state of suspended fear: many will not be rounded up for punishment, but at a moment's notice, any single one might. And indeed, when necessary, the coercive apparatus can still uncoil at a moment's notice to decisively smother a domestic threat with little compunction for human rights. The 100,000-strong teachers union suffered this fate in August 2020: less than a year after its nationwide strike paralyzed the public schooling system, the regime banned the group, curbed all its protests, and jailed its leaders. In April 2025, the Interior Ministry chose to ban the Muslim Brotherhood on extraordinary allegations that it had fostered terrorist activities, while permitting—at least for the moment—its IAF party to continue operating.

Less controversially, Jordan's royal autocracy has an unapologetic smash-mouth mentality in dealing with Salafi-jihadist terrorist movements like Al-Qaeda and the Islamic State of Iraq and Syria (ISIS).[23] While Western donors help fund counter-extremism programs focused on winning hearts and minds such as youth education, the regime prefers harder techniques. When terrorist attacks occur, from the 2005 Amman hotel bombings to the December 2016 shootings in Karak, the police and GID throw due process out the window as they hunt down not just the suspects but also wider circles of sympathizers. Endless interrogations and abusive detentions can follow, evincing a no-tolerance approach to ideological extremism.

The distinction between high-intensity and low-intensity coercion—between violent clampdowns versus stealthier suppression—is an essential one. Yet, they have the same effect, in terms of preventing any opposition within society from jeopardizing authoritarian order. Which techniques to use is a matter of strategic *choice* rather than physical capacity because the Hashemite regime commands the raw capabilities to control its populace all the same. It has simply become adept on choosing different approaches based upon its perceived threats. Three legs of its coercive apparatus ensure this: the military, the GID, and the police, each of which carries its own unique legacy and institutional role in sustaining authoritarian rule.

The Jordanian Armed Forces

The first leg of Jordan's coercive tripod is the military. The JAF is the modern descendant of the Arab Legion, the British-led army that policed Transjordan during the Mandatory period. British officers initially organized this armed force to secure its imported Hashemite crown, pacify resistant tribes, and defend the new emirate's borders. As legend avers, "The Legion virtually created the state of Jordan."[24] By the 1930s, the Legion—and its mostly Bedouin recruits—had become the biggest public institution within the colonial state, not only impressing tribal communities into royal service but also developing the capability to wage war.

And war it waged. The Legion supported British military campaigns across Iraq and Syria during World War Two. It next fought in the 1948 Arab-Israeli War, securing the West Bank and East Jerusalem for the newly independent Jordan.[25] After reorganization and expansion, the army fought again in the 1967 Arab-Israeli conflict, albeit in a losing effort that saw Israel capture those Palestinian territories. The JAF drove out insurgent Palestine Liberation Organization (PLO) guerillas during the short but bloody 1970 Black September civil war, but it largely sat out the 1973 Arab-Israeli War, deploying only an armored detachment to help defend the Syrian front.

In the half-century since then, the JAF has fought no major wars as a frontline combatant, for good reason. The monarchy has studiously avoided excessive entanglement in regional conflicts, not least because its military has always been dwarfed by larger or more powerful armed forces in neighboring Israel, Syria, and Iraq. Nonetheless, the JAF has grown over time. Today, its boasts nearly 115,000 personnel spread across a large army, small air force, perfunctory navy, and specialized units like its counterterrorism battalion and special forces. US and NATO allies provide extensive training and advising, while most of the JAF's weaponry are purchased or gifted by Western armories. Maintaining such a large armed forces is costly. Over the past two decades, the JAF's budget alone has equaled 5 percent of Jordan's gross domestic product (GDP), while its payrolls represent 4 percent of the national labor force; both figures put the kingdom among the top ten in the world.[26]

Why does the Hashemite monarchy need such an expensive military? Jordanians cannot openly ask such a delicate, but commonsensical, question. Perhaps it is because the answers have little to do with what militaries are supposed to do—defend national sovereignty from external attack and wage wars on behalf of the national interest. The JAF is a fighting force that does not fight much. Since the 1994 peace treaty with Israel, the United States has increasingly assumed the job of protecting Jordan from external attack, as Chapter 8 discusses. The country now hosts a major US military and security presence, having become a central node in the American war-making machine in the Middle East. While Jordanian soldiers dutifully interdict minor threats that enter the kingdom, such as Syrian drug smugglers or Salafi-jihadist terrorists, American forces would defend Jordan's territorial integrity against any regional belligerent foolish enough to attack it, or even momentarily violate it. For example, when Iran attacked Israel in April and October 2024 with waves of drones and missiles, American forces stationed in the kingdom dutifully shot them down once they crossed over Jordanian airspace. On other fronts, JAF units perform other tasks for the regime. For instance, they participate in United Nations peacekeeping missions around the world, which bring prestige and recognition to Jordan. At home, it has also helped train Palestinian Authority forces since the 1990s, along with Iraqi troops after the deposal of Saddam Hussein's regime in 2003.

The JAF only sporadically springs into military action abroad, and usually as a small part of Western-led campaigns. For instance, Jordan sent hundreds of troops to Afghanistan as part of NATO's operations in this Central Asian country after the 2001 fall of the first Taliban government. The JAF likewise joined the US-led campaign against ISIS. As Jordan hosted the US-led multinational coalition against the Islamic State group, the JAF launched limited airstrikes over Syria during 2014–2015; it also sent special forces units there, in addition to Libya and Iraq, to support Western operations in those zones. In recent years, the Royal Jordanian Air Force has also launched sporadic bombings of drug smuggling networks in Syria and Iran-supported militias in Iraq, assisted by US forces. Overall, though, the JAF has not engaged in much fighting. Resurgent conflict involving Israel, Hamas, Hezbollah, and Iran after the most recent Gaza war exploded in October 2023 captivated regional headlines but did not directly involve the Jordanian military.

The JAF's more important responsibilities are *domestic*. Historically, it has served as a constabulary of last resort, the ultimate enforcer of Hashemite order within Jordan. The JAF head, the chairman of its Joint Chiefs of Staff, stands as among the most prestigious regime figures who answers only to the king. Indicating its protective role over the monarchy, the army regularly subdued public demonstrations in the West Bank and Amman from the 1950s through mid-1960s. Palestinian-Jordanians recall the bloody days of Black September, when Jordanian soldiers rounded up thousands of Palestinians in Jordan in that civil war.[27] Even after martial law ended in 1989, the JAF continued to serve as the regime's coercive backstop, called into action when popular unrest or street protests overwhelmed the police. It curbed rural rioting over economic hardships in April 1989 and August 1996, and in 2002, it occupied the southern town of Ma'an after local violence there flared. While the JAF was never called to act against Jordan's Arab Spring–inspired peaceful protests of 2011–2013, it deployed once again during the Covid-19 pandemic. Then, authorities treated national lockdowns as military operations, with the army fanning out to enforce daily curfews. It is likewise telling that when King Abdullah ordered the arrest of Prince Hamzah and more than a dozen other alleged coup conspirators in April 2021, he assigned the awkward mission to the army.

That Jordan's leadership entrusts such sensitive jobs to the military reflects a second domestic function. As Joseph Massad has argued, the JAF connects East Bank tribes with the monarchical state, sheltering Transjordanian interests through symbolic and material channels.[28] For example, the JAF enshrines a highly professionalized identity upon its mostly tribal personnel, centered on serving the Hashemite throne—a sense of duty invented during the colonial period and one that still permeates its ranks. Lavish royal ceremonies and commemorative holidays personify the affinity between crown and soldier, as does the tendency of Hashemite kings to don military garb to signify their moral tutelage over the army.[29] The JAF also runs its own media services, including FM radio stations like Bliss and Hala, which propagate pro-government patriotism. Moreover, strict standards keep the military distanced from political controversy. JAF personnel cannot vote in parliamentary elections and are discouraged from openly discussing political issues. As one retired general expounded, "It is not that we have no political ideas. Some of us [officers] become politicians after we retire. But so long as we wear the uniform, we cannot be political. It is the understood rule. You will never hear an officer give a political speech attacking anyone, even with our American advisors."[30]

The JAF institutionally caters to Transjordanian interests in other ways. The monarchy has conventionally allocated its senior command positions among leading tribes, ensuring that the perks of promotion reach different East Bank constituencies. The officer corps also features a disproportionately high number of Circassians, signifying their privileged status. Moreover, the JAF provides significant social benefits to tribal communities. Since the colonial era, military employment has brought not only steady salaries to recruits but also housing assistance, subsidized foodstuffs, healthcare, and pensions that can support their families for generations.[31] Such sustenance has been historically vital in rural areas where few other employment opportunities exist. Thus, the monarchy has always been sensitive when soldiers and veterans grumble about living conditions. A small 1974 protest among army troops in Zarqa, for instance, resulted in King Hussein ordering pay increases to restore morale. In recent decades, rising living costs have led King Abdullah to frequently raise not only military salaries but also pensions for JAF retirees. Given that over 250,000 Transjordanian men today are army pensioners, these are steep but necessary concessions. Other forms of militarized welfarism are subtler but no less pervasive, taking the form of specialized programs that most other Jordanians cannot access. As a mundane example, tourists arriving at Queen Alia International Airport will find that legal airport taxis are driven by JAF veterans, who enjoy a monopoly on this service. Other retirees secure government-related business jobs.

Conversely, JAF veterans are protective of their political and social entitlements. In 2010, a committee of military retirees publicly disparaged Jordan's neoliberal economic reforms and accused Queen Rania and many technocratic elites of corruption. Such sentiments embody their aging vision of an older, more traditional Jordan defined by tribal identity and state-led development—not the more cosmopolitan, privatizing kingdom of King Abdullah, where inequality abounds and crony capitalism has blossomed. Such objections also reflect the communal schism described in Chapter 2. The JAF has always been a Transjordanian preserve, to the exclusion of most Palestinians in Jordan. After the 1948 Arab-Israeli War, for instance, the army segregated Palestinian volunteers into separate, lightly armed units stationed in the West Bank.[32] When national conscription came into effect during 1966–1992, most Palestinian recruits were again sequestered into technical positions rather than combat roles. The anti-Palestinian chauvinism unlocked by the 1970 Black September conflict made such prejudice so rampant that very few Palestinian-Jordanians today seek military careers, despite no formal laws barring them from doing so.

The JAF's third domestic function is economic. While it devours public resources, it also drives a small military-industrial complex that, over the past two decades, has spawned a cryptic web of new arms firms that have enriched the monarchy, JAF, and private investors.[33] One plank of this indigenous defense industry is the Jordan Design and Development Bureau, established in 1999 and which sells small arms and war materiel abroad—thus far, mainly to Iraq and Gulf militaries. Another is the King Abdullah Special Operations Training Center, built with US assistance and which generates profits in selling counterterrorism training services to foreign clients. Dozens of other military-related businesses exist. The most enigmatic is Mawared, a real estate firm created by the government in 2001. Mawared has made a fortune selling and commercializing army lands; it has directed some of Amman's largest developments, such as the $5 billion Abdali Boulevard, a luxurious commercial and residential megaproject that opened in 2014. However, its internal operations and precise financial relationship with the palace and armed forces remain wrapped in secrecy, despite an embarrassing corruption scandal in 2011 implicating its CEO.

The General Intelligence Directorate

The GID, or *mukhabarat,* is the second leg of Jordan's coercive tripod. If the JAF is the regime's sledgehammer, the mukhabarat is its scalpel. Since its founding in 1964, the GID has developed a mystique as an all-knowing secret police, one devoted to eliminating any perceived threat against Hashemite rule. Western fascination for the Jordanian mukhabarat runs deep. As Pete Moore has critiqued, from journalistic missives to the 2008 Hollywood thriller *Body of Lies,* glamorous portrayals frame the GID as Jordan's version of the American CIA or Israel's Mossad: a ruthless house of spies that infiltrates terrorist organizations and exterminates the fanatics who would endanger the kingdom.[34] The view from within Jordan is quite different. Many citizens dread the mukhabarat as a political animal with a checkered past that still stalks society by muzzling anyone who too insolently criticizes the government or evokes nonconformist political ideas.

The GID emerged during Jordan's martial law period, after ideological parties and popular opposition tested the army's control over the street during the 1950s and 1960s. Following the 1970 Black September civil conflict, it solidified its place as the palace's national security watchdog and charged its mostly Transjordanian staff to investigate and snuff out perceived troublemakers. Operating a wide network of informants, the mukhabarat surveilled all of society—students, activists, professionals, journalists, and even politicians and military officers. The GID often indulged in high-intensity repression against suspects, such as torture and abusive detentions, so much so that Western commentators grimly called its headquarters the "fingernail factory."[35] Given their duty as wardens of national stability, intelligence chiefs became more influential than prime ministers. After the 9/11 terrorist attacks in the United States, the mukhabarat focused its energies on Al-Qaeda. It worked closely with the CIA to infiltrate Salafi-jihadist networks during the War on Terror, turning Jordan into a dark hub for America's extraordinary renditions program. In the early 2010s, the GID entered the thicket of covert arms smuggling and counterinsurgency efforts in the Syrian Civil War, again in partnership with the CIA. Its expanding clandestine operations during these past decades came with quiet successes but also notable failures, such as the 2009 Khost suicide bombing ambush in Afghanistan and a June 2016 shooting attack outside Amman, both of which killed GID officers.

Today, the GID continues to fulfill two goals. As an intelligence agency, its many operational and analytical units hunt down terrorist groups, arms smugglers, foreign conspiracies, and other physical threats to Jordan. Where Jordanians shudder is at the mukhabarat's other role as an extrajudicial police force, one that can arrest and detain citizens at will if their speech or actions are considered politically dangerous.[36] As an institution, the GID abides by several cardinal beliefs: Islamism and other ideological opposition movements endanger Hashemite rule; Transjordanians, not Palestinian-Jordanians, are the rightful stewards of the kingdom; and democratization must be avoided at all costs. The GID has expansive coercive powers to enforce those ideas that are only partly inscribed in law. They exist because the king—to whom GID chiefs report, not to the prime minister or even the JAF—allows it. Times have changed, to some degree. The proliferation of Internet access means that mukhabarat agents cannot hear every utterance of political opinion, much less spy on all social media accounts. While tortuous interrogations and incommunicado detention still occur, the worst treatment tends to be reserved for terrorism suspects rather than mundane oppositionists.[37] The GID has also found hushing political dissidents easier through harassment and blackmail, the sort of intimidating measures easily conveyed with private conversation, rather than go through the hassle of openly arresting them in plain sight. Soft security, indeed.

Yet it is testament to the mukhabarat's fearsome reputation that many Jordanians still prefer not mentioning it in public, as if doing so would trip a hidden bug or alert a nearby informant. And indeed, stories of its menacing influence proliferate in daily life: A newspaper knows when to scuttle an editorial about political corruption after a terse phone call from a GID officer; an outspoken academic researcher will shush after running into her university's mukhabarat liaison. Being seen at the wrong protest can result in a citizen's "good conduct" certificate—a document that only the GID can issue—being revoked, thereby making it difficult to renew a passport, obtain public employment, or run in elections. A Jordanian tourist returning home can wind up being grilled about his political views merely because his passport has an Iranian visa. Youth activists know what a friendly request to drop by the GID's headquarters for a quick chat means: "The request is never friendly, and the chat is never quick. The next day, they'll do it again. And again. They grind us down until we sign a form pledging good behavior, and they hold that over us forever."[38] By the time of its final ban, the Muslim Brotherhood and its leadership had gotten used to scanning their ranks, knowing some among them were mukhabarat infiltrators. Major meetings of political parties and civil society organizations usually feature a conspicuous GID observer, who ensures that nobody raises too controversial of an issue.

The mukhabarat's reach even extends to the state itself. Given its privileged place by the king, the GID can sometimes veto the appointment of officials like ministers and senators if they carry views deemed excessively liberal or sympathetic to opposition ideals. Palace deliberations on democratic reform are always guided by mukhabarat warnings that too much political freedom will destabilize the kingdom and allow dangerous dissidents—such as Islamists or leftist ideologues—to destroy the monarchy. Its agents can plant stories in the media and orchestrate leaks to make haughty officials look like buffoons. GID chiefs in past decades also boasted of bribing as much as a third of the lower house's members of parliament (MPs), ensuring that they always supported government legislation and rebuffed opposition parties.[39] Parliamentarians not on their payroll face pressures to adopt pro-government positions. In 2007, the mukhabarat rigged the general elections altogether to engineer the IAF and other Islamists out of parliament.

There are downsides to having such a potent force. Sometimes, its actions become too aggressive, forcing the king to bridle this watchdog. In 2005 and 2019, for instance, King Abdullah abruptly fired the GID leadership after hearing too many uncomfortably public murmurs about senior officers meddling in the affairs of his government.[40] For another, the mukhabarat's massive growth during the US-led War on Terror—partly funded by CIA support—also created operational fiascos and financial corruption. Two former GID chiefs, Samih Battikhi and Mohammad Dhahabi, earned prison sentences from the Jordanian courts on criminal charges of embezzlement and fraud, although some Jordanians believe their downfall came only after personal disputes with the king. In 2016, international media reported that GID agents had enriched themselves by selling CIA-supplied arms destined for Western-backed rebels in the Syrian Civil War on the black market.[41] That perturbing news came after a string of local intelligence failures, including botched raids against militant hideouts and a shooting attack at a local GID office outside Amman, leading some to wonder if the mukhabarat had lost its touch.

In 2021, King Abdullah vowed to revamp the mukhabarat as part of a broader campaign of democratic reforms. The new GID would focus only on halting external threats such as terrorism, not snoop into the affairs of citizens or intercede into matters of government.[42] Yet few believed this, and rightly so. Not only did most royal promises for greater democracy in the past come to naught, but it made little sense for the regime to declaw its most effective weapon in controlling society. And so Jordanians went about their lives as mindful as ever, knowing that the GID could always be listening.

Civil Policing

The third leg of Jordan's coercive tripod is civil policing. Beside the monarchy's military carapace and intelligence directorate stands the Interior Ministry, which fields the sizable PSD, which includes the civil police and gendarmerie (*darak*). Alongside the JAF's coercive sledgehammer and the GID's repressive scalpel, Jordanian policing works like a chisel—always quietly chipping away at the rough edges of the social terrain.

Since its 1956 founding, the Public Security Directorate has served as Jordan's main law enforcement institution, doing everything from border control and traffic regulation to civil policing and criminal investigations. Its police units are the first to respond to major demonstrations. Internally, the PSD has uniquely militaristic features. It has an army-like ranking and promotion system, and even its directors are army generals rather than career police officers.[43] Like the JAF and GID, the PSD also embodies the regime's orientation toward Transjordanians, and not only because most of its personnel are East Bankers. For instance, rural police departments share close relations with many tribal communities, and they often resolve local crimes through informal mediation that allows feuding parties to privately resolve their grievances, no matter what the law requires.[44]

At the same time, the police also carry a reputation of abusing those caught committing undesirable public behavior. Stories of officers beating apprehended citizens within police stations abound, especially among protesters and activists. The LGBTQ+ community has been especially targeted in recent years, facing merciless outing and humiliation by PSD personnel as punishment for transgressing heterosexual norms. The PSD also brandishes a few hard-nosed units capable of violently suppressing public disturbances. Among them is the Royal Desert Police (*al-shurta al-baadiyyah al-malakiyyah*), a crack rural detachment that has sometimes deployed to urban centers to stamp out civil unrest. They crushed the 1986 student strikes at Yarmouk University in Irbid, and since then have menacingly loitered in Amman whenever public protests in the capital become raucous.

The PSD also fields the darak, the national gendarmerie founded in 2008. The darak serve as the regime's "internal strike force," more aggressive than civil police but less lethal than the army.[45] In quiet times, these paramilitaries—often donning black balaclavas and tactical vests—guard government offices, major hotels, and other sensitive locations. In times of protest, they rush to quell hotspots with close-quarter containment tactics. In early 2010, the darak assaulted striking port workers in Aqaba; in March 2011, they dismantled the largest Arab Spring protest encampment in Amman; and in November 2012, they subdued anti-austerity riots in Amman and other localities. Hundreds of operations since then have given them a reputation for stern efficiency that extends beyond the kingdom. Darak troops have trained the police of allied Arab states, such as Palestine and Iraq. Until 2015, a gendarmerie battalion also operated in Bahrain, helping authorities in this small allied Gulf kingdom deracinate their own disruptive oppositionists.

Whereas the GID operates in the shadows, uniformed police and darak paramilitary units serve as ubiquitous signs of authoritarian rule because they always occupy public spaces. Their anti-protest strategy exemplifies this. In keeping with the demands of soft security, Jordanian authorities tolerate most peaceful demonstrations and marches except during periods of emergency, like the Covid-19 lockdowns. This is no small feat; as Chapter 6 discusses, the kingdom has witnessed an efflorescence of public mobilization from many opposition groups under King Abdullah. However, the police and gendarmerie also execute a well-rehearsed strategy of control and intimidation to ensure protests do not spin out of control.[46] Typically, while police officers encircle protesters to prevent bystanders from joining, the darak stand in front of them with batons and shields at hand. Often, the main streets, public squares, and traffic circles in which crowds gather are pockmarked with concrete barriers and high fencing, further forcing protesters into narrow chokepoints. Such containment results in a handful of arrests, but more importantly can demoralize activists no matter what spirited grievance—solidarity with Palestine, demands for jobs, complaints about corruption, and so forth—prompted their mobilization in the first place.

Upgrading Repression

Most Jordanians—including peaceful oppositionists—do not suffer high-intensity repression. However, it is also true that many citizens hesitate to openly criticize their monarchical regime; and when they do, they seek safety in numbers through solidary protests and social movements. If Jordan's rule-makers truly believed that opposition within society posed no danger, then they would have little need to maintain such a large, well-armed, and expensive coercive apparatus.

What Jordanian authorities have called soft security since the 1990s has involved making coercion less violent but just as effective. It is an upgrade, not diminishment, of repression, which reminds "the population of the potential/reality of violence and other forms of coercive action."[47] As discussed earlier in this section, such soft security works by combining selective displays of public coercion—such as shutting down an organization or imprisoning a brash dissident—with subtler methods of discouraging opposition. Consider the weaponization of the judiciary. Thanks to convoluted laws that criminalize an impossibly wide category of speech and actions, prosecutors can outlaw offending organizations and arrest citizens for technical reasons, all under the mantra of rule of law.[48] For example, the 2014 Anti-Terror Law forbids any behavior or verbiage that "disturbs" public order, with the interpretation of that clause left open to officials. The 2023 Cybercrimes Law extended that sweeping mandate onto the online realm, banning all forms of online activity that could be seen as spreading "fake" news—with authorities very much willing to place sharp anti-government criticism in that category.

Moreover, administrative courts regularly approve executive requests to penalize civic groups, as when the Interior Ministry seized the Muslim Brotherhood's financial assets in 2016; they have likewise left intact the ministry's 2025 decision to prohibit the Brotherhood altogether. Criminal courts uphold flimsy charges against targeted opposition leaders that can result in imprisonment, which leaders of the now-defunct teachers union discovered after August 2020. And more than a few youth activists, protest organizers, and even litterateurs have been hauled into the notorious State Security Courts on baseless accusations of harming Jordan's national interests. These military tribunals are where the GID sends its suspects, and they routinely deprive defendants of due process in opaque proceedings.

Not all political critics suffer such lawfare through politicized prosecutions and trials. Yet they are still touched by the state's protean hands, which try to frighten them into obeisance.[49] They receive intimidating phone calls and visits from the GID; their friends, families, and even supervisors at work are pressured to disavow them. Nongovernmental organizations and parliamentary parties that complain too stridently are threatened with suspension. Journalists and human rights defenders find their smartphones hacked with the Israel-made Pegasus spyware, reputedly deployed by the Interior Ministry. Even on the street, protesters discover that authorities have found new ways to watch them. It was not long into the Arab Spring when young protesters in Amman began seeing an ominous sight: counterprotesters, typically goons paid by the GID or PSD, who jeered them as disloyal seditionists, all the while as government drones and facial recognition cameras tracked them from above.[50] Such judiciary chicanery and suppressive smokescreens embody much contemporary repression in Jordan, making even more impressive the unbending work of protesters and activism that Chapter 6 explores.

The Ruling (Transjordanian) Coalition

Jordan's coercive apparatus sustains authoritarianism by controlling opposition. It hammers, slices, and chisels away upon the populace, creating routines of public order and setting boundaries on political behavior. But this does not silence everyone. Indeed, as Chapters 5 and 6 show, opposition and dissent have existed on the East Bank for as long as the Hashemites have ruled. Durable autocracies need something other than threats of violence; they require a staunch coalition, a base of support drawn from other parts of society. They require some segment of citizens who believe that their regime, however flawed, represents a legitimate one worth endorsing and defending.

The Hashemite regime has such a coalition. The monarchy's main base of public support has always comprised Transjordanian constituencies, specifically East Bank tribes alongside small minorities like Circassians and Christians. A narrow elite stratum of wealthy merchants and business families also form this political bedrock. The concept that best describes this dynamic is ethnocracy, because it generally corresponds to the communal Transjordanian-Palestinian divide: with some exceptions, the coalitional structure underpinning Jordan's royal autocracy has given far more influence and privilege to Transjordanians, whereas Palestinians in Jordan have been excluded and marginalized in politics.[51]

That tribes form the social foundation of Hashemite rule became an orientalist shibboleth in older views of Jordanian politics. For decades, Western writers portrayed East Bankers, and especially the Bedouin tribesmen recruited by the JAF, as simpleminded desert folk—"fighting material par excellence"—historically destined to embrace their monarchy given their atavistic need for a grandiose Muslim chief.[52] Such mythology reeks of racial prejudice; its proponents facilely point to state practices in Jordan that propagate the affinity between tribe and crown. For instance, royal speeches and educational treatises celebrate the Hashemite king's implicit role as *shaykh al-mashaayikh* (sheikh of all sheikhs, or chief of all chieftains). If there is any Transjordanian ethos, such outmoded thinking goes, then it entails a love for the throne that seems almost genetically encoded into tribalism.

Such narratives are problematic. Cultural values do not magically will ruling coalitions in authoritarian states into existence. Rather, they are forged through painstaking bargains between leaders and supporters; they are the work of politics. Moreover, such arrangements evolve over time, because no coalitional alliance is permanent. In Jordan, many East Bankers initially endorsed Hashemite governance during the colonial period because they became enmeshed in its networks of patronage and protection, which maximized their prospects for survival and prosperity. Such Transjordanian support (and, conversely, Palestinian exclusion) deepened after the 1948 and 1967 Arab-Israeli Wars. Yet since the 2000s under King Abdullah, this coalition has begun weakening, as more tribal Jordanians feel their economic and political demands have become increasingly ignored. The monarchy still needs Transjordanians to operate its state and coercive apparatus, but it has also cultivated a newer elite class of technocrats and financiers enriched by privatization and neoliberal economics. This has produced tensions within its social base—not enough to produce major instability or change, but still different from past patterns.

The Tribal-State Compact, 1920s–1940s

The origins of the Hashemite regime's tribal coalition harken back to its imperial roots. In the 1920s, the British created an entirely new state and monarchy atop a rural landscape where tribal self-rule had been the norm. As local Arabic histories divulge, much like with Ottoman rule previously, many Transjordanians on the East Bank treated the new government with suspicion.[53] Indeed, some major tribes like the Bani Hassan had snubbed the Hashemite call to arms during the Great Arab Revolt years earlier. Throughout this first decade, many tribal communities resisted new taxes, anti-raiding laws, and other autocratic decrees. It took British firepower to squelch several major armed revolts, such as the 1923 Balqa uprising. Even so, paramount sheikhs from large Bedouin confederations like the 'Adwan and Bani Sakhr dismissed Emir Abdullah as an imported potentate whose Prophetic lineage meant little.[54] As the next chapter discusses, such local resistance also fueled early democratic movements in the form of the Transjordanian National Congress.

How did this enclave monarchy convince a reluctant population to obey? One explanation is that both sides came together due to conflict and insecurity. In the late 1920s, severe climactic and external shocks upended Transjordan.[55] Harsh droughts produced famine across the central steppe, decimating many villages and settlements. Bedouin and semi-nomadic tribes reliant on camel pastoralism were also devastated by the Great Depression, which dampened export markets for their livestock, as well as by the rise of motorized vehicles, which reduced transportation demand for camels. At the same time, foreign aggression loomed. Across the southern border, resurgent Saudi forces conquered Mecca in 1924, toppling the reign of Emir Abdullah's father and Britain's wartime ally, Sharif Hussein; the modern state of Saudi Arabia emerged not long after. Wahhabi militias employed by Saudi forces also marauded into the southern Transjordanian desert, skirmishing with its tribal groups.

Amid such weakness emerged a golden opportunity to reduce this mutual vulnerability. Emir Abdullah's fledgling regime needed to plant its roots into Transjordanian communities, which conversely sought the economic and political means to weather their privations. The British-funded Mandatory state allowed the monarchy to reach into local society with new policies that restructured public life, such as registering land, issuing censuses, building schools, and establishing courts.[56] Across impoverished rural areas, officials reduced widespread adversity through food subsidies, relief works, and public employment. At the same time, Abdullah's regime reached out to tribal sheikhs in strategic fashion, offering gifts and land grants in a bid to bring these notable elites to Amman and give them symbolic political voice. For many, it worked. Some tribal leaders began advising Abdullah directly, while others entered the Legislative Council, the semi-elected advisory assembly created by the 1928 Basic Law.[57] The Arab Legion was central to these efforts to secure tribal interests. The inchoate army patrolled tribal areas and guarded the southern frontier against Saudi incursions. It also provided education, healthcare, and housing to Bedouin recruits, becoming in effect a social welfare agency.

As it consolidated its economic reach across the East Bank, the Mandatory state extended patronage to other Transjordanian constituencies to incorporate their support. Circassians were heavily recruited as government functionaries and soldiers, while Christians received pledges that the Hashemite monarchy would protect their religious practices and social interests. As Chapter 7 observes, local merchants and business families who held considerable preindustrial wealth also earned favorable policies like tax abatements, regulatory loopholes, and lending opportunities in return for working closely with the monarchical regime.[58]

By World War II, all these pacts had created a coherent base for authoritarian power. Sheer necessity had spurred a coalitional arrangement: much as the monarchy needed local support to legitimate its rule, Transjordanian communities had become incorporated into the political institutions, economic routines, and social policies of their Mandatory state, thereby becoming stakeholders for Hashemite governance. Predicated on mutual dependency, this tribal-state compact constituted the political order that became independent of British imperialism in 1946.

Communal Ethnocracy, 1950s–1980s

No long after independence, Jordan experienced the earthquake of the 1948 Arab-Israeli War, which saw it gain control over the Palestinian West Bank. Given that territorial annexation and the displacement of other Palestinians onto the East Bank, the newly confederal Hashemite Kingdom tripled its prewar Transjordanian population; it was now a Palestinian-majority country. In the succeeding decades, though, the coalitional politics of autocratic rule failed to accommodate this demographic shift.

The postwar aftermath seemed rife with political opportunity. Publicly, the Hashemite monarchy proclaimed itself as caretaker for the Palestinian cause, which initially won applause from other Arab leaders in the region.[59] Abdullah's assassination in 1951 did not change this spirit of solidarity. Once enthroned in 1953, King Hussein inherited a liberal constitution overseen by his father King Talal during his brief reign, one that legalized political parties and established the bicameral parliament discussed in Chapter 3 that promised a modicum of popular participation. The 1954 Nationality Law allowed Palestinians to gain Jordanian citizenship, including those living in the West Bank. A small stratum of West Bank Palestinians thus integrated into the confederal kingdom's economic and political institutions by establishing close ties with the monarchy, including well-to-do landowners, merchants, and politicians.[60] The Nusaybah family of Jerusalem, for instance, contributed several ministers and ambassadors to the Jordanian governments from the 1950s onward. The Irshayd family of Jenin married one of its daughters, Firyal, to Prince Muhammad, King Hussein's younger brother, in 1964.

This spirit of national unity, however, fell short in assimilating most other Palestinians during the 1948–1967 period. Economically, Palestinians as a whole received little help from the Jordanian government. Outside refugee camps administered by the United Nations Relief and Works Agency (UNRWA), Palestinian communities faced significant hardships. Those on the East Bank initially struggled to acclimate in Amman and other cities, while West Bank towns and villages received only a paltry share of national development funding. This was intentional: state planners in Amman feared "the growth of a West Bank infrastructure" that might facilitate the emergence of independent Palestinian industries and political organizations.[61] Economic spending thus skewed heavily toward the East Bank, where most government employment, social services, and state-owned industries were located, to the benefit of Transjordanians.

The same communal inequality held within politics. Amman was the center of confederal power and treated the West Bank as an administrative appendage conquered through war rather than an autonomous area of equal importance to the East Bank. Government positions continued to be filled mostly by Transjordanian politicians, tribal sheikhs, Circassian personalities, and other non-Palestinian voices. With few opportunities for inclusion into the levers of state power, Palestinians helped lead the wave of democratic opposition that became the Jordanian National Movement in the 1950s, as Chapter 5 demonstrates. In the West Bank, such grassroots mobilization amplified a deep local tradition of political activism and civic organization.[62] After the regime crushed such mass mobilization, many Palestinians came to distrust royal authority even further. They saw the Hashemite monarchy's proclaimed custodianship over the Palestinian cause—embodied by the images of Jerusalem emblazoned upon national banknotes and postage stamps—as hollow rhetoric. As Kimberly Katz has adroitly shown, such symbolism did not promote national unity so much as *erase* the notion that Palestine could ever be an independent entity separate from Hashemite rule.[63]

By the 1967 Arab-Israeli War, thus, Jordan's coalitional politics had strayed only marginally from its Transjordanian moorings. King Hussein and his officials praised Palestinians as equal members of the Jordanian nation in public speeches, but in practice Palestinians faced economic and political exclusion. This trend deepened over the next two decades due to Black September. Jordan lost the West Bank and East Jerusalem to Israeli occupation in the 1967 war. Afterward, the PLO relocated much of its militant operations against Israel to the East Bank. What ensued was a chain reaction of broken agreements and escalatory violence that culminated in the Black September civil conflict of 1970, in which PLO guerillas unsuccessfully attempted to overthrow King Hussein.

The consequences of Black September resounded for decades. The tribal-staffed JAF succeeded in expelling PLO-affiliated fighters by early 1971, lionizing its status as the regime's unflagging sentinel.[64] After the conflict, as Chapter 2 mentioned, a virulent strain of chauvinism took hold among many Transjordanian politicians, writers, and public figures. They also blamed Palestinian-Jordanians for the conflict, despite most not participating in the PLO's insurgency or operations. They praised East Bank tribalism as Jordan's authentic heritage and rejected any Palestinian presence in its national identity: Palestine was Palestine, and Jordan was Jordan. Promoting an "East Bank first" mentality, such nativists portrayed all Palestinians in the kingdom as a treacherous fifth column—disloyal foreigners who had betrayed the very royal host that had granted then citizenship.[65] This conveniently fed into the Hashemite regime's advocacy for a sovereign Palestinian state across the Jordan River that was free of Israeli occupation, as tribal ultranationalists insisted that was the true home for Palestinian-Jordanians, not the East Bank.

This renewed ethnocratic impulse burrowed into politics. As the late Adnan Abu Odeh observed, an informal doctrine of *ardanna* (Arabic for Jordanization) took hold in the 1970s and 1980s, sidelining Palestinians while further raising the importance of tribal stakeholders.[66] Under martial law, the GID and police blanketed Palestinian-dominated urban areas like Amman with repression, treating any expressed sympathy with the PLO or the wider Palestinian cause as anti-Jordanian sedition. Transjordanians continued to fill the ranks of the government, Diwan, and coercive apparatus. Within education, discriminatory admissions and hiring practices elevated Transjordanian students and faculty within Jordan University and other institutions of higher learning, ensuring their overrepresentation.[67] Palestinian-Jordanians, by now, formed the bulk of Jordan's urban middle class, including its most talented engineers, technicians, pharmacists, and scientists—not to mention craftspersons, shopkeepers, and other small entrepreneurs. Yet, economic productivity brought them little political influence within the state, excepting the richest businesspersons protected by royal connections forged in decades past. Unsurprisingly, many Palestinians left Jordan altogether to seek work in the Arabian Gulf kingdoms.

Anti-Palestinian politicking went hand in hand with the regime's expanding patronage and protection for tribal constituencies, which redistributed public resources at a national scale. Economically, the public sector (including the civil service, public bureaucracies, and state-owned firms) expanded rapidly to meet Transjordanian job demands, wedding the material fates of many tribes to the Hashemite state. In 1975, the public sector encompassed roughly 157,000 workers; combined with the payrolls of the JAF, GID, and police, this meant that almost all Transjordanian families received some type of state salary.[68] In rural tribal-dominated towns like Ma'an and Karak, government-related jobs and pensions became primary sources of financial security for most households. Welfare policies likewise enhanced tribal livelihoods. Universal food and fuel subsidies enacted in the mid-1970s greatly helped Transjordanian families, given their dependence on modest public salaries; so too did targeted benefits, like cheap housing for soldiers and frequent wage increases for public employees, including the police.

Finally, the monarchy rekindled its political outreach to tribal communities. Donning the role of *shaykh al-mashaayikh,* King Hussein frequently consulted with tribal leaders, his ostentatious visits sometimes accompanied by gifts of cash, land, and other rewards.[69] Given the suspension of parliament under martial law, he also experimented with state-controlled organizations to ensure that Transjordanian figures enjoyed symbolic participation in politics. The 1971 National Union and 1978 National Consultative Council, for example, were figurehead institutions led by East Bank factotums intended to temporarily serve the place of the legislature.[70] They reminded Transjordanians that they were linchpins of Hashemite rule and more proximate to power than Palestinians. Also shoring up this tribal-state nexus were cultural and social privileges. For example, authorities in Amman afforded considerable independence to rural tribal communities to regulate their affairs through specialized tribal courts that applied customary laws to handle local problems. Even after their 1976 abolishment, the PSD and national judiciary continued allowing many tribes to adjudicate local crimes through informal mechanisms of mediation and justice.

By the 1980s, thus, a communal ethnocracy had been fashioned. Transjordanians, and above all the tribes, anchored autocratic rule. The costs of maintaining this social base rose over time as the population grew, but political payoffs were enormous. The price of such bargains, however, would soon become untenable for the royal autocracy.

Coalitional Narrowing, 1990s–Present

Ruling coalitions in authoritarian states always change. In Jordan, unexpected crisis weakened the tribal-state compact starting in the 1990s and precipitated a political shuffling of the cards. As Chapter 7 recounts, the economic collapse of the late 1980s exposed the fiscal precarity of the Hashemite regime, as overexuberant state-led development policies crashed under a heap of debt. Following its bailout by Western donors, the government enacted a new framework of neoliberal economic reforms, which King Abdullah enthusiastically implemented after his 1999 enthronement.

These policy changes brought widespread stagnation and hardship, as the government began scaling back its public expenditures and its redistributive commitments. They hit many tribal communities hardest, as reliance on public employment and welfare provisions left them vulnerable to cutbacks in those channels of protection and patronage. A tidy reduction of subsidy spending on food and fuel from 3.3 percent of GDP in 1989 to 1 percent in 1994, for instance, more than doubled poverty rates in rural areas.[71] Alongside impoverishment came soaring unemployment. Except for the coercive apparatus, no longer could public payrolls in other areas—such as municipal offices, national ministries, and government bureaucracies—keep pace with the long queues of East Bankers seeking government jobs. The privatization of state-owned companies after the 1990s further reduced public employment opportunities.

Concomitantly, King Abdullah paired these market-oriented economic shifts with a more technocratic political outlook, which diminished the luminary roles that tribal groups once played. Unlike his father, Abdullah entertained fewer consultations with major sheikhs and visitations to tribal gatherings; so too did royal largesse to tribal notables slow to a trickle. Instead, the palace promoted a new cohort of Western-trained officials and bureaucrats, who from their ministerial and Diwan perches preached the virtues of globalization and capitalism in the twenty-first century. The king's efforts to advance a new discourse of Jordanian identity centered on unity and loyalty also unsettled East Bank nativists, who interpreted this as eroding the Transjordanian-Palestinian inequality that had previously demarcated their ethnocratic superiority.

As Transjordanian grievances grew, so too did overt displays of tribal opposition. Rising food and fuel prices spurred riots in southern tribal areas in April 1989 and August 1996, for instance. Rural sheikhs and other East Bank figures began publicly criticizing King Abdullah in the late 2000s over ongoing privatization deals and rising corruption, even insinuating that Queen Rania and her Palestinian relatives were profiteering from the new economy. The 2011–2012 Arab Spring and the decade afterward likewise saw new swells of tribal opposition, much of it driven by grassroots movements and youth activists in rural areas angered by the high unemployment and political neglect of their communities.[72] Indeed, since the 2010s, as Chapter 6 highlights, it has become commonplace for Jordanians to hear of tribal critics—such as former MP Osama al-Ajarmeh, imprisoned in 2022 after insulting King Abdullah—who use social media or lead street protests to issue fiery complaints about the monarchy betraying its tribal bargain.

Such troubles are real, but they should not overstate reality. Recent tribal grumbling does not constitute a revolution, only a recalibration. The decades since the 1990s have not witnessed a complete abandonment of the tribal-state compact. Rather, the Hashemite regime has pruned its edges through market-based economics, keeping intact its bulk but no longer accommodating as many Transjordanians as before. Public employment still exists for East Bankers; there is simply less of it, given the slowdown in government hiring and privatization of state-owned firms. The JAF, GID, and Interior Ministry's police organs are the exceptions, as they have increased in size since the 1990s, to the benefit of tribal communities that depend on their salaries and pensions. The old merchant and business elite has retained its wealth and influence. Circassians and Christians likewise never lost their royal patronage and political standing. Conversely, despite the misgivings of some East Bank nationalists, most Palestinian-Jordanians have not suddenly found themselves favored by the monarchy under King Abdullah. Indeed, excepting the most prominent businesspersons and technocratic ministers, most Palestinians in Jordan have found conventional pathways to political advancement—government appointments, state patronage, royal favor—blocked as before. For all the king's talk of Jordanian unity, few Palestinians have been promoted to positions of political prestige, including the senior ranks of government and the Senate.

Transjordanians, thus, have seen their place in the monarchy's coalitional base modestly curbed. Hashemite rule still *needs* its tribes but is no longer willing or capable of providing as many goods and services to procure their support.

The new social class that the Jordanian regime has elevated after the 1990s is a small capitalist elite that many tribal critics regard as unfairly usurping their traditional importance. This new elite comprises a narrow stratum of investors, moguls, and industrialists who have amassed impressive fortunes as the kingdom adopted market-oriented economic policies. They include both Palestinian and Transjordanian entrepreneurs, many of them Western-educated and English-speaking, and for whom capitalism and profit matter more than communalism and identity. They staunchly support King Abdullah. In turn, the monarchy regards this sleek, globalized class as the face of modern Jordan, for they are the financial skippers attracting foreign investments, backing real estate megaprojects, embracing digital technology, and consuming luxury retail.

Wither the Ruling Coalition?

Over the past two decades, the emergence of tribal opposition through political petitions, public demonstrations, and online tirades against King Abdullah and his governments have startled Jordanian commentators. In their eyes, the Hashemite regime is playing with fire by ignoring its Transjordanian followers while favoring an elitist crowd of Palestinian businessmen, crooked courtiers, foreign investors, and other monied collaborators. Fears of instability peaked after the 2021 detention of Prince Hamzah, whose fellow alleged coup-mongers included East Bank tribal advisers who shared his revulsion with political corruption. Since that event, calls for a new tribal-state compact have circulated public discussions, one that would properly re-center the tribes within the monarchy's coalition. After all, if the monarchy's own tribal sons threaten to revoke their loyalty, then how can the crown endure?

Feeding off the tired survivalist trope of Jordanian politics, such alarmism makes easy headlines. It is also misleading. Typically, East Bank detractors bemoan state corruption, complain of economic inequality, and wax nostalgic about the glory days of tribal order many years ago. However, for all their protests, they have not risen in great numbers to demand an end to Hashemite governance or call for King Abdullah to step down. They criticize *how* this monarchy rules now—but not *that* it rules in the first place.[73] In other words, this is a loyal opposition, one that wishes the leadership do a better job in accommodating their interests rather than desiring an entirely new system of government. A few reasons account for this.

First, the coercive apparatus has effectively controlled tribal mobilization with the same strategies by which it treats all opposition: measured tolerance in the name of soft security, allowing many dissidents and demonstrators to let off their steam peacefully through protest, while resorting to selective repression only to stifle the most incendiary critics who cross the red lines. East Bank tribes still contribute manpower for the military, policing institutions, and GID, and in some communities large families may see their relatives both serving in the security forces and protesting on the street. Officials know better than to disturb that balance by brutalizing tribal critics indiscriminately.

Second, while old conduits of tribal patronage and protection have declined, they have hardly disappeared. The monarchy still does what it can to keep the livelihoods of Transjordanian households coupled with its own survival—just not as many as before. For instance, the total cost of public salaries and pensions has increased regularly since the 1990s, despite the financial burdens this puts on the Jordanian treasury. East Bank personalities still dominate the wider political system, from the appointed government to bureaucratic livery, despite the ascent of a handful of Palestinian technocrats under King Abdullah. The elected lower house of parliament, which both Chapter 3 and Chapter 5 discuss, continues boosting conservative tribal voices. So does the East Bank-dominated Senate. Clientelistic dealings between ministers, MPs, and bureaucrats still ensure that significant public resources benefit rural areas. King Abdullah himself prudently responded to Transjordanian criticism since the 2010s with well-coordinated campaigns of outreach. After the Prince Hamza controversy, for example, palace emissaries swiftly entertained prominent tribal clans and groups, praising their cultural importance and promising to give them greater representation in the future.[74]

Finally, for all but the most zealous tribal oppositionists, fears over the future outweigh frustrations about the present. Excoriating politicians and royals for elitist corruption is one thing, but toppling Hashemite rule altogether is another. Then what? Some East Bank nativists dread that without the monarchy, Jordan itself could disintegrate, auguring the internecine violence that has lacerated Syria and Iraq in recent memory. This would also play into Israel's hands, which make take that opportunity to seize the entire West Bank and displace its Palestinians onto Jordan. Other Transjordanian voices fear that should Jordan experience a revolutionary transition to democracy, Palestinian-Jordanians would be the ultimate beneficiaries, for their superior numbers would guarantee their dominance in future democratic elections.[75] Royal officials and GID officers alike shamelessly stoke both of these fears when privately engaging tribal representatives, underscoring the fatalist logic at the heart of Jordan's autocratic system. For the tribal-state compact, an imperfect Hashemite monarchy is far better than an uncertain future without the Hashemites. Thus, the East Bank coalition underpinning royal autocracy endures: frayed to be sure and occasionally combative, but persistent all the same.

Conclusion

Jordan is a stable Arab country because its authoritarian monarchy leverages a reliable toolbox of strategies to regulate, discipline, shape, and mobilize its populace. First, a large coercive apparatus regulates society, thanks to its well-armed military that no longer fights major wars, an intelligence directorate that specializes in chilling dissent, and policing institutions that ably contain unrest and monitor public life. The Hashemite regime has upgraded its techniques of repression as well. The high-intensity and oft-bloody crackdowns against opposition that occurred in decades past have been replaced with softer methods of intimidation, sabotage, and manipulation—tinged with violence when necessary.

Second, the monarchy stands upon a robust, yet selective, coalition of support. The Transjordanian tribes that have long resided on the East Bank, alongside smaller groups such as Circassians, Christians, and business elites, have been intertwined with the survival of this royal autocracy thanks to historical provisions of patronage and protection. Public employment, financial deals, social services, political promotion, and cultural endorsements have been the historical rewards furnished to these mostly tribal supporters, in return for their conditional loyalty to Hashemite rule. Such a social pact has conversely marginalized most Palestinians in Jordan, who excepting a privileged industrial elite have been excluded from the monarchy's circle of favor.

Both repression and coalition-building work in tandem. In Amman, a small number of unelected rule-makers command vast power, and they have no wish to surrender it. Coercion enables these powerholders to stop those who want change, while coalitional politics allows them to attract others in society to their side. Of course, there is an equally important external factor: Western allies, and specifically the United States, which have helped finance, arm, and legitimate the Hashemite regime for generations, as Chapter 8 unravels. But for domestic politics, these two strategies of coercion and coalitional politics keep authoritarianism in place.

Yet to be stable does not mean to be *static*. It is remarkable that the Hashemite monarchy has never been toppled, making Jordan the only Arab country in the Mashriq to have never experienced regime change. However, for all its repressive mechanisms and tribal exploitations, this regime has still weathered repeated opposition from its own citizens. The century-long story of Jordan is thus a tale of not just durable authoritarianism but also of democratic resistance from below—of public protests, creative organizing, and popular mobilization driven by ordinary people demanding more political and economic rights. This is the contentious, messy side of Jordanian politics, and it must now come into the limelight. As Chapter 5 narrates, democratic movements expressing the will of the Jordanian people nearly arrested the power of Hashemite rule in three special moments in time: the late 1920s, the mid-1950s, and the 1990s. These are the closest calls to real democracy that Jordan has had.

5

From Democratic Dreams to Liberalized Autocracy

What Happens When Jordanians Demand Democracy?

A wearisome ritual plays out when Western journalists ask Jordanian officials about the latest reports of human rights violations in the Hashemite Kingdom. No, they sigh in ornate ministerial conference rooms, Jordan has not yet democratized. It is not Sweden. But neither is it Syria or Saudi Arabia. Martial law ended decades ago, and Jordanians enjoy freedoms still scarce in other Middle East countries. They vote in elections, they protest government policies, and they form opposition parties. King Abdullah has himself praised European-style constitutional monarchism, vowing that a "Jordanian model of democratic transition" will deliver "unity, moderation, pluralism, and respect."[1] The problem, the royal hosts insist, is that Jordanians themselves are not yet ready for democratization. They are beset with economic hardship, regional terrorism, the Israeli-Palestinian conflict, and other treacherous crises. Give the Jordanian people too much choice, and maybe even the Islamists will win. Better to live with a mildly authoritarian system than gamble with the stability of this pro-Western bastion of Middle East calm.

And with that final talking point, the nodding visitors finish their tea and leave.

The curious thing about this ritual is not its scripted nature. For decades, the Hashemite monarchy has periodically proposed democratic reforms but then backtracked once the notion of ceding power became real—and thus retreating, as Chapter 4 explained, to crafty repression and coalitional politics to maintain its sway. It has justified such reluctance by valorizing how restrained Jordanian politics still looks when compared to far more closed dictatorships in the Middle East, such as Iran or Syria under the Assad regime. Rather, the most astonishing aspect is that despite this monotonous cycle of broken promises and disappointing excuses, hopes for greater freedom spring eternal from society. Jordanians know that political change will not happen without a fight. Yet, they never stop trying. Resistance to royalism, protests for participation, demonstrations for democracy: however it manifests, rowdy campaigns for democracy have been as ubiquitous to Jordan as Hashemite rule itself since colonialism—an unexpected find within this supposed island of placid stability.

In this sense, the story of Jordanian politics over the past century is not only one of kings and rule-makers who adapt and survive in a blustery region. It is also about rule-followers—the people and movements in Jordan who question those rules and imagine radical political alternatives. The history of Jordan, in sum, is also a history of democratic contention. This chapter unfurls this parallel history by showcasing three critical moments of popular struggle against royal authority. They represent the kingdom's closest calls with democratization. They illustrate not just how its autocracy has fought back in retaining power but also the defiance and creativity of opposition forces.

The first section lays the groundwork for this discussion by hypothesizing what real democracy in Jordan might look like. It has stark implications. It means denuding the Hashemite monarchy of its supremacy, grounding governance within elected bodies like parliament, and protecting a fuller spectrum of civil and political rights. Shallow excuses that Jordanians are not culturally or mentally ready for such changes hold little water; as public surveys show, most citizens in the kingdom want more democracy and less dictatorship.

The next three sections section connect the present to past by illustrating the kingdom's close calls with democracy—meaning "near-miss" moments of Jordanian democratization, in which popular opposition boldly challenged royal dominion and advocated for change. The first episode centers on the Transjordanian National Congress movements in the late 1920s, which pitted East Bank dissidents against Anglo-Hashemite authority. The second entails the Jordanian National Movement during the 1950s, which encased urban opposition drawing upon both Transjordanians and Palestinians, and which nearly upended Hashemite rule during Jordan's first decade of postcolonial independence. The third case was the renaissance of political opposition after the liberalizing reforms of the 1990s, which took place amid economic crisis and post–Cold War regional upheaval. To be sure, all of these movements failed to achieve their goals of transforming the political system and its structures of monarchical power, but they also inscribed their verve onto the shared memory of the Jordanian public, which still resonates today.

The fifth section settles on the present and explores the liberalized autocracy that delineates Jordanian politics under King Abdullah II. It highlights the curious mix of institutions and practices that compose this pseudo-democratic system. On paper, some desiderata of liberal politics exist, such as a bicameral parliament with an elected lower house, a lively civil society filled with opinionated voices, and an optimistic monarchy that pledges reform. But looks are deceiving, for a complex ecology of institutional control ensures that the royal leadership and its coercive apparatus continues to outflank popular pressures for change. Twenty-first century Jordan features a soft brand of authoritarianism, but it is authoritarianism all the same.

What Jordanian Democracy Augurs

Talk of democracy suffuses political chatter in Jordan. Every few years, authorities issue garrulous promises of political reform and ordinary folk bemoan how they never pan out. Lost in this shuffle is the deeper meaning of democracy in the Hashemite Kingdom. For some protesters and activists, democratization means justice (i.e., a responsive state that punishes the corrupt and provides more jobs). For others, democratic change connotes a government that more fairly represents their interests in foreign policy—a muscular stance to defend Palestine by ending the peace treaty with Israel, for instance. For still others, Jordanian democratization signals more everyday freedom, so that fewer people find themselves targeted by the mukhabarat for their critical political ideas.

All of these outcomes can result *from* democracy. However, they are not democracy itself. At heart, democracy centers on not specific policies but rather institutional procedures, or as political scientists term the "rules of the game" designed to make government accountable to the masses. It does not necessarily mean overthrowing the Hashemite monarchy and creating a republic; indeed, most Jordanians yearning for democracy prefer a constitutional monarchy, one where the king reigns as a national symbol but no longer rules. In this vein, democratization in Jordan would bring the following practical changes, all of which would dramatically transform the authoritarian power structures described in Chapter 3.

First, the Hashemite dynasty would concede its currently vast powers in favor of a more symbolic role, like the royal houses in Norway, Japan, the United Kingdom, and other constitutional monarchies around the world. In such a Jordanian democracy, executive authority would hail not from a hereditary king but rather from a government formed by parliament, with the prime minister—the head of government, and thus the most powerful political figure in the country—coming from the largest party or coalition of winning parties. Parliament would draft the laws that it cannot now, such as the national budget, and oversee all domestic and foreign policy issues, including oversight of the military and intelligence directorate.

Second, relatedly, elections would matter. Free elections enable vertical accountability, making politicians beholden to their voters. In a Jordanian democracy, general elections would be not the sideshows they are now, but meaningful contests in which unfettered parties and candidates would compete for parliamentary representation with the goal of forming the government. Such elections would be *fair*, unlike under the current system, which this chapter discusses. They would not under-represent Palestinian-Jordanians by apportioning more legislative seats to tribal-dominated rural areas.

Third, practices of power within the Jordanian state would transform. There would be horizontal accountability, in that no single elite actor or authoritative institution would be immune to constitutional oversight. Gone would be the sticky networks of royalists, technocrats, businesspersons, sheikhs, and other elites who have long monopolized political life. The rule of law would diminish corruption. The coercive apparatus could no longer operate with impunity, instead having to answer to the elected government and parliament. Imagine a Jordanian prime minister probing the General Intelligence Directorate (GID) about its latest interrogations, a parliamentary committee grilling military commanders over requested arms purchases, or a crack team of prosecutors and judges investigating suspicious patterns of royal spending: impossible scenes today, but part-and-parcel of democratic accountability in any other context.

Finally, a democratic government in Jordan would tolerate pluralism within society. Officials could not punish disagreeable speech, intimidate their critics, or stifle opposition movements so long as they are peaceful. This contrasts to the present day, in which the Hashemite regime—like many other post–Cold War autocracies—has learned to exploit the spirit of liberalization by tolerating some civil society and political dissent but still throttles public opposition through a jumble of repressive laws and judicial manipulation.[2] The doctrine of soft security discussed in Chapter 4 is one such example. Democratization would lift these restrictions, even if this means accepting the spread of Islamism and other ideologies that some dislike.

These drastic shifts represent only the start of the process. They drastically depart from the existing model of authoritarian rule, and it is little wonder why Jordanian authorities are so reluctant to democratize. Yet they represent, as veteran local commentator Labib Kamhawi suggests, "non-negotiables" in that any Jordanian democracy that does not limit monarchical power, reward electoral competition, and embrace pluralism cannot call itself democratic at all.[3] From these institutional foundations, Jordanians must decide among themselves what specific type of political order and set of public policies are best. Disagreements will be plenty. For instance, an elected government featuring more Palestinian than Transjordanian politicians would reflect the kingdom's social demography but may repel many tribal communities. An elected parliament led by Islamists might elicit outcry among secular parties, much as it did for Egypt in 2012 when the Muslim Brotherhood swept elections following the Arab Spring. Moreover, Jordanians will clash over what issues their elected leaders should tackle first. Many demand greater economic rights and social welfare measures; others focus on gender equality, religious freedom, or attaining a balanced foreign policy that no longer kowtows to US strategic interests.

These are mighty differences. Hashing them out would resemble how other democracies deal with similarly thorny divisions—through tenacious debate, bruised feelings, and political confrontations. But the underlying point is that the voices of Jordanians as a whole, rather than a narrow set of unelected powerholders, would steer the course of this litigious ship. They would bear that momentous responsibility, with all of its growing pains, but they would also reap all the fruit that comes from establishing such a bold democratic experiment in the Middle East.

The Fiction of Readiness

When presented with the prospects of such democratization, Jordanian authorities privately blanche. Democracy brings too much uncertainty to an already-shaky country, replacing the dependable rhythms of royal leadership with the nastiness of electoral politics and ideological competition. As they warn, empowering the leaderless masses in a country beset by regional conflicts, economic crisis, and social tensions could vent "passions and interests . . . that will spin out of control and take the Kingdom on an unpredictable and dangerous path."[4] Such is the received wisdom inside royal circles: Jordanians are not *ready* for democracy. If only the region were less violent and the Islamists were less menacing; if only the streets were quieter and citizens less poor. Defenders of authoritarianism even point to the Syrian Civil War to prove that, when gifted the taste of liberation, Arabs cannot handle freedom. Better instead to have what Curtis Ryan, an astute expert on Jordanian politics, aptly describes as a "*perpetually* liberalizing autocracy"—one where officials dabble in milquetoast reforms that give society some breathing room to protest, complain, and vote, but never fully surrender their grasp on power.[5]

The conceit that Jordanians are ill-suited for democracy needs debunking. It reeks of orientalism, the bigoted worldview that has always seen Muslim and Arab societies as "doomed to be eternally out of step" with the enlightened path of liberal democracy given their archaic culture and values.[6] Such ethnocentric bias lingers in the Western imagination, driven by equal parts fear and mystery about Islam as a faith and the Middle East as a geographic region. An August 2017 Pew survey, for instance, found that 44 percent of Americans believed that Islam and democracy were incompatible, while 41 percent believed it encouraged violence more than other faiths.[7]

It is incongruous that these ideas run in parallel with how Jordanian officials rationalize royal autocracy. Reasoning that Jordanians cannot handle democracy reproduces such cultural prejudice, which permeated how the British once treated this protectorate. In the colonial era, British observers mocked Transjordanians as incorrigible yokels incapable of grasping the mechanics of civilized government. The famous British commander of the Arab Legion, John Bagot Glubb—known honorifically as Glubb Pasha—bemoaned how "the primitive tribesman cannot apparently be transformed into an officer and a gentleman . . . we cannot send all the Howeitat [tribesmen] to Eton and Oxford."[8] More than seventy years later, an American diplomat in Amman offered me sadly similar thoughts when asked about the possibility of homegrown democracy: "Their biggest problem is themselves. The Jordanians don't understand how to build parties or deal with losing. So it's probably best that democratic reforms are very, very slow. Otherwise, we're playing with fire."[9]

This noxious paternalism makes little sense. In a historical perspective, every culture and religion has been chastised as hostile to democracy—until their countries democratized. For decades after World War II, for instance, scholars impugned Catholicism as an despotic faith, reasoning that the dictatorships ruling in Catholic-majority countries like Brazil and Spain mirrored the illiberal theology and hierarchical structure of the Vatican.[10] That silly notion dissolved once those autocracies disappeared during the Third Wave of Democratization, which during the 1970s through 1990s saw over sixty authoritarian regimes transition to democracy around the world. Moreover, today there exists little evidence that either Islam or "Arabness" hinders a desire for freedom. For instance, witness Indonesia, the world's largest Muslim country as well as its third largest democracy—or the stirring protests of the Arab Spring, when millions of Arabs mobilized for greater rights in the face of stubborn dictatorships. In a purely theoretical sense, as well, political scientists know well that democracy requires no single precondition. Across time and space, innumerable factors like economic development, labor mobilization, elite bargains, and external support have been tied to the downfall of tyrants and the rise of elected government.[11] Perhaps the only consensus from this body of knowledge is that for democracy to transpire, some citizens must *believe* it is worth a shot—and they must fight for it.

Jordanian Views on Democracy

Jordanians certainly believe in it. The Arab Barometer delivers crucial evidence here. As Figure 5.1 illustrates, six survey waves since 2007 divulge two consistent patterns about popular opinion in the kingdom. Many Jordanians report that democratic politics can be messy, indecisive, and problematic (between 35

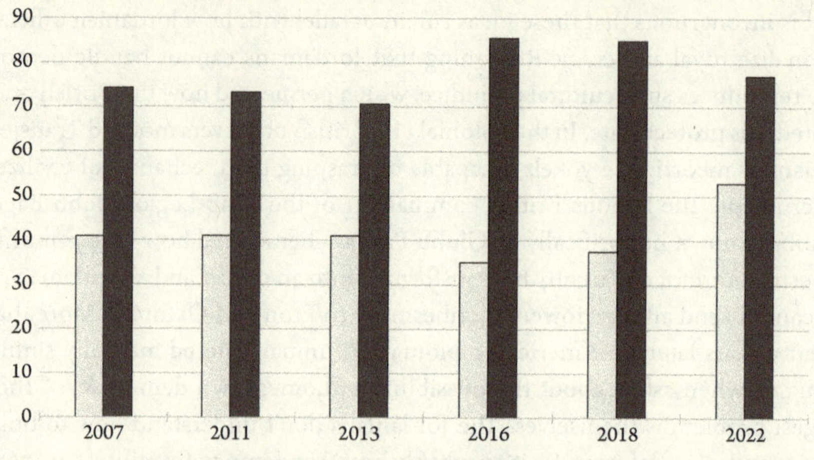

Figure 5.1 Support for Democracy among Jordanians, 2007–2022. The light bar represents the proportion of respondents who agreed or strongly agreed with some variant of the statement, "Democratic regimes are indecisive and full of problems." The dark bar represents the proportion who agreed or strongly agreed with some variant of the statement, "Democracy is better than other political systems, despite its problems." Source: Arab Barometer, https://www.arabbarometer.org/.

to 53 percent). They have no delusions that an elected government, even one that respects their liberties and rights, will satisfy all their assorted grievances. Yet despite this, the overwhelming majority still sees democracy as the best political system, for all its warts—to the tune of 70 to 85 percent. Indeed, every major opinion poll of Jordanian political attitudes taken by other survey organizations such as Pew Research Center, the International Republican Institute, and the Konrad Adenauer Stiftung since the 2000s emits similar findings.[12] Citizens here mistrust officials, fret over corruption, and grumble about the economy. And, clearly, a majority desires democracy.

Moreover, many Jordanians not only believe in democracy but have also struggled for it for generations. Ever since the kingdom winked into existence, opposition movements have mobilized for greater freedoms and advocated alternative visions of political order oriented around public representation rather than royal power. The most intense confrontations between such popular forces and Hashemite authority came in the late 1920s, mid-1950s, and early 1990s. These are Jordan's closest calls with democratization. Though the regime leaned on its usual strategies to emerge victorious—such as brute repression, coalitional lures, and Western support—such conflicts were so threatening that they made real the tantalizing possibility that the ruling monarchy would surrender at least some of its power.

While Chapter 6 will discuss the ongoing pulse of protest and dissent during and after the 2011–2012 Arab Spring, these three historical showdowns highlight a more pertinent point. Democratic aspirations are no less authentic or indigenous to the East Bank than the Hashemite monarchy that governs it, and *both* Transjordanians and Palestinians alike have driven these bottom-up campaigns for change. In doing so, they laid down enduring legacies that still permeate the collective memory of citizens.

Transjordanian Congress Movements, 1928–1933

Jordan's first close call with democracy occurred not long after its imperial creation, as the fledgling Hashemite regime encountered calls for self-rule among local East Bank communities. Those efforts climaxed in the Transjordanian National Congress (TNC) movements, which starting in the late 1920s mobilized to demand greater political participation. The TNCs did not compose a single unified front, but shared a common dream of self-government, bounded by anti-colonial militancy and committed activism. They left behind a rich bequest of disobedience that would impregnate the imaginations of future opposition for good reason: such protestations came from Transjordanians. The very communities whom future observers would uncritically portray as bulwarks of conservative pro-monarchical loyalty also generated shrill, early challenges to Hashemite authority.

Tribal Resistance and Mobilization

The tribal residents of the East Bank defied foreign powers well before the British established the Transjordanian Mandate in 1921. In the late nineteenth century, when the area was under Ottoman rule, Ottoman administrators grafted themselves onto major towns like Salt and Ajloun to control this imperial expanse more firmly. Yet, they frequently met pushback, as many Transjordanians rejected the tax laws, military conscriptions, and other bureaucratic demands they imposed.[13] Impassioned dissidents resisted Ottoman rule by publishing illegal newspapers, holding public gatherings, and sometimes organizing armed rebellion. Especially bloody revolts occurred in the towns of Shobak and Karak; tribes there today still recall their violent suppression, which ended with the execution of local opposition leaders.

Such defiance underscored that the East Bank's diverse populace had never before formed, or been treated as, a coherent nation or state. Peasant and nomadic tribal communities, alongside small Circassian and Chechen minorities, each carried their own cultural histories and political identities, bound together by a shared economy of petty trade, small agriculture, and pastoralism.[14] To be sure, many Transjordanians grasped the inexorable arrival of British colonialism after the 1916 Great Arab Revolt, whose military campaign against the Ottomans meandered across much of the East Bank. However, few still welcomed it. When British officials held public conventions in several East Bank towns in 1920 to gauge local sentiment about the prospect of imperial government, they met jeers from tribal sheikhs and merchant representatives who instead demanded self-rule. When the British converted the East Bank into a colonial state the following year, they hence fundamentally transmuted the social reality of Transjordanian life. East Bank residents became subjects within a newly constructed state they did not craft, bounded by borders they did not draw and nominally ruled by a monarchy whose leader, Emir Abdullah bin Hussein, they did not elect.

For Emir Abdullah and his British minders, the 1920s brought considerable tribal opposition. In the early years, British-led forces squashed armed uprisings in their bid to pacify the most restive tribes. At the same time, peaceful political resistance came from more organized Transjordanian networks. One was the Istiqlal, an early Arab Nationalist party founded in Syria; some of its intelligentsia accepted invitations to serve in Abdullah's first cabinet governments, while more combative members decried the new Anglo-Hashemite state as a foreign occupation.[15] Worried about domestic stability, Abdullah and his British minders impressed two new laws in 1928. The first was the Anglo-Transjordan Treaty, which reaffirmed the emir's standing as absolute ruler while safeguarding Britain's military and financial tutelage; the second was the Basic Law, which allowed for an elected but powerless sixteen-seat Legislative Council. As Chapter 4 noted, such measures occurred as authorities simultaneously sought to establish a popular base for Hashemite rule by enmeshing tribes in militarized welfarism while patronizing local merchants, Circassians, and other constituents.

Still, not all Transjordanians were content. The Anglo-Transjordan Treaty and Basic Law provoked a groundswell of criticism from outspoken sheikhs, writers, and protesters, who disparaged the absence of popular consultation in their governance.[16] They drew upon liberal ideals swirling in international circles at the time, such as Woodrow Wilson's Fourteen Points and potent anti-colonial ideologies. Among such formidable dissent was the poetry of Mustafa Wahbi al-Tal, a popular teacher from Irbid. Known by his pen name 'Arar, al-Tal's writings called for an independent Transjordan unshackled by any Western power. A deepening campaign of demonstrations and petitions culminated in July 1928, when 150 East Bank notables gathered in Amman, styling themselves as the Transjordanian National Congress. Five further TNC conventions would follow, with the last meeting in June 1933. Over this five-year life span, the TNCs functioned as people's movements propelled by grassroots support, with well-to-do traders, rural tribal figures, and Istiqlal activists all playing a role in their rapid growth.[17]

The TNCs were knit together by a solidary commitment to a fearless goal—self-determination in Transjordan, or, barring that, a truly representative government where Emir Abdullah and his British patrons would have far less say. Their social pressures and political statements thus repudiated the proclaimed authority of the Mandatory state. For instance, the first TNC sent its National Charter (*al-Mithaaq al-Watani*)—an anti-colonial declaration calling for constitutional governance and which notably referenced the self-determination principles raised by Wilson's Fourteen Points—to the League of Nations. TNC supporters likewise pioneered Jordan's first autochthonous political parties, such as the aptly named Executive Committee, to institutionalize and coordinate their activities.[18] Such mobilization undercut the Legislative Council, the centerpiece of the new regime's efforts to symbolically grant its subjects a limited opportunity for popular participation. Many TNC members boycotted the council's founding elections in April 1929, and they also garnered the sympathies of some elected deputies afterwards. For the first two years of its existence, thus, the council often bogged down in embarrassingly stormy quarrels over public spending and government perquisites—the sort of issues that a proper ruling monarchy backed by British firepower was not supposed to bear.

Repression and Coalitional Politics

During the first decades of the British Mandate, the TNCs represented the most sustained opposition against authoritarian rule and Western colonialism. Their activists based much of their writings and meetings in Amman, which sent a thunderous message: "Amman may have been the seat of the Anglo-Hashemite state, but it was not a space that they controlled completely."[19] Unwilling to brook such a challenge, the monarchical regime with British approval responded with repression. New laws passed by 1929, particularly the Crime Prevention Law and Deportation Law, allowed the government to arrest, fine, and exile dissidents for uttering critical political speech. Censorship muzzled the East Bank's embryonic literary scene, closing opposition newspapers like *Al-Shari'ah*. In 1931, Emir Abdullah suspended the bickering Legislative Council altogether, previewing the punishing blows of royal power in future decades against elected representatives who refused to cooperate. In addition to heavy-handed policing, internal disagreements emasculated the unity of the TNCs, with issues like Jewish land purchases and calls to unite Transjordan and Syria into a single Arab union proving especially divisive to their members.

Through the early 1930s, the regime succeeded in containing these movements, while also expanding its reach over the populace. While welfarist protections and targeted patronage drew more Transjordanian communities and tribes into the ruling coalition, tactics of co-optation quieted individual adversaries. For instance, the general secretary of the Executive Committee, Tahir al-Joqah, accepted an appointment to become mayor of Amman in return for exiting the ranks of opposition. Mustafa al-Tal himself ultimately accepted a government job after repeated detentions, eventually serving within the emir's Diwan and as a respected judge.[20] (Decades later, Mustafa's son Wasfi would become one of the most famous prime ministers and confidantes of King Hussein.) The waning of the TNC moment was felt within the Legislative Council: once reconvened, the assembly proved more submissive to the emir, with its members' docility secured with appointments and gifts. Between 1931 and 1946, the Legislative Council's collective roster hailed from just thirty-six Transjordanian families, all favored by royal largesse.[21]

By the mid-1930s, the TNCs had dissipated as an organized force. Local dissent was restricted to "pockets of independent influence and pressure groups" that occasionally made their voices heard, as in protests supporting the revolts in neighboring Palestine during the late 1930s.[22] By World War II, national politics settled into a more predictable cadence, with the Hashemite regime having consolidated its authority atop its tribal-led coalition, military protection from the Arab Legion, and British financial assistance. Still, the TNCs had achieved a remarkable feat. They enabled East Bankers to question the legitimacy of their rule-makers during Jordan's colonial genesis and also percolated habits of dissension and critique in public life that would not be forgotten. When King Hussein granted liberalizing political reforms nearly sixty years later—another democratic moment that this chapter discusses—the 1991 National Charter that he endorsed illustriously referenced the TNCs as proof of Jordan's liberal heritage.

The Jordanian National Movement, 1950s

Another intimate brush with democracy came during the 1950s, the first post-independence decade. What kicked off this era of opposition was the 1948 Arab-Israeli War, which recast Jordan's territorial and social composition through the absorption of Palestinians. One byproduct was the Jordanian National Movement (JNM), an umbrella of opposition parties and civic movements that, like the TNCs, promoted a more liberal vision of politics. The JNM sought to replace royal dictatorship with a parliamentary democracy infused by leftist, anti-imperial ideals. JNM activists enjoyed meteoric success in bringing the palace to its knees, but for that reason also suffered harsh repression when the Hashemite regime fought back.

Mobilization and Coordination

Several titanic events set the stage for the JNM. First, the 1948 Arab-Israeli War reinvented Jordan, turning a mostly tribal kingdom into a confederal domain with a Palestinian majority. The annexation of the West Bank and the arrival of Palestinian refugees in the East Bank metamorphosed politics through sheer strength of numbers. For instance, whereas the 1947 elections for the new parliament, the legal successor to the old Legislative Council, had 100,000 Transjordanian voters, the 1950 elections featured 304,000 registered voters across the country thanks to the Palestinian influx.[23]

Second, royal succession and constitutional changes shook politics. The assassination of King Abdullah in 1951, the new constitution of King Talal in 1952, and the enthronement of a young King Hussein in 1953 augured an opportunity for the Jordanian public to reimagine their state as one of democratic principles, not just an authoritarian dynasty. The 1952 constitution, in particular, dripped with liberal rhetoric that gave oppositionists hope that officials would tolerate their activism.[24] For instance, it laid out the separation of executive and legislative powers, established a new bicameral parliament with an elected lower house, and spoke brightly of expressive and associational freedoms being guaranteed.

Third, urban centers like Amman, whose population soared from 26,000 in 1946 to 120,000 in 1955, gave rise to a flourishing civil society. Leading the charge by the early 1950s were leftist ideological parties, such as the Arab Nationalists, Communists, and the Ba'th, and new civic organizations like professional syndicates, worker groups, and student clubs.[25] Public fora nurtured vivacious debates about provocative topics like the future of Palestine, political freedom in the kingdom, and the problem of Western imperialism. A critical print press hummed, catering to a growing audience of hungry readers. So too did demonstrations and strikes become frequent occurrences, with protesters on the street drawing inspiration from pan-Arab sentiments rumbling from Egypt's Nasserist regime, which called for the collective struggle of all Arabs against Western domination—including those governments and kingships left behind by colonial rule, like the Hashemites of Jordan and Iraq.

Critically, the JNM drew both Palestinian and Transjordanian supporters. Among its members were middle-class Palestinians like teachers, lawyers, writers, and clerks.[26] Many were suspicious that the Hashemite monarchy had no intention of treating Palestinians as equal citizens, or the West Bank as an entity equal to the East Bank, within the kingdom's confederal union. However,

Transjordanians were no less important. East Bank activists revived the TNCs' tradition of grassroots mobilization, coordinating with West Bank counterparts to establish independent labor unions; among their achievements was establishing the General Federation of Jordanian Trade Unions (GFJTU) in 1954. The JNM also attracted support from sympathetic soldiers in the Arab Legion, similar to other Arab countries roiled by the powerful call of Arab Nationalist ideology. In Jordan, this small military circle—the Free Officers (*al-dhubaat al-ahraar*)—gravitated to the JNM.[27] They especially supported its campaign to liberate Jordan from its dogged British alliance cemented in the 1948 Anglo-Jordanian Treaty, which preserved the United Kingdom's political influence over the newly independent country through military basing rights and economic aid.

Despite its variegated membership and parties, the JNM converged on the bold goal of trimming the Hashemite monarchy's powers and installing a popularly elected government held accountable to parliament and the street. As Betty Anderson's definitive treatise explains, the JNM dreamt that such blanket change could enact the sort of policies that Jordanians deserved, such as more social spending, equitable economic development, greater civil and political freedoms, and a new foreign policy to replace the kingdom's pro-Western orientation with closer relations with Egypt, Syria, and other Arab Nationalist states.[28] This, of course, was anathema to the Hashemite palace and its conservative powerholders, which set the stage for intense conflict.

Clashes, Coercion, and Defeat

The early 1950s saw a tit-for-tat dynamic of escalating tensions between the monarchy and society in both the East Bank and West Bank. As the JNM held protests, organized strikes, rallied for elections, and issued antigovernment condemnations, authorities responded in kind with increasing repression. The 1953–1954 period was especially violent, featuring high-profile political arrests, newspaper suspensions, and martial decrees issued by cabinet governments led by Hashemite loyalists like Tawfiq Abul-Huda. Rioting after the October 1954 parliamentary elections, which Abul-Huda rigged to undermine the JNM's parties, triggered the widescale deployment of the Arab Legion to quell unrest. In late 1955, though, mass demonstrations compelled a reluctant King Hussein to reject the Baghdad Pact, a British treaty aiming to fold Jordan into a new anti-Soviet defense alliance. Not long after, Hussein acceded to popular pressures to sack Glubb Pasha and thus end British leadership of the Arab Legion—a major opposition demand.[29] To the JNM, this represented a long-awaited severance of the colonial yoke.

The crisis reached its apogee after the October 1956 parliamentary elections. Then, the JNM won more than half of the lower house's forty seats, producing a historic opposition majority. A cornered King Hussein appointed Sulayman al-Nabulsi, of the JNM's National Socialist Party, as prime minister. The resulting leftist government marked the only time in Jordanian history that political parties, rather than the Hashemite palace, controlled the cabinet. In its brief life, it pursued radical domestic and foreign policies.[30] For instance, the Nabulsi government began guiding Jordanian foreign policy toward closer relations with the Arab Nationalist states and the Soviet bloc—a shocking turn amid the Cold War, as Chapter 8 discusses, given Jordan's longstanding pro-Western stance grounded in British colonial history. In January 1957, such maneuvers enabled Jordan to ink the Arab Solidarity Agreement, which severed British foreign aid and replaced it with joint economic assistance from Egypt, Syria, and Saudi Arabia. Domestically, the Nabulsi government began restructuring political institutions and rethinking national policy priorities. For instance, it engineered the dismissal of conservative royal officials like Diwan Chief Bahjat Talhuni. As parliamentary minutes during this period reveal, it also sought to reverse press censorship, investigate wasteful spending, and prioritize economic development in the West Bank.[31]

Had the Nabulsi government been allowed to continue, it could have inaugurated a full-fledged transition to constitutional monarchism, using its popular backing to steadily marginalize the royal autocracy even further. Alas, it was not to be. In April 1957, a series of chaotic events, including a bungled coup attempt by the Free Officers, resulted in King Hussein sacking the Nabulsi government. Its tolerance exhausted, the monarchy cracked down on all opposition, backed by its tribal supporters and—thanks to Hussein's avowed anti-Soviet stance—the United States.[32] Under martial law, the army detained thousands of JNM members and democratic activists, while purging its own ranks of Free Officers. Officials suspended parliament, closed independent newspapers, and banned all parties. Within a year, such heavy repression had shredded the JNM, reminding citizens of a sobering lesson: "not parliament, democracy, or even some abstract and well-meaning notion of constitutionalism" could ever imperil Hashemite primacy.[33] Despite such actions causing strains with Arab Nationalist governments in Egypt, Syria, and Iraq (after the latter's own Hashemite dynasty was deposed in 1958), King Hussein doubled down by leaning on the United States, which replaced the British as Jordan's new great power patron.

The JNM's defeat laid a long chain of consequences. It strengthened the tribal-state compact, as the monarchy deployed its Transjordanian-staffed coercive apparatus to police society and quash criticism. It also put political opposition into a slumber. Organized parties remained prohibited for decades, while major civil society associations, like the GFJTU, came under government control.

By the early 1960s, the regime felt secure enough to co-opt some dissidents to secure their compliance. It worked. King Hussein pardoned many former opponents, including even Sulayman al-Nabulsi, who was appointed to the Senate in 1975. Rank-and-file critics were likewise rehabilitated. One famous example was ʿAbdel Hamid Sharaf. An Arab Nationalist, Sharaf was jailed in 1959, but he worked his way back into politics with an astounding result: he served as prime minister twenty years later, a reformist politician entrusted by King Hussein despite wariness from more conservative figures.[34]

However, memories of this democratic conflict from the mid-1950s persisted in the ensuing decades of martial law. On occasion, veteran activists emerged from underground to call for political change. Old Arab Nationalists reappeared during the Black September civil conflict of 1970 to support the Palestinian *fida'iyin*, for instance. In the early 1980s, an uptick of university student unrest was likewise inspired by the leftist parties that abounded three decades earlier. Most of all, the efflorescence of political activism in the 1990s would recall the JNM by sharing its same belief—that a participatory public, expressed through parliamentary elections and street mobilization, could force their monarchy to grant citizens greater voice and freedoms.

Political Liberalization and Pluralism, 1990s

Jordan's final democratic near miss came as the Cold War ended. In the late 1980s, economic crisis compelled the monarchy to end martial law and enact a bevy of bold political reforms to assuage an angry public. In the resulting interregnum, a tempest of empowered citizens pushed against the frontiers of royal authority. Hashemite rule-makers responded in a novel way. Whereas past democratic confrontations ended with violent clampdowns, the regime restored its dominance with a façade of openness. The partially liberalized authoritarian system that typifies Jordan today emerged this period, with state officials learning how to regulate opposition with a new arsenal of legal chicanery and reformist smokescreens.

Economic Crisis and Political Opening

As Chapter 7 expounds, Jordan's economy sharply contracted in the late 1980s. Buried in debt, the government drained its financial resources in maintaining the public employment, militarized welfarism, and other expensive protections expected by its Transjordanian coalition. When the World Bank and International Monetary Fund bailed out Jordan with emergency loans, they also imposed structural adjustment policies that heralded the advent of market-oriented economic reforms, or neoliberalism. Officials immediately cut public spending, with fuel subsidies the first to go.

In April 1989, a sharp rise in gas prices triggered irate reactions among truck drivers in southern Jordan. Protests rocked tribal-dominated rural governorates like Ma'an, Tafileh, and Madaba, and soon spread to several urban areas and university campuses. In the rural areas, riotous clashes with police killed a dozen and injured more than 100. This legendary uprising—the April unrest, or *habbat nisaan* as Jordanians recall—represented the biggest civil disturbance in decades.[35] The most aggrieved were tribal communities, because Transjordanians dependent on public sector work and government services had been most harmed by the economic crash. Subsidy cuts represented a jolting violation of the tribal-state bargain that had trussed their fate to the monarchy for generations.

The Hashemite regime speedily restored order. King Hussein deployed the army and coordinated with tribal sheikhs to quiet restive areas; he also sacked wildly unpopular Prime Minister Zeid al-Rifa'i. Yet after the riots, officials needed a new strategy to ensure calm in a context of worsening economic deprivation. It could not inflict high-intensity coercion on the very tribal communities whose sons staffed the military and state, but neither could the insolvent treasury spend its way out of calamity. The solution was political liberalization. The monarchy relaxed repression by ending martial law and pardoning political prisoners. In November 1989, it allowed the first lower house elections in two decades, restoring a parliament suspended since the 1967 Arab-Israeli War. In June 1991, the monarchy issued a National Charter pledging a democratic future, drafted in concertation with civil society representatives. In 1992, authorities dropped the ban on political parties, while the 1993 Press and Publications Law ended formal censorship and legalized a broad range of nongovernmental media. In 1995, King Hussein boasted to CNN that unlike Saddam-led Iraq "where democracy is missing," Jordan had become "a democracy which we hope will offer an example to others in the region."[36]

From their position, the palace and its coercive apparatus never intended such cautious reforms to produce democratization. Officials talked of *islah* (reform) and *ta'addudiyah* (pluralism), but in reality, they hoped that replacing lost economic bread with the crumbs of limited freedom could temporarily mollify Jordanians aggrieved from the financial downturn. Such liberalization also accompanied major foreign policy moves in these post-Cold War years, as Chapter 8 explains, by strengthening Jordan's Western-friendly stance and entertaining peace with Israel. King Hussein's regime, however, did not anticipate how fervently the public would take this opportunity by pushing for more democracy. In the 1989 elections, a hodgepodge of leftists, Arab Nationalists, and Islamists captured a majority of the eighty contested lower house seats—an opposition victory that stunned royal observers.[37] As the largest bloc, the Muslim Brotherhood claimed the position of parliamentary speaker, as well as several ministerial posts in the government. This emboldened the emergent climate of activism. The Brotherhood created its own political party, the Islamic Action Front (IAF), in 1992. Other opposition parties, from the old leftist and Arab Nationalist groups from the 1950s to newer liberal and centrist organizations, were not far behind. In Palestinian-dominated cities like Amman, civil society organizations like the professional syndicates and nongovernmental organizations (NGOs) assembled to advance political debates in open view. Independent news magazines and lively newspapers like *Al-Arab Al-Yawm* and the Brotherhood's *Al-Sabeel* proliferated, giving citizens new channels of unfiltered information.[38]

Certainly, this refulgent current of dissent was not revolutionary. The old red lines held: talk of toppling the monarchy, much less reproaching the military and other sensitive institutions, was still forbidden. Repression continued to target the brassiest dissidents; in 1992, for instance, authorities arrested Layth Shubaylat, a well-known Islamist member of parliament (MP), on flimsy charges of conspiring against the monarchy. The mukhabarat was still capable of intimidating and silencing critics. Nonetheless, the opposition forces that coalesced by the early 1990s were sizable and ambitious. Journalists, ideologues, organizers, and other voices breathed freely after decades of hibernation.[39] They did not cry for sudden regime change, but they did intrepidly poke the monarchy in public ways that were unthinkable during the previous decades of martial law. They decried Jordan's economic penury, lambasted the inept and corrupt bureaucracy, and questioned the king's choices of politicians. They monitored Jordan's foreign policy, debated when parliament would gain enough clout to form the government, and called for a new generation of elected representatives in the lower house. Through the inexorable weight of popular organization, they embarked on an open-ended campaign to win more political and civic rights.

In the end, this post-1989 opposition failed. As the late Musa Kilani, a veteran Jordanian commentator, recounted in an interview, "Nobody thought democracy would come instantly. But those [post-1989] years were different. The government admitted it could not handle the economic crisis. This was an opening, a message from the people. Many of us believed this was the start of something new."[40] In retrospect, something *was* new—but it was not democracy. Rather, Jordanian authoritarianism adapted. It upgraded its mechanisms of control in order to temper popular sentiments and end any potential that the outpouring of opposition could spiral into an uncontrollable pressures for democratization. Returning to martial law was too costly, given not only King Hussein's bombastic talk of democracy but also the regime's external desire to retain a reformist, progressive image with the West. The authorities needed softer tactics to regulate society, as too much violence would contradict its liberalizing veneer. And so they invented them.

Subverting Opposition

After the early 1990s, the Hashemite regime developed a sophisticated arsenal of legal and political instruments to squash challenges to its authority. First, officials maintained their commitment to elections, but also stacked the electoral system after 1989 to ensure that opposition would never commandeer parliament again. The monarchy had no intention of vesting more power in the lower house such that it could form governments and contest its will, as a true parliamentary democracy would stipulate. Therefore, before the 1989 elections, officials malapportioned electoral districts, such that sparsely populated rural tribal areas—still seen as conservative founts of monarchical support—received far more seats per voter than the Palestinian-heavy urban centers of Amman, Irbid, and Zarqa.[41] The authorities reasoned the latter could be hotbeds of opposition, much as they were in the past; they hence preserved this electoral imbalance throughout the 1990s and beyond. For instance, in 1989, rural Ma'an received one deputy for every 5,600 eligible voters, whereas Amman received one for every 25,000; by 2016, the Ma'an ratio had increased to 13,000 voters per seat, compared to Amman's high 53,300 citizens per seat. Malapportionment therefore gave Transjordanian rural voters more weight, helping to keep the tribal-state compact intact while marginalizing Palestinian-Jordanians. Moreover, the 1989 elections retained special quotas for Christians and Circassians that provided them with more seats than their demographic size warranted—an obvious concession to favored minorities with close royal ties, as Chapter 2 discussed.

However, malapportionment combined with the special quotas was not enough to prevent opposition groups from dominating the 1989 elections. A second scheme thus took effect for the 1993 elections, which adopted the obscure single nontransferable voting method (SNTV)—or more commonly "one-person, one-vote" balloting. SNTV limited every voter into casting just one vote in their multimember electoral districts, unlike the block voting system used in 1989. This favored conservative and usually pro-government independents, such as tribal sheikhs and local magnates, who could capture voters on account of clientelistic favors or familial appeals.[42] It conversely undermined opposition parties, who struggled to attract the precious single votes of citizens through policy agendas or ideological messages. The regime cared little for the Islamist boycott in the 1997 elections in protest of SNTV, as it got what it craved: a skewed electoral system plus balloting method that looked competitive from afar, but whose internal rules silently crippled oppositionists.

The third countermeasure was handicapping political parties. The 1992 Party Law legalized parties, but it also constrained their campaigning and membership. Their policy proposals and ideological statements could not criticize the monarchy or government policies; neither could they raise much financing beyond the paltry public funds allocated to them. More lenient party laws passed in 2007 and 2012, but these early curbs fatally sabotaged opposition parties in the 1990s, when they needed to quickly consolidate their status after decades of lying fallow. Consequently, excepting the IAF, which could draw upon the Brotherhood's loyal cadres, neither older leftist and Arab Nationalist parties nor newer liberal and centrist groups could attract enough followers to stand a chance during elections.[43] Jordanian parties did themselves no favors, for many lacked effective strategies despite receiving support from civil society and technical assistance from Western donors. However, these top-down restrictions did not help their cause, particularly for upstart parties hoping to create democratic momentum. They ensured that many citizens saw political parties as weak and untrustworthy associations. That sad legacy persisted for decades. One 2018 report revealed that Jordan's four-dozen licensed parties had only 34,957 registered members, or less than 1 percent of more than 4.1 million registered voters that year.[44]

All these moves ensured that oppositionists would never claim more than a minority of lower house seats from the 1990s onward. Authorities tinkered with the electoral law in other ways to polish their pseudo-democratic imagery. For instance, for the 2003 elections, a female quota came into effect, reserving a fixed number of seats for women. This was a shrewd government effort to claim credit for advancing feminist ideals while flaunting its progressive credentials to global audiences.[45] Beyond elections, however, officials went further by trimming the pluralism and freedoms promised by the 1991 National Charter.

Such limitations came to a head in the mid-1990s, when complaints over electoral manipulations, economic crisis, and political corruption grew feverish. The tipping point was the 1994 peace accord with Israel. While King Hussein insisted that normalizing ties with Israel would bring abundant geopolitical and financial payoffs, few Jordanians supported this shocking decision. Speedily, an opposition alliance of the Muslim Brotherhood, leftist and Arab Nationalist parties, professional syndicates, and student groups formed.[46] Across public meetings and street protests, they harangued Jordan's perceived capitulation to an Israeli state that still occupied Palestine and Jerusalem.

This quarrel touched raw nerves within the regime. As Jordanian historian Ali Muhafazah argued in a heavily censored book, by attacking the royal decision to normalize relations with Israel, opposition forces assertively questioned who steered Jordanian foreign policy: the monarchy or the people.[47] Raising memories of the JNM from the 1950s, this crossed a sacrosanct line, spurring authorities to harass, penalize, and detain more activists and groups in the name of national security. Such intolerance soon spread to other parts of society in obvious ways, from the heightening frequency of police and GID arrests to the growing number of civil society associations wilting under government pressures to disband.

New legal regulations also stifled the media sector. Under martial law, the Ministry of Information had monitored and gagged publishers, while the state-run Jordanian Press Foundation ensured that all licensed journalists hewed to state narratives. The 1993 Press and Publications Law ended such censorship, but authorities soon backtracked by narrowing the margins of press liberty. The 1997 amendments to this law, for instance, criminalized any publication alleged to cause strife, offend public decency, and other bleakly vague categories. Increasingly onerous bureaucratic regulations convinced newspapers and publishers to restrain critical opinions lest they suffer de-licensing. The government also continued quietly banning hundreds of books every year, from political tracts to literary novels, deemed too risqué for public consumption; this practice continues today.[48] By the end of the 1990s, dozens of new groundbreaking papers like *Al-Majed* had closed under these pressures, and hundreds of reporters and writers had been browbeaten into euthanizing their public views.

After King Abdullah was enthroned in 1999, Jordanian observers realized that the democratic moment had ended. All the heady reformist talk of years prior was merely a defensive strategy to help the monarchy to weather economic troubles, for now the kingdom was "de-liberalizing."[49] Still, like the TNCs and the JNM, the post-1989 renaissance of opposition left a lasting imprint. It showed that democracy was not alien to Jordan, and that citizens were always ready to speak, assemble, and publish in boisterous defense of their interests. It also forced authoritarianism to adapt. The Hashemite monarchy had praised democracy in the early 1990s and elevated the kingdom's international reputation by inking the 1994 peace treaty with Israel. Jordan's rule-makers were stuck with a citizenry that would no longer accept martial law and expected tangible further democratic change consonant with their leaders' assurances. The decades since have hence been marked by a perpetual effort to keep the democratic genie in the bottle.

Liberalized Autocracy under King Abdullah

The historical episodes of the late 1920s, mid-1950s, and 1990s prove that political contestation runs deeply throughout Jordanian history. The TNCs pushed against unyielding colonialism in the name of self-government; the JNM aimed to curtail royal power through unifying nationalist appeals. A reawakened civil society after 1989 fought to expand political rights at a time of economic disarray.

Given this heritage of struggle, many Jordanians hoped that, upon his enthronement, King Abdullah would restore the democratizing verve of the early 1990s. The young, Western-educated son of King Hussein reaped positive coverage in the global media given his avowed promise to modernize the country. However, while the new monarch implemented neoliberal economic reforms that called for market-based capitalism, he dashed popular hopes in edging away from the waning democratic agenda of his father. Under his leadership, officials continued curtailing opposition in new ways, perfecting a formula of liberalized autocracy—that is, a regime that allows for limited pluralism and freedoms but never surrenders the reins of executive sovereignty.[50] After the Al-Aqsa Intifada in Palestine erupted in September 2000, authorities harshly dispersed many protests waged in solidarity with the uprising, fearing that popular criticism of Israel could turn into anti-government dissent—much as the anti-normalization movement years earlier had. Following the 9/11 terrorist attacks in the United States and subsequent worries about domestic unrest as Washington invaded neighboring Iraq years later, the king suspended parliament from June 2001 to June 2003. During this period, the government passed many new laws by decree. Well-known critics, like former MP Toujan al-Faisal, the first woman elected to the lower house, were arrested after complaining too sonorously about corruption and other regime failings. Within years, Jordanian academics saw the writing on the wall. Though the king still spoke brightly about political reforms, bold talk of democratization was off the agenda. The new catchphrase in royal circles by the mid-2000s was *tanmiyyah siyaasiyyah* (political development)—a fuzzy phrase that meant little, save for preserving national stability.[51]

The 2011–2012 Arab Spring stirred another eruption of popular mobilization. Yet this was no close call with democracy, because by now the Jordanian regime had developed ample tools to manage its clamorous public—unlike dictatorships in Egypt, Tunisia, Libya, Syria, Yemen, and Bahrain, whose bloody crackdowns turned public demonstrations into revolutionary insurrections. The royal autocracy outlasted thousands of peaceful protests by employing its proven repertoire of selective repression, coalitional outreach, and external support.[52] Authorities tolerated most demonstrations, but they still targeted thousands of the loudest activists for arrest. The GID infiltrated and sabotaged opposition movements, King Abdullah raised public salaries to reward Transjordanians on government payrolls, and Jordan reaped a flood of Western and Gulf foreign aid to keep the monarchy afloat. Officials also chilled the mood of dissent by warning that prolonged unrest could only produce anarchy and violence, as in neighboring Syria, which plunged into civil war. By 2013, most of Jordan's large Arab Spring–inspired protest campaigns had faded away.

However, political activism and opposition persisted. Chapter 6 delves into Jordan's contentious rumbles during and after the Arab Spring. More relevant here is the broader picture of how King Abdullah's regime has gone about its business since 1999, such that even thousands of protests during 2011–2012 did not truly endanger it. Its formula of liberalized autocracy, which mixes some accoutrements of pluralism and limited freedom with the obstinate structure of authoritarian power, has continued to *prevent* democracy. It has done so through three institutional mechanisms: subverting competitive elections, inhibiting public activism, and choreographing superficial reforms.

The Gilded Cage of Elections

One way that democrats in Jordan could erode authoritarianism is by winning parliamentary elections. Despite its faint legislative powers, a lower house—the sole nationally elected body—controlled by opposition parties could still spearhead change by holding fearless debates, berating the government, and encouraging popular protests to bring immense pressure on the monarchy. Under King Abdullah, general elections appear healthy enough. These are no plebiscites, where handpicked minions win 99.9 percent of the vote. Many politicians run lively campaigns, and legal parties stump for votes. The conduct of elections has also become increasingly transparent, excepting the infamous 2007 contest that was reputedly rigged by the intelligence directorate. The Independent Election Commission, founded in 2013 as part of the monarchy's political reforms during the Arab Spring, has admirably prevented systemic abuses, such as large-scale voter fraud. US and European electoral monitors have vigilantly observed elections since 2010 and have noted with satisfaction that most elections are free of glaring irregularities like ballot stuffing.

Yet, herein lays a vital lesson. Even when the process of elections seems fair and reasonable on the surface, engineered rules can stealthily handicap opposition forces so grossly that the results matter little. This keeps political change out of reach by preventing opposition groups from winning outright control over the lower house. Consider chronic malapportionment, which ensures that Transjordanians are overrepresented in parliament. Jordan's electoral system has evolved since the 1990s, despite frequent tinkering with the elections law that often confuses voters.[53] Officials have done away with the worst flaws, such as ending the STNV balloting method in 2016, and since then have also allowed for some list-based proportional representation (PR) open to parties. The latter satisfies a longstanding demand of democratic advocates. But at the district level where most parliamentary seats originate, rural tribal areas still receive far more seats per voter than Palestinian-heavy urban districts in Amman, Irbid, and Zarqa. Today in Amman's large Second District, for instance, roughly a half-million voters receive six seats, whereas in rural Tafileh or Ma'an, less than 60,000 voters receive three seats. In effect, it takes many more Palestinian-Jordanians to elect far fewer parliamentarians, making them feel even more like second-class citizens.[54]

Malapportionment goes hand in hand with other deficiencies that favor monarchy's East Bank base at the cost of fairness. Several Baadia districts in the east and south of the kingdom, populated almost wholly by tribal communities, receive a general allotment of lower house seats—in essence, an implicit tribal quota. Another example lays in the practice of holding informal primaries. Months before elections, some tribal communities coordinate among themselves to preselect the representatives who will eventually run in their district, and so likely win. While upstarts can still compete against these consensual candidates when elections arrive, the more relevant point is that these primaries are technically illegal. However, officials have tolerated them for decades. They give Transjordanian stakeholders room to organize their affairs and reinforce local networks of tribal patronage that limit the reach of opposition parties.[55]

Even ignoring these distorting factors, other substantive flaws persist within elections. Table 5.1 lists every lower house election held during 1989–2024. It illustrates how built-in systemic defects have gutted the meaningful contestation necessary for opposition to grow stronger. A few disconcerting trends stand out.

First, exemplifying the Jordanian regime's proven coalitional tactics as Chapter 4 discussed, special parliamentary quotas have consistently privileged minorities tied to monarchical largesse. Today, Christians and Circassians enjoy a reserved allocation of nine and three seats, respectively, which likely overweighs their demographic size. The women's quota has risen from six in 2003 to eighteen in 2024—a move that advances gender equality against patriarchal norms in many ways, but which also exposes the royal autocracy's calculated embrace of feminism to earn public and international acclaim. That liberal position hardly extends to the rest of politics, since the palace still appoints relatively few women to the government (and never in the most senior positions of influence, such as prime minister, interior minister, foreign minister, or finance minister).

Second, despite being legal, opposition has suffered from anemic representation since the early 1990s. The combined weight of malapportioned districting, SNTV balloting until 2016, and political restrictions has eviscerated the capacity of opposition parties to attract more members and develop organizational backbones. As a result, for decades most lower house sessions have been filled with what the palace and its security minders prefer: tribal notables and independents who spend more time bickering or jockeying for favors than debating political issues and demanding legislative authority.

The IAF, the political wing of the Muslim Brotherhood, represents a case in point. This broad Islamist faction serves as a decent proxy for all parliamentary opposition; not only has the IAF frequently allied with other opposition groups in elections, but it has served as the largest and best-organized party. However,

Table 5.1 **Lower House (Parliamentary) Elections in Jordan, 1989–2024.**

	Turnout[*]	*Total Candidates*	*Total Seats*	*Percent Seats Won by Muslim Brotherhood*	*Quota (Reserved) Seats*	*Major Flaws*	*Positive Takeaways*
1989	53.1	647	80	41.3[**]	12 (9 Christians, 3 Circassians/Chechens)	Malapportioned districts, parties not yet legal	Opposition candidates (Islamists and others) win majority
1993	54.8	534	80	21.3	12 (9 Christians, 3 Circassians/Chechens)	Malapportionment; SNTV system begins	
1997	47.5	524	80	0 (boycott)	12 (9 Christians, 3 Circassians/Chechens)	Malapportionment and SNTV; political freedoms restricted; weak parties	
2003	57.8	765	110	15.4	15 (9 Christians, 3 Circassians/Chechens, 6 women)	Malapportionment, SNTV, and political restrictions; weak parties excepting Islamic Action Front	Two-year parliamentary suspension ends

Continued

Table 5.1 **Continued**

	*Turnout**	*Total Candidates*	*Total Seats*	*Percent Seats Won by Muslim Brotherhood*	*Quota (Reserved) Seats*	*Major Flaws*	*Positive Takeaways*
2007	54	880	110	5.4	18 (9 Christians, 3 Circassians/Chechens, 6 women)	Malapportionment, SNTV, and political restrictions; weak parties; widespread vote rigging	
2010	53	763	120	0 (boycott)	24 (9 Christians, 3 Circassians/Chechens, 12 women)	Malapportionment, SNTV, and political restrictions; weak parties; "subdistricting" scheme confuses voters	International election monitors begin observing
2013	56.5	1425	150	0 (boycott)	27 (9 Christians, 3 Circassians/Chechens, 15 women)	Malapportionment, SNTV, and political restrictions; weak parties	Closed-list PR system for 27 party-based seats
2016	36.1	1252	130	10	27 (9 Christians, 3 Circassians/Chechens, 15 women)	Malapportionment and political restrictions; weak parties not benefiting from revamped open-list PR system	SNTV replaced by hybrid system of bloc voting and open-list PR

2020	29.9	1674	130	6.1		27 (9 Christians, 3 Circassians/Chechens, 15 women)	Malapportionment and political restrictions; weak parties; in-person voting required despite Covid-19	Open-list PR system continued
2024	32.3	1634	138	22.4		30 (9 Christians, 3 Circassians/Chechens, 18 women)	Malapportionment and political restrictions; mostly weak parties; large new parties aligned with the regime	New mixed PR system, with 41 seats allocated to party-based national list

Note: * Turnout means percentage of eligible, registered voters who cast ballots.
** In the 1989 elections, all candidates ran as independents given that parties were not yet legal. Prevailing estimates suggest twenty core Muslim Brotherhood members, thirteen pro-Brotherhood Islamists, and at least a dozen non-Islamist oppositionists as among the winners

Sources: International IDEA, *Voter Turnout Database*, https://www.idea.int/data-tools/data/voter-turnout-database, and author's data.

as Table 5.1 charts, its share of seats won has remained low, even during elections that it does not boycott. Critics argue this reflects the waning popularity of Islamist ideals in Jordanian society. However, this ignores the stunning reversal seen in the September 2024 elections, in which the IAF stormed back to win nearly a quarter of all seats (over 22 percent). Islamist candidates astutely capitalized on anti-Israel anger over the latest Gaza conflict, which drove much of their spirited platform, and also ran well-organized outreach campaigns that resonated with many voters.[56]

However, such success may not last given the regime's efforts to suppress the wider Muslim Brotherhood movement, as Chapter 6 outlines. Even if the IAF escapes the same prohibition that befell the Brotherhood in 2025, the IAF faces a wrenching no-win dilemma that symbolizes the bigger problems of all opposition groups before elections: boycott or participate?[57] Boycotts in 1997, 2010, and 2013 conveyed a forceful message of dissent, namely that elections under autocratic rule in Jordan were so stacked and unfair they were not worth entertaining. However, this also froze them out of parliament. Participation guarantees that at least some oppositionists among them will enter the lower house, but this also legitimizes the regime's charade that this elected legislature proves that Jordan is democratizing because all parties willingly compete for its seats.

Third, the number of total parliamentary candidates has risen over time, from 647 in 1989 to 1,634 in 2024. While this partly stems from the lower house's increasing size, it also shows that powerful personalities have long trumped party politics. In competitive multiparty electoral systems, party organizations serve as gatekeepers that control resources and influence: to win office, an aspiring politician must first win over their party. Most democracies hence have relatively few legislators willing to compete for seats as independents. The opposite holds true in the Hashemite Kingdom. Because one can succeed in Jordanian politics without joining a party, would-be MPs enjoy lower entry barriers to run for office. In tribal communities, candidates do not need party slogans to attract local voters; in many urban areas, money and connections count for more than policy promises.

This highlights a deeper problem. Excepting the IAF, decades of autocratic machinations have made opposition parties small and frail. King Abdullah has repeatedly extolled the importance of developing stronger parties to fill the political spectrum, but with a catch: the parties that the palace and its coercive guardians prefer would be bland pro-government entities, with no ideological identities or critical ideas.[58] The regime abhors partisanship almost as much as it fears authentic mass-based parties—such as those that drove the JNM in the 1950s—becoming powerful enough to eclipse its sway. The problem is that within an unconstrained environment, this is what many party entrepreneurs *desire*: to mobilize the masses, advance ideological programs, and necessarily clash with other parties that take opposing positions. Partisanship is part-and-parcel of modern democratic politics.

Thus, conditions remain dire for opposition parties in Jordan. While amendments to the laws governing political parties in 2015 and 2022 made their organizational tasks easier, such as allowing for more independent financing, an implicit political restriction remains: parties cannot too openly criticize the monarchy, coercive apparatus, or even the government. Since the 1990s, therefore, of the several dozen Jordanian parties licensed at any given time, most have lacked a popular base and ideological identity. Some are vanity projects for their founders; others dissolve after each election, having failed to secure any seats. As local research director Ahmad Awad explained, Jordanian parties have become "organizational dinosaurs," irrelevant to national politics for an obvious reason: excepting the IAF, party membership seldom advances one's career.[59] This is another reason why most lower house candidates have long preferred to run as independents, forming loose blocs with other like-minded independents when necessary. This has only marginally changed in recent years. Elections since 2016 have incorporated a PR component that reserves some seats for parties, which can also run candidates in local districts. In 2024, for instance, dozens of new parties competed for seats in this way. However, most were pro-government entities that scored only middling results. The largest one—the National Charter Party—secured twenty-one seats across the PR list and local districts, well below the IAF's thirty-one seats.

Finally, voter turnout is low. Despite royal exhortations to participate in elections, most Jordanians do not vote. As Table 5.1 tracks, turnout has plummeted from its peak of nearly 57.8 percent in 2003 to 32.3 percent in 2024. There are wrinkles here. Turnout often broaches 70 percent in rural districts, where locals respond well to promises of copious benefits from tribal candidates or else to kinship and tribal appeals from sheikhs requesting their votes.[60] In the urban districts of Amman, Irbid, and Zarqa, however, abstention is rife, with turnout hovering at 20–30 percent.[61] Skeptical citizens believe that, given the weakness of parties, constraints on opposition, ongoing curbs on their freedoms, and the parliament's ineffectual nature, voting is a waste of time. Such apathy runs deepest among youth, as Chapter 2 described. In Amman's biggest districts, turnout among those under thirty barely reaches double digits—an implicit boycott of sorts.

In all these ways, this gilded cage of parliamentary elections has produced a self-reinforcing cycle of authoritarianism. As the regime orchestrates schemes to favor its tribal coalition and subvert competition, weakened opposition parties have little chance of gaining many seats. Dejected citizens and especially young people do not vote, leaving the lower house filled with compliant deputies who, in turn, repel more voters and dissuade new parties from organizing. All the while, the fact that elections take place remains a cornerstone of Jordan's democratic mirage.

Regulating Ideas, Penalizing Speech

In August 2023, King Abdullah proclaimed, "Jordan was never an oppressive country and will never be one."[62] That is true—for Westerners. Here, international NGOs like Human Rights Watch and the Open Society Foundations operate openly; no injunctions prevent visiting journalists from interviewing locals. Humanitarian workers, diplomats, and Western students throng about Amman's leafy cafes and ritzy restaurants. This is, by such accounts, a remarkably unconstrained place by Middle East standards.

The story is different for Jordanians. Since the 1990s, their regime has not only immobilized political competition but also carefully policed public life to demoralize and atomize opposition. The media sector no longer has the independence it regained after 1989. To be sure, writers can still cover mundane issues. Officials allow for routine reporting of Jordan's frequent protests, economic problems, or bureaucratic malaise. Modest criticism of government policies even enters quiescent state-affiliated outlets, such as the Arabic daily newspaper *Al-Rai* and the public television channel Al-Mamlaka.

However, old red lines loom large. As before, nobody can spread exposés on the royal family or question the palace's handling of national security. The authorities still gags coverage of delicate issues, such as the April 2021 coup-mongering episode involving Prince Hamzah. Over last two decades, however, the regime has created even more legal tools to deter and punish critical speech through the doctrine of soft security. The repeatedly revised Press and Publications Law and other penal statutes allow officials to prosecute journalists and shutter media outlets for ambiguous offenses, such as publishing "fake" news, insulting religion, or defaming public figures. Anti-terror laws provide another cudgel. The 2006 and 2014 Anti-Terror Laws widened the definition of terrorism to include an impossibly arbitrary spectrum of recondite speech, such as any published or spoken words that stir public discord or even injure Jordan's foreign relations. Terror-related charges shuffle the accused into the dreaded State Security Courts, which usually convict them. Jordanian writers, in essence, do not feel free. In 2022, the Center for Defending Freedom of Journalists found that over 90 percent of local journalists practice self-censorship, and that most also recall being questioned by authorities over their work.[63]

The online world has fared only slightly better. Broadband access to the Internet has been widespread since the late 2000s. Officials boast of Jordan's digital connectivity to foreign investors and Western aid donors as proof that the kingdom is a moderate, open place. However, they have also criminalized many online spaces. Draconian cyber-regulations since the 2011–2012 Arab Spring have allowed state bodies like the Media Commission to ban hundreds of critical blogs, news portals, and other independent websites in the name of protecting public morality.[64] Some online entrepreneurs left Jordan, as in the case of 'Alaa Fazaa, whose blistering *KhabarJo* news website drove him into exile. Other online media platforms, such as the vivacious, youth-driven platform *7iber*, were forced to sanitize their political content to obtain an official media license and escape being blocked. The authorities also periodically block access to foreign media platforms in retaliation for publishing embarrassing stories about Jordan, as happened to London-based *Middle East Eye* and nearly a dozen other mostly Arabic-language news and analysis websites in May 2025.[65]

The 2023 Cybercrimes Law took such paternalistic supervision to the extreme, as it allowed all social media content to be treated as political speech: now, even reposting X (formerly Twitter) posts or sharing YouTube videos that incense the regime can be prosecuted as equivalent to shouting anti-government slogans on the street. Unsurprisingly, such digital restrictions have entrapped many oppositionists.[66] In 2015, for instance, senior Muslim Brotherhood figure Zaki Bani Irsheid was imprisoned for publishing a Facebook post that disparaged the United Arab Emirates, with which Jordan shares close ties. Hundreds of activists, protesters, and journalists since then have similarly been arrested and punished, with their online activities used as the basis of their criminal convictions. What makes online speech modestly freer than offline media, at least for now, is its sheer volume. The Interior Ministry and GID vigilantly monitor local IP addresses with dedicated cyber-teams, but there is simply too much online activity to monitor all at once.

In the twenty-first century, Jordanian authorities have defended all these restrictions as necessary to preserve national security and political stability. In reality, these statutes provide more judicial cover to castigate those who upset the regime's sensibilities. This produces wrenching uncertainty among content producers—authors, filmmakers, journalists, and the like—who never know whether their work will irk the government. The safest route is self-censorship. Thus, television producers refuse to touch anything political in their shows, local journalists refuse to grill officials in their reporting, and professors halt uncomfortably honest debates in seminars. Isam Uraiqat, proprietor of the now-banned *AlHudood* satirical website, has lamented how this "desire not to offend" has come to permeate public life, dragging the spirit of creativity in Jordan into a "pit of mediocrity."[67]

Two other realms of opposition, civic organizations and grassroots protests, suffer similarly frustrating limitations, as Chapter 6 more fully discusses. Certainly, activists can *try* to establish new groups and organize a mass demonstration. Most will not be brutalized for doing so, but neither will they find success given the obstacles confronting them. For instance, the 2008 Law on Societies and Social Bodies reaffirms the right of Jordanians to found independent civil society organizations. However, it also places them under continual scrutiny from the Interior Ministry, Ministry of Social Development, and other state bodies, because such entities must be licensed by the government. Minor infractions like financial irregularities or overtly political activities can result in steep fines and organizational suspensions, with authorities having the final say in determining whether an NGO or civic association will survive.

The same holds for protests. Intimidation, containment, and targeted repression ensure that citizens marching in public fall under the stern gaze of the police, gendarmerie, and GID. When all else fails, the royal autocracy can ban public gatherings during sensitive times, as happened most recently during the Covid-19 pandemic. When this happens, critics suffer the heaviest blows. During the 2020 public health lockdowns, for instance, authorities took advantage of calm streets to arrest renowned cartoonist Emad Hajjaj, after he penned a cartoon admonishing the new UAE-Israel peace treaty; suspended the 100,000-strong teachers' union, given its refusal to stop organizing events; jailed Ahmad Oweidi al-Abbadi, a stubborn tribal critic of the monarchy; and arrested the heads of Roya, an independent television outlet, after it aired a story about jobless citizens suffering during the pandemic.

Endless Reformism

Besides engineering elections and throttling public speech, the Hashemite regime has perfected a third strategy of liberalized autocracy: rhetorical double-speak. In this ruse of reformism, officials regularly deliver grandiloquent reforms that promise democratization, but that they never deliver.[68] The margins of political freedom wax and wane, but the institutional structure of autocracy does not change. Such an approach makes democracy not a vigorous buzzword of opposition but instead the dreary refrain of national officialdom—thereby diluting its power and meaning. Three examples span King Abdullah's reign. All share the same sequence of oscillating events: a royally convoked committee filled with eminent figures issues democratic reforms to public fanfare, within years such pledges are forgotten, and finally restrictions on civic and political rights tighten, resetting politics back to the start.

First, in November 2005, former Foreign Minister and deputy Prime Minister Marwan Mu'asher unveiled a sweeping reform package called the National Agenda. Among the dramatic changes proposed were better social services, economic upgrading, overhauling elections, and, most controversially, reversing Palestinians' marginalization in politics in order to create a more inclusive democratic system. However, despite having been summoned by royal decree, Mu'asher and his committee saw their optimistic project shelved by the monarchy and its security chiefs. Officials insisted that the dangers of Islamists winning elections, the ongoing Iraq War, and threats of terrorism proved too formidable to experiment with any political change. Within months, as Mu'asher himself recounts, "the reform engine had lost all of its steam" given this mountain of "old guard" reluctance.[69] Instead, King Abdullah invited 700 mainly young Jordanians to the Dead Sea in July 2006 under the "We Are All Jordan" initiative to discuss economic and political problems. However, the conference did little except produce a spectacle of public loyalty to the monarchy, and perhaps help participants forget about the National Agenda issued less than a year earlier.

Another cycle of reform started during the Arab Spring. Amid national protests in March 2011, King Abdullah mustered a fifty-two-person National Dialogue Committee to brainstorm a new raft of reforms. In June, as street demonstrations continued, the king astonishingly vowed in a televised speech to implement European-style constitutional monarchy. He even began issuing his own personal discussion papers about democratization.[70] However, like before, these moves produced little results. Among them was creating the Independent Electoral Commission and making a few electoral concessions, such as dropping the much-maligned SNTV balloting starting with the 2016 general elections. However, in other ways, authoritarianism *deepened*. During 2015–2016, the monarchy ratified constitutional amendments that expanded the king's uncontested powers, such as enshrining his implicit prerogative to appoint key officials like the GID chief without oversight from either the government or parliament.

For Jordanian critics, such amendments composed definitive proof that King Abdullah's June 2011 democratic speech—now almost forgotten—had been smoke and mirrors.[71] Such retreat from reforms occurred even as public demonstrations continued. For instance, in December 2018, amid a new wave of protests against economic hardship, King Abdullah announced a general amnesty in a bid to win public favor. Thousands of prisoners jailed for petty crimes, and their families, were understandably elated. However, the pardon excluded political critics ensnared under the Anti-Terror Law. It also came with a royal warning: the palace had grown tired of public agitation, and no more clemency would be forthcoming.

The third cycle of reforms started in June 2021, when the king charged another royal committee with modernizing the political system. Featuring an ensemble of ninety-two political elites and civic representatives, the group circulated dozens of public proposals on decentralization, women's rights, youth engagement, and economic development. It also unveiled a new roadmap for democracy: within a decade, Jordan would become a constitutional monarchy through an incremental reform process, in concert with broadening freedoms for citizens.[72] In particular, lower house elections would allow a progressively larger share of seats through PR-based lists for political parties; eventually, a revitalized parliament filled with thriving parties would assume full legislative authority and even relieve the burden of forming governments from the king.

However, such ambitious plans dithered. Soon after endorsing this democratic roadmap, the regime incongruously imposed more authoritarian dictates. In early 2022, King Abdullah ratified new constitutional amendments that enlarged his executive prerogatives even further, such as creating a National Security Council that further centralized royal control over foreign policy. The 2023 Cybercrimes Law made these reformist pledges look even more futile. In this context, the September 2024 lower house elections did little to win back skeptics; the worsening Gaza War, which incited popular outrage, did not help. Those elections featured many new political parties that formed with the palace's blessing, and in the end, candidates from ten parties secured a record of over 100 (out of 138) seats—surely a positive development.[73] However, excepting the IAF's surprising victory, the details betray a result that was anything but democratic. Most new parties were docile pro-government entities. And as before, there was no parliamentary consultation when the king appointed his new cabinet. Just two party heads, from the National Charter and Taqaddum parties, were selected as ministers; despite having won the most seats, the IAF was excluded from the government. Much as before, royal powerholders had created an impression of democratization without conceding its most inviolable requirements of accepting the results of elections, no matter how distasteful, and giving citizens real input in choosing who ruled them.

Conclusion

For over a century, Jordanians demanding political rights have been stymied by a recalcitrant autocracy, despite some close calls with democracy. It is this repeated conflict, and not just the resilience of Hashemite rule, that defines the kingdom's political history. The regime's excuses for ignoring such pressures from society are always the same. Too much change will destabilize this brittle land, and Jordanians themselves are unready for what democracy entails, including the responsibility to select who governs them. Such apologetics are to be expected: no autocracy concedes its vast power and authority without a fight.

Yet Jordanians have never been convinced of such hollow talk. It took a combination of repression and tribal outreach, backed by British muscle, to suppress the TNCs that dreamt of self-governance and popular participation by the early 1930s. Only a vicious military crackdown and political co-optation ended the JNM's democratic ascent after the mid-1950s. Halting the post-1989 renewal of civil society and political opposition required more adaptive strategies of control, including carefully engineered elections and a new framework of liberalized autocracy. Now, a peculiar holding pattern of pseudo-democracy has taken hold. Officials intermittently unveil promises of democratic reforms while capriciously constricting the boundaries of pluralism and freedom. Lest another large national campaign for democratic reforms mobilizes, the monarchy can lean on its coercive apparatus and core Transjordanian coalition to keep order.

Can this equilibrium last? The Hashemite state's defenders would insist that it *must*—or else uncertainty and chaos will consume the East Bank. Jordanians have other ideas. They are not revolutionary, as few seek to overthrow their monarchy. Yet neither are they content. As Chapter 6 shows, for all the authoritarian machinations of their stubborn regime, ordinary people under King Abdullah have pioneered new forms of dissidence to prod and push their rule-makers. They join organizations, disobey laws, and rowdily protest. Their passionate mobilization has come to define the public arena, entrenching innumerable capillaries of resistance that embody a citizenry unwilling to surrender its voice. Resurrecting fragments of the past but oriented toward a hopeful future, Jordanian activism has become an intriguing example of what happens when a seemingly irresistible force collides with an immoveable object.

6

Opposition and Protest in the Twenty-First Century

Who Fights for Political Change in Modern Jordan?

In *Bending over the Corpse of Amman*, an Arabic novel published in 2014, Jordanian writer Ahmed al-Za'atari imagines an alternative reality in which the Hashemite Kingdom is reduced to rubble. In this post-apocalyptic tale, a powder keg of popular frustrations unmet by a totalitarian dictatorship detonates into civil war. Lawlessness and death reign as warring classes fight over the ruins of once-proud Amman, divided between rich militarized fiefdoms and devastated wastelands run by warlords. The protagonist, a middle-class Jordanian named Ahmad, bounces between overflowing infirmaries and restaurants without food amid surreal flashbacks of how mass protests and unchecked corruption destroyed the country. In this tale of dehumanizing survival, life itself becomes meaningless: "None of us was born in Amman," bids one militia leader to Ahmad, "but surely we will all die in it."[1]

It is little wonder that the Jordanian government's Press and Publications Department banned the book. Not only does talk of revolutionary meltdown qualify as sedition and cancel the Hashemite Kingdom's global image as a citadel of calm, but the novel brims with thinly veiled references to this reality—down to patriotic hymns that few sing and a ruler named Abdullah. For many Jordanian readers, the story struck a nerve, allegorically capturing how so many feel suffocated by their authoritarian order. They are incensed by pseudo-democratic reforms, rampant state corruption, and economic hardships. Some already feel like they subsist in a dystopia where, for all their complaints and anger, they are merely told to wait for a better tomorrow. As one young tribal protester declared in 2016 from Dhiban, a downtrodden rural town rocked by unemployment and poverty, "We are tired of living like the dead."[2]

These raw emotions tug at contemporary Jordanian politics, putting ordinary people in frequent confrontation against their regime and state. While Chapter 5 showcased organized campaigns for democracy over the past century, this chapter explores the tempo of everyday dissent under King Abdullah. What counts as contentious opposition—protests, marches, occupations, petitions, strikes, boycotts, vigils, and other campaigns—transpires in public spaces, beyond the confines of parliament and periodic elections. Those who speak out have different ideas about what can fix the country's economic and political ills, but they agree that something about the present is profoundly rotten. This should not imply that Jordan tiptoes on the precipice of chaos, a familiar trope that Westerners impose upon the kingdom. As Chapter 4 explained, the monarchy handily maintains its power through its coercive cudgels and tribal stalwarts. Western support likewise bolsters its financial and military resources. Nonetheless, the wider point is that while Jordan's streets are not burning, they are *churning*. The contentiousness that has marked social life since King Abdullah was enthroned in 1999 is neither revolutionary nor violent. But it is diffuse, showing a society in constant motion as citizens articulate their resentments and test the boundaries of permissible disobedience.

These ideas guide this chapter. It brings society back into the analytical picture by surveying Jordan's contemporary topography of activism and protest in five sections. First, it illuminates useful theories of popular mobilization and contentious politics. That individuals fight for change embodies a fundamental aspect of social life under all governments, as perceived injustices catalyze people to pioneer new movements, articulate criticism, and disrupt political routines. Such activism has punctuated how many Jordanians relate to politics under King Abdullah. Second, the chapter tracks the major grievances that have fueled public protests and opposition in Jordan since the 2000s. These include foreign policy, economic hardship, authoritarian abuses, and widespread corruption. The Arab Barometer surveys show that popular perceptions of such problems have grown worse over time, signifying a major gap of expectations between what many Jordanians want from their leadership versus what their leadership has delivered.

The chapter then shifts into identifying *who* mobilizes in contemporary Jordan. Two major types of activism exist. The third section explores formal opposition forces, meaning legally licensed groups that have led the way in pressuring and criticizing the Hashemite regime since the liberalization of the 1990s. These include civil society organizations such as professional associations, as well as the Muslim Brotherhood, which until its 2025 prohibition served as one of the largest social movements. The fourth section weighs the other side of contentious politics—informal activism, led by newer grassroots networks and agile groups of youthful protesters who do not belong to any political party or civil society organization. Embodied by the rise of *hirak* (movement) groups during the Arab Spring, this newer style of opposition continues to defy autocratic authority.

The final section tracks the widening trail of contentious politics since the 2010s onto the present. Outside of parliament, both traditional, formal opposition and newer, informal activists have driven protest campaigns and sustained campaigns of dissent. Such mobilization crosscuts the Transjordanian-Palestinian divide, revealing that, just as autocratic power endures, so too do efforts at change and reform within society.

The Meaning of Mobilization

As social scientists aver, popular mobilization means the process by which individuals join forces to make public claims for change. This produces social movements—sustained campaigns of activism built on a shared purpose and solidarity. Movements can be large or small, religious or secular, formal or informal, continuous or sporadic. To have maximal impact, they partake in contentious politics, defined as "episodic, public, collective" acts that disrupt public routines.[3] Under dictatorships, contentious events like protests, strikes, marches, boycotts, rallies, and occupations transgress political authority. They fill public spaces with the din of defiance, which mindful rulers must appease or suppress.

Crucially, not all disturbances of public order are evidence of political mobilization. Sometimes, they communicate social problems or cultural concerns that do not explicitly target the state. For instance, during the 2011–2012 Arab Spring, Jordanian universities recorded nearly 300 brawls between students. Such fighting had little to do with the broader protests unfolding elsewhere in the country, as most stemmed from personal grudges or long-simmering tribal feuds.[4] Likewise, some organized movements do not challenge the regime so much as raise awareness over important social issues, like when local Jordanian women's groups hold rallies against honor crimes and gender inequality. In fact, the authorities encourage such "apolitical" protestations, as they buff their Western-facing repute: if Jordanian women can freely rally for more rights, then surely the kingdom is a progressive and liberal place.[5]

Moreover, one does not have to mobilize publicly or in large numbers to make a political impact. As anthropologists know, oppressed peoples often practice "everyday resistance," meaning localized and often invisible acts of disobedience.[6] Such actions microscopically chip away at authoritarian power without inviting public confrontations. For instance, some Jordanian farmers have long drilled illegal wells to circumvent aloof officials who reserve precious water resources for industries—a cunning act of insubordination, but not obvious rebellion. Humor, too, conveys a subversive soul. For example, while sardonic jokes have always been part of Jordan's mass culture, online satire has bloomed over the past two decades. A leading purveyor is *AlHudood*, a popular website that explained the November 2020 lower house elections (which required in-person voting despite the coronavirus pandemic) this way: it was part of a new health strategy.[7] By exposing everyone to Covid-19 through the patriotic act of voting, Jordan would be the first global country to obtain herd immunity. *AlHudood*, unsurprisingly, was blocked by authorities several years later.

Beyond these subtle forms of sabotage, popular mobilization worries autocrats the most because it brings contentious commotions into full view. Few rulers want to see their streets and airwaves brimming with clamorous discontent in full view of the world. Whether protesters and activists campaigning from below triumph is a thornier question. In a historical perspective, the most successful movements tend to be not only nonviolent in method but also sturdy in organization.[8] Even when pounded by repressive measures or goaded by political enticements, they remain driven in their mission: forcing their governments to concede meaningful reforms and new policies or even inducing some powerholders to resign. Such commitment guides much popular mobilization in Jordan.

Evolving Mobilization

Jordan's varied residents have always banded together to advance their interests. The crusades for democracy from Chapter 5 are but the biggest signposts in the century-long history of Jordanians leading bold movements and fresh ideas.[9] By the late 1920s, for example, Transjordanians had populated their colonial state with new civic associations like the Orthodox Club, business groups like the Amman Chamber of Commerce, and educational societies. Repressive backlash following the Transjordanian National Congress movements dampened such activities until the late 1940s. Then, the annexation of the West Bank and absorption of Palestinians inspired new forms of organizing. Activists across both banks stimulated not only the leftist and Arab Nationalist parties that led the Jordanian National Movement, but also civil society entities such as trade unions, women's leagues, and student associations. Martial law imposed in the late 1950s stifled these organizations. After martial law ended in 1989, however, popular mobilization was efflorescent, as citizens used new organizational platforms to demand economic justice, political freedom, and Palestinian rights. Reinvigorated civic forces reclaimed public spaces through protests and campaigning, while previously pro-government movements like the Muslim Brotherhood joined the ranks of the opposition.

Since then, Jordan has entered a new phase of popular mobilization, mirroring the rest of the Middle East. Its greatest display was the Arab Spring. During 2011–2012, mass uprisings toppled tyrants in Tunisia, Egypt, Libya, and Yemen, came close in Bahrain, and precipitated a civil war in Syria that ended only in 2024 with the downfall of its dictatorship. The memorable chant of those revolutions—*al-sha'b yurid isqaat al-nizam* (The people want the downfall of the regime)—shook the Arab world.[10] Alas, civil conflicts and vengeful autocrats choked off democratic transitions in all but Tunisia. In Jordan, the Hashemite monarchy endured thanks to its repressive capabilities and coalitional strategies, but not before citizens had their say. From January 2011 through early 2013, the kingdom's homegrown protest wave, or the "Jordanian Spring," sprouted thousands of weekly protests for economic relief, democratic change, and anticorruption measures. Such contentiousness ranged from large urban occupations to small rural demonstrations and drew upon Palestinian-Jordanians and Transjordanians alike. It was mostly peaceful, save for a March 2011 youth rally in Amman that was violently dispersed, resulting in one participant's death, and the November 2012 rioting that followed a hike in fuel prices.

As Chapter 5 described, the royal autocracy did not budge despite these pressures, preserving its visage of liberalized autocracy while issuing more shallow reform promises. Jordanians thus continued mobilizing and protesting, again in concert with their Arab peers. During 2018–2019, a new wave of popular uprisings erupted in Algeria, Sudan, Iraq, Lebanon, and Palestine, with presidential dictators suffering overthrow in Algiers and Khartoum. In Jordan, citizens similarly stayed active on the street. Hundreds of small demonstrations have occurred every year since then, with the largest public protests sparked by explosive government controversies: the government purchase of Israeli natural gas in October 2016, higher taxes imposed by the International Monetary Fund (IMF) in May 2018, the suspension of the teachers' union in August 2020, rising gasoline and food prices in December 2022, Israeli bombardments against Gaza after October 2023, and so forth.

Still, a cynic might interpret this impressive record of resistance as one of failure. The regime has seldom altered its policy agenda in response to domestic pressures thanks to its coercive apparatus, coalitional supporters, and Western backing. Yet Jillian Schwedler, a leading observer of Jordanian activism, proffers a far better interpretation. Every outburst of public opposition is not a life-and-death moment of revolution; instead, it is one episode of a long-running battle over who controls public spaces in Jordan—the regime or the people.[11] That open-ended struggle is ongoing and is the effervescent currency of daily politics. The police shutter traffic circles, fence off squares, and block roads as part of its civil efforts to contain protests. The General Intelligence Directorate (GID) intimidates activists and infiltrates youth groups; the judiciary convicts dissidents and criminalizes social media. But citizens still find ways to organize, showing that two contradictory things can be true. An authoritarian regime can wield superlative power, and its subjects can object incessantly to that power. This is yet another paradox within this outwardly stable country.

Beyond Mobs

Journalists who have never visited Jordan (or worse, visit for a few days to interview friendly officials in their hotel lobby before jetting out) often describe local protests and opposition in frenetic terms. Any large demonstration is described as an unruly mob, whose fury and rage jeopardizes the kingdom's stability.[12] In such facile portrayals, activism is a bad word—a portent of chaos; activists, hence, are single-minded agents of anarchy.

Some basic truths cry for attention given this misunderstanding. First, there is no prototypical "activist" (in Arabic, *naashit*) in Jordan. An activist can be a first-time protester from a bourgeois, mostly Palestinian neighborhood in Amman, or a grizzled tribal nonconformist with a long arrest record from poor, rural Ma'an. She can be a university student roused by a meeting, a creative artist publishing online, or a wage earner shaped by workplace complaints. Activists may belong to formal organizations like political parties and civil society associations, or they may have no affiliation to any licensed group at all. They may represent entire neighborhoods and tribes, or they may be loners from nonpolitical communities.

Second, activism has changed in the era of King Abdullah. While protests have always been part of its toolkit, the pathways through which Jordanians mobilize have changed drastically in the twenty-first century. Activism has become less ideological and more informal. Historically, many Jordanian oppositionists mobilized through formal entities like civic associations and political parties. These are *physical* organizations, with official headquarters, hierarchical leadership, founding charters, and membership rules. Many also center on ideologies like socialism, Arab Nationalism, and Islamism. Ideologies, here, mean philosophical doctrines that can inculcate lifelong commitments among adherents, because their revolutionary ideals promise utopian emancipation through collective struggle.[13] For instance, during the 1950s and 1960s, leftist and Arab Nationalist parties declared that only by eliminating every vestige of Western colonialism—including the monarchy's immense power—could Jordanians have dignity. In the 1990s, Islamism became a leading purveyor of dissent, with the Muslim Brotherhood and its Islamic Action Front (IAF) party advancing its creed of political salvation through faith-based work.

These ideological torchbearers led political opposition in the 1990s, when political liberalization modestly widened space for activism. They formed alliances, as when Islamists, leftists, civic groups, and student groups rallied against the 1994 peace accords with Israel. And they still work with one another. By the 2000s, however, political manipulations and repressive measures from the regime had taken their toll on these parties and organizations, as Chapter 5 explained. During the Arab Spring, hence, a new generation of youth dissidents stood in full view. Representing both Palestinian-Jordanians and Transjordanians, their grassroots movements—the hirak—were far more formless and fluid. Their vocabularies abjured from grand ideologies like socialism and Islamism, evincing instead a practical desire to fix immediate problems like corruption and repression. Neither did they create parties and civil society organizations, instead mobilizing through community collectives, social media, and other informal channels.

Third, much as purveyors of political activism have evolved, so have their strategies. Contentiousness takes many forms. It shows not only in rural protests against unemployment that have dozens of participants, but also in national campaigns of solidarity that draw hundreds of thousands of people, like the December 2023 professional strike that condemned Israel's war on Gaza—perhaps Jordan's largest general work stoppage ever. It could mean intellectual political declarations that took months to craft by an alliance of political parties or rowdy slogans raised by youthful coordinators who arrange a public occupation in a day through word of mouth. Some incendiary acts flagrantly violate the red lines, as when tribal activists deface pictures of the king or accuse Queen Rania of corruption. Other protests have become so routinized as to not merit news despite drawing thousands, like the once-familiar sight in decades past of the Muslim Brotherhood holding methodical Friday marches in downtown Amman. Activism can also be digital, expressed through social media such as Facebook, X (formerly Twitter), and WhatsApp, where fiery political criticisms can go viral in a heartbeat.

Finally, Jordanian activism is vociferous, but also fissiparous. Under King Abdullah, there has been no national, unified opposition movement drawing together all ends of the protesting spectrum—Islamists and non-Islamists, youths and elders, Palestinians and Transjordanians, and others.[14] This would be a nightmare for the Hashemite regime, which is why, as Chapters 3 and 4 unpacked, its targeted repression and coalitional strategies work hard to silence and fracture activism. However, extant divisions among Jordanians also account for the absence of such opposition unity. Some Transjordanians sound populist in their bitter attacks on capitalist elites and economic inequality, but they also traffic in xenophobia against Palestinian-Jordanians by accusing the wealthiest among them, like Queen Rania, of financial corruption that has caused tribal impoverishment. Islamist leaders echo most Jordanians when they denounce American militarism and criticize Israel for its military operations in Gaza or the West Bank, but they alienate secular-minded citizens in calling for gender segregation and shari'a-inspired public education. A grassroots hirak group and old opposition party may attend the same anticorruption rally, but that does not mean they will join forces to compete in the next election, not least because youths see little point in voting at all.

Sources of Popular Discontent

Concrete grievances drive this terrain of popular mobilization. For all the different identities and ideas delivered by their contentious politics, a common theme emerges when speaking to many Jordanians: their country suffers from endemic problems and mismanagement, which make life *hard*. One 2023 global report suggested that Jordanians rank as the second-unhappiest society in the entire Middle East and North Africa (MENA), just behind Lebanon.[15] Digging deeper, public survey data illuminate four major complaints that have kindled opposition and activism for the past quarter-century: foreign relations, political freedom, economic well-being, and corruption.

Foreign Relations

Jordan's post–Cold War foreign policy stands on two untouchable pillars: its close alliance with the United States and normalized ties with Israel. As Chapter 8 explains, these are interlinked principles. The 1994 Wadi Araba peace treaty with Israel brought this already pro-Western monarchy into closer orbit around American hegemony. It unleashed more torrents of US diplomatic support, economic aid, and security assistance, while making the regime an accomplice to future American-led wars in the Middle East.

However, many in Jordan regard the United States as an imperial power, intent on bullying the rest of the region by force. Anti-US protests occurred during the 1990–1991 Gulf War, as most Jordanians sided with Iraq during that conflict. When the wildly unpopular Iraq War commenced in March 2003 with the American invasion, only emergency security laws imposed two years earlier, which had suspended parliament and banned most demonstrations, prevented similar agitation. Washington's ongoing military interventions across the MENA and staunch support for Israel have continued spurring public enmity, although brigades of Jordanian police and gendarmerie ensure protesters never endanger the US Embassy in western Amman (or, for that matter, the Israeli Embassy). It makes little difference who sits in the White House: President Obama held just a 22 percent approval rating among Jordanians after his first term, while President Trump's approval rating in 2019 bottomed at a dazing 2 percent.[16]

However, anti-US sentiment pales in comparison with antipathy toward Israel, shared among Palestinian-Jordanians and Transjordanians alike. Dozens of public opinion polls since the 1994 peace treaty show that most in Jordan reject the normalization of relations with Israel and support Palestinian statehood.[17] They see Israel as a colonial usurper of Palestinian lands and as an untrustworthy neighbor that cares little for Jordan. The list of anti-Israeli rallies, petitions, and campaigns runs long. For decades, they have targeted the 1994 peace treaty, Israel's bloody reoccupation of the West Bank during the Al-Aqsa Intifada after 2000, the importation of Israeli natural gas in 2016, the expansion of illegal Israeli settlements in the West Bank over the past fifteen years, and repeated Israeli military operations in the Gaza Strip. The grisly humanitarian toll of the latest Gaza conflict upon the territory's Palestinian populace, which began following the October 2023 Hamas attacks in Israel, set off the most bellicose mass protests since the 1994 peace treaty and involved tens of thousands of marchers.

Jordanian officials privately share these sentiments. They have long abandoned their trust in Israel to facilitate Palestinian statehood as envisaged by the 1993 and 1995 Oslo Accords, and they also bristle at right-wing Zionist proposals to massively displace Palestinians from the West Bank and Gaza Strip onto Jordan and thereby annex all of Palestine. They also recognize that too much anti-Israel criticism among citizens brings another danger. For citizens, the next step after panning Jordan's foreign policy is blaming their royal leadership for *maintaining* that foreign policy. As Chapter 8 confers, domestic pressures have previously influenced the monarchy's external stances, as in King Hussein's surprising support for Iraq during the 1990–1991 Gulf War. Today is a different story. The Hashemite regime risks alienating Western support should it abandon the peace treaty with Israel, which many Jordanians advocate. So, it does what it can, tolerating many anti-US and anti-Israel demonstrations but curbing the most raucous marches that test the limits of "permissible" dissent and so could turn into anti-government uprisings.[18]

Political Concerns

Domestic problems weigh heavily on public opinion. The thousands of Arab Spring protests in Jordan during 2011–2012, after all, hardly mentioned the United States or Israel. Failed democratic reforms, shrinking margins of freedoms, and ineffectual governments have bred widespread political disaffection.

Figure 6.1 compares Arab Barometer surveys from the pre–Arab Spring years to the 2021–2022 Wave VII round. The data illustrate tattered public faith in political institutions. Roughly 16 percent of Jordanians trust parliament, a precipitous drop from 55 percent in 2007, and only 31 percent trust the prime minister–led government, an incredible decline from 66 percent in 2007. Growing legal and political restrictions have also pummeled perceptions of freedom. Now, about 36 percent of citizens believe the right to express free opinions is guaranteed, a far cry from 71 percent in 2011; only 25 percent believe the freedom to participate in peaceful protests is guaranteed, down from 36 percent in 2011; and just 39 percent think the freedom of the press is guaranteed, nearly halving the 71 percent figure in 2011.

The numbers are startling. Since the first decade of King Abdullah's tenure, Jordanians believe that their civic and political rights are shrinking. Their regime's democratizing rhetoric, described in Chapter 5, has not fully obscured this autocratic reality. Relatedly, far fewer Jordanians than before regard

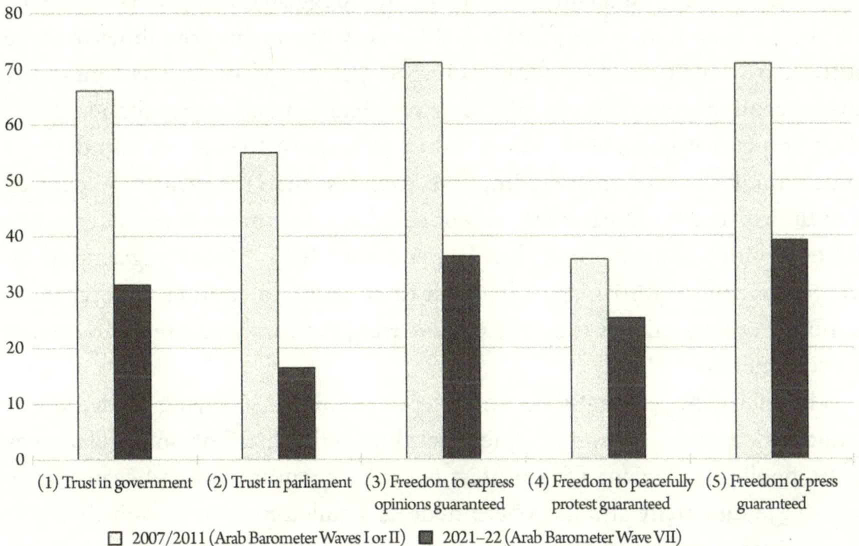

Figure 6.1 Declining Perceptions of Trust and Freedom in Jordan, 2007–2022. Public trust in government (1) and parliament (2) report the percentage of respondents who, between the Arab Barometer's Wave I (2007) and Wave VII (2021–2022) surveys, reported having some or a great deal of trust in these institutions. Freedom to express opinions (3), freedom to peacefully protest (4), and freedom of press (5) report the percentage who, between the Arab Barometer's Wave II (2011) and Wave VII (2021–2022) surveys, believed these rights were guaranteed to a medium or great extent. Source: Arab Barometer, https://www.arabbarometer.org/.

their political figures as accountable, transparent, and responsive. Declining trust in parliament reflects recognition that hamstrung elections have produced a feckless legislature that has little role in national decision-making. That less than a third of citizens now trust the government is more telling. Public surveys cannot ask citizens about their true feelings regarding the monarchy. Because it is royally appointed, the prime minister–led government is a crude proxy to the kingship—and its stature has palpably dropped over time.

These findings reverberate when speaking with writers and activists. Mohammed Ersan, a prolific journalist and community radio pioneer, described this political disconnect: "Jordanians feel like *subjects* and not citizens. They feel like the government talks *at* them, not with them. They feel like the government treats them like children. And they can only take so much of this."[19] Jordan's feisty protesters and dissidents would agree.

Economic Hardship

Public dissatisfaction also stems from the creeping poverty, high unemployment, and widening inequality produced by the sluggish economy. As Figure 6.2 reveals, the Arab Barometer's 2021–2022 survey shows dire trendlines in these attitudes over the preceding decade. Over 85 percent of Jordanians believe the current economic situation to be bad or very bad—much higher than in 2011, when 56 percent thought so. When asked to forecast the future, less than 24 percent think the economy will improve, even less than the meager 30 percent of optimists in 2011. Nearly 80 percent see the government as not adequately addressing inequality, compared to 59 percent in 2011. Most staggering of all, over 93 percent of Jordanians who wish to emigrate to another country cited economic opportunity as their reason, dwarfing the barely quarter who carried this sentiment in 2011.

While Chapter 7 investigates the deeper problems stymying Jordan's economic growth and development, these data hint at the distributional preferences of the public. Jordanians who protest over the economy do so because they believe the monarchy and its government have failed in their responsibility to ensure citizens enjoy fair livelihoods and opportunities. For their part, officials blame external problems for ravaging the economy, such as unexpected refugee flows, neighboring wars, and global pandemics. These are not irrelevant—the Covid-19 crisis ratcheted up already-high unemployment until it peaked at a record 25 percent in 2021, for instance. Nonetheless, the end result is the same: popular mobilization. In June 2018, for example, an IMF-backed law that raised income taxes for the cash-strapped government sparked national strikes and urban demonstrations. As economic protests persisted through the fall, one

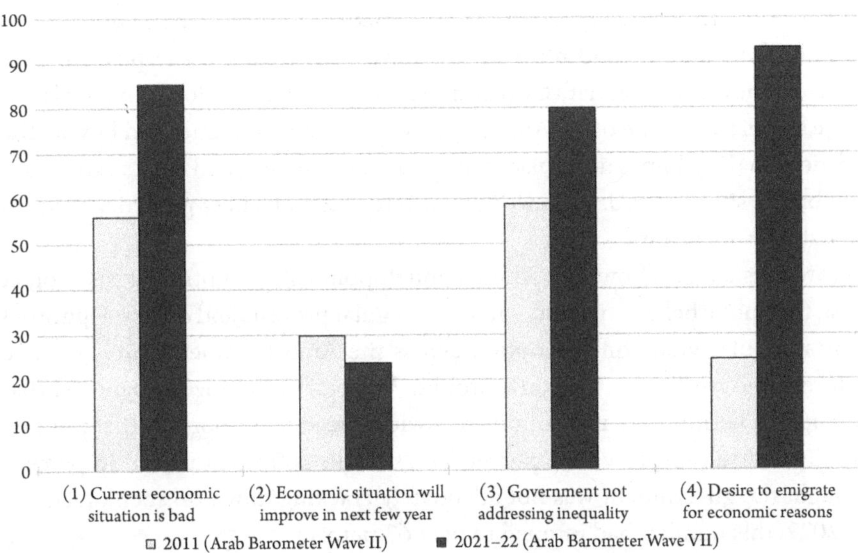

Figure 6.2 Worsening Views on Economic Conditions in Jordan, 2011–2022. The first cluster (1) reports the percentage of Jordanians who, between the Arab Barometer's Wave II (2011) and Wave VII (2021–2022) surveys, evaluated the current economic situation as either bad or very bad. The second cluster (2) reports the percentage who believed the economy in the next few years would get somewhat or much better. The third cluster (3) reports the percentage who gauged the government's efforts to narrow the gap between rich and poor as bad or very bad. The fourth cluster (4) reports the percentage who had a desire to emigrate for economic reasons. Source: Arab Barometer, https://www.arabbarometer.org/.

mantra among young activists became viral—*ma'nash* ("We're broke," in colloquial Jordanian Arabic).[20] Reproduced through street slogans and social media hashtags, this refrain resonated among tribal communities that had been dislocated by neoliberal economic changes like privatization since the 2000s. The diminished supply of government jobs and public services has spawned pockets of dissent within these traditional bases of regime support, much as grinding hardships and worsening inequality have exasperated residents of Amman and other cities.

Corruption

Perhaps the biggest source of popular anger in recent decades is corruption (in Arabic, *fasaad*). Corruption means the abuse of public office for private gain. As Chapter 3 noted, corruption takes many forms, including the *wasta* (favoritism) that lubricates daily dealings with the state. What provokes sharper indignation is grand corruption, meaning high-level bribery, extortion, embezzlement, graft, and other crimes enriching powerful politicians and their corporate cronies. It is impossible to accurately measure such practices in Jordan: corruption flourishes in the shadows, and most of it is never reported. On the positive side, Transparency International's Corruption Perceptions Index does rank Jordan as more lawful than some other Arab countries, like Lebanon, Iraq, and Egypt. The Hashemite Kingdom is not a place where judges, teachers, and clerks extract undue bribes simply to come to work or where every business pays kickbacks to predatory bureaucrats.

Jordan is a place, however, where enough political corruption exists—or, at least, the public believes it does—to incite regular protests and outcry. Figure 6.3 charts popular views on corruption across the Arab Barometer surveys since before the Arab Spring. In 2007, around 31 percent of citizens believed that corruption within state institutions was widespread, a proportion that jumped rapidly and settled at over 88 percent in 2022. In 2007, just under 36 percent thought the government was not adequately cracking down on such practices; by 2022, this number had jumped to over 62 percent.

These numbers are glaring. Across King Abdullah's reign, virtually *everyone* has come to associate corruption with their ruling state, while nearly two-thirds see the government as neglecting the problem. Chants and signs against fasaad have become ubiquitous at major demonstrations, and anticorruption fervor unites all dissenters—from leftists and Islamists to civic associations, opposition

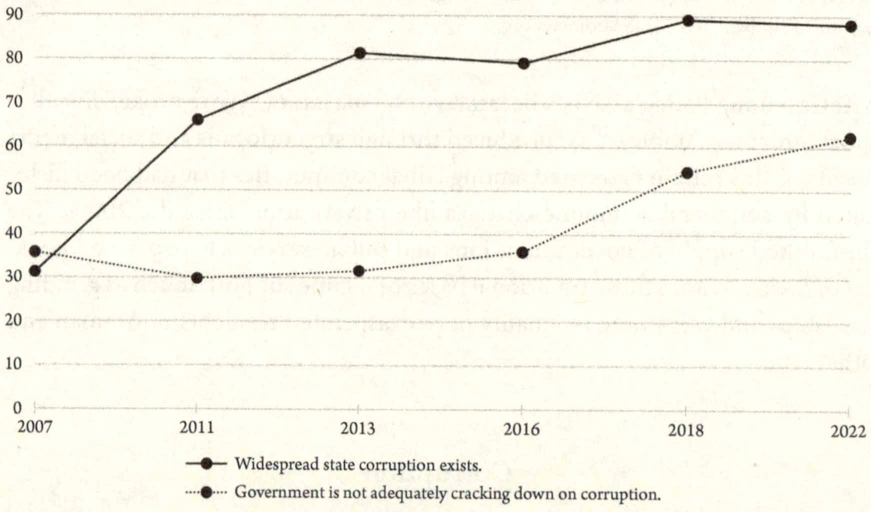

Figure 6.3 Public Attitudes on Corruption in Jordan, 2007–2022. The solid line represents the percentage of Jordanians who believed that corruption existed to a medium or large extent within state agencies and institutions. The dashed line represents the percentage who believed that the government was working to halt corruption to a small extent or not at all. Every year represents a distinctive round (i.e., wave) of the Arab Barometer survey. Source: Arab Barometer, https://www.arabbarometer.org/.

parties, and grassroots youth movements. As one civil society leader averred, locals see corruption as an "insult to dignity: why should we work hard and feel proud of Jordan, like the king always demands in his speeches, if everything will be stolen from us by the crooked politicians that serve him?"[21]

Such frustration has worsened despite the regime taking visible, if half-hearted, anticorruption measures. In King Abdullah's royal addresses, promises to punish the corrupt come as frequently as pronouncements of democratic reforms. To this autocracy's credit, after the 2000s, officials inaugurated an official anticorruption agency—the Jordanian Integrity and Anti-Corruption Commission (JIACC)—to investigate public corruption complaints and tightened laws penalizing corrupt acts.[22] However, while the JIACC has caught some civil servants engaging in low-level wrongdoings, only a handful of mighty figures suffered prosecution for their financial malfeasance. Among the most notorious are a former GID chief, a dozen former ministers, business tycoon Khalid Shahin, and the king's uncle (by marriage), Walid al-Kurdi.

In the eyes of many Jordanians, however, such elites are just a drop in the bucket. During the 2000s, the neoliberal transformation of the previously state-led economy spawned financial abuses at the highest levels. As Chapter 7 notes, a new stratum of fat-cat cronies and capitalist investors benefited from privatization, free trade, and business deals, while the middle class and poor experienced rising joblessness and living costs. It is not hard to find Jordanians who can attest to having seen signs of such corruption: public funds for a development project disappearing, ministers and deputies suddenly purchasing ritzy mansions on their meager civil salary, and humble shopkeepers' and young entrepreneurs' dreams dissolving because they cannot pay their fixers enough bribes to make their licensing problems disappear. While the JIACC and the courts began whittling down upon many petty financial abuses after the Arab Spring, public confidence was still shaken by suspicions that corruption had become so systemic that the Jordanian state lacked the capacity to effectively uproot it.[23]

Periodic corruption scandals implicating high-level political figures have not helped. They have triggered popular acrimony, and some massive misdeeds were exposed only after years of murky profiteering. Over the past two decades, these controversies have involved sordid deals: for instance, an abortive Dead Sea casino complex (later termed "Casinogate"), the embezzlement-tainted privatization of the state-owned phosphate company, sham housing development schemes, and even counterfeit cigarette production.[24] Whispers of corruption have even embroiled the monarchy itself. In October 2021, the Pandora Papers—the leaked document dump detailing the offshore wealth of many global leaders and billionaires—revealed that King Abdullah had a trove of wealth in luxurious overseas real estate and European bank accounts. While public reporting about this was forbidden, such revelations riled some Jordanian activists, who had long complained of the seemingly lavish lifestyles of their royal leadership.[25]

Formal Activism: Civil Society and Islamism

These varied economic and political grievances have propelled contentious politics in Jordan in the twenty-first century. The mantle of mobilization falls upon two types of activism: formal groups, such as civil society associations and well-structured organizations like the Muslim Brotherhood; and informal movements, borne of grassroots networks and youth activism that shuns ideological labels. Each contributes to the broader cacophony of protest and resistance under authoritarianism.

Outside of opposition parties, which save the IAF have been immobilized by the rules of liberalized autocracy, civil society has birthed the most traditional activism. Civil society refers to associational life distinct from the state, economy, and family—in other words, nonprofit groups that connect citizens and promote their interests. Civil society organizations (CSOs) are formal, in having internal structures like identifiable leadership, membership rules, financial budgets, and brick-and-mortar offices. Being licensed by the government, they have abounded since martial law ended in 1989. In 2023, the Ministry of Social Development counted over 4,000 registered CSOs, but they vary greatly.[26] The largest are professional syndicates and labor federations, whose hundreds of thousands of members span the country. Most, however, are much smaller, and take the form of local cooperatives, charities, clubs, and research centers. Among them are impassioned groups advancing many different causes, such as women's rights, childhood education, social justice, climate change, media rights, and refugee accommodation.

Ideally, CSOs serve public ends by empowering citizens. One prominent civic leader furnishes this optimistic view: "We [CSOs] do what the state cannot. We try to be independent platforms that bring Jordanians together to help solve problems, like training youths and improving public services. Our events let people create new ideas, and sometimes even talk to the government so they have a voice."[27] Foreign aid donors agree with this sanguine optic. Since the 1990s, Western governments and nonprofit foundations have provided financial assistance and organizational resources to many Jordanian CSOs. Major donors such as German foundations like Konrad Adenauer Stiftung, the US Agency for International Development, and various United Nations agencies have underwritten huge swathes of local civil society.[28] For more than a few CSOs, writing grant proposals and securing outside funds rank as the most important annual tasks.

In turn, these mostly Western donors celebrate local civil society as a vector for political reform, given their assumption that a healthy Jordanian democracy also needs a well-organized sector of voluntary associations to represent the interests of the populace.[29]

However, civil society cannot be the sole handmaiden of democratization in Jordan. One reason is that most CSOs focus on social or cultural issues. For example, many charitable foundations have emerged since the 1990s to redress Jordan's worsening economic challenges, but their purpose is not to confront state power so much as improve the quality of life in local communities.[30] Others are so dependent on foreign funding that they care more about pleasing those donors than focusing on domestic politics. Above all, as Chapters 4 and 5 laid out, the regime places CSOs within a labyrinth of hobbling regulations. For instance, authorities can freely attend their meetings to oversee their political speech. They can audit their budgets and arbitrarily disband the most irksome organizations on account of finding alleged misdeeds or financial irregularities. CSOs also risk suspension—and with it, the loss of their offices, resources, and mission—if they are deemed too critical of the government. Moreover, even if allowed to operate autonomously, civil society groups advocating policy change have little institutionalized access to the state; bureaucrats and officials can simply ignore their phone calls and meeting requests, making them twist in the authoritarian wind.[31]

As another tact, the Hashemite regime has found varied ways to co-opt civil society. The government institutionally manages several large associations, which were once independent but placed under state sponsorship during the martial law decades that followed the 1950s. For instance, the Jordanian state financially and politically controls the General Federation of Jordanian Trade Unions (GFJTU) and its nearly 140,000 worker members, thereby keeping the traditional sector of organized labor on a tight leash. Other civic entities require intimate government relations to operate, as with the Amman Chamber of Commerce and other business societies that lobby for favorable financial and trade policies. Still other civil society groups need to build contingent partnerships with the monarchy to promote their interests. Women's movements—which include not only the state-run General Federation of Jordanian Women, but also many smaller women's CSOs—face this dilemma.[32] Advances for gender equality, from the lower house's female quota to the long-overdue 2017 repeal of the marital rape law, have come with sympathetic backing from Queen Rania and other Hashemite figures. Women's rights activists welcome such royal help to overcome resistance from socially conservative opponents, such as urban Islamists as well as rural tribes, but this dependence also makes them more vulnerable to the regime's influence and pressures.[33]

Finally, the Jordanian state has created its own CSOs in order to monopolize eminent issues. In 2006, the government established the National Centre for Human Rights as a clearinghouse to investigate alleged human rights abuses. Yet, this official organ has little authority to criticize the regime or probe too deeply into the very bodies, like the GID, that citizens hold responsible for many egregious violations. The regime has also created royal nongovernmental organizations (RONGOs), such as the Hashemite Fund for Human Development (formerly the Queen Alia Fund), Jordan Media Institute, Jordan River Foundation, and Crown Prince Foundation.[34] With superior financial resources and political sway thanks to their monarchical ties, RONGOs undertake work in vital areas, such as youth entrepreneurship, community enterprise, and environmental protection. Yet in doing so, these quasi-state bodies also crowd out truly independent CSOs from the public sphere. RONGOs relegate them to the sidelines because these more authoritative organizations can dictate how social and political problems are discussed, adjudicated, and framed for outside audiences.

Professional Associations and Labor Unions

Despite these limitations, some CSOs do engage in contentious politics. They push for incremental reforms by pressuring the regime, making public statements, and mobilizing protests.[35] Of these, the more than dozen professional syndicates—or official unions for salaried professions—stand out. These licensed independent groups represent many fields, such as medicine, law, and art, and have not yet been absorbed into the Jordanian state. They also include Jordan's largest CSOs, whose national membership can defensibly claim to represent much of the public. For instance, the Engineers Association, established in 1948, has over 160,000 members today.

Over time, Jordanian syndicates have developed an impressive capacity to organize for political causes. Some were historically aligned with the leftist and Arab Nationalist ideologies that underpinned the popular uprisings of the 1950s and continued harboring these opposition sympathies under martial law.[36] Over time, most became dominated by Palestinian-Jordanians—understandably so, given their urban middle-class base—including Islamist-leaning members. Starting in the 1990s, these demographic and ideological shifts thrust the professional associations into the forefront of democratic opposition. Led by a new generation of outspoken leaders, they rallied against the 1994 peace treaty with Israel, opposed the 2003 Iraq War, and pressed authorities to grant fairer elections and greater freedoms. Solidarity marches with Palestine became common, as did demonstrations against corruption and economic difficulties. The associations supported the Arab Spring protests during

2011–2012, and later they led the June 2018 anti-austerity unrest by organizing a national strike against the proposed tax laws.

However, because they are so large and easily identifiable, these syndicates are also vulnerable to repression and manipulation from above. New tactics of government surveillance and control, such as the digital hacking of smartphones belonging to civic leaders, have become the norm over the past decade.[37] Yet the old ways of coercion are still the most effective. During the early 2000s, officials took advantage of the two-year period of emergency law decreed by King Abdullah to muzzle the syndicates. They ordered targeted arrests of members and threatened the organizations with closure, on basis that their political activities violated the kingdom's nebulous associational laws.[38] Such authoritarian encroachment eventually claimed one prominent group in the Teachers Association. After years of petitioning, Jordan's over 100,000 public school teachers obtained the right to establish their own syndicate in 2011. Their association quickly entered the political fray by criticizing state corruption and government mismanagement. In September 2019, the syndicate coordinated a school strike to obtain long-overdue pay raises for educators. In July and August 2020, authorities retaliated by closing the organization and arresting its leadership, alongside over 1,000 other teacher-activists and supporters.

That episode illustrated the lopsided fight that professional associations wage. While the royal autocracy cannot prevent all their activities, it can ensure the syndicates do not grow into a credible threat. Organized labor, too, has suffered this. In comparative perspective, working-class organizations like labor unions have directed popular opposition under many dictatorships, as in Latin America during the 1970s and 1980s. However, Jordan never had this experience. Its earliest labor unions supported the Jordanian National Movement in the 1950s, and thus after the 1957 crackdown suffered intense repression.[39] By the mid-1970s, the regime limited unionization to just seventeen industries, such as transportation, textiles, and construction; in turn, all unions were mandated to join the state-controlled GFJTU. Public-sector wage earners, such as civil servants, were forbidden from unionizing at all. Under the autocratic thumb, workers hence lacked the right to collectively bargain and strike, and so could not participate in the oppositionist campaigns as the professional syndicates could in the 1990s.

In the late 2000s, some labor activists fought back. In response to stagnant wages and job losses wrought by neoliberal economic reforms, thousands of Jordanian wage earners formed independent (and technically illegal) unions, defying GFJTU pressures to stand down.[40] They demanded competent management, higher wages, and full-time job contracts—the latter especially important for day laborers, who were employed through part-time contracts that did not afford them insurance, pensions, and other basic protections. Such illicit unionization drew agricultural laborers, port workers in Aqaba, and phosphate miners into wildcat strikes and disruptive sit-ins. Their actions spread into other industries like tourism and healthcare; by the Arab Spring, these workers regularly launched demonstrations for economic relief and fed the currents of activism spreading elsewhere throughout Jordan. During 2011–2013, over 2,600 unlicensed labor protests took place, whereas there were virtually none a decade earlier.[41] However, the irascible regime stamped out these campaigns, ensuring their sharp reduction. It detained and prosecuted many labor organizers, while allowing the police and gendarmerie to mistreat defiant strikers. Such repression shows that while authorities cannot halt all worker mobilization, they can throttle such actions enough to prevent their uncontrolled growth.

Enter Islamism

Besides professional syndicates and organized labor, Islamists also drive civil society and associational life in Jordan. In this regard, the kingdom mirrors bigger regional trends. By the late twentieth century, Islamist organizations had become leading opposition in many MENA countries.[42] After the Iranian Revolution showed a rare example of Islamism—albeit of the Shi'a variety—seizing power, the Sunni-led Arab states diverged in their responses to Sunni Islamist groups. Some, like Saudi Arabia, Syria, and Libya, banned them. Others, like Jordan, Kuwait, and Egypt, warily tolerated them, so long as they did not call for revolution and stuck to sponsoring minor reforms. Within the Hashemite Kingdom, Islamists thus compose a key part of the political landscape. They have participated in elections, rallied followers, and coordinated protests, but they have also experienced repressive backlash and autocratic suffocation.

As an ideology, Islamism promises political salvation by renewing the Muslim faith. The goal is to Islamize state and society by making religious traditions and values—such as shari'a, or Islamic law—guiding principles in government and social life. In Jordan, the biggest Islamist movement comprises the Muslim Brotherhood (*jama'at al-ikhwan al-muslimin*) and its IAF party, which during the 1990s became a vanguard of formal opposition. Other varieties of local Islamism exist. The non-Brotherhood Wasat Party has operated since 2001, offering a more centrist (that is, less opposition-oriented) alternative to the pious. Still other Islamists eschew the corridors of power, preferring instead community-based work rather than any political activism. For example, hundreds of Islamist-inspired CSOs abound and see God's purpose in providing social services to the masses, rather than making political statements about the regime.[43]

Salafists represent another branch of Islamism. Salafism expresses the most conservative interpretation of Islam, rejecting modernity in favor of restoring literalist understandings of the Qur'an and classical religious practices. As

Joas Wagemakers has pointed out, most Jordanian Salafists are "quietist," as they propagate their beliefs through cultural and educational programs—not through elections, protests, or opposition.[44] Overshadowing this quietist majority is Salafi-jihadism, a radical subset of Salafism that calls for achieving its stringent vision through violence, including terrorism against all perceived oppressors of Islam. To Salafi-jihadist groups like Al-Qaeda and the Islamic State in Iraq and Syria (ISIS), those oppressors include the Hashemite monarchy, portrayed as an apostate regime that has sold out its Muslim faithful to the West. Salafi-jihadist networks have attracted thousands of Jordanian youths estranged by economic deprivation and political voicelessness.[45] Indeed, the Jordanian militant Abu Musab al-Zarqawi helped found the predecessor militant group to ISIS on the battlefields of Iraq in 2004. Al-Qaeda and ISIS have engaged in sporadic terrorism against Jordan. Most Jordanians accordingly back stern efforts to end their violent activities, and the Hashemite regime eagerly hosted the US-led military coalition to destroy ISIS during the Syrian Civil War.

In domestic politics, though, it is not Salafi-jihadism but mainstream Islamism in the form of the Muslim Brotherhood that looms largest. The Brotherhood is a moderate Islamist group: it seeks influence and power through peaceful methods and recognizes the Hashemite monarchy as the rightful leadership of Jordan.[46] The organization started in 1945 as a branch of Egypt's original Muslim Brotherhood, and adapted its mission to fit the royal landscape of Jordan. During the 1950s and 1960s, the Brotherhood struck a close alliance with the monarchy. Its mostly Transjordanian members rejected the secularist call of Arab Nationalism and defended King Hussein during periods of domestic unrest, such as the 1970 Black September civil war. In return, the monarchy spared the Jordanian Brotherhood from high-intensity repression during the martial law decades. Somewhat quiescent to the kingship, the movement thus expanded its charitable work with little interference, even as its membership became increasingly Palestinian. By the 1980s, the Brotherhood had developed an effective hierarchical structure, with its governing body, the Shura Council, guiding disciplined cadres of followers. It steadily grew thanks to adherents who proselytized its alluring Islamist creed across university campuses, religious networks, and CSOs like the professional syndicates.[47]

This royal alliance frayed during the liberalization of the 1990s. After finding success in the 1989 elections, the Brotherhood asserted its political independence by assailing unpopular policies, which in turn attracted more members. For instance, its mantra of defending Palestine—as the group shared ties with Hamas until the latter's 1999 expulsion from Jordan—made it a leading detractor of the Israeli peace treaty. Coordinating innumerable protests and wielding its own media arm, the Brotherhood also joined with leftist groups, professional syndicates, and other movements in decrying the regime's economic policies, rollbacks of press freedom, and electoral manipulations.[48] The IAF found its pathway to the lower house stymied starting with the 1993 elections by the same soaring barriers that restricted all opposition parties, as Chapter 5 discussed: malapportioned districting that privileged rural tribal communities, the single nontransferable vote (SNTV) balloting method until 2016, and bureaucratic constraints on party activities. Still, the monarchy accepted the presence of the Brotherhood and its party, perhaps fearing the backlash if it outright banned such a large and well-organized Islamist sector after generations of peaceful coexistence.

However, these tensions turned acerbic under King Abdullah, who showed less tolerance for Islamism than his father, King Hussein. Driving these frictions was fear—shared by some within the monarchy, as well as its coercive apparatus—that if left uninhibited, the Muslim Brotherhood would become a political juggernaut and eventually seek to topple Hashemite rule. Particularly after 9/11 and the US-led invasion of Iraq in 2003, the palace and GID began seeing the Brotherhood and Salafi-jihadists like Al-Qaeda as two sides of the same coin: all Islamism imperiled national stability, and even moderate movements could not be trusted. As the 2000s wore on, the monarchy thus became increasingly hostile to the Brotherhood. The rigged 2007 general elections trimmed the IAF's presence, leading to the party boycotting the 2010 and 2013 contests. The regime arrested and tried Islamist critics, removed Islamist preachers from mosques, and used the official press to smear the Brotherhood. Still, the Brotherhood persisted. It became adept at organizing its disciplined cadres and civic allies to hold weekly marches that tackled resonant issues like corruption, economic hardship, and Israel's occupation of Palestine. It also led many of the urban demonstrations calling for democratic reforms during the 2011–2012 Arab Spring.

Islamist Evolution and Downfall

After the Arab Spring, Jordan's royal autocracy more successfully sheared the influence of the Muslim Brotherhood, culminating in its abrupt prohibition in April 2025. Early on, officials took advantage of the Brotherhood's internal divisions. The Brotherhood was never an ideological monolith, and political differences had long split its Shura Council.[49] Some leaders, the "doves," favored cooperating with the regime despite its hostility, believing Islamizing reforms to be possible only through dialogue and compromise; more skeptical "hawks" advocated more rigid opposition through electoral boycotts, fervid protests, and public dissent. Within the rank-and-file membership, younger followers similarly harbored deviating ideas. For instance, hoping to emulate other Islamist groups in the Arab world, such as Tunisia's Ennahda movement and Morocco's Justice and Development Party, some called for the Jordanian Brotherhood to redefine its mission by emphasizing social justice and religious pluralism over any further political battles with the Hashemite regime.[50]

In 2015, one dovish faction within the Brotherhood, the Zamzam Initiative, created a new Islamist political party distinct from the IAF and established their own civic organization confusingly called the Muslim Brotherhood Society. They attracted younger Islamists, having positioned themselves as resourceful reformists open to new ideas.[51] Most hawks stuck with the IAF and the original Brotherhood, which still commanded thousands of hardline devotees. Some suspected the GID had orchestrated this rift through infiltration and sabotage. Clearer is what happened afterward, when the regime exploited this schism to weaken its Islamist opponents—much to the delight of Jordan's more conservative Arab allies in the region, such as Saudi Arabia, which had long regarded all branches of the Muslim Brotherhood as ideological and political threats. In 2016, the Interior Ministry anointed the new Zamzam group as the true Muslim Brotherhood. Officials abrogated the old Brotherhood's legal status as a charitable organization; they seized its financial assets, closed its headquarters, and even delicensed its satellite TV channel, Al-Yarmouk. Having partly defanged the original Brotherhood, the regime felt comfortable enough to experiment with the 2016 lower house elections by finally ending the much-derided SNTV balloting method.[52] It presented that contest as Jordan's most democratic yet, a claim tinged with irony: it was opposition to SNTV, after all, that previously had invigorated Islamist opposition.

The Islamists quickly regrouped from these setbacks, resulting in a final crackdown. The old Brotherhood enjoyed far more popularity than the upstart Zamzam, and still possessed considerable resources through its large membership, charitable enterprises, and property holdings. Its public protests and political activities finally crossed the regime's dreaded red line, however, after the onset of the Gaza conflict in October 2023. The Brotherhood led the most vigorous anti-Israel demonstrations as the war raged on, evincing bold demands that upset the monarchy—such as ending Jordanian ties with Israel and supporting Hamas in its resistance to Israeli military operations in Gaza. A handful of members, whom the Brotherhood's leadership disavowed as rogue elements, were implicated in several security-related controversies in 2024, such as an arms smuggling ring connected to Hamas in June and a cross-border shooting attack against Israeli soldiers in October. Meanwhile, the IAF enjoyed a political resurgence thanks to an internal decision to downplay its religious messaging and craft new alliances with secular opposition groups. While the party fared badly in the 2016 and 2020 parliamentary elections, nearly half of its more than 150 candidates won local positions in the 2017 municipal elections. In the 2024 parliamentary elections, the IAF roared back by securing nearly a quarter of all lower house seats, partly due to its hearty campaigning centered on national solidarity with Gaza.

In April 2025, Jordan's royal autocracy dropped the hammer. In a decision that stunned many citizens, it completely banned the Muslim Brotherhood, forbid any public mention of its ideology, and confiscated its last resources. The technical reason reflected national security concerns: several weeks earlier, the police had arrested 16 Brotherhood members after the GID discovered a putative plot to manufacture drones and explosives intended to attack domestic targets, such as government offices. Major regional allies, such as Egypt and Saudi Arabia, applauded the move, not least because they had also outlawed the Muslim Brotherhood. Local cynics, however, not only questioned this conspiracy but also rejected the insinuation that Jordan's largest Islamist group—one that had never attempted armed uprising before—had come to embrace terrorism overnight, and so merited a sweeping prohibition.[53] The palace did not initially dissolve its IAF party, for instance, although its future certainly became more uncertain. Neither did officials detain the Shura Council leadership and many other Brotherhood members, which would have been the logical move if the movement had indeed become beholden to Salafi-jihadist extremism.

The likeliest explanation is the simplest one. An authoritarian regime finally had enough of a well-organized opposition movement, and used the most convenient evidence—rightly or wrongly—to justify its elimination. This does not spell the end of Islamism in Jordan, however. Other Islamist groups that generally refrain from political dissent, such as Zamzam as well as the kingdom's many non-Brotherhood Islamist CSOs, still exist. Brotherhood activists may yet attempt to reorganize themselves. Nonetheless, the legal demise of Jordan's Muslim Brotherhood signifies a hard lesson about formal activism. In autocratic settings, traditional organizations that mount contentious struggle are susceptible to bureaucratic and repressive stratagems because they precariously depend upon legal recognition from powerful rule-makers: they only exist if the regime *allows* them to exist. This divulges a powerful reason why many younger Jordanians today have gravitated to informal networks of activism, which do not require government licensing or recognition at all.

Informal Activism and Youthful Dissent

Youth activists in Jordan were surprised to witness the Muslim Brotherhood's downfall—but not shocked. In truth, they had long witnessed signs that conventional opposition groups no longer commanded the public mood as they did in the 1990s. For instance, in 2018, Brotherhood-affiliated Islamists were trounced in the internal elections of both the student union at Jordan University and the Engineers Association within civil society. While the Brotherhood's student bloc, *Ahl al-Himma,* clawed back half the open leadership seats at the university's student union years later, this marked the first time in decades that Islamists no longer held the leaderships over these flagship civic institutions. While this stunned Western observers, many young Jordanians saw this moment coming—and not just because the Brotherhood was wilting under regime pressures. Islamism represented the old-fashioned style of formal activism. Younger citizens wanted more practical ways to get involved, without having to absorb ideological refrains and organizing structures that felt so disconnected from their daily routines. As one Jordan University student remarked at the time, "Why should we go and liberate Jerusalem [a traditional Brotherhood slogan] when we need a job next year to survive? All the old groups have big ideas. But ideas are for philosophers. Who will help us in our lives now?"[54]

This illuminates a vital part of Jordan's contentious landscape: informal, grassroots activism steered largely by younger people. Many Jordanian youths like students, writers, artists, and entrepreneurs vocalize their opposition not through political parties and civil society organizations, but new protest groups and social movements. Like their older associational counterparts like the syndicates and Muslim Brotherhood, they are not revolutionary, as few call for violence or ousting the monarchy.[55] However, this novel generation of opposition more directly assails institutions of royal power, questions the writ of the coercive apparatus, denounces corruption, bemoans the economy, and defies warnings to stay quiet. Despite the touchy politics of communal identity that Chapter 2 described, both Transjordanians and Palestinian-Jordanians have propelled these activities, because the economic, political, and foreign policy grievances discussed earlier have elicited acute opposition among many citizens—not just one corner of society.

Over the past two decades, the novelty of this new activism has manifested in three ways. First, it takes the form of popular groups that are horizontal in structure.[56] These new youth movements are not organized hierarchically, with top-down leadership committees and strict membership charters; rather, they are "leaderless" networks that operate through consensus and discussion. What ties them together are not hard-and-fast rules or any supercilious ideology, but shared anger about the status quo—and, even more, frustration with the regime's responses such as repressing outspoken critics and appointing fruitless royal committees. This generation sees through the superficial reforms so often issued from above as a stop-gap solution to appease the public. Instead, it seeks *taghyir al-nahj* (Arabic for changing Jordan's path) by contentiously reimagining its political rules, economic structures, and foreign relations.

Second, the zeitgeist of such activism prizes informality. These protest forces do not aspire to become CSOs or political parties. Instead, they value the suppleness that comes with being unsanctioned movements; there is no license that officials can suspend and no physical offices for police to barricade. Therefore, such groups do not bother with the bureaucratic drudgery of incorporating themselves as legal organizations, or applying to a government ministry for official recognition. Instead, these young activists cherish their authentically popular (*sha'bi*) and inclusive disposition. There is no educational credential or litmus test needed to join their cause. Neither is there a complicated ideology or philosophical platform that one must memorize. Supporters need only a willingness to make themselves heard at meetings and protests. This egalitarian strategy also attracts more women and other vulnerable communities, who might otherwise be deterred from attending the public meetings of closely monitored parties and civic associations.[57]

Finally, these activists favor fluid, street-level action. They eschew participating in elections, which they regard as illiberal travesties. Their goal is far more direct: people power. Such protesters aim to assemble citizens through word of mouth and online messaging, and inundate authorities with pressures from the street. Older activists dismiss such tactics as counterproductive; to them, it sounds like protesting for the sake of protesting. Yet this new generation stands on solid ground in using disruptive actions as their elementary tool of resistance, for this has become the regional norm. Horizontal, informal, and protest-laden movements—and not professional syndicates, labor unions, and Islamists from civil society—pioneered the 2011–2012 Arab Spring uprisings across the MENA.[58] The popular insurrections that shook more Arab countries during 2018–2019 and overthrew presidential dictators in Algeria and Sudan likewise drew upon grassroots movements. So too did the 2022–2023 women's rights demonstrations across Iran emanate from leaderless mobilization from below.

The Arab Spring's Forge

In Jordan, major rumbles of informal activism under King Abdullah began in the late 2000s. At that point, neoliberal economic shifts and the rising inequality it engendered had aggravated many East Bank conservatives. Military veterans, tribal sheikhs, and public intellectuals published manifestos and coordinated small protests that complained of these developments.[59] Some felt betrayed by the cronyism and corruption afflicting the Jordanian state; others fell back on ethnocratic canards by accusing the monarchy of betraying its tribal sons while enriching rich Palestinian businessmen. Despite such nationalistic chauvinism, this new opposition made a striking impression on other Jordanians, especially when compared to the staider image of older CSOs and political parties withering under authoritarian rule. By 2010, wage-earning labor had launched the first of many wildcat strikes, while student activists on university campuses directed online movements calling for constitutional monarchy.

These initial efforts morphed into wider episodes of unrest during the Arab Spring. Jordanian activists launched their first major protests in January 2011, complaining of high living costs so stridently that King Abdullah quickly sacked Prime Minister Samir al-Rifa'i. But citizens did not stop there. In solidarity with the spreading wave of regional uprisings, Jordanians launched weekly marches, demonstrations, and sit-ins that called for economic justice and democratic reforms.[60] Islamists, professional syndicates, and some parties led some events, but the majority came from young informal activists—many of whom had never protested before but felt sufficiently moved to participate. Their grassroots movements occupied public spaces, created online platforms, sang patriotic songs, and chanted reformist slogans. In Amman, among the biggest early campaigns was a bold pro-democracy rally on March 24, 2011. In a rare display of high-intensity coercion, the Interior Ministry's darak troops violently disbanded thousands of participants there, leaving one dead and many others injured. Knowing that such bloodshed had only made opposing crowds larger in other Arab countries such as Tunisia, Egypt, and Syria, officials wisely chose to tolerate most other protests for the next two years.

How Jordan experienced the Arab Spring can be thus told in two ways. The first is a story of authoritarian resilience, of how the Hashemite Kingdom escaped revolution and maintained stability in tumultuous times. During 2011–2012, King Abdullah's regime utilized its conventional tactics—selective repression, tribal outreach, government shuffling, pseudo-democratic reforms, royal dialogue committees, and new parliamentary elections—to fend off domestic pressures.[61] These schemes essentially allowed the monarchy and its coercive apparatus to outlast the opposition.

Yet the other story about Jordan during the Arab Spring centers not on autocratic power but on the revival of popular mobilization through informal activism, whose contentious politics channeled deeper grievances shared across the country. The best evidence of this comes from hirak groups. These grassroots movements personified the spirit of those giddy years. They comprised horizontal, leaderless networks whose young activists—typically in their twenties—rejected ideological labels and excelled in leading extemporaneous protests.[62] They came in many varieties. The largest, such as the Amman-based Jordanian Youth Hirak, had thousands of Palestinian-Jordanian and Transjordanian members. Smaller hirak groups came from tribal communities, from Amman's Hay al-Tafaileh neighborhood to more rural settings like Tafileh, Karak, Ma'an, Jarash, and Mafraq. In fact, the first hirak movement originated in Dhiban, a poor tribal town forty miles south of Amman.[63]

During the Arab Spring, these dozens of hirak movements never united to create a national opposition coalition. This partly reflected the pragmatic attitudes of youth activists, who saw themselves as not leading an historic revolution against the state but as signaling the discontent and frustration of their local communities to the monarchy. Their multiflorous protests reverberated with chants for dignity (*karamah*), justice (*'adl*), and bread (*khubz*), and adroitly used social media to issue stinging statements. However, their views also diverged in fascinating ways.[64] For instance, while some tribal hirak leaders worked with Palestinian-Jordanian activists in the cities in common cause, others brought identity politics into the mix by blaming Queen Rania and other wealthy Palestinians for destroying their livelihoods through corruption. Hirak movements in Amman and Irbid, representing urbane middle-class protesters, saw constitutional reforms and political rights as the most pressing goal, while those from poor rural areas clamored for economic redistribution in the form of equitable jobs, affordable food costs, and better infrastructure. Some hirak groups allied with the Muslim Brotherhood or leftist parties in coordinating protests together; others disdained such collaboration, seeing all the elements of the existing political system—down to legal opposition forces whose leaders had not accomplished much at all—as so unpardonably polluted by authoritarian rule that they could not be trusted.

Despite these differences, the hirak trend as a whole served as a piercing wake-up call to the Hashemite monarchy. Jordan's rule-makers had long expected opposition from the usual suspects of Islamists, CSOs, and leftist parties. They never foresaw how youth activists, each channeling a rivulet of local dissent, could generate so much spontaneous collective noise. The hirak's methods of contention during 2011–2012 certainly broke the mold, because their movements did things that civil society and opposition parties had seldom done before.[65] For example, they held mock trials of corrupt politicians, burnt their election cards to signify political disgust, and held daring public debates about national identity, constitutional monarchy, and other explosive issues. Their social media profiles and online chats insulted, mocked, and derided their regime through language unfathomable to many older activists. In the streets, they also occasionally crossed the red lines. Notable hirak rallies intoned poetic affronts against King Abdullah, lampooning his awkward Arabic and alleged gambling habits. Tribal activists also garnered popular attention when they performed a *dabke* (a traditional folk dance) titled "Ali Baba and the Forty Thieves," which likened King Abdullah and his ministers as the legendary plunderers. Indeed, it was during these years that some tribal detractors began pondering whether the king should step down in favor of his half-brother Prince Hamzah, reputed to be far less corrupt—discussions that the palace and its security chiefs never forgot.

Hard Lessons

Jordan's hirak movements faded after the Arab Spring, exhausted by the obstinate regime's repressive blows and coalitional strategies. Targeted arrests from above—usually conducted well after protests, so as to preserve a public image of political tolerance—smothered some dissidents, while the monarchy's loyal tribal constituencies refused to defect to mass opposition. Geopolitics also did not favor this generation of activism. That the 2011–2012 uprisings elsewhere in the Arab world did not create new democracies, save for Tunisia, discouraged many youthful dissidents. So too did influxes of Syrian refugees into Jordan fleeing from their civil war, which tragically reminded them about the consequences of too much domestic conflict and political unrest.[66] By the spring of 2013, most had ceased their weekly activities.

However, the hirak's decline also stemmed from an inherent weakness of informal activism. What makes this style of contentiousness so nimble and unpredictable—its leaderless, horizontal, and spontaneous nature—also made it impermanent.[67] Without organizational structure, such youth groups were prone to fading once their ranks thinned out from arrests and apathy; Facebook and SMS texting alone could not hold people together. Thus, while newer hirak groups have continued to pop into existence well into the 2020s, they also frequently melt away once their campaigns of protests end. This puts formal civic actors like Islamist movements and opposition parties into fascinating relief. They look like lumbering, inflexible organizations when compared to this novel style of grassroots mobilization. Yet some of those groups are still here, because the very structural traits that leave them exposed to autocratic pressures—fixed budgets, physical offices, government licenses—also ensures their legal existence during quiet times. Informal activism embraces agility at the cost of durability, while older opposition forces prefer the opposite.

This comparison raises piquant insights into contemporary political activism in Jordan. There is no perfect style of mobilization or method of opposition because different approaches carry unique tradeoffs. If there is any dictum, it is this: Jordanians have learned that different times call for different methods, and that they must continually adapt—much as their own regime has evolved to better regulate them.

Persistent Mobilization

As the Arab Spring recedes into national memory, the firmness of Hashemite rule belies the teeming layers of potential mobilization that persist within society. Jordan's public sphere continues to feature old and new forms of activism expressed through contentious politics and pitched against King Abdullah's regime.[68] Most protests are small, getting little media coverage despite expressing passionate grievances by their local communities. The largest demonstrations drive global headlines that stereotypically portray them as mutinous mobs wreaking instability in Jordan, but they neglect the real issue: many Jordanians are unhappy and want change.

Economic hardships, for instance, still kindle popular distress. When the professional syndicates led a national strike against an IMF-imposed tax law in June 2018, they had little idea that so many other sympathetic campaigns would follow.[69] Inspired by that burst of contentiousness, Amman-based youth activists organized weekly demonstrations throughout that summer. However, rural hirak networks sent protesters to the capital well into the winter, when they mounted boisterous sit-ins and rallies.[70] In February 2019, hundreds of tribal youths took their resistance further by marching from Aqaba and other southern towns to the royal palace in Amman. The sight of so many jobless, hungry Transjordanian men supplicating their king for work left an indelible impression. So did loud demonstrations in several rural towns in December 2022, prompted by a spike in fuel prices and which resulted in the death of a police officer. So long as the economy languishes in privation and inequality, and Jordanians among the middle class and poor alike feel like they have few opportunities to prosper, such agitations will continue.

Pro-Palestinian campaigns, led by both grassroots movements and older civic associations as well as Islamists, have also expanded. Many tens of thousands of Jordanians, representing both Palestinian-Jordanians and Transjordanians, participated in weekly protests against Israel after the latest Gaza war began in October 2023. Against such disruptions, the authorities employed their usual balance of tolerating the public mood of anti-Israel sentiment, while arresting the most ardent activists who could turn their anger against the monarchy next. The outlawing of the Muslim Brotherhood silenced one key organizing node of such mobilization. However, provocative forms of opposition have not disappeared, even if they no longer garner Western media mentions—from neighborhood assemblies, hunger strikes, and student sit-ins to creative online campaigns calling for more economic boycotts, human barricades around the Israeli Embassy, and other acts of resistance.[71] As long as Jordan maintains its normalized relations with Israel, anchored as always by American support, such restiveness will go on.

Pleas for democracy still suffuse activism, too. The short but blazing trajectory of the Teachers Association, ending in its coercive dismemberment in August 2020, signifies how attuned that citizens have become to authoritarian overreach. Corruption remains the omnipresent concern, tinging many marches and rallies with damning accusations about how crooked ruling elites within the palace and state enrich themselves with impunity.[72] The dream of democratization similarly refuses to expire. In March 2021, for instance, youth movements across the kingdom mounted solidarity demonstrations in remembrance of the March 2011 pro-democracy occupation in Amman. Even though police and darak forces quickly halted their mobilization and detained dozens of organizers, calls for political change persevere. Women's rights groups hold animated protests against gendered violence in public areas such as in front of parliament, while wildcat strikes within agriculture and other sectors continue without the blessing of the state-controlled labor unions. Such actions endure because many Jordanians do not believe that their government is protecting their social and political rights, and because they see no other way of flagging down their ruling monarchy besides putting their literal bodies on the line within heavily policed public spaces.

It is easy to conclude that such contentious episodes "fail," insofar as not convincing the Hashemite regime to change its ways by completely reconfiguring the underlying structure of Jordan's economic institutions, political system, and foreign policy. But such expectations of success are unfair, because by that criterion virtually all protests against all types of governments fail. In Jordan, authoritarian rule-makers have upgraded their techniques of public management; their repressive touch, coalitional politics, and Western backing are more than enough to override popular resistance. Yet if the goal of the royal autocracy is to demobilize society into obeisance, then it has also faltered, because Jordanians are not buying that all is well. Activists, protesters, and critics are not unified. They are not revolutionary. But they are also not *quiet*, and their invectives show an inexhaustible capacity to scramble onward.

Conclusion

The throes of popular mobilization across Jordan show no signs of abating. As this chapter portrayed, the sources of protests, petitions, and other opposition under King Abdullah are not monolithic. They span all of society because economic problems, political restrictions, and foreign policy controversies have shaken public sensibilities for decades. Civil society has harbored considerable dissent, from the Islamist cradle of the Muslim Brotherhood to professional associations and other formally licensed organizations. Grassroots activism has taken its rightful place, generating hirak movements, youth networks, and tribal criticism. Both Palestinian-Jordanians and Transjordanians have participated in these tides of contentious politics; they may not always work together, but they share common grievances. What they yearn to achieve is what past generations of oppositionists advocated during their close calls with democracy: in the words of renowned journalist Lamis Andoni, a "new social contract" between the Hashemite state and its diverse society, one that redefines the boundaries of royal power and makes them feel like their voices *matter*.[73] Their ongoing work suggests that the rest of King Abdullah's tenure may make for a bumpy ride.

National politics in Jordan is dynamic, imbued by exciting unpredictability not ordinarily found in authoritarian countries praised by the West as bastions of stability. However, the opposite holds true with the economy, an enormously important aspect of everyday life. As this chapter discussed, material grievances have sullied the public mood for decades. The Hashemite Kingdom's financial travails are legion, and its government expends inordinate energy—not to mention foreign aid—merely keeping its sluggish economy afloat. Yet too many people still feel that for all their toils and demands, there are far too few opportunities to prosper. Explaining why Jordan's economy struggles so much to grow and develop, from its historical origins under British colonialism to its neoliberal transformation in the twenty-first century, is the next step in fully grasping how its state and society cohere.

7

The Little Economy That Stayed Little

What Explains Jordan's Economic Underdevelopment?

For decades, Western governments have stacked tributes upon Jordan for being the little kingdom that could—the faithful Arab ally whose valiant monarchy has backed the United States and its allies in their Middle East adventures while steering clear of extremism and revolution. Jordanians wish the same praise applied to their economy. The Hashemite Kingdom has a little economy that has stayed little. Indeed, Jordan's biggest foreign aid donors—like the United States, European Union, World Bank, and International Monetary Fund (IMF)—use a standard wordlist when describing it: fragile, battered, lethargic, stalled, and sclerotic.

These are depressing terms, but they are not wrong. For many Jordanian families, the most pressing issue is not how institutionally stable or politically progressive their country looks to outsiders, but rather their day-to-day livelihoods—how to get jobs, how to pay off debt or educational costs, how to secure food and housing. In every Arab Barometer poll since 2007, Jordanians have marked economic difficulty as the biggest national problem, well ahead of terrorism, corruption, and other challenges. A February 2024 survey by the US-based International Republican Institute (IRI) found that for 70 percent of Jordanian households, monthly incomes did not cover their basic needs.[1]

It did not have to be this way. Jordan's economy has historically oscillated between exuberant booms and wild busts. The last few decades have been mostly bust-worthy despite the implementation of neoliberal economic reforms, such as privatization and free trade, promising mass prosperity. Pressed too by regional misfortunes and environmental adversity, Jordan remains a middle-income country stricken with high unemployment, rising poverty, and deepening inequality. Meanwhile, royal technocrats preach to global audiences that the kingdom could one day become an Arab simulacrum of Sweden or Singapore—a high-tech wonderland of capitalist innovation and productive markets, if only it received more foreign aid. Most Jordanians would prefer instead the modest goal of sustainable and inclusive development; their economy will never be the world's richest or largest, but it can still improve everyone's living standards and provide fair opportunities for all.

In this way, Jordan provides an intriguing glimpse into how a small, resource-poor economy in the Global South hangs on to dear life. It is also a microcosm for the bigger puzzle for why so much of the Middle East and North Africa (MENA), at least outside the wealthy Gulf states, has economically underperformed relative to its potential.[2] These conundrums are not just theoretical, as economic privations routinely spur political unrest across the region; the Arab Spring is Exhibit A. In Jordan, as Chapters 5 and 6 discussed, problems like widespread joblessness and unaffordable food prices have likewise spurred swells of contentious opposition, from the 1989 rural riots to the 2011–2012 Jordanian Spring protests to the 2018 anti-tax strike. Indeed, the Jordanian street would be much quieter if the economy actually worked.

What explains Jordan's economic doldrums? Regional specialists have suggested a lengthy list of academic reasons why the Arab world has been mired in economic misery for several generations, such as colonial legacies, sectarian conflict, authoritarian corruption, costly wars, foreign interventions, and globalization.[3] These are fine theories, but this chapter takes a more fine-grained approach to tackle the unique case of Jordan. Its sorrows are rooted in more specific factors, among them the regional context, environmental burdens, and misguided authoritarian policies that privilege the authoritarian regime's political interests over long-term development.

To that end, the first section reviews major features of the Jordanian economy, including its small size, historical origins, limited wealth, and sectoral composition. It also explores the problems of high unemployment, stubborn poverty, and gendered inequality that have distressed many for decades. The second section investigates structural constraints on economic development, meaning harmful factors that the Jordanian state cannot control. One is the region: nearby conflicts and geopolitical shocks undermine the trading, investing, and producing that this economy needs to function. Another is the natural environment. Ecologically, an arid landscape lacking oil encumbers Jordan with water scarcity, energy shortages, and food imbalances. These make achieving prosperity harder, but not impossible.

The third section explores the political underbelly of economic underdevelopment. More than anything else, policy choices reflecting domestic political priorities have failed to enrich most Jordanians. Early decades of state-led growth following independence, in which the government took a significant role in building the economy, generated impressive gains. However, such modernization ended with the financial crisis of the late 1980s, resulting in neoliberal reforms that preached market-based capitalism. Though guided by Western donors, these new policies—which have influenced national economic decisions since the 1990s—have backfired.

The fourth section explains why. The one constant throughout Jordan's economic journey has been the constant prioritizing of political interests by the royal autocracy over all other concerns. As a result, four destructive patterns of policymaking have persisted during quarter-century tenure of King Abdullah: militaristic overspending, favoritism to business elites, public sector bloat, and dependency on external financing. Since the 2000s, these commitments have consumed massive resources, and only some benefit from them. The kicker is that Jordanians themselves have little way of changing course: this is, after all, an authoritarian state.

As the chapter concludes, the solution to this morass is not another package of IMF-endorsed reforms or Western aid. Neither is it returning to the past, restoring the state as the center of economic activity. Revamping the economy so that Jordanians themselves benefit requires completely rethinking how money, markets, and people should coexist here—and how, above all, autocratic policies can do more harm than good. The recipe for success may not be fully known, but this much is clear: the status quo is failing most people on the East Bank.

Jordan's Modern Economy

A few traits characterize Jordan's economy. First, it is small, even for the MENA. According to the World Bank, in 2024, Jordan's nominal gross domestic product (GDP), which measures total economic production and output, measured about $52.1 billion. Excluding those nearby states stricken by civil war, only Tunisia, Bahrain, and Palestine have smaller GDPs; the largest regional economies of Türkiye and Saudi Arabia surpass well over a trillion dollars each. Globally, this puts Jordan in the same neighborhood as countries like Uganda, Turkmenistan, and Bolivia. Such smallness only partly correlates with populational size: Finland, for instance, has half Jordan's population, but its GDP is six times as large.

Second, Jordan's economy is middle-income. This is a glorified way of describing a country with some auspicious businesses and monied elites, but most of whose people qualify as middle class or poor. Consider nominal GDP per capita, a rudimentary gauge of living standards. The kingdom's 2024 figure was roughly $4,600, which regionally fares better than large oil-poor countries like Morocco and Egypt, but well below rich oil-rentier Gulf states like Qatar and United Arab Emirates—the latter of which enjoys a nominal GDP per capita of over $50,000, about the same as Canada and Germany.[4] Globally, Jordan stands

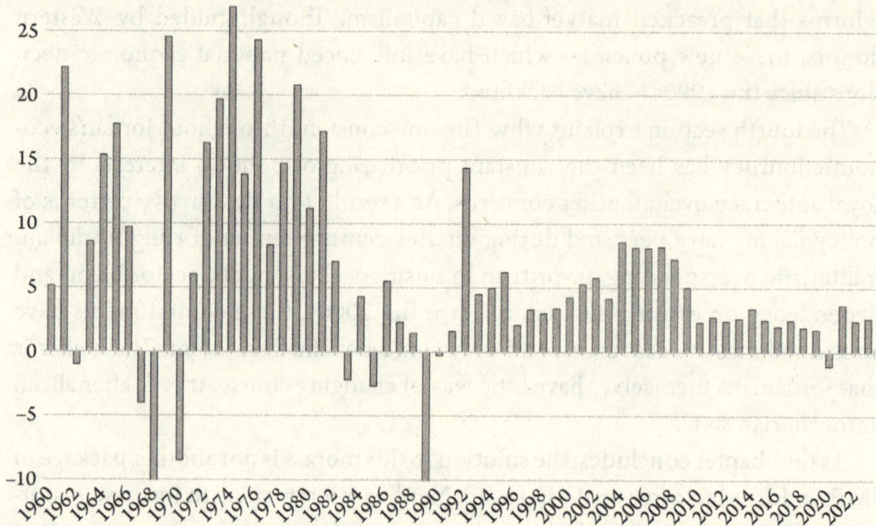

Figure 7.1 Economic Growth by GDP in Jordan, 1960–2023. Source: World Bank, *World Development Indicators* (IBRD, various years).

in the middle of the pack, matching the levels of other developing countries like Vietnam, Namibia, and Sri Lanka.

Third, the Jordanian economy has never grown consistently, oscillating for generations between booms and busts.[5] Figure 7.1 maps out eye-catching trends in GDP growth since 1960. The data show how the economy quickly expanded in the 1960s as state-led modernization strategies took hold, only to plummet due to the 1967 Arab-Israeli War and the 1970 Black September civil conflict. Blustery growth then returned, propelled by foreign aid, worker remittances, and public spending, but ended with the financial collapse of the late 1980s. Since then, the economy has plodded at a painfully slow clip. It has averaged 4 percent annual growth across King Abdullah's reign since 1999, but only 2.3 percent since the 2011–2012 Arab Spring. "Economic growth" is a loaded term, but it is nonetheless one that governments covet; an economy that grows briskly is more likely to create jobs, raise living standards, produce value, and overall make its populace content.

Fourth, the Jordanian economy is a hodgepodge of mostly light, modestly productive sectors. Table 7.1 compares five domestic sectors by their contributions to GDP for the past 60 years. For the most part, the economy has not drastically changed, with just one exception: agriculture. In 1965 (when Jordan controlled the Palestinian West Bank's fertile lands), farming activities generated 15.4 percent of GDP, but in 2022 they yielded just over 5 percent. Such a drop is not unexpected, given the rapid urbanization described in Chapter 2.

Table 7.1 **Key Sectors in Jordanian Economy by Percentage of Contribution to Nominal GDP, 1965–2022**

Year	*Agriculture*	*Heavy industry (manufacturing, mining, construction)*	*Hotels, restaurants, shops, (including tourism)*	*Finance (banking, insurance, real estate)*	*Government activity (including military)*
1965	15.4	18.5	13.8	26.9	12
1970	11.9	18.4	12.4	28.6	19.4
1975	7.9	22.9	12.5	22.2	20.3
1980	7.8	23.5	13.6	20.9	17.6
1985	5.5	22.8	12.3	21.3	18.6
1990	7.7	25	10	19.9	18.2
1995	4.3	26.5	10.1	20.6	18.8
2000	2.4	22.9	11.4	20.8	20.2
2005	3.1	26.2	10.5	21.9	17.9
2010	3.6	28.5	10.5	19.1	22.8
2015	4.4	26.7	12.1	20.5	22.5
2020	4.6	25.3	10.5	22.2	16.5
2022	5.1	26	13.7	21.6	16.1

Note: Figures in nominal (i.e., current) prices. The latest year available is 2022.

Source: Central Bank of Jordan, *Annual Statistical Bulletin* (CBJ, various years).

Among Jordan's most valuable agricultural products are export-ready fruits and vegetables.

Heavy industries have reliably composed a quarter of Jordan's GDP. They include construction, mining (mainly for potash and phosphates, perhaps Jordan's only abundant natural resources), and manufacturing. Manufacturing encompasses many types of products, such as cement, chemicals, fertilizer, garments, paper products, processed foods, and pharmaceuticals, the latter being the rare local industry that has become regionally competitive. These fields generate most exports to outside markets, the largest of which now are America, followed by China, India, and other Arab countries. Even so, those exports never offset Jordan's huge import bill, as the economy consumes far more of what the region and world provides than the other way around. Since the 1970s, Jordan has run large trade deficits, with the annual value of imports often measuring twice or more of all exports. These industries also do not create many Jordanian jobs. They are either highly mechanized and need more machines than workers or else—especially in the case of clothing factories and construction companies—employ low-cost foreign workers. For all these reasons, they do not stimulate much technological innovation.

Retail services such as shops, restaurants, and hotels have comprised 10 to 14 percent of GDP since 1965. This is a sprawling sector, as it should be: where people shop, eat, and congregate outside their homes drives much of this private commerce. This also includes the large tourism industry, given the popularity of Amman, Petra, Wadi Rum, Jerash, and the baptismal sites of the Jordan River to foreign visitors. Finance, which includes real estate, insurance, and banking, is another service engine. The businesses and families that dominate it are among Jordan's richest. Like heavy industries, though, it creates relatively few jobs; finance is capital-intensive, requiring more technical skills than raw labor.

Finally, the government itself has contributed around 15–20 percent of GDP since 1965 through its consumption and operation. This reflects the colossal resources expended by state institutions, from ministries and bureaucracies to the coercive apparatus (i.e., the military, police, and intelligence directorate). It also underscores the enormous number of Jordanians—today, nearly 40 percent of the salaried labor force—who work in the public sector, such as the civil service, public schools, municipal administrations, and utility companies.

Fairly, Jordan hardly has the only small, lightweight economy in the MENA. Many other Global South countries also face what experts call the "middle-income trap," in having sufficient industrial activity and functional markets to escape mass poverty, but not quite enough growth and innovation to reach the much higher living standards associated with wealthy, technologically advanced economies.[6] But, such intangible debates mean little for ordinary Jordanians, worried squarely about how to pursue lives free of constant financial worry.

This has political consequences. The economic abundance that the Hashemite regime promised when it began implementing neoliberal policies like privatization and other market-oriented reforms a generation ago has not materialized. Figure 7.2 compares responses from the Arab Barometer's Wave I (2007) and Wave VII (2021–2022) public surveys on two key questions and reveals a startling downward trend in how Jordanians see their economic future and opportunities. In 2007, there still existed some optimism, with over half of respondents seeing the economy as good or very good; by 2022, though, more than 85 percent saw Jordan's economic situation as bad or very bad. In 2007 as well, 37 percent of Jordanians believed the economy would improve in the next few years, but in 2022 more than half of respondents thought the reverse—that the national economy would become a little or much worse.

As Chapter 6 explored, economic grievances have driven much popular opposition throughout King Abdullah's reign. However, one does not have to observe street protests to see this, as the signs of material woes have permeated public culture. For instance, some youths pining to leave Jordan for opportunities elsewhere have resorted to ever-desperate measures, including hiring human traffickers to smuggle them into North America and Europe.[7] Few other topics incite as much satire, as well. In January 2011, as local protests sprouted in solidarity with the Arab Spring, well-known cartoonist Emad Hajjaj drew

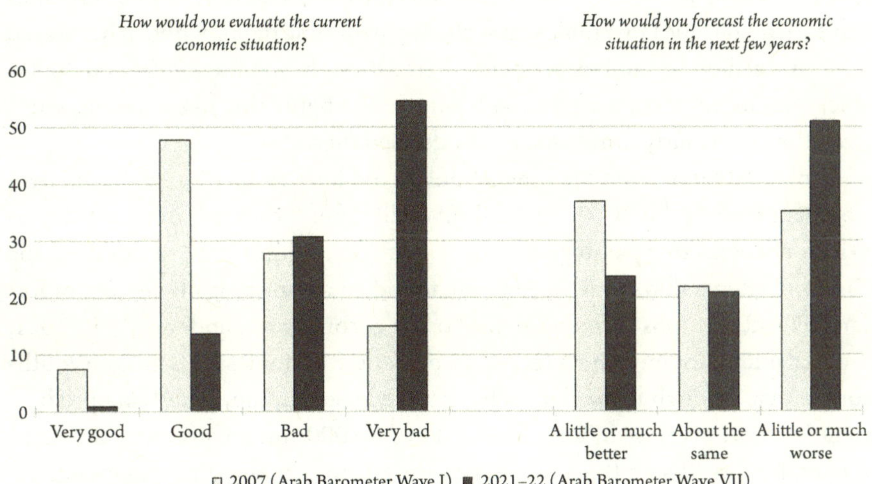

Figure 7.2 Public Perceptions of the Economy in Jordan, 2007–2022. The first cluster compares responses to the displayed question about the current economic situation between the Wave I (2007) and Wave VII (2021–2022) Arab Barometer surveys. The second cluster compares responses to the displayed question about the economic future between the Wave I (2007) and Wave VII (2021–2022) Arab Barometer surveys. Source: Arab Barometer, https://www.arabbarometer.org/.

a droll entry in his online *Abu Mahjoob* comic series.[8] The eponymous character, a hapless Jordanian man, stands by a petrol pump with an empty fuel canister and sadly utters that he too wished to light himself on fire, inspired by Mohamed Bouazizi's self-immolation in Tunisia that sparked the Arab Spring revolutions. The punchline: like so many other Jordanians, he had no money to buy gas.

More recently, in May 2023, Jordanian Muslims celebrating Ramadan were likewise stunned to see a local financial company advertise that they could secure platters of mansaf, the lamb-and-rice national dish, for their iftar feasts through special loans to be repaid in three-month installments. Such was the morose poverty of many families that now securing food for iftar—the holy evening meal of breaking the daytime fast, and often a festive occasion—would require indebtedness. Social media commentators were aghast at this "loans for lamb" deal, given that in Jordan unpaid debts are criminal offenses.[9] As local observers quipped, now it was no longer the mukhabarat but sheep that would imprison Jordanians.

Jobs, Poverty, Inequality, and Gender

Of all the problems that rankle Jordan's economy in the twenty-first century, unemployment ranks highest.[10] There are too few jobs for too many Jordanians. The last time that the kingdom enjoyed full employment (i.e., when virtually every citizen who wanted a job had one) was during the mid-1970s boom. Once that ended a decade later, joblessness shot up to double digits, where it has stayed since. According to the Department of Statistics, during the 1990s and 2000s, official unemployment averaged 14.5 percent—a figure that likely undercounts, given the notoriously unreliable methods used then.[11]

Neoliberal reforms under King Abdullah did little to ameliorate this. Unemployment rose in the 2010s and fell off a cliff after Covid-19, not least due to strict lockdowns that paralyzed economic activity. A June 2020 report from the Phenix Center, a think tank in Amman, found an astonishing 40 percent of Jordanians had lost jobs or income due to the coronavirus pandemic.[12] In 2021, national unemployment hit a record 25 percent, with joblessness among youths double that. Though these figures have since lessened, the underlying predicament has not: every year, around 65,000 to 70,000 Jordanians enter the labor market, but less than a third obtain full-time employment. This experience especially demoralizes many of the kingdom's young people, as Chapter 2 noted. Those envisaging a bright future know that transitioning into adulthood requires a financially secure job, without which marriage (especially for men) and independent housing are out of reach. For others, the grinding of daily survival can be overwhelming. When a poor street vendor in Irbid committed suicide in February 2020 after the police confiscated his food cart, his only means of earning money, Jordanians despaired that this was not an isolated incident.

Why is unemployment so high? Most obviously, a sluggish economy generates less demand for labor; jobs accompany growth. But other factors also matter in distorting the labor market, such as the lagging educational system.[13] Jordan's public schools and universities overproduce graduates in technical fields like engineering, which outstrip the number of job openings in those areas. This skills mismatch is dire: as of 2023, whereas Jordanians without a high school diploma have a 20 percent jobless rate, those with university degrees suffer 27 percent unemployment—among the highest such rates in the world.[14] In effect, there is an unemployment *penalty* for higher education. This creates ripple effects. Educated Jordanians eschew unskilled positions they see as unworthy of their credentials, such as those in construction and hospitality. Those local employers hire foreign laborers instead, who often endure more abusive conditions and lower pay. This helps explain why Jordan hosts nearly a million Arab and Asian expatriates, who are not refugees but instead economic migrants who fill low-wage jobs, from garment factories and farm fields to restaurant services and household work.

Moreover, those who do find employment experience unequal conditions. The vast public sector provides job security and good benefits—a strategic necessity since the majority of government employees are Transjordanian and satisfying their political interests constitutes a coalitional priority for the monarchy. However, much of the private sector involves informal work. Informal employment refers to unregulated labor not covered by laws on workplace safety, minimum wages, insurance, and pensions. The Jordan Strategy Forum, an Amman-based think tank, estimated in 2023 that 44 percent of all private sector jobs came from the informal sector.[15] This covers an enormous category. Examples include "under-the-table" jobs in lesser-skilled fields like agriculture, construction, and food services, which often prefer to hire non-Jordanians. It further includes Jordanian micro-enterprises that support entire families, such as street vendors, transportation drivers (including both taxicabs and rideshare services), and small shops. It also encompasses contract-based assignments (i.e., the "gig" economy)—such as those offered by private companies, social organizations, or even government institutions, which prefer to hire short-term workers cheaply rather than create more costly full-time positions. Such employment is better than none at all, but it is still unfair to many.

The second source of economic adversity is poverty. As of 2025, the official minimum wage is 290 Jordanian dinars (JD) (about $409) monthly, while the national poverty line—a floating figure based upon indirect government estimates and international donor calculations—hovers at JD 168 per person monthly. While the majority of Jordanians are not poor, impoverishment has nonetheless been rising. In 2022, the government conceded that 24 percent of the populace lived below the poverty line, a startling rise from the 13 percent rate seen in 2006; a less-forgiving World Bank report suggested the real poverty rate at 35 percent.[16] Depleted incomes have much to do with this. According to the government's Department of Statistics, in 2023 the average monthly income among jobholding Jordanians was just JD 543, barely twice the minimum wage, while 70 percent earned less than JD 500 (about $705) per month.

As a result, many families feel crushed by living costs, as low salaries depress their purchasing power. A 2019 IRI survey asked Jordanians what items constituted the heaviest burdens on their household budget; they were food (31 percent), electricity (22 percent), housing (13 percent), automobile fuel (13 percent), and education (10 percent).[17] This is not surprising. Food and energy prices have risen due to the high cost of imports as well as vanishing government subsidies, which in turn result from cutbacks in social spending under neoliberal economic policies since the 2000s. Likewise, unaffordable housing stems from outdated urban planning schemes, as high mortgage interest rates and profit-driven real estate developers often prefer building luxurious properties rather than modest homes that middle-class families can purchase or rent.[18] To stay afloat, many Jordanians withdraw private loans from local banks and informal lenders. But debt defaults run high, bringing threats of criminal prosecution and imprisonment to many. One Human Rights Watch report estimates that a quarter-million Jordanians face debt delinquency, and that 16 percent of the kingdom's total prison population is incarcerated due to nonpayment of loans.[19]

These pressures bring a third economic weakness: escalating inequality. Under King Abdullah, Jordan has become one of the most unequal countries in the MENA. According to the World Inequality Database, the top 10 percent of Jordanian income earners in 2022 claimed 48.4 percent of national wealth, leaving the bottom 50 percent with just 14.3 percent.[20] On social media and through public chatter, Jordanians fret that their economy has become cleaved between the suffering masses and an ultra-wealthy elite. Indeed, over the past two decades, many families considered middle class—with at least one educated parent having a salaried job—have been forced to shift their consumption patterns, such as buying less food or forgoing use of their car (if they have one). At the bottom of the economic hierarchy, refugees usually face the worst conditions. Many Iraqi and Syrian refugees who arrived here over the past two decades have experienced much gloom given their social isolation, housing shortages, and lack of work. The 2016 Jordan Compact, an international aid deal intended to integrate Syrians into the local economy, misfired due to shoddy implementation and inadequate monitoring, and most refugees as of the mid-2020s still live below the national poverty line.[21]

Such torpid differences do not just aggravate popular frustrations. They also deepen various forms of social inequality, like that of gender. Jordanian women already face lifelong hurdles such as legal prejudice, religious strictures, and political underrepresentation. There is more than meets the eye to this, of course. As anthropologists have shown, girls and women in the Hashemite Kingdom are hardly passive victims, and they fight back against patriarchy by subverting male domination and expressing their voices in creative ways.[22] Nonetheless, economic conditions weigh disproportionately on them: an economy that provides little mobility enables the worst social biases and marital pressures to deter women from entering the workforce, no matter how educated. In 2024, despite that more than half of all students at Jordan's three dozen universities are female, Jordan exhibited just a 14 percent female labor force participation rate (i.e., the proportion of women either seeking or having employment).[23] Across the world, only Afghanistan, Iraq, Yemen, and Syria—countries devastated by recent conflict—rank lower.

Unforgiving Environments

Why is successful economic development so ephemeral in Jordan, preventing it from "taking off" as in some other non-Western countries that became rich industrializers by global standards, like Taiwan or Singapore? Perhaps the easiest answer relates to the structural context. By no fault of its own, Jordan's regional surrounding and natural environment have constrained its economic growth. Nearby conflicts wreak detrimental fallout, while water scarcity, food imbalances, and energy deficits impose serious strains.

Conflict, Water, Food, and Energy

Jordan must constantly adjust to exogenous shocks given its regional milieu. Statistical studies show that every major nearby conflict since the 1948 Arab-Israeli War has distressed Jordan's macroeconomic health in some measurable way (e.g., by limiting trade, reducing tourism, and dampening investments).[24] Adjacent wars have also brought waves of refugees, whose accommodation unsettles the labor market, stresses infrastructure, and raises the cost of public goods like education. Whereas the Arab-Israeli wars displaced Palestinians onto the kingdom, the Iraq War and Syrian Civil War over the past two decades begot well over a million newer refugees. All these spillover effects can sideline the best-laid economic development plans. As one Jordanian economist joked, "Try building a house when all your neighbors are catching fire."[25]

Jordan is also susceptible to other regional crises, thanks to its close ties with other Arab countries. When the Middle East sneezes, the kingdom catches a cold. For example, as Chapter 8 explains, vital foreign aid from Gulf allies like Saudi Arabia can disappear if Jordan rejects their foreign policy demands or if oil prices tumble. Remittances open another window of external vulnerability. Today, 750,000 Jordanians live and work in the hydrocarbon-rich Gulf kingdoms, and the monies they remit back home prop up the economy. Remittances give domestic households additional money to save, spend, and invest; at a higher fiscal level, they provide foreign exchange earnings that extenuate the current account imbalance caused by the hefty trade deficit.[26] In 2023, Jordan recorded over $4.5 billion of remittances, equivalent to nearly 10 percent of the GDP. This ranked higher than all other MENA states save Lebanon and Palestine. Therefore, any geopolitical drama that cuts off the labor markets that employ Jordanian expatriates who send remittances wreaks havoc. Jordan experienced this with the 1990–1991 Gulf War, when the expulsion of Jordanian workers in the Gulf kingdoms—retribution for King Hussein's support for Iraq during the conflict—starved its already reeling economy of much needed capital.

Besides the regional context, the Jordanian economy also subsists within an unforgiving natural environment. Officials fondly pronounce that the Jordanian people are the kingdom's most valuable resource. That is a roundabout way of saying it has few other resources. Take, for example, water. In economic terms, water is a production factor whose cost rises under conditions of scarcity: limited water means that the government must subsidize it, industries cannot upgrade, and farms lose efficiency. That applies to Jordan, one of the world's most water-stressed countries. Most residents here never see more than a few inches of rainfall per year, and only about a dozen other countries receive less annual precipitation.[27] Just 2 percent of Jordan's parched land is arable, mostly near the fertile Jordan Valley. What freshwater exists comes mainly from the Jordan River basin, which stretches from the Sea of Galilee to the Dead Sea, and a dozen aquifers. However, climate change and overuse have pummeled their levels, making it impossible to find the 1.3 billion cubic meters of water that the Jordanian populace needs annually. The Jordan River and Dead Sea are shriveling, and most groundwater reserves will dry up within two decades. As Jordan's environmentalist movement has pointed out, rising temperatures are also desiccating the agricultural sector.[28] Signaling the fragility of its ecosystem, Jordan's own national flower, the black iris, became an endangered species in 2014.

In historical perspective, aridity has long shaped life on the East Bank. Well before the British arrival following World War I, the absence of arable land foreclosed large-scale agriculture. The tribal populace was therefore poor but egalitarian: unlike Egypt or Syria, no feudal class of landowning elites existed, as there was not much productive land worth accumulating. Transjordanian peasants often worked off communal plots, while more nomadic tribes—the Bedouin—practiced seasonal herding of camels, sheep, other animals. The situation changed in the 1950s, when an urbanizing population swollen with Palestinian refugees needed water at a mass, orderly scale. The United States and other donors helped build canals, pipelines, and storage tanks of the national water infrastructure, but the underlying problem was always absolute scarcity.

In 1987, authorities declared an emergency, claiming all water as state property and implementing strict rationing. Households suffered. After agriculture and industry drew their lion's share of the water grid, municipal taps supplying residents dried up. Many homes resorted to buying from private water tankers to fill their cisterns, now a ubiquitous sight across Jordan. Rural communities exercised more illicit coping strategies, such as drilling private wells or siphoning off public pipelines. Today, these toils continue. Between thirsty farms and factories, leaky pipes and theft, and needy communities, finding enough of this dwindling resource is difficult. The largest overland water project to date—the Disi Water Conveyance system, which began pumping from the Disi-Mudawarra aquifer underneath the Jordanian-Saudi border in 2014—has alleviated the problem for now, but this will not last forever.[29] Ambitious plans to build new desalination facilities on the Red Sea give hope, but like other short-term measures do not address the long-term dilemma of climate change.

A second juncture of ecology and constricted development lies in food. The farming sector cannot produce enough of it to feed Jordan. In the 1960s, ambitious irrigation and mechanization schemes like the US-funded East Ghor Canal sought to revolutionize agriculture. Even so, Jordan never attained food self-sufficiency. What little arable land existed was thrashed by overcultivation and overgrazing, and over time government investments went more to large-scale cultivation of water-needy produce like tomatoes for lucrative export, rather than to basic commodities like wheat for local consumption. Agribusinesses reaped massive profits from this policy at the expense of small farmers, which in turn contributed to the depopulation of rural areas in favor of urbanization. For several generations now, most of the cereals, sugar, oils, meats, and other basics of the Jordanian diet have been imported at considerable cost. In 2002, for instance, Jordan imported 2.31 million tons of food while exporting under 583,000; in 2022, it imported 5.29 million tons (worth one-fifth of its total imports) and exported about 818,000.[30]

This food deficit has economic ramifications. Beholden to fluctuations in global markets and trade disruptions, high food costs expose poorer households to nutritional insecurity. Covid-19 showed the wrenching side of this: in August 2020 at the height of the pandemic, a United Nations survey showed that less than half of all Jordanians were fully food secure, while 28 percent of children went to bed hungry.[31] Such privation also hits the refugees the hardest. Their presence increases the kingdom's total food needs, but they are least likely to obtain enough to eat.

An undernourished society is not only economically unproductive but also politically unsatisfied. The Hashemite regime recognized this early on, and in the mid-1970s authorized its now-defunct Ministry of Supply to control and subsidize the production of staple consumables such as wheat and sugar. As José Ciro Martínez has argued, the monarchy flaunted the availability of cheap bread as a sign of its strength and compassion.[32] However, the government has incrementally lifted those subsidies since the 1990s as part of the public spending cuts required by neoliberal economic reforms. Regular protests have resulted. A controversial decision in 2018 to replace the venerable bread subsidy with a US-designed targeted cash payment system did not inspire public confidence, given the decline of many households' purchasing power due to low incomes and rising inflation. In 2022, a rapid hike in imported food costs due to the Ukraine War forced the government to increase its subsidization of wheat flour so that bakeries could continue making affordable bread. Still, the relative cost of food has still increased over time. When the Arab Barometer fielded its Wave VII survey in 2021–2022, a jarring picture emerged: 47.9 percent of Jordanians reported that the food they had purchased over the past month did not last and that they lacked the money to buy more.

The natural environment also hinders economic development through Jordan's energy deficit. Jordan has less oil than water—and it has no water. It must import crude oil and natural gas to run its electricity plants, provide cooking fuel, and produce gasoline for automobiles; since 2000, fossil fuels have composed an average of 16 percent of its total imports.[33] The country does have huge reserves of shale oil (among the world's largest, in fact), but most efforts to commercialize these rocky deposits have failed. A Chinese-built shale energy plant opened in May 2023, but only after securing a multi-billion-dollar Chinese loan so onerous that electricity prices may need to rise just to break even. Otherwise, domestic energy production is slim. Some technocrats have dreamt of nuclear power as an alternative, but this brings its own geopolitical and environmental risks. The kingdom has no coastal access to the Mediterranean Sea, and so cannot siphon from its large offshore gas fields. Renewable energy, such as solar and wind farms, has scalable potential but need far more investment.[34] As of 2022, renewables supplied just 10 percent of domestic power usage.

This reliance on expensive energy imports has long-ranging effects. On the plus side, Jordan has dodged what political economist call the "oil curse" that befalls rentier states, in that the profundity of hydrocarbon wealth can sow excessive corruption and violence in many dictatorships.[35] In the negative side, oil-poor Jordan also had no financial shortcut to riches, unlike the flush oil-rentier countries like Saudi Arabia and the United Arab Emirates. It could never export "black gold" to generate rapid wealth or guarantee cradle-to-grave welfare to citizens. Local industries had no access to cheap energy either, which further reduced their productivity.

Domestically, energy costs also bring political repercussions. The Jordanian government has long subsidized electricity and petrol to make them affordable, but the slow withdrawal of those subsidies due to their unsustainable expense has instigated as much popular outcry as rising food prices. The April 1989 riots described in Chapter 5 and the November 2012 protests mentioned in Chapter 6 both stemmed from jagged increases in fuel costs. Geopolitically, as well, this energy shortage requires the royal autocracy to view regional affairs through an economic lens, as Chapter 8 outlines. The 2003 invasion of Iraq sent Jordan dashing to the Gulf to replace lost Iraqi oil with Kuwaiti and Emirati shipments. A cut-off in Egyptian natural gas in 2012 hastened a $10 billion gas deal with Israel in 2016, spurring stinging dissent from civil society.

Beyond Structural Constraints

Neither the Hashemite monarchy nor its people had much choice in choosing their regional neighborhood and natural environment. However, while immoveable forces constrain Jordan's economy, they do not entirely predetermine its fate.[36] Structure is not destiny. If it were, then Jordan would not have experienced clips of astonishing growth prior to the 1990s. Moreover, in comparative perspective, many countries have overcome equally daunting barriers. The absence of natural resources did not foreclose the wild industrializing success of South Korea and Taiwan. Botswana has earned plaudits for its surprising prosperity despite being lodged in conflict-prone southern Africa. Costa Rica has sustained robust development partly by reducing energy costs by switching entirely to renewable sources. As economists know well, the policies enacted by governments—that is, *agency*—matter as much as structure in shaping economic trajectories. This casts the spotlight onto the strategic choices made by the Jordanian leadership and underscores how policies that prioritize the maintenance of authoritarian rule seldom have the best economic interests of society at heart.

From State-Led Development to Neoliberal Dreams

The most important explanation for Jordan's economic distress is the state itself, and thus the royal autocracy that directs its policies. While Chapters 3 and 4 discussed the institutional features of Hashemite rule, a crucial point is that the historical consolidation of authoritarian governance involved not only *political* strategies—for instance, repressing opposition and rallying public support—but also economic interventions into society. Much like other "late-developing" states during the twentieth century, the Jordanian regime took a leading role in economic planning. It harnessed the state to create industries, employ workers, build infrastructure, protect markets, oversee trade, and fix prices. Such state-led development was not a uniquely Jordanian or Middle Eastern phenomenon; after World War II, it characterized many countries wishing to catch up with larger, more advanced Global North economies.[37] Only the guiding hands of government could compensate for the lack of capital, technology, and knowledge that stymied their preindustrial economies.

However, while state-led development helped modernize Jordan's economy, it also deposited a caustic legacy. It privileged the political interests of an authoritarian regime. Over time, those interests—expensive militarization, commercial favoritism, public sector overspending, and reliance on foreign aid—became too costly to sustain. Yet officials refused to discard them, even when implementing neoliberal economic policies starting in the 1990s, because they were considered integral for Hashemite rule. As promoted by the World Bank, the IMF, and Western governments, neoliberal principles hold that not the all-mighty state but market-based capitalism can rescue ailing economies by privatizing industries, encouraging free trade, and cutting public spending (i.e., austerity).[38] Free enterprise within the private sector rather than government-directed activity represents the engine of progress, though with a titanic tradeoff: the imperatives of profit relentlessly seek to reduce the costs of labor and minimize social protections. Thus, in the twenty-first century, Jordanians have received the worst of both worlds: they experienced the unforgiving excesses of market capitalism combined with obdurate government policies that prioritized autocratic survival over all else.

This section reviews how the Jordanian economy evolved along these lines, from its early promise to contemporary stagnation. It traces the growth and success of state-led development until the late 1980s financial meltdown, followed by the painful turn toward neoliberal reforms.

State-Led Development, 1940s–1980s

State interventionism in the Jordanian economy began as quickly as the emirate formed. Prior to the British Mandate, preindustrial life on the East Bank entailed subsistence-based farming and nomadic pastoralism among the tribes, as well as modest overland commerce led by a small merchant class.[39] After the 1920s, the colonial state expanded its infrastructural power through the Arab Legion, the precursor to today's Jordanian Armed Forces, and other institutions to incorporate these Transjordanian communities into its political order. Tariq Tell calls this economic transformation as "military Keynesianism," in how it imposed a new system of dependence centered on the Hashemite monarchy paying soldiers, distributing food, reorganizing farms, and providing social welfare.[40] Officials sought not to industrialize the East Bank or maximize agricultural productivity but to tether the livelihoods of local communities to the economic practices of burgeoning state institutions. This was part-and-parcel of the coalitional strategy that Chapter 4 discussed, which gave Hashemite rule a base of Transjordanian support. The military in the form of the Arab Legion stood at the heart of this strategy; led and financed by the British, it recruited loyal tribesmen to serve the palace, enforce order, and police the frontiers of this new country.

The same economic interventionism extended to another key social force, the merchant families. This storied group comprised transplanted traders from Palestine (mostly Nablus) and Syria, alongside local Transjordanian businesspersons. In this preindustrial period, this East Bank stratum dominated the small-scale commerce linking local villages and towns. Some of these families—like the Asfour, Tabba, Mu'asher, Abu Jabir, and Tuqan families—remain influential in Jordan today. As a whole, these clans adapted to Hashemite rule quickly during the 1920s and 1930s. Organizing their interests through the Amman Chamber of Commerce, the merchants worked with colonial authorities to secure favorable policy concessions to further elevate their profits.[41] Officials handed out merchandising agreements, tax loopholes, moneylending, land acquisitions, and trade licenses. In return, this business class backed Emir Abdullah and provided loans and resources to his administration whenever necessary.

Upon Jordan's independence after World War II, this nascent economy was growing but still underdeveloped. Though it had assembled political support from the populace by making crafty deals, the Hashemite leadership had paid scant attention to deeper economic problems, among them limited infrastructure, little industrialization, and public spending still reliant on British foreign aid. Even more challenges would crystallize with the 1948 Arab-Israeli War. Afterward, the staggering economy struggled to accommodate so many Palestinian refugees given Jordan's overall paucity of jobs, housing, services, and infrastructure. A 1955 World Bank mission estimated unemployment at nearly 20 percent (and reaching over 50 percent among Palestinian refugees).[42] At the same time, however, Palestinians introduced much-needed capital and skills into the economy. At the top were well-connected Palestinian merchants from the West Bank. They founded profitable new financial and commercial houses with the monarchy's blessing, and so joined the older East Bank merchant class as Jordan's premier business elites. Among them were storied families that still hold prestige (and fortunes) now, like the Masri, Nuqul, Shoman, and Sukhtian families. Down the class ladder, middle-class Palestinian entrepreneurs established smaller businesses such as printing presses, cigarette factories, and retail shops. Much as Palestinian activists invigorated civil society by leading new political parties, social movements, and cultural clubs, the Palestinian bourgeoisie breathed new life into a largely agrarian economy.

As Jordan's post-war economy gained its footing in the 1950s, the government accepted its charge of guiding its development. Royal officials inaugurated ambitious campaigns to reorganize the economy, and state-led development commenced under powerful planning institutions like the Jordan Development Board.[43] The public sector became the centerpiece of their strategies. Alongside the military, the civil service and bureaucratic officialdom expanded to soak up unemployment, particularly among Transjordanians. The government created and financed new industries, such as phosphate mining, potash production, cement, oil refining (for imported crude), electricity, and communications. The state-owned firms that operated these sectors yielded many jobs. Elsewhere, central planners invested in other companies to extend their top-down economic influence; by the 1970s, the Jordanian state either owned or partly owned most of Jordan's 100 biggest companies. In the private sector, Transjordanian and Palestinian merchants thrived as an oligarchic class. Friendly public policies like tax leniency, trade licenses, and import controls protected them from competition.[44] With royal encouragement, they also helped create Jordan's financial sector through new banks (e.g., Arab Bank, Bank of Jordan, and Ahli Bank) that remain large and profitable today. They coordinated frequently with royal officials and government ministers, ensuring that private capital and public investments flowed wherever the economy needed and the regime demanded.

Jordan's economy expanded rapidly, until the 1967 Arab-Israeli War and the 1970 Black September civil conflict. However, as Figure 7.1 depicted, overall growth rebounded from these costly interruptions in the early 1970s. Those years inaugurated a historic, feverish boom: the GDP grew by an annual average of 17 percent during 1972–1982, giving Jordan one of the world's fastest growing economies. Transjordanian and Palestinian business magnates amassed fortunes in merchandise trade, industrial supply, and credit markets; occasional disagreements with officials about currency rules or price controls were handled with behind-the-scenes negotiations, which preserved the influential status of this elite class.[45] Below them, the Palestinian middle-class majority found economic success, despite being politically voiceless given the anti-Palestinian backlash following Black September. In Amman and other urban areas, their small businesses and professional activities stimulated private commerce. Hundreds of thousands of Palestinian-Jordanians also emigrated to work in the soaring Gulf kingdoms, which generated valuable remittances for the economy.

Such state-guided development could be described as worker-friendly, albeit not in conventional terms. As Chapter 6 observes, the government controlled all major unions by the 1970s, foreclosing an organized labor movement. However, economic policies did favor generous economic redistribution customarily associated with worker interests, thanks to a vast but expensive public sector. During the 1970s, East Bank tribal sons found ready employment within the ever-enlarging payrolls of government ministries, national bureaucracies, the military and police, state-owned firms, and municipal administrations. By mid-decade, most Transjordanian men worked for the government in some capacity; that, plus the emigration of hundreds of thousands of Palestinian-Jordanian workers, resulted in national unemployment plummeting to a record-low 2 percent.[46] Essentially, the Hashemite Kingdom reached the rarified economic air of full employment. By then, some sectors, like construction and agriculture, were encouraged to hire migrant workers from other Arab countries, given their labor shortages.

In other areas, state interventionism ensured a rising tide of living standards for much of the populace. In particular, social policies conveyed generous welfarism. Within education, authorities rapidly enlarged public schooling and the university system, which not only reduced illiteracy but also churned out degree holders who could quickly transition into government-related work. To allay inflation, officials regularly raised public salaries and unveiled targeted benefits, like low-cost military housing and food cooperatives for government employees. Generous subsidies for bread, fuel, and other basic commodities kept living costs affordable, especially for Transjordanian households dependent on public salaries, which relied heavily on such economic provisions.

Economic Bust and Neoliberalism, 1990s–Present

Such roaring growth could not last forever. In the late 1980s, a tempest of factors triggered severe financial crisis.[47] Domestically, core manufacturing activities, such as fertilizers and potash, hit their industrial ceiling due to technological obsolescence. Smaller sectors like agriculture could not pick up the slack. Both were stymied by the Central Bank's insistence on high exchange rates, which advantaged the regime's merchant allies but depressed demand for Jordanian exports. In addition, a real estate bubble burst, and tourism leveled off.

Above all, the collapse of oil prices in 1983 threw the economy into a tailspin. So long as oil prices stayed high, the Gulf kingdoms led by Saudi Arabia could deliver to Jordan the over $1 billion in annual aid payments they had promised at the 1978 Arab League summit in Baghdad—a geopolitical reward for King Hussein's rejection of the Camp David Accords between Egypt and

Israel. Like manna from heaven, such outside financing allowed the Jordanian treasury to avoid serious arrears caused by politically driven overspending on public employment, social services, and the military.[48] It also enabled officials to keep domestic taxation—and especially income and property taxation—low, an important concession to its base of tribal communities and merchant elites. During 1980–1988, for instance, Jordan's budget deficit excluding foreign aid ran a whopping average of 44 percent; only Gulf aid payments plus public debt covered that gaping shortfall to sustain profligate government expenditures.[49] Moreover, strong oil prices had underwritten the Gulf kingdoms' own economic expansion, and with it allowed Palestinian-Jordanians to find steady work there. Their remittances not only boosted the incomes of many Jordanian households back home but also sustained the overall economy by supporting local banks and palliating the effects of extreme trade deficits.

When oil prices dipped and the Gulf economies crashed after the early 1980s, two things happened: Jordanians working there remitted less money, and generous foreign aid payments dwindled. Gone was the easy money that had financed Jordan's pyretic development, and with it came recession. By the late 1980s, joblessness had risen to nearly 20 percent, exposing a generation of Jordanian families accustomed to middle-class lifestyles to unexpected hardships.[50] The dam burst in 1989. Currency devaluation, double-digit inflation, capital flight, and crushing public debt—which had grown to double the GDP—forced the government to secure emergency loans from the World Bank and IMF. While these multilateral institutions helped rescue Jordan's finances, they also imposed acute austerity measures, such as reducing public spending by retracting consumer subsidies and other social welfare policies, as the initial condition for this bailout.

This had an immediate impact. Without government subsidies, fuel and food prices rose rapidly, instigating rural rioting in April 1989 and a smaller bout of rural unrest in August 1996. The forced return of nearly 300,000 mostly Palestinian-Jordanians from the Gulf after 1991 ramped up poverty and unemployment, as the freefalling economy could not absorb these returnees.[51] As the economic crisis deepened, royal authorities began the painful process of structural adjustment under neoliberalism—that is, moving the state-led economy toward more laissez-faire principles of market-oriented capitalism, in line with the Washington Consensus approach of the World Bank, IMF, and Western governments. King Hussein's mild democratic reforms discussed in Chapter 5, such as restoring parliamentary elections and relaxing repression, were intended to offset the pain of economic change. Yet the Jordanian public remained frustrated with worsening material conditions, their discontent animating the renaissance of political opposition and civil society during the 1990s.

After his 1999 ascent to power, King Abdullah enthusiastically embraced the idea that neoliberalism could salvage the Jordanian economy. A new cohort of young, Western-trained technocrats and royal ministers swiftly masterminded the momentous shift away from the old state-led paradigm of development, coordinating with Western officials as well as economists from the World Bank and IMF.[52] Among the most controversial of their measures was privatization. Easily overcoming parliamentary resistance, the government divested its ownership or stakes in many public firms spanning industries like phosphate mining, cement production, and telecommunications. By 2008, it had netted over $2.3 billion in proceeds from these sales. However, this sometimes resulted in steep job losses among Transjordanian communities that had long staffed these companies, because new corporate managers sought to maximize revenues by shedding redundant workers.[53] As part of their reform push, officials also sold off many public lands to private investors eager to build extravagant real estate and commercial projects using cheap labor. Such policies reflected the new mantras of capitalism and globalization that prevailed inside the Diwan and royal committees: if only Jordanians could all become pioneering entrepreneurs and business owners overnight, then the kingdom could become a veritable twenty-first-century tale of how free markets could flourish, even in the heart of the Middle East.

Elsewhere, the regime pruned public spending in the name of fiscal austerity, such as slowing civil service hiring and reducing social services. To raise domestic revenues for the pinched treasury, authorities also introduced a general sales tax (GST) in 1994, while floating plans to increase income and business taxes in the future. After the 2008–2009 global financial crisis, they also quickened the phaseout of public subsidies for electricity, fuel, and bread, despite that this would raise living costs.[54] Finally, royal planners adopted free trade policies, starting with pegging the Jordanian dinar to the US dollar in 1995 and then with incrementally cutting import tariffs. In 2000, under King Abdullah's direction, Jordan joined the World Trade Organization and signed a free trade agreement with United States. In 2003, the World Economic Forum began holding star-studded international conferences on global affairs on the Jordanian side of the Dead Sea, signifying the kingdom's sudden and dazzling rise as a pro-Western darling of neoliberal dogma.

Wither Neoliberalism?

From a distance, Jordan followed the neoliberal playbook with aplomb. In the mid-2000s, the World Bank and IMF declared Jordan as a model reformer, praising King Abdullah's commitment to privatization, free trade, and fiscal austerity.[55] Alongside United States, these multilateral institutions helped guide this process, often working directly within government ministries and public institutions so that Jordanian bureaucrats and administrators understood precisely how to execute their recommended reforms.

Decades later, these changes have not fashioned sustainable and inclusive development. As Figure 7.1 depicted, except for a growth spurt in the mid-2000s ending with the global financial crisis, the Jordanian economy never launched into stratospheric heights. Problems of unemployment, poverty, and inequality forced citizens to find new coping strategies. As Anne Marie Baylouny discovered, for instance, many Jordanians responded to neoliberal dislocation by establishing new mutual aid associations and local charities, whose services filled the gap left by the retreating state.[56] Many others turned to protest and opposition, including some tribal communities. Most Transjordanians have not deserted their authoritarian regime, as Chapter 4 discussed. However, those who dissent see privatization, the withdrawal of subsidies, and other market-oriented shifts as a betrayal of the social contract that previously bartered tribal loyalty to the state for economic protection. They accuse King Abdullah's regime of prioritizing profitable investments and trade deals that benefit only a wealthy elite, not furnishing social welfare or secure job opportunities.

As the optimism of the 2000s faded, Western donors and the IMF began describing the Jordanian economy as experiencing "market failure." Many studies pinpoint the technical reasons for this and why the economy never became a capitalist powerhouse as dreamt by neoliberal visionaries.[57] They point out, for instance, that despite being exposed to greater market-based competition, Jordan failed to create sophisticated new industries, improve its labor productivity, and construct advanced infrastructure. The private sector did grow, but was still filled with too many inefficient businesses, while new wealth that did accumulate in narrow fields like finance and banking never trickled down to the masses. The few exports that swelled in the 2000s thanks to free trade, such as ready-made garments for American firms like Gap and Victoria's Secret, centered on low-skill work rather than high-tech innovation that could uplift other economic areas by sparking more integrated value chains. In essence, Jordan experienced what many countries in the Global South underwent upon implementing neoliberal economic reforms: not instant affluence but a jarring, painful transition.

Despite these shortcomings, Western donors continue to push the neoliberal creed, believing that just a few more policy tweaks can push the Jordanian economy over the hump. The World Bank and IMF have become even more involved in Jordan's economic decisions since the 2000s. Every periodic IMF loan over the past two decades has mandated increasingly aggressive reforms, such as deeper public spending cuts and higher tax rates. Meanwhile, the World Bank's presence in Jordan has diversified. While its lending arm still provides financial loans to the government, its investment arm has directly funded technical projects—such as entrepreneurship incubators and infrastructural schemes—in hopes of stimulating the economy.

Jordanian officials have also doubled down on neoliberalism. Much like their empty pledges of democracy, royal committees regularly issue national development strategies that incorporate ultra-modern economic jargon but whose optimistic goals are the stuff of fantasy. In 2015, for example, the government launched a national growth framework called Vision 2025, which vowed to revamp the private sector so that it could sustain a "dynamic and competitive economy" driven by digital entrepreneurship practiced by every citizen.[58] It quietly shelved that tone-deaf rhetoric—with the insinuation that Jordanians could escape their financial funk only if they all became Silicon Valley gurus—within years. The latest grand strategy was the Economic Modernization Vision, rolled out in 2022 to much fanfare given its pledge to revolutionize the country through foreign investment and green technologies. Unsurprisingly, most Jordanians have learned to ignore such proposals, which do more to divulge the reveries of Western donors and Jordanian technocrats than to reduce unemployment or jump-start growth.

Jordan's arduous experiences over the past few decades offer two lessons. First, neoliberalism is no panacea for countries that suffer economic difficulty. In comparative perspective, transforming state-based economies is a risky endeavor requiring slow and costly adjustments. For every so-called success story of market-based turnarounds of previously state-led economies, like Chile and Malaysia, there exist countervailing horror stories from the rest of the Global South, where capitalist policies brought modest growth but at the cost of higher poverty, corruption, inflation, and other ills.[59] It should not be surprising, therefore, that Jordan is no exception to this pattern, and that its transition toward market-based capitalism has been bumpy.

Second, agency matters. Regardless of neoliberalism's inherent limitations, the Jordanian regime's own political impulses have limited what economic development *could* come from chasing market-based capitalism. Policies birthed in the older era of state-led planning—such as using government jobs to reduce unemployment—made sense when the population was smaller and economic conditions were poorer. Now, however, these commitments have become corrosive, draining Jordan's financial and human resources at a time when the flailing economy can least afford it.

The Sabotaging Effects of Authoritarian Priorities

Neoliberalism has been an enormous gamble in Jordan, one that many citizens are not winning. However, the regime of King Abdullah has not helped by retaining obsolete policies that sabotage what growth and development could be realized in the new market-based economy. Four such policies—military overspending, commercial favoritism, public sector bloat, and external financial dependency—warrant closer attention. These commitments not only clash with what neoliberalism supposedly entails in terms of downsizing the state in the name of private enterprise, but they also prolong dangerous authoritarian habits that crowd out the economic opportunities made available to society.

Militarism Redux

Given its small economy, the Hashemite regime still spends far too much on its coercive apparatus (i.e., its armed forces, civil policing, and intelligence directorate). While Chapter 4 elucidates the finer details of why coercion has always defined Jordanian authoritarianism, two relevant facts brandish relevance here. First, since the 1960s, more than 40 percent of all government spending has flowed toward these organs of repression, an indefensibly high rate that starves public resources needed to improve infrastructure and furnish social goods that facilitate inclusive development. Second, over 220,000 Jordanians—nearly a fifth of all formally employed male citizens—still work in these institutions. The coercive apparatus deprives the economy of both financial and human capital.

Curiously, such coercive spending should have slimmed once authorities began implementing neoliberal reforms during the 1990s, since fiscal austerity requires reducing all public expenditures. However, the opposite happened. Far from diminishing, military and security spending rose from 32.7 percent of the state budget in 1995 to over 48 percent in 2010. Western donors like the World Bank and IMF knowingly looked the other way as this happened, due to higher geopolitical interests: Jordan became a peace partner of Israel in 1994 and served as a strategic ally of the American war-making machine after the 9/11 terrorist attacks.[60] Convinced that curbing the coercive apparatus could destabilize this hardy pro-Western oasis of moderation, they allowed this destructive autocratic habit to persist.

Commercial Favoritism

Within the small private sector charged with leading Jordan's capitalist transformation, regime politicking has misshapen economic outcomes. Theoretically, neoliberalism favors private business: with less regulation and more competition, creative profit-driven actors have freedom to make goods, sell services, and transact contracts that produce value. In practice, though, such fetishizing of free markets paradoxically requires careful government guidance, especially after a half-century of state-led development.

The plight of small businesses illustrates this. Jordanian officials were slow in updating the bureaucratic rules and laws regulating private commerce in the 2000s, despite their public rhetoric championing the private sector as the kingdom's new motor of growth. As privatization renovated creaky state-run firms during the 2000s, small business entrepreneurs discovered that they still needed political connections (or *wasta*, as Chapter 3 mentioned) to grease the wheels of even basic tasks, such as obtaining construction permits, registering their company, and accessing loans and credit.[61] While new government programs have arisen since the 2010s to nurture more entrepreneurship, the system as a whole does not reward risk-taking. Given that most of Jordan's full-time jobs in the private sector come from medium-sized and small firms employing fifty or fewer workers, such inflexibility has ratcheted up unemployment while discouraging start-ups, especially among youths.

Yet, Jordan does have considerable wealth within the private sector. It is just concentrated in the hands of a small elite favored by the monarchy—magnates and millionaires whose record profits have not filtered downstream to the rest of the economy. After the 1990s, the kingdom's traditional band of rich merchant and trading families adapted to neoliberal reforms. Some lobbied royal authorities to protect their businesses, while others diversified their corporate empires or took on foreign investors to expand.[62] They hence largely kept their wealth; the rich got richer. For instance, their banks and commercial houses maintained an oligarchical grip over the financial sector, in return for favors like providing loans and investments to the government whenever necessary. In this context, it is easy to see why many of Jordan's premier business captains retain a central place within the Hashemite regime's ruling coalition: the prospect of radical political change through democratization carries little appeal when compared with the material benefits gained from their ongoing partnership with the prevailing autocratic state.[63]

This logic of dependency applies to newer industrial elites in Jordan. In the 2000s, the monarchy cultivated a younger echelon of investors, financiers, and traders. This nouveau elite included a new generation of Palestinian and Transjordanian capitalists eager to exploit financial deregulation and liberalized investment rules to carve out space for their commerce. As with the older merchant stratum, rent-seeking prevailed as they worked with officials to coordinate investment and business deals, who in turn facilitated their success—and sometimes pocketed handsome kickbacks in return.[64] The royal calculation was simple: it was better to have wealthy elites in its pocket than risk them amassing fortunes independent of royal patronage. Among the richest tycoons from this class, for instance, is Ziyad Manasir, who leveraged Russian energy ties to establish one of Jordan's largest industrial conglomerates, including over 100 gas stations now dotting major roads.

Such crony capitalism has inevitably unleashed corruption. In comparative perspective, crony capitalism occurs whenever political regimes manipulate economic reforms to unfairly advantage business allies.[65] Of course, cozy ties between rulers and the rich have always existed in Jordan; merchant industrialists could not have otherwise thrived in the past era of state-led development. Neoliberalism, however, produced more systemic corruption. The huge amounts of money exchanged between politicians, businesspersons, and intermediaries through privatization sales, investment deals, real estate contracts, and trade arrangements gave rise to new practices of bribery, graft, and embezzlement. For instance, officials deliberately slowed the privatization of some state-owned firms in the 2000s in order to find the most attractive, and likely bribe-laden, deals with handpicked investors.[66] Many commercial megaprojects have been likewise plagued with corruption scandals. Consider the Casinogate affair from the early 2000s, a failed scheme to build a touristic casino complex on the Dead Sea that involved huge kickbacks to government ministers. It is easy to see why complaints of corruption prod public anger, as Chapter 6 explained. Too many Jordanians believe their politicians have enriched themselves in shadowy cahoots with faceless investors, while ordinary people struggle to afford housing.

Public Sector Bloat

Under state-led development, the public sector exemplified the tight relationship between political interests and economic planning in Jordan. Until the 1990s, the Hashemite regime directed the incessant expansion of government payrolls in order to intertwine the livelihoods of its Transjordanian supporters with its own survival. In other words, political interests fueled the public sector. This authoritarian social contract also solidified the ethnocratic division of economic labor that still shapes how many Jordanians see their political order: whereas Transjordanians are expected to work for the state as clerks, bureaucrats, and soldiers, Palestinians have little proximity to power and so toil away in the commercial economy.[67] For generations, this sheltered tribal communities from poverty, while ample social services like universal education were designed to turn them into a well-credentialed workforce for the public sector. However, this arrangement also engendered an oversized administrative system in which state-owned firms, the civil service, and public institutions became shot through with redundancy, inefficiency, and clientelism. Such a system was extremely costly, as well. From the 1960s onward, after military and security spending, the majority of all public expenditures went toward the salaries, benefits, and pensions of the mostly Transjordanian government workforce.

Despite the neoliberal adjustments initiated in the 1990s, the Jordanian regime only lightly trimmed this public sector. Its most aggressive measure came through privatizing state-owned companies. In 2001, it also cut the number of municipal administrations from 328 to 94, narrowing a common source of public jobs at the local level. More salient, however, is what the palace did *not* order: slashing civil service payrolls altogether and drastically shrinking the physical size of government ministries and national bureaucracies to streamline its operation. Much like its refusal to downsize its coercive apparatus, the royal autocracy did not risk inciting even more wrath from Transjordanians who, atop rising fuel and food prices, might treat early retirement from their bureaucratic sinecures as a hostile act.[68] Despite mild reforms, neither did it restructure hiring practices to fully eliminate nepotism, in which personal connections and favoritism determined the allocation of government-related jobs to eager applicants.

Such political forbearance has severe implications. First, the overcrowded public sector continues to devour financial resources that could be spent on other economic initiatives—for instance, building a national public transit system to provide affordable travel between homes and workplaces or comprehensive programming to reduce gender inequality and incentivize equal pay for women. While Jordan does spend less on its public sector than before, it is still large, even within the MENA. The percent of government spending earmarked for compensation to public sector employees only modestly fell from nearly 60 percent in 1990 to just over 44 percent in 2024.[69] Among other Middle East countries, only Iraq and Saudi Arabia have higher ratios. When added to the coercive apparatus, a sobering fiscal picture emerges: for all its talk of austerity, the Jordanian state still allocates roughly three-quarters of its public budget to the military and security institutions plus the salaries and pensions of government staff. Moreover, the share of the formally employed labor force working in the public sector has not budged much in the twenty-first century, slightly dropping from an average of 42 percent during the 2000s to about 37 percent in 2024.[70] As of 2024, nearly 589,000 Jordanians—the majority of whom are Transjordanian—receive a government salary, out of over 1.5 million total employed citizens.

Second, this public sector distorts the labor market. Government-related jobs, such as in the civil service, often carry an aura of prestige for many educated Jordanians because they offer lifelong salaries, workplace insurance, and guaranteed pensions. In a vacuum, such economic security seems laudable, providing benefits and protection that neoliberalism sacrifices on the altar of profitability. The problem is that the Jordanian state has sought to have it both ways: it chides citizens for not entering the private sector to seek jobs, while preserving a public sector that lures those job-seekers away from the private sector in the first place. This aggravates unemployment, because many university graduates are willing to stay jobless until they can land a government-related position rather than venture into the very private sector that Western donors and Jordanian technocrats proclaim will save them.[71] It is a long wait indeed, measured in decades for some. In 2021, the Civil Service Bureau divulged that 388,000 qualified applicants awaited placement for a government position, but that it could offer just 7,000 new jobs annually.[72] This massive mismatch between supply and demand intensifies political dissatisfaction, especially among Transjordanians raised on the principle that public employment was their birthright.

Finally, the political mandate of preserving the public sector has aggravated shaky budgetary practices. Market-based reforms did not erode the Jordanian regime's tendency to spend—or rather, overspend—its scarce financial resources. This has produced a vicious circle of fiscal unsustainability and made the country even more dependent on external financing.

External Financial Dependency

While Jordan's fiscal health has been unsteady since its colonial days, the twenty-first century has aggravated its worsening imbalance. To bankroll crushing financial obligations, most developing states have three choices: extract more domestic revenues through taxes, take on debt, or secure outside financing like foreign aid. The Hashemite regime has repeatedly demurred on the first option. Under state-led development, it calculated that imposing higher income and business taxation would risk political backlash from its coalitional base of tribal communities and merchant elites: no taxation without representation, indeed. Neoliberal restructuring marginally changed this. Officials relented to donor pressures by implementing indirect taxes, as in the 1994 GST, but only slowly increased direct income and business taxes over time. When they finally proposed more stringent tax laws in 2018 at the IMF's behest, national strikes and livid protests erupted. While they eventually ratified those taxes months later once public fury had lessened, that polemical event signified the political costs of raising more domestic revenues. Indeed, Jordan's income taxation system remains so spindly today that evasion is rampant, driven by widespread mistrust and matter-of-fact refusals to pay which officials are unwilling or unable to halt. For every Jordanian dinar collected as income tax, more than one other is missing.[73]

Jordan's second option is amassing debt. Most governments take out loans by issuing public bonds and other debt instruments, which raise temporary funds. Yet when repaying those debts saps the treasury, the potential for default results, which can result in financial catastrophe. In 1989, Jordan escaped this fate thanks to a World Bank and IMF bailout. However, since then, the government has become heavily indebted once more. Since 2015, Jordan's national debt has nearly equaled the entire GDP, and repaying the interest or principal for these loans requires 10 to 20 percent of public spending in any given year.[74] Combined with military and public sector expenditures, this leaves only a paltry slice of the national budget that could be spent boosting the economy directly, such as unemployment assistance, job training programs, targeted stimulus packages, and small business credit.

The third option has become Jordan's favored resort: external financing. As Chapter 8 lays out, foreign aid has long swayed the Hashemite monarchy's outlook on the world. Its foreign policy aims to maximize alliances with key donors, from Western powers like the United States to regional allies like Saudi Arabia, whose economic assistance helps underwrite its domestic expenditures. A second source of outside capital is remittances from Jordanians working abroad. For political economists, this dual dependency on aid and remittances makes Jordan a "semi-rentier" state.[75] Partially resembling true oil-rentier states like the Gulf kingdoms, which rely on revenues from hydrocarbon exports, the easy availability of foreign income for Jordan obviates pressures to extract more domestic taxes and encourages reckless overspending.

Figure 7.3 illustrates the depth of external financing over the past half-century. The total value of Jordan's economic aid plus remittance inflows has equaled large parts of its GDP since 1973. This ratio peaked during the boom that ensued; in 1980, for instance, aid and remittances equalled over 60 percent of Jordan's GDP. However, this dependency on outside funding has persisted even during the neoliberal reign of King Abdullah—and has outpaced the rest of the MENA (excluding Israel and the oil-rentier Gulf kingdoms, whose economies rely on neither foreign aid nor worker remittances). In 2021, for example, foreign aid and remittances represented over 18 percent of Jordan's GDP. This seems like an ample drop from the 1970s but was still more than double the regional average of 8.3 percent.

As these data show, the Hashemite regime's financial capabilities—and with it, the overall state of the economy—precariously turn upon external flows of money. To an ordinary citizen, such tradeoffs may seem immaterial: foreign aid transfers or IMF loan agreements do not have an immediate impact on whether they land a coveted job or if they can secure an affordable home. However, they have a gargantuan influence over the wider economy, because fiscal mismanagement from above dictates what public resources are left for the rest of society.

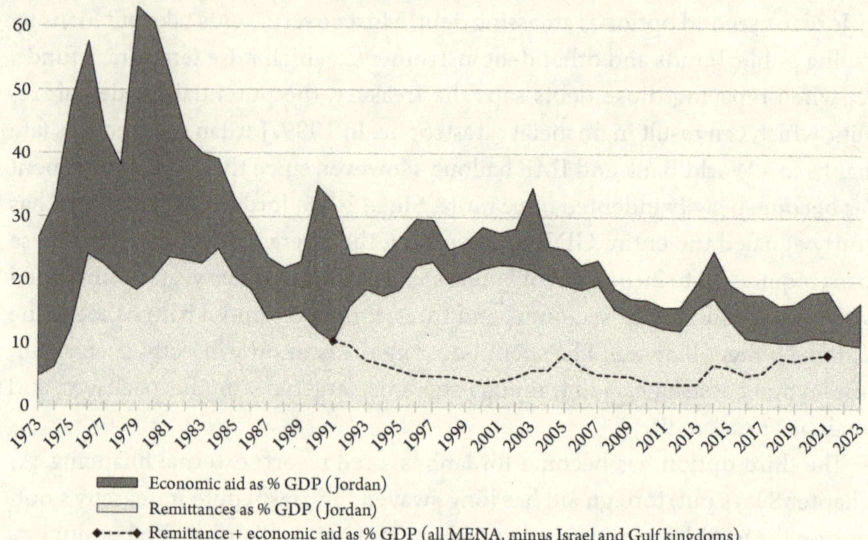

Figure 7.3 External Financial Dependency in Jordan versus MENA, 1973–2023. Collective figures for aid and remittances to the MENA (dashed line) are incomplete; all available data are shown. Sources: Central Bank of Jordan, *Annual Statistical Bulletin* (CBJ, various years); and World Bank, *World Development Indicators* (IBRD, various years).

The Jordanian state overspends on inefficient items for the obvious reason that it *can*—and if economic disaster strikes, then surely Western donors will intervene to save it. Such thinking resonates with how this autocracy prioritizes other interests, such as business cronyism. Shielded from the consequences of their political choices, royal authorities have learned to kick the putative bucket of responsibility down the road, even if this means weathering another inevitable swell of popular protest and democratic opposition.

Conclusion

Economics is a dismal science only when those who dictate its rules make bleak choices that leave most people worse off. Jordan encapsulates this lesson. As this chapter divulged, its economy labors under notable constraints. It is small, does not grow consistently, and has few dynamic industries. The abject challenges that have confronted Jordanians during King Abdullah's quarter-century reign include high unemployment, substantial poverty, and rising inequality. Part of the problem stems from regional and environmental limitations, which manifest through geopolitical conflicts, water shortages, energy costs, and food imbalances. All of these impose considerable costs and make inclusive, sustainable development more elusive.

Beyond these exogenous factors, though, the trials of the Jordanian economy are also political in nature. The country once experienced impressive growth and modernization, especially during the postcolonial decades when the authoritarian state oversaw national development by organizing economic life and regulating industrial output. However, this state-led strategy also hinged upon the political interests of the Hashemite monarchy. Those self-destructive commitments—overspending on the military and security, patronizing a narrow business elite, maintaining a large public sector, and relying on external financing—survived the dramatic shift toward neoliberal economics following the late-1980s financial crisis. Under King Abdullah, not only has market-based capitalism exposed the populace to the vicissitudes of privatization, subsidy cuts, deregulation, and other risky policies, but the Jordanian state is still constrained by the same autocratic imperatives that guzzled its financial and human resources from earlier decades. The result is an economic riddle imprinted with political blame. The recipe to revitalize this moribund economy is still a work in progress. Nonetheless, this much is clear: the status quo is not sustainable, and the Jordanian leadership must rethink its own directives, such as spending less on coercion, supporting businesses beyond the wealthiest elites, and rethinking the logic of government employment.

The outside world will have much to do with such a turnaround. Jordan's biggest allies, particularly the United States, provide massive flows of foreign aid and security assistance that have become inextricably intertwined with how the Hashemite regime functions. More broadly, the royal autocracy's pursuit of security and stability runs through its foreign policy. Thorny external dilemmas like inter-Arab rivalries and the Israeli-Palestinian conflict have consumed the attention of Jordanian leaders as much as domestic governance and economic policies. Like most aspects of national decision-making, Jordanians have little voice in these external relations. But they must still bear the brunt of it.

8

Foreign Policy in a Small State and Rowdy Region

How Does Jordan Engage the World?

A classic metaphor in political science holds that modern states are "Janus-faced." They not only govern their societies, but also interact with an international system filled with like-minded governments thirsting for prestige and power. How they navigate this external realm is foreign policy. Here, Jordan offers insights no less incisive than its domestic politics. For such a diminutive state, its foreign relations have traversed mountains of challenges in the Middle East: wars, peace, alliances, rivalries, bargains, and the lure of Western hegemony.

Playing on geopolitical tropes, Jordanian officials describe their foreign policy as the embodiment of moderation (in Arabic, *'itidaal*). The kingdom is the "calm eye of the infernal storm," as one former ambassador preached: despite being surrounded by treacherous crises, it steadfastly rejects extremism and endorses peace through diplomacy.[1] Jordan, according to this view, is a linchpin of Middle East stability, the consummately temperate country whose collapse would be calamitous for the region. Such arguments are half right. A Jordan that implodes due to, say, civil war or economic breakdown would indeed make neighbors like Israel, Syria, and Iraq worse off. Yet the chances of this happening are remote, given how much economic aid and military assistance that the United States and its allies give to ensure the country holds together.

By contrast, like all platitudes, proclamations that Jordan's foreign relations are moderate are deceiving. This royal autocracy maintains cordial ties with most other countries and global organizations; it has not fought a major war in a half-century, and it prefers resolving nearby conflicts through compromise rather than violence. But then, the same thing could be said for virtually all small states lacking economic affluence and military power—which is to say, *most of the world*. Most countries reject terrorism, avoid wars, and embrace diplomacy. To suggest these are Jordan's hallmarks misses the trees for the forest, ignoring the intricate opportunities and austere tradeoffs its leadership weighs in dealing with a rowdy region and bigger world. As with all things in the Hashemite Kingdom, there is far more than meets the eye.

This chapter explores this rich topic, beginning with the premise that foreign policy is a matter of choice. It entails how sovereign governments make friends, confront foes, and negotiate complex dilemmas to fulfill their interests. In Jordan, the singular interest that matters over all else is regime security, meaning whether the ruling monarchy feels relatively safe from any threat that could undermine its grip on power. Some perceived perils are external, as in regional belligerents and revolutionary ideologies; others are domestic, as in public opposition incensed by the floundering economy. Foreign policy choices thus pivot against these dangers, from making canny alliances in the Middle East to crafting brassbound ties with the United States. The girding principle is not moderation so much as pragmatism.

This chapter unfurls this framework in four sections. It does not record the historical chronicles of Jordanian diplomacy, which fill many bookshelves (and they do, within the internal libraries of the Ministry of Foreign Affairs and its Institute of Diplomacy). Rather, it descriptively captures how foreign relations are made and why certain decisions are done. First, it identifies the royal structure of foreign policymaking in Jordan. It also assesses how the monarchy uses external strategies to protect its regime security from three types of threats: foreign aggression, domestic opposition, and ideational challenges.

Second, it reviews Jordanian foreign policy stances in the Middle East and North Africa (MENA) region. Rather than blindly adhering to any single position, the monarchy has practiced naked flexibility when dealing with other countries, realigning alongside whatever state or alliance best reduces the most immediate threat to regime security. Jordan has no eternal friends in this region—only constant calculations about which side offers the most benefits by striking closer relations. Third, it dissects Jordan's biggest foreign policy challenge, that of the Israeli-Palestinian nexus. More than any other issue, this conflict dominates the external outlook of this authoritarian state and has proven the most resistant in resolving. The Hashemite leadership and the Jordanian people alike are wary of this problem. Under King Abdullah, Jordan's keen advocacy for a two-state solution, which calls for a viable and independent Palestinian state that coexists with Israel, has had little effect. Instead, fears of Israel annexing the West Bank and displacing more Palestinians onto Jordan have become rampant, creating more bitterness over the 1994 peace treaty with Israel.

The last section unpacks the US-Jordanian special relationship, a vital but misunderstood pillar of the kingdom's foreign policy. Though Jordan has many allies, America is its great power patron par excellence. It has sustained Hashemite rule for generations through not just diplomatic support but also economic and military assistance—in fact, over $30 billion worth since 1957, making Jordan the second-largest recipient of US aid in the Middle East after Israel. This also accounts for how the monarchy has earned its reputation as a stalwart pro-Western regime, having defended US-led wars, interventions, and counterterrorism across the region despite such actions estranging the Jordanian public.

Foreign Policymaking and Regime Security

In autocracies, the same ruling elites who cartelize domestic power also control foreign relations.[2] In Jordan, foreign policy flows from the regime's inner circle, which Chapter 3 details. The core decision-maker is the king, backed by his Diwan and the Ministry of Foreign Affairs. He sets the overall agenda, directs diplomatic goals, and executes high-level summitry with other foreign leaders and delegations.[3] Much like in domestic affairs, no major policies happen without his authorization. Consider Jordan's cooperation with the United States in the 2003 Iraq War or its decision to host the Western military coalition against the Islamic State of Iraq and Syria (ISIS) in the early years of Syria's civil war. These controversial moves occurred not because parliament approved them or the government debated them but because King Abdullah ordered them so.

Other elite actors play into foreign policy by contributing ideas and handling specific problem areas. The king is not a one-man show; he leans on foreign ministers, Diwan chiefs, General Intelligence Directorate (GID) heads, and prime ministers to undertake diplomatic missions on his behalf.[4] The Jordanian Armed Forces (JAF) leadership makes its voice heard for military issues like border security and arms deals. The GID steers royal thinking about how to counter security threats, such as Palestinian Hamas and Salafi-jihadist terrorism. The Ministry of Finance, Ministry of Planning, and Central Bank likewise guide the monarchy in its approach to foreign aid, outside investments, and other external financing that affect Jordan's economic capacity, as Chapter 7 discussed.

Ordinary Jordanians have little input into this elite process, given the absence of elected government and the limited authority of parliament. Of course, public opinion does matter; as Chapter 6 noted, hot-button issues like peace with Israel and Jordan's close American ties raise frequent protestations. However, while popular sentiments can occasionally constrain the regime, citizens have no institutional way of influencing foreign policymaking. This partly explains why the United States and its allies pale at the prospects of Jordan truly democratizing. An elected government in Amman might prefer a more independent foreign policy that directly reflects the will of voters—say, one that pauses military cooperation with Washington or rethinks the wisdom of normalized relations with Israel. For Western governments, the Hashemite regime is imperfect, but better to deal with the devil they know.

What does the Jordanian monarchy seek in its foreign policy? Since the 1950s, officials have espoused a doctrine of openness to the world, tempered by advocacy for a lawful international order that avoids war and protects the weak. King Hussein frequently invoked themes of humanitarian justice and Arab solidarity in his international addresses, while King Abdullah has advocated good governance, sustainable development, and moderate views on Islam. Like most small states, Jordan has also readily participated within the architecture of global governance. It has been an enthusiastic member of regional and multilateral institutions like the Arab League, Organization of Islamic Cooperation, World Trade Organization, World Bank, and International Monetary Fund (IMF), while signing most major United Nations–based treaties (though not, pointedly, the 1951 Refugee Convention). Within the UN, the kingdom punches far above its weight. The JAF has contributed to peacekeeping missions for decades, and Jordan has been a nonpermanent member of the Security Council three times (1965–1966, 1982–1983, and 2014–2015). During 2014–2018, Prince Zeid bin Ra'ad, a cousin of King Abdullah who descends from the Hashemite branch that once ruled Iraq, served as the UN High Commissioner for Human Rights.

In practice, though, the Jordanian leadership does not fixate on this pensive dream about a just global order. Its foreign policy focuses on a more solitary goal: how to maximize regime security, meaning relative freedom from credible threats that jeopardize its capacity to maintain power.[5] Traditionally, three threats have compromised the Hashemite regime's sense of security: external aggression, domestic opposition, and ideational pressures. At any given time, Jordan's foreign policy seeks to offset at least one of these pressing dangers.

External Threats

In Jordan, foreign policy calculations often hew closely with neorealist thinking. As imparted by perhaps the richest tradition in international relations theory, neorealism argues that ceaseless conflict and brutal competition shape the anarchic interactions between national states of varying capabilities; as the smallest fish in the global pond, the smallest states always suffer at the hands of bigger predators.[6] Foreign relations therefore entail a constant struggle for security and survival. This approach may be bleak, but it frequently captures the stoic mood whenever Jordanians gaze upon the latest geopolitical dramas and conflicts within their Middle East neighborhood. As one recent editorial in the daily *Al-Ghad* opined, Jordan long ago surrendered any fantasy of becoming a great power, and its real triumph has been braving the "evil geography" of the Middle East where "crises and wars never stop."[7]

The MENA region is full of volatility affecting all countries. Jordan, though, is more vulnerable because it qualifies as a classically "small" state, in terms of its diminutive population, weak economy, defensive military, and irregular borders with Syria, Iraq, Saudi Arabia, and Israel that are difficult to seal.[8] In other words, the kingdom cannot dictate regional affairs by imposing its will on others, much less singlehandedly squash a rival state or transnational terrorist organization like ISIS. Neighboring instability can impose wrenching costs. For instance, the major conflicts that have rocked nearby states since the late twentieth century—the Iran-Iraq War, the Gulf War, the Iraq War, Palestinian uprisings, the Syrian Civil War, and Israel's wars on Gaza and Lebanon—all thrashed Jordan's economy by disrupting trade, reducing energy imports, and deterring tourism. Its boundaries are also permeable in a social sense. Jordanian society has been deeply transformed by outside forces over the past century that have catalyzed profound change, such as refugee flows, revolutionary ideologies, and protest movements.[9]

Another external threat to Jordan comes from potential attack by foreign belligerents. In the colonial years, tribal raids from what is now Saudi Arabia helped precipitate the British creation of the Arab Legion, the precursor of today's JAF. From the late 1940s through 1960s, the Hashemite regime not only fought two wars against Israel, but also engaged in recurrent hostility against Arab Nationalist states like Egypt, which saw the monarchy as a hangover of Western imperialism and supported various conspiracies to overthrow it. During the 1970 Black September civil conflict, the JAF repelled an ill-fated incursion of Syrian tanks sent to support the Palestinian commandos rebelling against King Hussein. After the Cold War, terrorism from Salafi-jihadist organizations targeted Jordan. Since the 1990s, both Al-Qaeda and ISIS have struck the kingdom. The former engineered the 2005 Amman hotel bombings, the worst terrorist strike in Jordanian history, while the latter instigated a campaign of smaller attacks starting in the mid-2010s, including shooting sprees, suicide bombings, and border assaults. ISIS also recruited several thousand Jordanian youths into its militant networks within Syria.

Recent years have renewed the Jordanian regime's sense of external insecurity, as new strains of regional violence have spilled over onto its soil. In January 2024, an Iranian-backed militia in Iraq bombed a secret US military base just inside Jordan's border with Syria. That drone strike followed years of border skirmishes with Iran-backed drug smuggling gangs based in Syria, which galvanized officials like former Interior Minister Hussein al-Majali to declare that Jordan would "strike with an iron fist" against these new enemies.[10] In April and October 2024, Iran attacked Israel amid the worsening Gaza War with hundreds of drones and missiles, many of which flew over Jordan. US forces in Jordan shot down much of this armada. Still, these unsettling incidents raised memories of the 1990–1991 Gulf War, when Saddam Hussein's regime in Iraq similarly lobbed missiles against Israel over Jordanian airspace.

Over many decades, Jordan's leaders have neutralized these outside pressures in several ways. As neorealists would predict, they have plied the circuits of regional diplomacy, craftily making alliances with other Arab countries to "balance" against whatever external threats seem most dangerous.[11] They have also leaned on the special US-Jordanian relationship, espousing pro-Western positions in return for diplomatic support, economic aid, and military assistance. While these strategies garner more attention later in this chapter, an underappreciated aspect of Jordanian foreign policy lays in its framing—meaning, how rulers present their plight to the world. Hashemite kings have deployed the survivalist trope beautifully, warning foreign audiences that their fragile kingdom stands on the brink of collapse, and so deserves more international support. In the Cold War, King Hussein played on American and British fears that should Jordan fall, then the reactionary forces of Arab Nationalism and Soviet Communism would march across the Mashriq until they conquered the Arabian oil fields and breached the Mediterranean shores of NATO. In the post–Cold War era, King Abdullah has counseled the United States and its allies that a shattered Jordan would become haven to their worst enemies—Hezbollah, Hamas, Al-Qaeda, ISIS, Iran, and the like—all intent on wreaking chaos and annihilating Israel. Jordan is held hostage to dark and malevolent forces, and if the kingdom falls then the Middle East "will burn."[12] Such admonitions sound hyperbolic, but they work.

Domestic Challenges and Foreign Aid

Domestic opposition represents the second major threat to regime security. In contravention to neorealist theories, many autocracies in the Global South fear not so much external conflict or invasion but rather being overthrown by social movements and rebel groups at home.[13] The Jordanian monarchy knows this well given all the contentious uprisings that have contested its authority. One logical response has been to "omnibalance," or using foreign policy to advance positions that assuage popular discontent at home and so reduce domestic opposition.

Thus, external choices facilitate internal order. King Hussein did this in the 1980s when he embraced the Palestine Liberation Organization (PLO) under Yasser Arafat, despite sour memories of its efforts to overthrow him during the 1970 Black September civil war. Palestinian-Jordanians, representing the majority of the populace, welcomed the move, believing that any future Palestinian state would require cooperation between the two sides. During the 1990–1991 Gulf War, King Hussein supported Iraq and refused to endorse Western military intervention to liberate Kuwait, in contrast to most other Arab states. This caused rare tension with the United States, which savaged the decision as "erratic, unpredictable, inconsistent, even counterproductive."[14] It was entirely logical, though: at a time of severe economic turmoil, as Chapter 7 discussed, Hussein needed to win plaudits from a Jordanian public reeling from an economic downturn. They indeed cheered his decision, for they saw Saddam Hussein's regime in Baghdad as an icon of Arab resistance against Western hegemony.

However, Jordan's regime usually does not bend completely to the demand of satisfying public opinion. So, it steers foreign policy toward another goal: acquiring economic resources from the world. Laurie Brand famously called this strategy "budget security," meaning convincing allies to give up trade deals and foreign aid to keep the economy afloat.[15] A prominent example came with Jordan's staunch support for Iraq amid the 1980s Iran-Iraq War. This alignment surprised many, because Jordan had bitter relations with its neighbor following the 1958 Iraq coup, which exterminated a related branch of the Hashemite monarchy. However, the alliance made economic sense in Amman, for it gave Jordan access to cheap Iraqi oil and augured profitable trade with what was then the region's second biggest economy.

The quest for foreign aid has played a larger role in Jordanian foreign policy. The Hashemite regime relied on British financial subsidies not only during its colonial decades but well into the 1950s. At the end of that decade, the United States became Jordan's biggest patron and has since delivered dollops of economic and military assistance, as this chapter later explains. However, the kingdom also receives help from other donors so long as it caters to their interests. For example, since 1949, the UN Relief and Works Agency has financed humanitarian services like education and housing for Palestinian refugees. When hydrocarbon prices are high and geopolitical frictions are absent, oil-rich Arab states like Saudi Arabia, Kuwait, and the United Arab Emirates have delivered lavish aid packages, such as during the 1970s and again after the 2011–2012 Arab Spring. Since its late 1980s financial crisis, Jordan has also received billions of dollars in World Bank and IMF concessional loans and technical development support. Finally, since the 2000s, the European Union and Japan have provided significant development funds and technical assistance. The 2016 Jordan Compact, for instance, was a lofty EU-led initiative offering more foreign aid intended to integrate Syrian refugees into the local economy. While that project stumbled, the kingdom did receive other humanitarian aid during the Syrian Civil War to cushion the costs of absorbing its mushrooming refugee flows.

All this foreign aid has bolstered Jordan's regime security. Economic breakdown and public insolvency, after all, would not only trigger mass opposition but also endanger the royal autocracy's capacity to underwrite the coercive

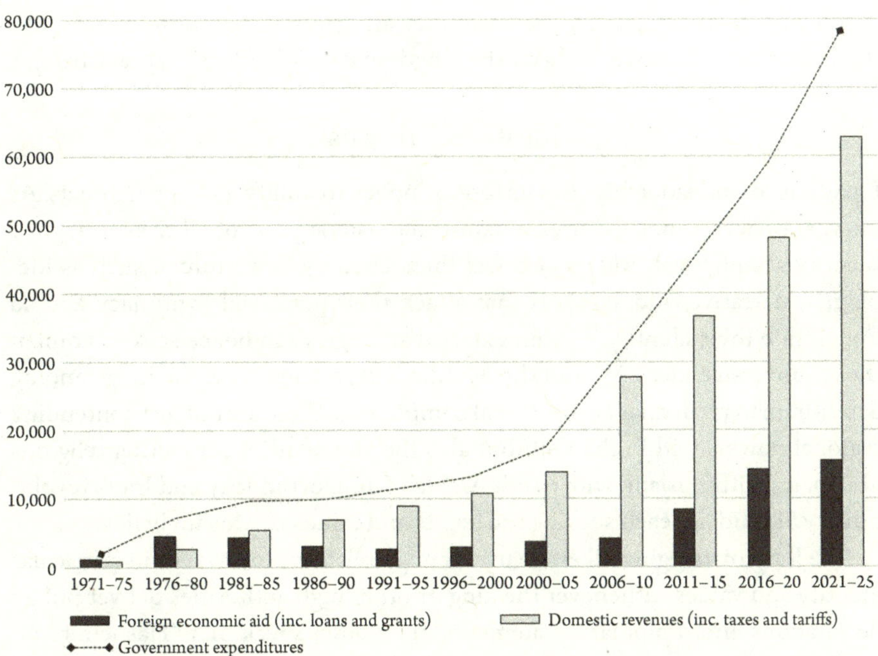

Figure 8.1 Jordan's Economic Aid Dependency in Five-Year Sums, 1971–2025 (in millions, current USD). Data are sums for each five-year period. Budgetary figures for 2025 are projected. Sources: Central Bank of Jordan, *Annual Statistical Bulletin* (CBJ, various years); World Bank, *World Development Indicators* (IBRD, various years).

apparatus that regulates dissent, as well as coalitional entitlements like public employment that sustain its Transjordanian tribal base. As Chapter 4 discussed, these are the twin domestic pillars of authoritarian rule. However, it has also made the kingdom the living definition of aid dependency, to the point where the regime could not function without foreign assistance—something commonly seen in very poor countries but not in middle-income ones like Jordan. Figure 8.1 illustrates this pattern since 1971 and compares total foreign aid with domestic revenues raised by the government, and tracks both amounts next to overall public spending in five-year increments. These aid figures notably exclude military assistance, and count only economic loans and grants from donors.

The data paint an astonishing picture: only with foreign aid can the Jordanian state sustain its ever-rising public expenditures. Indeed, during the 1970s, the government recorded more economic assistance than all domestic revenues collected via taxes, tariffs, and other income. More broadly, from 1971–2025, Jordan collected about $65 billion in total foreign economic aid, equaling nearly 30 percent of domestic revenues; in essence, almost one in four Jordanian dinars spent by the treasury over this time period originates from an external donor. As Chapter 7 explained, such dependency creates a vicious circle by encouraging chronic overspending under the hazardous assumption that those donors, like the United States or IMF, will save the kingdom if it suffers financial catastrophe.

Ideational Threats

Finally, Jordan's leadership uses its foreign policy to nullify ideational threats. As international relations theories of constructivism argue, not all risks to regime security are physical. Rulers also feel threatened by "soft" forces, such as ideologies, narrative, and symbols that attack their perceived legitimacy and so undermine their identity.[16] Their external strategies can hence seek to combat those subversive ideas. Within the Middle East, for instance, the longstanding Saudi-Iranian rivalry has an ideational component. These are not just contending regional powers within the Gulf but also the vanguard of competing religious ideologies within Islam, with Saudi Arabia's Sunni orthodoxy and Iran's revolutionary Shi'a ideals each seeking the hearts and minds of Muslim believers.

The Jordanian regime likewise uses foreign relations to advance its particular identity and values. Whenever the king or other high authorities deliver public declarations and diplomatic statements, they often speak of a "Hashemite vision." This vision anoints the Hashemite monarchy as a just, wise, and proud Muslim leadership whose legitimacy predates the creation of Jordan itself. It claims lineage from the Prophet Muhammad, as well as prestige from its historical leadership of the 1916 Great Arab Revolt, which sought to create a unified pan-Arab state. Since the 1948 Arab-Israeli War, the monarchy has also served as custodian over the Al-Aqsa holy compound in Jerusalem, Islam's most venerated site after Mecca and Medina; it has administered this sacred place since the 1948 Arab-Israeli War.

Such historical and religious symbolism influences how this royal autocracy sees regional issues. As Marc Lynch has argued, the monarchy deeply cares about how citizens and outsiders alike consume its self-conception as a regal Muslim dynasty.[17] The Hashemite vision demands stability and order within Jordan proper; indeed, as Chapter 2 touched on, King Abdullah's early efforts to propagate a new national identity centered on civic loyalty conveyed the notion that Jordanians should always treat their dynasty as the centerpiece for their own personal identity. However, the regime also seeks respect from other Arabs within regional affairs. It understandably bristles whenever rival Arab states deny its revered past and historical identity. For instance, what amplified political animosity with Nasser's Egypt in the 1950s and 1960s was the Arab Nationalist ideology it broadcast, which viewed the Jordanian Hashemites as a British-installed sham potentate undeserving of historical recognition. Likewise, Jordanian-Saudi relations have always been tinged with unspoken tensions regarding which royal house held more religious esteem, as the original Hashemite dynasty ruled Mecca as its Islamic steward until its conquest by Saudi forces in December 1924.

However, no other regional dynamic shows how Jordanian foreign policy tilts against ideational threats more than the Israeli-Palestinian conflict. As this chapter later discusses, King Abdullah has tirelessly sponsored a two-state solution for good reasons. First, the regime fears that Israel's attempts to annex all of the West Bank could end its custodial claims over the Muslim holy sites of Jerusalem and thus destroy an inviolable pillar of its identity. Royal authorities see such custodianship as a *national* interest for all of Jordan. In June 2020, the Royal Aal al-Bayt Institute, the state body charged with issuing official interpretations of Islamic doctrine, even claimed that since Arabs were the original inhabitants of biblical Palestine, the Hashemites enjoyed an ancient right over Jerusalem that precedes the modern state of Israel.

Second, the Jordanian leadership sees the noxious "alternative homeland" (*al-watan al-badil*) project, which Chapter 2 discussed, as an ideational menace. Right-wing Zionist ideologues in Israel have long conspired to not just annex the Palestinian territories but displace its Palestinians onto the East Bank, thereby making Jordan the new Palestine.[18] Jordan's kingship walks in lockstep with citizens in rejecting this abysmal idea, because this possibility constitutes an *existential* threat. Should this scenario materialize, it could spur domestic tensions within Jordan between Transjordanian nativists and a greatly-enlarged Palestinian supermajority. Who counts as Jordanian, what is Jordanian identity, whom do the Hashemites serve—all these loaded questions problematize the monarchy's own identity, and they would be dislodged with yet another mass refugee wave that would change the demographic composition of the kingdom. Moreover, if Jordan becomes a substitute homeland for all Palestinians, then the monarchy would serve as an accomplice in destroying the dream of Palestinian self-determination, thereby contradicting one of its orienting doctrines. For this reason, the Jordanian regime insists upon a two-state solution within the Israeli-Palestinian conflict, for only the promise of Palestinian statehood centered upon a West Bank and Gaza Strip free of Israeli occupation can snuff out the alternative homeland delusion.

Flexibility and Opportunism in the Middle East

Jordan's royal autocracy uses foreign policy to address external aggressors, domestic opposition, and ideational forces. Importantly, though, it does not see the world as an undifferentiated canvas. Excepting ties with the West, the regime's external outlook has heavily focused on its *regional* environment, because that is what generates the most threats and pressures.[19] Within the MENA, the Hashemite monarchy has maneuvered through a long parade of alignments, rivalries, and conflicts. In the past, wistful commentaries commended this "art of survival" as an outgrowth of royal cunning or monarchical wisdom.[20] Today, a more objective term is *flexibility*. As Curtis Ryan has observed, while Jordan has always needed Western support, within the Arab world it has no permanent commitments or sacrosanct friends—just a practical desire to neutralize whatever external, domestic, or ideational threat seems most urgent.[21] Such opportunism and flexibility have ably resolved most crises, excepting one: the Israeli-Palestinian conflict, which has encaged Jordan with an irrevocable peace treaty with Israel and fading hope for a two-state solution.

Competition, 1950s–1960s

Jordanian foreign policy in the MENA has evolved in broad three stages since the 1950s: competition, rapprochement, and entrenchment. Each phase shows the changing face of the kingdom's security dilemmas over time.

The first phase, competition, befell Jordan not long after its independence. It coincided with the "Arab Cold War" that consumed regional politics in the mid-1950s through 1960s.[22] The Arab Cold War began with the rise of Arab Nationalism, in which forefront states like Egypt and Syria promoted pan-Arab unity under its ideological banner and rejected Western involvement. This threatened Jordan's regime, as its British-backed monarchy would have been subsumed within a secular pan-Arab state ruled by magnetic republican presidents like Gamal 'Abdul Nasser. Underscoring Jordan's permeable boundaries, the Jordanian National Movement (JNM) through the 1950s channeled Arab Nationalist ideological fervor in its resistance to Hashemite rule. Indeed, as Chapter 5 explicated, the foreign policy advanced by the opposition-dominated government of 1956–1957 attempted to realign Jordan away from the West and toward the Soviet-supported Arab Nationalist bloc.

After crushing the JNM in 1957 and forging closer bonds with the United States, the royal autocracy continued bearing fallout from the Arab Cold War. In response to the February 1958 merger of Egypt and Syria into the United Arab Republic, the Hashemite kings of Jordan and Iraq established their own tepid union, which ended when the July 1958 Iraq Revolution snuffed out its monarchy.[23] Over the next decade, King Hussein faced a plowing campaign of propaganda, saber-rattling, and conspiracies organized by Arab Nationalist states and movements hoping to destabilize his reign. Among the most brazen events was a 1960 mail bombing that killed Prime Minister Hazza' al-Majali—father of the aforementioned former Interior Minister Hussein al-Majali and eulogized by *Time Magazine* as "one of the West's best friends in the Arab world."[24]

To weather such stress, Jordanian foreign policy adopted a few different tactics. It leaned on the United States as its new Western patron. However, King Hussein also exploited common opposition against Israel to find common cause with its Arab Nationalist rivals, using the inaugural 1964 Arab League summit in Cairo to mend relations with Nasser. He also struck closer ties with other Arab monarchies like Morocco, Saudi Arabia, and Kuwait. Safety lay in numbers, particularly against an Arab Nationalist bloc that saw all these royal houses as anathema to its modern call for a unified pan-Arab republic. This was not easy; Jordanian-Saudi relations in particular had been dogged by prickly mistrust over the other's claimed religious heritage and territorial ambitions.[25] King Hussein assured his Saudi counterparts, however, that he had little aspiration to reclaim Mecca, which his family lost in 1924 to Saudi conquest; this temporarily lubricated these ties.

Rapprochement, 1970s–1990s

The second phase of Jordanian foreign policy, rapprochement, began after the 1967 Arab-Israeli War, when the Arab Cold War gave way to more regional cohesion and cooperation. Though disputes still spoiled some bilateral relations, the Hashemite regime enjoyed more regime security. Collective enmity against Israel soothed inter-Arab tensions leading up to their June 1967 conflict, during which King Hussein put Jordanian forces under Egyptian command. The Arab defeat in that war created an opening for the Hashemite palace to lead more assertive diplomatic initiatives, not least because Jordan had just suffered the loss of the West Bank and East Jerusalem. At the September 1967 Arab League summit in Khartoum, King Hussein pledged to ceaselessly oppose Israel in the spirit of Arab solidarity, and in return the Arab Nationalist states agreed to halt all subversion against Jordan.[26] By the 1970s, with its previous external and ideational threats (save Israel, of course) gone, the Jordanian monarchy enjoyed closer relations with most Arab countries. The Gulf kingdoms rewarded Jordan with foreign aid, subsidized oil, and trade agreements, all of which helped propel its economic boom during the decade. They also welcomed Palestinian-Jordanian expatriate workers in their prospering rentier economies.

This rehabilitated standing paid dividends. After the Black September civil conflict, which expelled the PLO from the East Bank, most other Arab states criticized—but did not sanction or isolate—Jordan, despite its army having killed thousands of Palestinians. The regime felt confident enough to sit out the 1973 Arab-Israeli War, sending only a small brigade to defend Syria while letting Egyptian forces lead the battle charge. The 1978 Arab League summit in Baghdad gave the kingdom more standing within regional affairs. There, King Hussein rejected the Camp David peace process between Egypt and Israel, reiterating that Jordan as a frontline state to Israel would never seek peace without firstly achieving the corollary promise of a sovereign Palestinian state. In return, Saudi Arabia and other wealthy oil-exporting Arab states promised the kingdom a staggering $1.2 billion in annual aid.

Though its regional position improved, Jordan continued alternating its alignments between larger Arab states as it angled for the best returns. For instance, it was the first Arab country to restore relations with Egypt in 1984, ending the latter's estrangement from Arab diplomatic circles after Camp David. That move indicated Jordanian realization that Cairo remained the Arab world's biggest political and military player, and it was prudent not to alienate it. Rocky relations with Syria—which had mounted a military intervention into Jordan during the 1970 Black September conflict to support the PLO—began smoothing in the mid-1970s under new bilateral commercial and trade agreements.

This Jordanian-Syrian détente crumpled when King Hussein supported Iraq during the Iran-Iraq War of the 1980s, while Syria backed Iran. Jordan benefited from its pro-Iraqi stance; as wartime Iraq's financial outlet to the outside world, Jordan reaped a gush of cheap oil shipments and new business investments.[27] Many Jordanians hailed this new Jordanian-Iraqi alliance and came to see Saddam Hussein as a kindred leader. They likewise cheered the decision to back Iraq during the 1990–1991 Gulf War. However, this pro-Iraqi position would bring blowback after the war. Saudi Arabia, Kuwait, and the other Gulf states retaliated against Jordan's perceived betrayal by deporting their nearly 300,000 Palestinian-Jordanian expatriates, which further distressed its reeling economy. King Hussein spent much of the 1990s repairing these diplomatic wounds by reaching out to Gulf leaders. The 1994 peace treaty with Israel was, likewise, critical to Jordanian efforts to upgrade relations with the United States.

Entrenchment, 2000s–present

The latest phase of Jordan's regional dealings—entrenchment—began with King Abdullah's ascension to power in 1999. In this ongoing era, the Hashemite regime has enjoyed relative peace and cooperative ties with most MENA countries. Gone are external threats and ideational challenges from competing Arab states; the prime danger to regime security instead has come from domestic opposition, partly reflecting the listless economy, as well as terrorism and spillover from nearby wars. King Abdullah set the tone for this confident stance with whirlwind diplomacy early in his reign, visiting most Arab states to reinforce relations and establish his judicious positions: no to war, yes to peace, and regional stability over all else.[28]

As always, though, unpredictable events have required pragmatic responses. When the United States waged new wars across the Middle East after 9/11, the kingdom could not afford to disaffect Washington as it did in the Gulf War. King Abdullah therefore enlisted Jordan as a keen supporter of the US-led War on Terror, even allowing US forces to transit through the country during the invasion of Iraq in March 2003. The Iraq War battered Jordan's economy, which not only lost its cheapest source of oil but also received a half-million Iraqi refugees within years. US and Western foreign aid cushioned the blow, while Jordan struck expedient agreements with Egypt and the Gulf kingdoms to secure new energy supplies. This became the calling card of Jordanian diplomacy in the new century: cautious collaboration in the Arab world, with reliance on American support as its ultimate backstop.

This strategy gained momentum in the late 2000s, as regional order fractured around the new geopolitical schism between a coalition of Sunni Arab states, led by Egypt and Saudi Arabia, and a resurgent Iran hoping to dominate the Middle East. New flashpoints of conflict implicated Iranian-backed actors, from Hezbollah's 2006 war against Israel in Lebanon to the rise of Shi'a parties and militias in post-Saddam Iraq.[29] Given these tensions, the Hashemite monarchy joined the Sunni-Arab bandwagon's campaign against Iran. In 2004, King Abdullah famously stoked these sectarian fires by decrying that a "Shi'a crescent" of Iranian-led extremism would annihilate the entire MENA unless the Sunni Arab bloc—backed by the United States, of course—could punish and contain Tehran. Such hyperbole was well calculated; Jordan never faced any credible threat of Iranian aggression, but it secured more regional applause and Western goodwill in aligning with what it perceived as the winning side.

Such bandwagoning paid dividends during the 2011–2012 Arab Spring uprisings, when Arab autocrats suddenly remembered that domestic opposition could just as easily overthrow them as distant foes like Iran. As it weathered thousands of peaceful protests, the Hashemite monarchy leveraged its anti-Iranian credentials to lean even more on its Gulf allies. It flirted with an invitation to join the Gulf Cooperation Council, which had sought to evolve from its origins three decades earlier as a security alliance of oil-rentier states into an unapologetic club of Arab monarchies.[30] Jordan did not ultimately join, but nonetheless in 2012 received a five-year, $5 billion foreign aid package from Saudi Arabia, the UAE, and Kuwait. The United States and its allies also continued endorsing Hashemite rule, unwilling to embrace the idea of true democratization on the East Bank.

Soon, Jordan's rule-makers pivoted once more against new constraints. In its early years, the Syrian Civil War not only burdened the kingdom with 750,000 refugees but also gave rise to ISIS's ghastly campaign of militancy and terrorism. The Jordanian regime gladly hosted the US-led international military campaign against ISIS; it also froze relations with Syria and called for the end of its ruler, Bashar Assad, while warning Iran and its proxies like Hezbollah to halt their meddling in the region. Yet revealing its penchant for caution, the Hashemite monarchy also rebuffed Saudi-led pressures to declare outright war on Syria in order to hasten Assad's downfall. King Abdullah tried to thread the needle. His regime had little compunction in banding with the Western consensus against Syria, but it also had little desire to be dragged into its civil conflict, particularly given the flood of Syrian refugees entering the kingdom. Neither did he trust the new Saudi leadership of Crown Prince Muhammad bin Salman, whose impulses would launch Saudi Arabia's disastrous military intervention in Yemen in 2015 and an ineffectual blockading of Qatar in 2017.

Such hedging cost Jordan. In 2018, Saudi Arabia refused to renew its five-year Gulf aid package, relenting (alongside the UAE and Kuwait) only with a much smaller $2.5 billion aid pledge. Refusing to be sidelined, the Jordanian monarchy sniffed out another geopolitical opening by leading efforts to end Syria's isolation in the Arab world as its civil war settled down. To much fanfare, Jordan reopened its commercial border crossings with Syria in late 2021. Like past realignments, this gesture came with strategic intentions. Royal officials hoped smoother coordination with the Assad regime could not only help repatriate the kingdom's many refugees but also staunch Syrian drug-smuggling operations, which had elicited increasing clashes with the Jordanian military across the Jordanian-Syrian border.[31] Such assertive thinking continued after the collapse of Syria's Assad regime in December 2024, as King Abdullah quickly welcomed the new government in Damascus and offered the kingdom's support for its post-war rebuilding efforts. As events in the Arab world continued to outpace all predictions, the Hashemite position thus preserved the same strategy as before: look for opportunities, side with the strong, and offset all known threats.

From Opportunism to Entrapment

Though painted in broad brushstrokes, this historical review illustrates how the Hashemite monarchy has never bound itself to any single viewpoint or issue in Middle Eastern affairs apart from its own survival. Its external relations have always aimed to reduce imminent threats to regime security, and it has experimented with different alliances, rivalries, and commitments since the 1950s. Jordan's foreign policy has succeeded in this regard, despite, given its small size and modest capabilities, never being able to set the regional agenda.

Such pragmatic opportunism would make Jordan an unqualified success story save for one harrowing problem: the Israeli-Palestinian conflict. Given its neighboring location and Palestinian-majority populace, Jordan has never escaped the reality that what happens within Israel and the Palestinian territories of the West Bank and Gaza Strip—protests, terrorism, annexation, displacement, colonialization, and violence—reverberates within its own borders. Since 1994, the monarchy has maintained a peace treaty with Israel that it cannot revoke for fear of alienating the West, but it lacks the ability to advance the cause of Palestinian statehood over Israeli hostility and Western insouciance. This is the prickliest dilemma in Jordanian foreign policy.

The Israeli-Palestinian Yoke

Jordan and Israel historically share a symbiotic relationship, rendering them the best of enemies and now worst of friends. It began in secrecy. During the 1930s, as clashes worsened between Jewish and Arab settlers in British-run Mandatory Palestine, Emir Abdullah and some tribal notables quietly reached out to Zionist leaders across the Jordan River to establish mutually beneficial ties.[32] Such clandestine relations continued through the 1940s, driven not only by the ruler's ambitions to expand his influence but also anxiety that any new Zionist state (or, alternatively, a Palestinian one) could infringe on the East Bank.

Such covert diplomacy continued even after the 1948 and 1967 Arab-Israeli conflicts made Jordan and Israel formal belligerents. Publicly, King Hussein stood against Israel. He endorsed the Arab League's 1967 Khartoum Resolution with its "three no's"—no peace, no recognition, and no negotiations—and likewise repulsed US-sponsored peace initiatives.[33] Indeed, Jordan rejected any possibility of normalizing ties with Israel without the implementation of UN Security Council Resolution 242, the 1967 land-for-peace proposal that called for Israeli withdrawal from the occupied Gaza Strip and West Bank in return for Arab peace and recognition of Israel. Even so, behind the scenes, Jordan and Israel continued to engage one another through secret meetings. Envoys coordinated on issues like border security and especially water usage of the Jordan River, which the two countries shared.[34] Generations of Israeli leaders also trusted King Hussein enough to furtively meet with him dozens of times well into the 1980s, sometimes to air their grievances and other times to float potential peace settlements.

The PLO Challenge

What facilitated such Jordanian-Israeli cooperation was not only their shared border but also their mutual problem of Palestine. Israel's occupation of the Palestinian territories made it the biggest obstacle to any future project of establishing a sovereign Palestinian state. Conversely, the 1948 war turned Jordan into a Palestinian-majority country, and by the 1967 conflict, more than half of the Middle East's 2.35 million Palestinian Arabs lived under Jordanian rule across both banks of the Jordan River. This demographic reality enabled the royal autocracy to claim leadership over the Palestinian cause, offering citizenship to its Palestinian subjects in the early 1950s and acting as custodian over the Muslim holy sites of Jerusalem. For King Hussein, only through Hashemite stewardship could the Palestinians reach their promised land of independent statehood. However, many Palestinians doubted that Jordan could serve as their conduit to self-determination, not least because the kingdom would need to eventually surrender its sovereign control over the West Bank should a future Palestinian state come into existence.[35] Their own political plight in Jordan did not conjure much confidence, either. The 1951 assassination of Emir Abdullah in Jerusalem and the JNM's contentious opposition afterward, as Chapter 5 discussed, presaged the increasing marginalization of Palestinians within Jordanian politics and the ethnocratic order that re-centered autocratic power around Transjordanian interests.

In this context, the rise of the PLO in 1964 posed a serious conundrum to Israel and Jordan alike. Under guiding voices like Ahmad Shuqayri and Yasser Arafat, this umbrella organization threatened Israel in its armed operations and terrorism waged in the name of the Palestinian cause. However, it also implicated Jordan's regime security. The PLO asserted transnational leadership over *all* Palestinians, including those living in the kingdom as Jordanian citizens. Though he never fully trusted its leadership, King Hussein acceded to pressures from other Arab states and allowed the PLO to construct its headquarters and a large militant infrastructure in Jordan. This would soon bring untenable backlash. After the 1967 war, PLO commandos staged many armed raids into Israel from their operating bases in the East Bank, which triggered Israeli retaliation that sometimes targeted Jordanian forces in costly battles. Indeed, one such skirmish, the 1968 Battle of Karameh, has become etched into Jordanian lore as a gallant episode of military resistance against Zionist aggression.[36] As Chapter 2 discussed, bitter disagreements between the monarchy and PLO climaxed with the 1970 Black September civil conflict, which resulted in the latter's defeat and expulsion to Lebanon.

The bloody casualties inflicted on PLO militants during Black September at the hands of the Jordanian army soiled the Hashemite regime's pro-Palestinian credentials in the Arab world. Eager to repair this image, King Hussein agreed to the Arab League's 1974 Rabat declaration that the PLO was the sole, legitimate representative of all Palestinian people. No longer would the Jordanian monarchy pose as the principal keeper of the Palestinian cause. However, it still coveted the West Bank after its loss to Israel in the 1967 war. Hence, Jordan maintained administrative and financial ties with this occupied Palestinian territory after the conflict. It recognized West Bank Palestinians as Jordanian citizens, replete with passport privileges and educational rights, and paid salaries for local civil servants. The Israeli government needed little convincing to accept this arrangement: still worried about ongoing PLO militancy, it trusted the Hashemite regime to continue influencing local affairs in the West Bank. Only in July 1988 did the Jordanian state terminate these responsibilities in a momentous decision known as *fakk al-irtibaat* (severance of ties). While the Hashemite palace maintained its custodianship over Jerusalem's Muslim holy sites, no longer would it claim sovereignty over the West Bank or consider its residents as citizens.

Like all foreign policy moves, this disengagement from the West Bank aimed to fortify the Hashemite monarchy's perceived regime security. By 1987, the uprisings against Israeli occupation known as the First Intifada had broken out across the Palestinian territories, raising the specter of unrest spreading into the East Bank. Untethering the West Bank helped shield Jordan from this conflict while also satisfying the PLO, whose leader Yasser Arafat had long clamored for this severance in his meetings with Jordanian officials throughout the 1980s. The decision also sent a blunt message to Israel: having relinquished its lingering claims over Palestinian land, the Hashemite Kingdom now put the onus of satisfying Palestinian demands for self-determination squarely on the Israeli state.[37]

Peace, Negotiations, and Failure

All this puts the October 1994 peace agreement between Jordan and Israel, signed at the southern border crossing of Wadi Araba, into historical perspective. Crafted after the groundbreaking 1991 Arab-Israeli peace conference in Madrid, the Wadi Araba Treaty is celebrated in the annals of Jordanian diplomacy as a triumph of valiant Hashemite leadership over a hostile, obstinate Zionist enemy.[38] In reality, although it triggered widespread criticism among the Jordanian public, the accord was simply the next logical foreign policy step for this authoritarian regime. After generations of covert ties predicated on shared interests, publicly normalizing relations allowed Jordan to drop its pretense of hostility. The treaty observed the monarchy's custodianship over Jerusalem's Muslim holy sites. It enabled more seamless coordination on border security, water allocation, and other critical bilateral issues. For Jordan, it also portended domestic economic payoffs—urgently needed, given the financial crisis of the late 1980s—through rejuvenated American foreign aid, alongside new trade, investment, and tourism opportunities with Israel.

Above all, the peace treaty reaffirmed Jordan's central importance in resolving the Israeli-Palestinian conflict. The 1993 Oslo Accords between Israel and the PLO commenced bilateral negotiations for a two-state solution, which might finally satisfy the Palestinian dream of self-determination so long as it also abided by Israel's own existence. Having surrendered its claims over the West Bank in 1988, the Hashemite palace needed to shape this process, given its perpetual fears that without a guaranteed framework for an independent Palestinian state, radical Israeli voices would continue advancing the alternative homeland project. With the Wadi Araba Treaty, the royal autocracy believed it could be the fulcrum in a triangular relationship climaxing in the two-state solution, pressuring Israel to honor its promises on one side while assisting the Palestinian Authority (PA), the Palestinian governing body created by the Oslo process, on the other. To that end, in 1999, King Abdullah expelled Hamas, the Palestinian Islamist movement that rejected the Oslo process, from Jordan.[39] Though Hamas would maintain private contact with Jordan's Muslim Brotherhood, and covertly even its Foreign Ministry and GID, this formal ejection signaled Jordan's preference for a two-state solution wrought through legal negotiations, not armed resistance.

Three decades later, the aspirational hopes for peace and prosperity embodied by the Wadi Araba Treaty have evaporated, leaving behind only a cold peace. On shared security concerns like counterterrorism and Iran, Jordan and Israel still warily align under US guidance. For instance, Israeli aircraft received safe passage through Jordanian airspace to attack Hezbollah and Iranian targets within Syria during the Syrian Civil War. Bilateral dealings continue on some issues, such as the kingdom's 2016 agreement to import Israeli natural gas, while the two sides have floated various proposals on water, scientific, and energy exchanges.

Beyond this, however, Jordan under King Abdullah has seen few dividends of peace beyond increased Western foreign aid. Economically, more than a dozen bilateral tourism and trade agreements have brought meager returns, while joint investment projects through Jordan's Qualifying Industrial Zones have had limited impact in creating jobs within the kingdom.[40] Politically, peace has also caused the monarchy more headaches. The Wadi Araba Treaty becomes a domestic liability whenever crises give voice to angry anti-Israeli demonstrations demanding the king abrogate the peace agreement. Sometimes, diplomatic incidents spur public outrage; examples include Israel's attempted assassination in 1997 of Hamas official Khalid Mish'al in Amman and the 2017 shooting deaths of two Jordanians on Israeli Embassy grounds. More often, outbursts of horrific violence after Israeli military incursions into the Palestinian territories—from the Al-Aqsa Intifada during the early 2000s to periodic Gaza-centered conflicts since the late 2000s—bring out agitated popular mobilization. As Chapter 2 and Chapter 6 discussed, few other issues unite Transjordanians and Palestinian-Jordanians in contentious protest as denouncing Israel.

All these costs could be offset if crafting peace with Israel yielded a massive payoff, such as giving Jordan influence to sustain the Oslo process. It has not. For reasons beyond Jordan's control, Israeli-Palestinian negotiations after the 1990s sputtered to a halt, interspersing false starts with prolonged periods of violence. By the 2010s, Israel's creeping militarized dominion over the Gaza Strip, the West Bank, and Jerusalem effectively created a "one-state reality" that all but foreclosed the possibility of Palestinian statehood.[41] And here, the royal autocracy has felt helpless in halting the death of the two-state solution. Jordanian objections have not stopped Israel's many aggressions onto the West Bank, such as building illegal settlements, mass political detentions, restrictions on Al-Aqsa Mosque, and financially suffocating the PA.

Neither have royal pressures curtailed escalating wars between Hamas and Israel, despite the humanitarian catastrophe they have unleashed on Hamas-run Gaza. At each step of this downward spiral, Israel's right-wing governments have simply shrugged off Jordanian entreaties. The usual punitive measures available to Amman, such as withdrawing its ambassador, reducing already-meager trade, and issuing livid statements, fall on deaf ears. In 2018, Jordan refused to renew Israeli farming permits in Al-Baqura and Al-Ghamr—two patches of East Bank land whose sharing after the Wadi Araba Treaty symbolized bilateral cooperation—but to little effect. Only terminating the 1994 peace treaty would make a difference to Israeli decision-making, perhaps by forcing it to reconsider the two-state solution. However, Jordanian officials reject this option, for this would bring harsh US and Western backlash, including the drastic reduction of foreign aid, that the kingdom cannot afford.[42]

Violence and Extremism

What has magnified Jordanian insecurity since the 2010s is rising conflict and violence within Palestine. Despite supporting the Hashemite Kingdom through economic and military assistance, the US has also sponsored Israeli expansionism into Palestine, despite the dangers posed by the extremist alternative homeland project. The Trump administration has had much to do with this. During his first term, President Donald Trump recognized Jerusalem as Israel's undivided capital—a provocative move, as Palestinians have long dreamt of making the holy city as the capital of their own future state—and slashed US foreign aid to the Palestinian Authority. Yet his January 2020 "deal of the century" peace plan shocked Jordan's monarchy and people the most.[43] The plan terminated the Oslo two-state framework in favor of Israel. It called for Palestine to exist as a tiny rump state, leaving much of the West Bank for Israeli annexation; all Palestinian refugees would lose their right of return, and the Hashemites would lose custodianship over Jerusalem's holy sites.

This embryonic scheme emboldened right-wing Zionists and their alternative homeland ideology. They insisted the writing was on the wall: on the verge of losing their lands, Palestinians might as well relocate to East Bank and make Jordan the new Palestine. The US-brokered Abraham Accords in September 2020 brought this dreadful scenario one step closer to reality. With four new Arab peace partners—the UAE, Bahrain, Morocco, and Sudan—and talk of negotiating another groundbreaking peace treaty with Saudi Arabia in the air, the Israeli government could now claim support from other Arab states in advancing its one-state reality. Though the deal of the century was never fully implemented, its brief consideration demoralized the monarchy, for it showed how marginalized that Jordanian interests had become within the Israeli-Palestinian nexus.

More recent years have shown how the Israeli-Palestinian quandary has become virtually unwinnable for Jordanian foreign policy. The Gaza conflict that began in October 2023 killed more Palestinians than the 1948 and 1967 Arab-Israeli Wars, plus both major intifadas, combined. Wracked by domestic protests against the devastation of the Gaza Strip, Jordanian authorities could do little to stop the Biden administration from financing Israel's war machine; they could only plead that such unbridled aggression would eventually wreck the kingdom's own stability.[44] In February 2025, early in his second term, President Trump further alarmed Jordan's monarchy and citizens alike by proposing to end the Gaza war by transferring its two million Palestinians to Egypt and Jordan, who would be expected to accept those expelled peoples for humanitarian reasons, and then turn the emptied Palestinian land into a US-owned touristic megaproject.

Though absurd, the scheme underpinned Jordan's dilemma. For the monarchy to accede to this wild venture would be "political suicide," as former Information Minister Samih Ma'aytah argued, because it essentially facilitated the alternative homeland project—the very scenario that all Jordanians seek to avoid.[45] However, Jordan has little leverage on its own to neutralize such disruptive ideas, much less reverse the terminal decline of the Palestinian dream by ending the Gaza war or restarting negotiations between Israel and the Palestinian Authority. In the spring of 2025, King Abdullah worked with the leaderships of Egypt and the Gulf kingdoms—all equally perturbed by the volatile Trump proposition, which they interpreted as ethnic cleansing—to formulate an alternative plan to create a permanent truce, rebuild Gaza, and hence allow its Palestinian residents to stay. That they needed to conjure this joint counterproposal highlights how the wider Israeli-Palestinian conflict remains the rare regional peril that Jordan cannot ameliorate through diplomatic creativity. It can only pivot to different options in hopes of delaying far bigger forces.

If anything girds Jordan's efforts to weather this unending crisis, it is its longstanding relations with the United States, which precede recent events. For all of America's support for Israel, Jordan does enjoy its own special ties with Washington that extend back for many decades. Why the United States has such long reach into a small Middle Eastern country nearly 6,000 miles away implicates the last tenet of Jordanian foreign policy: its strategic attachment to the West, and the role this plays in buttressing the political, economic, and military stanchions of authoritarian rule.

The Shadow of American Hegemony

Beyond its maneuverings in the Arab world and the Israeli-Palestinian conflict, Jordan's foreign policy rests upon a close relationship with the United States. No other alliance matters as much, for American support, aid, and arms have been central to Hashemite rule since the late 1950s. From the US perspective, Jordan is a curiously useful friend, despite having none of the oil resources of bigger regional allies like Saudi Arabia. "There is no ruler in this area for whom we have greater admiration and affection," Secretary of State Henry Kissinger fawned to King Hussein in a meeting at the Diwan in 1975.[46] A half-century later, President Joseph Biden effused similar panegyrics when he welcomed King Abdullah to the White House, introducing him as a "good, loyal, and decent friend" providing "vital leadership in . . . a tough neighborhood."[47]

For generations, critics have raised eyebrows at Jordan's intimate ties with the United States and savaged its monarchy as an "obedient" lapdog of the West.[48] In the 1950s and 1960s, for instance, Arab Nationalists won plaudits by accusing the Hashemites as being Arab quislings to British and then American imperialism. Today, Jordanians wonder why their autocracy continues facilitating US-led interventions in Iraq, Syria, and other Middle East countries—and how their kingship can claim to support Palestine while requesting help from the very global hegemon that also arms and finances Israel's military. Washington's towering presence in Jordan certainly does not help this image. The US Embassy sits like a giant garrison in Amman's wealthy enclave of Abdoun, flanked by layers of militarized security so thick that diplomats once called it Fort Apache. The US Ambassador's words are monitored more closely by the Jordanian media than any domestic figure save the king, the prime minister, and the heads of the military and intelligence directorate. King Abdullah has been the first Arab leader to visit every US president since the Obama administration (during President George W. Bush's first term, only the late Hosni Mubarak of Egypt beat him to the punch). A Jordanian Foreign Ministry official put it best: when the Hashemite palace ponders any bold external initiative, "The first question is what could happen if it fails. The second question is what do the Americans think?"[49]

In truth, Jordan is dependent on the United States—but it is no American colony or puppet. The best term for this relationship is *cliency*. The kingdom is a client state of American power, an outcome wrought by strategic choice. The royal autocracy has opted to back US, and broadly Western, interests in the MENA for many decades, because this brings diplomatic protection, economic aid, and military assistance that help preserve its security and stability. Such international patron-client ties resemble clientelism in domestic politics, which Chapter 3 introduced. They are transactional hierarchies: a powerful state (i.e., the patron) secures the alignment and loyalty of the smaller client state in return for providing resources and support.[50] On one side, foreign patronage makes weak client states stronger, because they help immunize them from external threats and domestic opposition. For example, diplomatic sponsorship boosts the confidence of struggling autocrats. Economic aid and trade deals support their economies and fiscal health. Military assistance like arms transfers and intelligence cooperation strengthen their coercive apparatus. On the other side, great powers extract concessions from client states that aggrandize their own interests. They use smaller allies to establish military bases, access new markets, obtain resources like oil, wage regional wars, and expand their prestige and power.

Given their mutually beneficial nature, these transactional relationships are a common feature in global politics. During the Cold War, the Soviet Union and United States formed many clientelist partnerships with smaller, developing countries as part of their efforts to amass competing blocs of alliances.[51] Today, America still has many client states, not only in the Middle East—including Lebanon, Iraq, and Egypt—but elsewhere across the world, as in Taiwan, South Korea, and Ukraine. So do Russia (as in Belarus, Armenia, Kazakhstan), China (as in Cambodia, North Korea, Tajikistan), and even France, with African states like Mali and Chad. Thus, Jordan's position as a client state under American hegemony is not unique. It is, though, long and deep.

The Evolution of a Special Relationship

Jordan's engagement with the West began during the colonial period. As a protectorate, the fledgling monarchy received British financial subsidies and military protection, although in return Emir Abdullah also had to surrender his personal ambitions to march upon French Syria, which the British felt would have disturbed the post–World War I regional balance.[52] Abdullah's regime retained British support after gaining independence, and the 1948 Anglo-Jordan Treaty provided for British military basing rights, economic aid, and other areas of high influence: the kingdom graduated from protectorate status to British client state. As Chapter 5 described, these ties came under fire by domestic opposition as well as Arab Nationalist rival states. Such pushback was so intense that King Hussein was forced to terminate the British treaty relationship in March 1957, marking a stunning turn. For the first and only time in the history of Jordanian foreign policy, popular resistance shattered the formal bonds between the Hashemite palace and a Western power.[53]

America quickly stepped into this critical breach. When the royal autocracy cracked down on political opposition in April 1957, it forged a new clientelist pact with the United States, which under the Eisenhower Doctrine was eager to enlist Middle East allies in its superpower struggle against the Soviet Union. The United States declared Jordanian sovereignty as a national interest, signaling its approval for domestic repression while moving a naval fleet to the eastern Mediterranean Sea—a show of force, as well as a contingency plan for potential intervention to restore King Hussein to power if democratic opposition prevailed.[54] Within months, the United States also delivered cash grants to rescue Jordan's bankrupt government, as well as emergency arms shipments to augment the army's morale and capabilities.

Jordan was now an American client state. Prior to the late 1950s, few in Washington considered the Hashemite Kingdom important, apart from the now-defunct Trans-Arabian oil pipeline crossing its territory. However, as the Cold War unfolded, American policymakers came to see the country as part of its grand strategy in the Middle East, which aimed to keep as much of the region as possible—including the oil-rich Gulf, which fueled the NATO economies and Japan—from falling under the sway of Arab Nationalism and Soviet Communism. Jordan was a convenient friend, given its proximity to Israel, Syria, Iraq, and other crisis zones. Keeping the little country within the American orbit would prevent hostile forces from dethroning the monarchy, while conversely the Hashemite regime was happy to receive American support in return for adopting anti-Communist positions. This bilateral relationship stayed firm throughout the Cold War, with King Hussein acting as a stately Arab interlocutor with every US president.[55] Occasional disagreements never derailed these ties. For instance, Jordanian participation in the 1967 Arab-Israeli War frustrated the United States, but did not dissuade the Nixon administration from intervening during the 1970 Black September civil war with a renewed spurt of diplomatic outreach, economic assistance, and arms transfers to ensure the monarchy's victory over PLO militants.[56] For US policymakers, the Hashemite leadership was fallible—but far more reliable than, say, a revolutionary leftist regime enticed by Moscow.

The post–Cold War years intensified Jordan's gravitation toward Washington. The demise of Soviet Communism gave the United States uncontested paramountcy in the MENA. Jordanian diplomacy took notice and pursued new ways to make the kingdom indispensable to Washington. The 1994 peace treaty with Israel helped relieve lingering sourness from the Gulf War, when King Hussein broke from the United States in backing Iraq. The United States also rewarded Jordan by forgiving its debts and ramping up foreign aid. In 1996, the Clinton administration designated Jordan as a Major Non-NATO Ally—a rare status held then only by five other countries—and which gave the JAF access to more advanced US arms and security programs. In 1996, US strike jets flew from Jordan to enforce Operation Southern Watch over Iraq, and in 2003 some American forces used its eastern desert as a conduit for the Iraqi invasion. Intelligence cooperation likewise deepened after 9/11, when Jordan's leadership marketed itself as an unswerving comrade in the battle against Salafi-jihadism. During the War on Terror, Jordan became a hub for the controversial US extraordinary renditions program, with the GID serving as the CIA's most trusted Arab partner in its operations against Al-Qaeda. As Secretary of State Condoleezza

Rice proclaimed in 2005, the United States "had no closer ally than Jordan in the war on terror, and Jordan will find no better friend."[57] In the mid-2000s, King Abdullah's implacable hostility against Iran also fed into the Western campaign to isolate Tehran's expanding sphere of influence.

The past two decades have witnessed even more Jordanian entanglements with American foreign policy in the Middle East. King Abdullah has visited Washington more than any other Arab leader, each time playing up his kingdom's stable, moderate image—even when feeling slighted on the Palestinian issue, as during the Trump years.[58] In 2010, Jordan began hosting Eager Lion, which has since become the largest US-led military and training exercise in the MENA. The Syrian Civil War made the country even more integral to the United States and its allies. In 2013, Jordan began serving as the regional headquarters for Western involvement in the conflict. It helped coordinate the CIA's arms smuggling and training operations for Syrian rebels fighting the Assad regime and housed the coalition of Western military forces campaigning against ISIS. Meanwhile, to better defend Jordanian sovereignty, the United States quietly built a surveillance and defense network on Jordan's Syrian and Iraqi borders, making these frontier zones the most secure they had ever been.[59]

By the late 2010s, the United States recognized that a militarized Jordan would be integral to its other geopolitical interests, particularly any future war with Iran. Thousands of US troops and security contractors therefore stayed in Jordan long after the campaign against ISIS ended, some in major military installations like Muwaffaq Salti Airbase (just sixty miles east of Amman) and others in undisclosed combat and training facilities so secretive that most Jordanians do not know of their existence. The 2021 US-Jordanian Defense Cooperation Agreement facilitated this, as it gave American troops visa-free rights to enter and operate in the kingdom. British, French, and German forces also remained at smaller bases in the eastern desert and near Aqaba.

Collectively, this Western military infrastructure in the Hashemite Kingdom is impressive. It encompasses spies, soldiers, drones, jets, air batteries, and other crack equipment intended to not just defend Jordan but also intervene into nearby regional conflict zones, from Lebanon and Syria to Iraq and Iran.[60] In early 2024, NATO opened its first Middle East liaison office in Amman, signifying Jordan's entrenched importance for Western governments as a secure, stable perch from which to channel their strategic interests upon the region. Jordan's role in assisting US military forces within the country in shooting down much of the Iranian drones and missiles attacking Israel throughout 2024 further cemented its status as a dutiful client state that solidifies the hegemonic reach of the United States.

Patronage and Protection

Jordan's militarized integration into American grand strategy has not gone unnoticed by its people. Far from it, as Chapter 6 notes, Jordanians regularly protest against their kingdom's chummy ties with the United States, particularly when it comes to Israel. Yet the monarchy refuses to budge, for good reason: as a client state committed to American interests, the royal autocracy has received patronage and protection from Washington that ensure its regime security. Fairly, other global stakeholders factor into Jordanian foreign policy too. The European Union and Japan have given substantial and increasing volumes of economic assistance over the past two decades, alongside multilateral donors like the World Bank and United Nations agencies. In recent years, royal watchers have also paid more attention to China and Russia, given the increasingly multipolar structure of global politics and the prospect of securing more profitable relations with both. For all these audiences, Jordanian officials adopt the same diplomatic message: their country is a cornerstone of regional stability and needs more international support in the form of aid, trade, and investments.

However, the United States stands above the rest. It has given the most support to Jordan since the 1950s, and other Western allies tend to follow its strategic lead. To be sure, there are occasional tensions. In early 2025, for instance, President Trump insinuated Jordan could lose much of its American aid and support should King Abdullah refuse to entertain his bizarre proposal to depopulate the Gaza Strip. However, the weight of history favors the Hashemite Kingdom in standing pat: every time the US has downgraded ties with Jordan over a foreign policy disagreement, from the 1967 Arab-Israeli War to King Hussein's 1990 decision to back Iraq during the Gulf War, relations have always bounced within years given the distinctiveness of this alliance. The US needs a compliant Arab ally to support its Middle East adventurism, while Jordan needs a powerful foreign patron to proffer the resources and protection that keep its autocratic institutions humming.

The latter point is worth parsing out. Since the 1950s, the United States has buttressed Jordan's authoritarian order and regional position in six crucial ways. First, it has interceded during crises to insulate Jordan from outside aggression or to boost the monarchy's confidence to retain power. Washington has never launched a coercive intervention here against domestic opposition, like it did with Iran in 1953 or South Vietnam during the 1960s. That dubious honor falls to the British, who in July 1958 landed paratroopers in Amman to reassure a shaken King Hussein after an Arab Nationalist takeover in Iraq killed his cousin, King Faisal II. Instead, it has used other means to flex its muscle and back the kingship. During the Cold War, the United States deployed forceful diplomacy—such as threatening hostile Arab states and declaring Jordanian sovereignty as a national interest—whenever it felt Hussein's rule imperiled by domestic foes or regional rivals, as in the April 1957 crackdown and the 1970 Black September conflict. The April 2021 coup conspiracy involving Prince Hamzah illustrated subtler methods of support. US intelligence alerted King Abdullah to his half-brother's dealings, while President Biden issued full-throated statements of support for the king after the army had detained all the alleged conspirators.

Second, the United States and its allies discourage democracy and publicly valorize authoritarian rule in Jordan. They offer only muted criticism over Jordan's uninspiring human rights record, knowing that a truly representative government—such as one dominated by Islamists or liberals—could be far less pro-Western. As Benjamin Schuetze has pointed out, since the 1990s, when democracy promotion became part of many Western foreign policies, the United States and European donors have therefore played a game of double-speak.[61] They operate many democracy assistance programs. Yet while these programs improve public life, they do not confront the monarchy's vast powers, as Chapter 6 touched upon. Instead, the sliver of Western foreign aid that supports democratic reforms by funding civil society associations, training political parties, and monitoring elections ultimately back "regime-compliant" activities.[62] They do not aim at encouraging Jordanians to protest against the government or adopt opposition ideologies like Islamism, much less question the basis of Hashemite rule

Similarly, the United States has never rebuked the Hashemite palace after its reneging on repeated democratic reform promises since the 1990s. Neither has it punished repressive backsliding—such as draconian restrictions on basic freedom, such as the 2023 Cybercrimes Law—by issuing public warnings that embarrass officials or withholding aid and arms in the name of human rights principles. The result is diplomatic sophistry. The regime knows its democratic pledges mean little; the West knows they mean little; the regime knows the West knows; and the West knows that the regime knows.[63] So it goes for the Arab world's oasis of moderation.

Third, the United States has historically provided technical economic resources that have strengthened the Jordanian state's capacity to administer and govern the populace. Since the 1960s, the US Agency for International Development (USAID) has financed, designed, or managed many public institutions to alleviate the burden of national governance for Jordan's cash-strapped state. Critically, much of USAID's development programs were dismantled by the Trump administration in early 2025, but this came as part of the agency's across-the-board downsizing rather than any specific targeting of Jordan. Nonetheless, the legacy of its historical involvement endures. For instance, large swathes of local infrastructure partly or wholly originate from USAID schemes, such as highways and roads, agricultural networks, sanitation plants, and business parks—what Anne Mariel Zimmerman has tellingly called Jordan's "parallel institutions."[64] Indeed, over time, USAID development projects have come to touch virtually every major public service, such as education, healthcare, women's rights, and youth programs. USAID even designed and oversaw much of Jordan's national water systems, such as the King Abdullah Canal (formerly East Ghor Canal) and the Disi Water Conveyance project.

Beyond USAID, American planners and consultants in recent decades have branched out to improve other areas of governance such as business registration, tax collection, and judicial training—in effect helping to build and operate the Jordanian state itself. Even purely social policies bear American thumbprints. For instance, in 2018 the US Department of Agriculture helped Jordan replace its longstanding bread subsidy with a more targeted welfare program, which combatted rising wheat and bread prices by transferring cash payments to poor families. The controversial neoliberal move intended to cut public welfare spending, and was directly modeled on the US-based Supplemental Nutrition Assistance Program, otherwise known as "food stamps."

Fourth, the United States has provided direct economic payments to the Hashemite regime. Jordan receives assistance from many donors, but America's aid spigot has been the largest and most consistent. From 1957 to 2024, the United States delivered more than $30 billion in foreign assistance, of which two-thirds has been economic.[65] Despite fluctuating over time, such aid payments have historically filled the Jordanian state's budgetary chasm caused by low domestic revenues and high public spending, thus staving off insolvency. During 1957–1962, when King Hussein reasserted autocratic power after years of political unrest, Amman received more US economic aid payments than *all* domestic revenues from taxes, tariffs, and other local income.

That pattern continued under King Abdullah. For instance, Jordan backed the 2003 Iraq War, despite it causing considerable financial damage due to lost trade and oil imports with its neighbor. To cushion the blow, the US gave an unprecedented $1.8 billion economic aid package during 2003-2005, equivalent to $540 per person in Jordan. Since then, US financial subventions have been dispensed through multiyear aid guarantees coordinated between the two governments, each one growing in size. Whereas the 2009–2014 US-Jordanian aid agreement provided the kingdom with $600 million of economic assistance per year, the latest 2023–2029 agreement delivers an economic aid baseline of $1 billion annually—a huge sum given that in 2024 the Jordanian treasury collected about $10 billion in national taxes. The only other countries where US economic assistance is equivalent to double-digit percentages of domestic government revenues are allies at war, like Ukraine during its conflict with Russia, and very poor states like Somalia or Afghanistan prior to its 2021 reclamation by the Taliban.

US aid to Jordan is indispensable because it contains a special cash component. Historically, American economic assistance has come in many forms, such as the technical support described earlier, food shipments, soft loans, and humanitarian funding. However, the biggest component has always entailed cash grants called Economic Support Funds (ESF), which entail money transfers directly to the Jordanian government. Jordanian officials, in turn, treat those incoming funds like any other revenue stream—as fungible resources to be spent on normal budgetary items like paying public salaries. That the US has delivered such budgetary grants so consistently for many decades signifies their importance. Wealthy Gulf states like Saudi Arabia can generously wire cash to Amman as well, but they also capriciously rescind such aid payments whenever oil prices dip or Jordanian foreign policy veers from their demands. The World Bank and IMF have loaned Jordan billions of dollars since the late 1980s, but under the condition of Jordan implementing neoliberal economic reforms that bring political tradeoffs, such as reducing price subsidies. Even purely humanitarian programs, such as the 2016 Jordan Compact, require stipulated aid funds to be allocated to specific projects and communities, so as to prevent its misuse. By contrast, ESF grants from Washington are literally money in the Jordanian bank. They illustrate how there are "no strings attached" to American foreign aid, as one recent US ambassador assured to the Jordanian media.[66]

Fifth, since the 1994 peace treaty with Israel, the United States has also helped advance King Abdullah's neoliberal reform agenda to revivify the previously state-led economy, although with only modest success. Some efforts have come through USAID projects aimed at job creation, such as small business funding and youth entrepreneurship programs. Others entail high-level American policies affecting all of Jordan. For example, since 1995, the Jordanian dinar has been pegged to the US dollar at a fixed rate, foreclosing any currency volatility that might harm trade and investment. American advisors guided Jordan's accession the World Trade Organization in 2000, and that year Jordan became just the fourth country to sign a US free trade agreement.[67] Within years, the United States had become Jordan's top export destination, and new US-Jordanian investment, aviation, and technology treaties followed. Another exceptional indicator of American help came in 2013, the Jordanian government began issuing billions of dollars in Eurobonds on the international market. This, by itself, was not exceptional. Many sovereign states raise money through public bonds to assuage short-term fiscal crunches; but like all loans, these require eventual repayment. Uniquely, the US Treasury Department guaranteed Jordan's bond issuances: if its government were to default on these debts,

Washington would repay them itself. Such a privilege currently extends only to a handful of other American client states and allies, like Israel and wartime Ukraine.

Sixth, US security assistance has helped militarize Jordan. The expansion of Western military forces based across the East Bank over the past two decades has made the kingdom the most secure from foreign aggression it has ever been. However, the United States has also directly bolstered the capacity of the Hashemite regime's coercive apparatus, which, as Chapter 4 described, underprops its *domestic* power. Within the intelligence field, the CIA has provided the GID with funds, technology, and skills for decades, expediting their cooperation since the US War on Terror. The CIA has its own sordid history in Jordan, running much of its regional clandestine operations from Amman.[68] It has fervidly supported Hashemite rule, from secret cash payments funneled to King Hussein to the regular sharing of high-level information. One American official observed that the Jordanian king "had a closer relationship with the local CIA station chief than with the American ambassador."[69]

Equally impactful has been aid to the JAF. The United States has helped arm and finance the Jordanian military since the late 1950s. The goal has not been to make the armed forces a sleek and competent fighting machine that can dominate the Middle East; Washington, after all, has long guaranteed the Israeli military's superiority over any Arab army. Neither does the United States need the JAF to singlehandedly defend Jordanian sovereignty from outside attack, given its own military bases and defense networks in the kingdom. Rather, US security assistance ensures that the JAF undertakes small operations when necessary, enjoys high morale, and can seamlessly work with American advisers and troops should war come close.[70] Such militarized aid manifests through assorted measures. For decades, the United States has transferred knowledge and skills by training thousands of JAF officers in exchange programs. It has also delivered weaponry and technology to the armed forces, such as small arms, guided missiles, warplanes, vehicles, artillery, and radar systems. Importantly, most of these American arms transfers are not sales: they are grants, mostly given through special credits (termed Foreign Military Financing) that allow the JAF to procure US weaponry at no real cost.

As Figure 8.2 tracks, the overall value of US military assistance over time has been enormous. Since 1965, it has equaled 24 percent of Jordan's own military spending—a proportion unseen outside wartime countries under US occupation. In some post-conflict years, as in following the 1970 Black September civil war and Iraq War, this coercive support spiked; during 2003 alone, it outpaced the entire JAF budget. All this assistance has defrayed the regime's internal cost of sustaining its oversized armed forces. When Jordan receives over $400 million annually in foreign military financing, as it has for the past decade, it means that

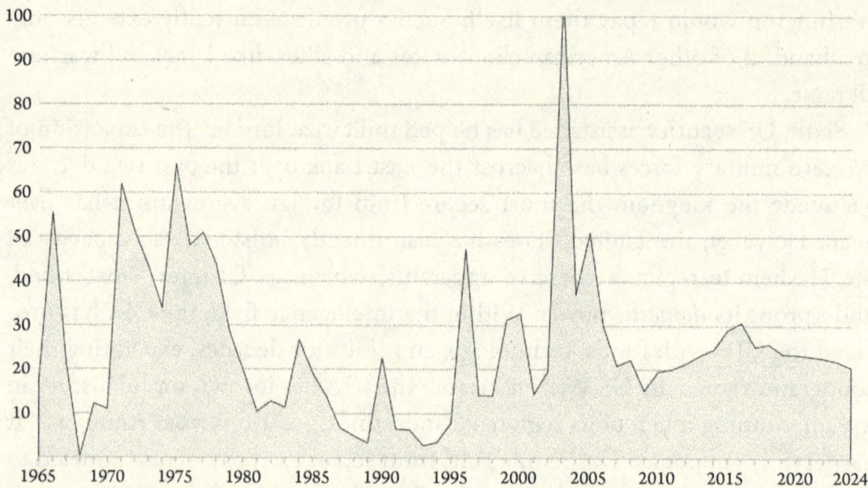

Figure 8.2 Value of US Military Assistance Compared to Jordanian Military Budget, 1960–2024. Sources: Central Bank of Jordan, *Annual Statistical Bulletin* (CBJ, various years); World Bank, *World Development Indicators* (IBRD, various years).

the royal autocracy does not need to spend that much of its own scarce finances to purchase arms and technology on the commercial market.

In totality, these six mechanisms of patronage and protection represent Jordan's geopolitical payoffs for aligning with the United States and the West. By shoring up Hashemite rule, they have made America not just complicit with, but an active participant in, Jordan's authoritarian order. For its part, the United States has gained much from this patron-client relationship. So long as the Jordanian monarchy maintains peace with Israel, cooperates on military issues, and reaffirms strategic goals like containing Iran, Washington will stand by the monarchy—and conversely, see any "serious threat to regime stability" as endangering "core US and allied interests."[71] That, in a nutshell, is why Jordanian foreign policy remains so invested in American hegemony, despite its contemporary wars across the Middle East, blind favoritism of Israel, and most recent unpredictability under the Trump administration.

Conclusion

Jordanian foreign policy cannot be essentialized into the one-line descriptors that punctuate popular portrayals of the country. Objectively, it is not simply (or even at all) the keystone to all stability in the Middle East, because the kingdom is too small and weak to lead the regional agenda. Neither is it simply a monument to Hashemite moderation, because this imbues mysterious qualities into a concrete and logical strategy of dealing with threats to regime security. At heart, this royal autocracy engages the external world through the prism of pragmatism. Its ever-changing friendships, rivalries, and engagements in the MENA have aimed to reduce whatever external threat, domestic opposition, or ideational challenge most immediately imperils regime security. Just like coercing dissent within society as well as maintaining a sticky coalition of mostly Transjordanian support, the ruling monarchy uses its foreign policy to gain breathing room by which to exercise power, project its interests, and plot the future.

It has seldom been easy, though. The kingdom's constant maneuverings around various Middle East crises since the 1950s attest to the success of its flexible outlook. Yet no amount of Jordanian politicking has mitigated the fallout of the Israeli-Palestinian conflict. That unresolved predicament poses an existential threat to Hashemite rule, dredging up the possibility of the alternative homeland scenario while kindling incendiary domestic anger over Israel's demolition of Palestinian self-determination. The other constant in Jordanian foreign policy has been the United States. Historically, this great power patron has proffered mammoth help to its client regime through savvy diplomacy, economic aid, and military assistance, in return for the regime's pro-Western advocacy and commitments. Certainly, the US sometimes displeases the Hashemite palace with its own regional endeavors, as recent dealings with the Trump administration attest. In all, however, nailing the Jordanian flag to the American mast provides the monarchy with the surest guarantee of international support. For all these reasons, Jordan's foreign policy encapsulates much of the engrossing nuance and complexities that characterize its politics as a whole.

9

Expect the Unexpected . . . and Nothing Is Unexpected

What Does Jordan's Future Behold?

During a summer 2024 visit to Jordan, I gathered with local friends in our favorite Amman café to hungrily discuss the Hashemite Kingdom's latest political events. There was much to ponder. Israeli bombs were falling upon Palestinian Gaza, national unemployment exceeded 21 percent, Islamists and grassroots activists were leading street protests, a half-million refugees still lived in poverty, a journalist colleague had just been arrested for publishing online criticism against the government, and gossip coursed that the king would abruptly fire his unpopular prime minister.

In other words, it was a typical year in Jordan.

As the confab adjourned, I wondered to my companions what distant Western audiences should think about this unassuming Arab country. It was so easy to repeat the distorting tropes of global media coverage—that given all its latest troubles, Jordan teetered on the brink of disaster, but this geopolitical oasis of stability and pro-Western moderation might well survive if its valiant monarchy steered through the coming storm. As we all recognized, though, such trite stereotyping was useless, replacing meaningful ideas with tired clichés. Was there any decent direction by which to gaze into the future? One friend chortled the parting wisdom: "Expect the unexpected. But remember, nothing in Jordan is unexpected anymore."

That refrain perfectly summarizes the endless nuance of Jordanian politics, which this book has sought to capture. Jordan is not a big, rich, or democratic state. It has never been regarded as a dominant player in Middle East politics over its century of history. Yet, thanks to its strategic locale (and its preposterously zigzagging borders), the country influences, and is influenced by, almost every major crisis in the Arab world that captivates Western readers and policymakers. Jordan's fate should hence matter to anyone remotely curious about the Middle

East. It abuts civil conflict and warring states. It is party to the Israel-Palestinian conflict, and it has one of the highest rates of refugees hosted per capita in the world. At the same time, enigmatic puzzles lurk within the country. Here, a system of authoritarian governance under the ruling Hashemite monarchy thrives, and it has stayed remarkably constant over many generations despite facing various shocks and ruptures. Opposition movements, refugee influxes, economic meltdown, sharp inequality, mass protests, terrorist attacks, Islamist mobilization, identity disputes, palace intrigues: these are no strangers to Jordan, no less so than the constancy of Hashemite rule.

That *permanence* can be ascribed to Jordan, this diminutive Arabian hinterland long regarded as a byproduct of British colonialism, is tribute to how nothing indeed is unexpected anymore in this modest corner of the Middle East—least of all its own existence. The late Wahib al-Sha'ir, a prolific Jordanian intellectual, ruminated over this mystifying fact in his controversial (and banned) 2004 book.[1] As he wrote, few other creations of modern sovereignty brim with as many paradoxes as Jordan. It beholds one of humanity's last ruling monarchies that commands vast repressive powers, but which publicly preaches its fondness for democracy and civil society. Its oil-poor economy produces little of global value despite worshiping on the altar of market-based capitalism, and it somehow averts financial ruin through a steady diet of foreign aid and sheer luck. Jordanian nationhood centers on flags, rituals, and patriotic myths, but few citizens can pinpoint what being Jordanian truly means across their many social differences, such as the Transjordanian-Palestinian divide.

Even by the volatile standards of the Middle East, few countries present such a curious conurbation of puzzles. This happens to be one that borders Israel, promotes Western strategic interests, and sports a king whose family descends from the Prophet Muhammad. Given these complications, it is critical to reassess what, overall, can be gleaned from such a place. As this volume has expounded upon, Jordanian politics are fascinating because its furrows hold illuminating lessons about much broader themes in regional affairs and international politics—specifically, the nature of authoritarian rule, the throes of democratic contention, and the challenge of making do in the contemporary Middle East.

Authoritarianism Is Not Mysterious

Unlike much of the Arab world, Jordan has never experienced regime change since its formation as a sovereign state. No revolutionary uprisings or military coups have overthrown its royal leadership, unlike the fate of so many other monarchical dictatorships and despotic republics around the world since World War II. It is tempting to ascribe this resilience to some mysterious quality, such as the cultural essence of royalism or the dauntless tenacity of the Hashemite pedigree. But doing so would miss the bigger picture.

Understanding how political systems endure over time, particularly the endangered species of authoritarianism known as ruling monarchism, requires unpacking the institutions and practices that organize power. In Jordan, political power centers on predictable rhythms and structures, not haphazard caprice. As Chapter 3 discussed, a small core of unelected decision-making elites—the rulemakers—operate a monarchical regime with tentacular influence. At the center stands the king, who brandishes incontestable authority. King Abdullah, who has ruled since 1999, is like his predecessors. He bears the pomp and regalia of a rarefied Muslim dynasty, but in practical terms is also an imperfect politician who, as the head executive, will reign until abdication or death, after which his son, Crown Prince Hussein, will take over. The king does not rule alone, of course. Responsibility for key functions within this system falls upon other entrusted figures, from the military and security chiefs to the Diwan's royal officialdom. Parliament and its elected lower house command much attention, but has little role in determining domestic or foreign policies, much less overseeing this highly centralized state's bureaucracy; that job goes to the royally appointed government, whose prime ministers answer to the monarchy. Within this framework, ordinary Jordanians cannot freely choose their political leaders through elections, much less meaningfully constrain how their autocracy creates the laws that regulate their public lives. This is no democracy.

Yet for all its flaws, this authoritarian political order has endured across many generations despite breeding a fair bit of corruption, clientelism, and abuse. As Chapter 4 showed, entirely rational mechanisms explain this. Autocracies can last a long time with successful strategies that balance controlling opposition with rallying public support. The Hashemite regime has done this ably. It operates a colossal coercive apparatus. Its armed forces, civil police, and intelligence directorate monitor, regulate, and punish those who speak out too brazenly. These days, Jordanian officials prefer using softer, defter methods of repression to chill dissent, avoiding the ghastly bloodshed that doomed tyrants like Assad in Syria or Qaddafi in Libya. At the same time, the monarchy has also drawn the conditional loyalty of Transjordanian tribal communities by incorporating them into its economic and political institutions. It has patronized other groups too, from well-to-do merchants and business elites to minorities like Christians and Circassians. Some of these coalitional pacts that helped build the Jordanian state are now fading, as King Abdullah has embraced a sleeker, narrower model of technocratic governance in the twenty-first century. However, they are sticky enough to ensure that this regime maintains robust linkages with its social foundation, and compels not just reluctant compliance but also support from significant parts of the populace.

Such arrangements impart an enduring message. From a distance, Jordan's regime and state may seem to wobble whenever subjected to sudden crisis, such as economic turmoil or external conflict. Since it has few natural resources and a diverse society where disgruntled voices frequently protest, perhaps it has been inevitable that, for decades, Western onlookers have repeated the same tired question at the first sign of unrest: will the monarchy survive, or will everything collapse? Such cyclical anxiety has added little to our collective knowledge. Jordan pulls through every time not because its royal backbone willed it or the historical gods foretold it, but because its levers of autocratic governance manage to balance the containment of opposition with the selective cultivation of public support. It is an ageless formula for resilience: quash enemies and reward friends, with the right balance between the two. Rulers who stray too far from these precepts do not last long. The growing graveyard of deposed dictators in the Middle East since the 2011–2012 Arab Spring attests to this.

Stability Is Not Stasis

When evaluated against the depressing benchmarks of its Middle East surroundings, foreign observers often see Jordan as a calm and peaceful place, like a geopolitical fortress of solitude. Its leadership stokes this image vigorously when pitching the kingdom to foreign investors, Western tourists, aid donors and other global audiences. When compared to the state-wrecking crises in nearby Palestine, Lebanon, Syria, and Iraq in recent years, Jordan indeed looks like the consummate island of stability. However, stability is not *stasis*. In matters of domestic politics, the absence of violence or revolution does not mean the absence of change and struggle. The political equilibrium that has cohered on the East Bank of the Jordan River for the past century boils down to a stolid dynamic: an unelected government practices authoritarian power over an ever-aspiring populace, whose own dreams and demands often produce opposition and resistance. Jordanians of all stripes—secular or Islamist, Muslim or Christian, Transjordanian or Palestinian—have campaigned for democratic reforms and ideals of justice since the kingdom's founding.

Jordanians mobilize and protest for many reasons. As Chapter 2 recounted, one is that the story of Jordanian nationhood itself is unfinished. The country's history inverts the classical model of Western modernization theory. Here, no primordial embryo of nationhood coalesced organically, giving rise to a cohesive people that sought self-determination in a homeland they cherished as their own. It was British imperialism, not ancient nationalism, that invented the Jordanian state in 1921, which in turn tried to weave a mostly Muslim nation out of disparate social threads running across this desert patchwork on the eastern bank of the Jordan River.

Today, this task of defining and realizing Jordanian nationhood remains a work in progress. Many Transjordanian tribes and communities learned to accommodate their implanted Hashemite monarchy early on, despite its foreign origins. So too did traders, merchants, Circassians, Christians, and other local groups, though never at the cost of forgetting their own identity and history. The situation with many Palestinian-Jordanians is more convoluted. Their experiences reflect not just their origins as refugees from the Arab-Israeli conflicts but also their marginalization in national politics. Frictions with Transjordanian nativists, who are worried about a Palestinian takeover of the East Bank, stoke wider debates over what being Jordanian means and who authentically represents Jordan-ness. Meanwhile, fears of Israel annexing all of historic Palestine on the other side of the Jordan River and the prospect of the Hashemite Kingdom being forced to absorb millions more Palestinian refugees panic everyone. In this social terrain, there is pluralism and diversity, but also disagreement and contention, the sort of mishmash that makes many Jordanians wonder whether their own leaders have made the best decisions.

Often, they conclude otherwise. Jordan may be a putative stronghold of political moderation when compared to its neighbors, but this bastion also beholds constant confrontation between rule-makers and rule-followers (i.e., this authoritarian regime and its vocal society). As Chapter 5 explained, the indomitable capacity of ordinary people to contest their autocratic regime by organizing and mobilizing their own interests in public spaces is a hallmark of Jordanian politics. In the early 1930s, the Transjordanian National Congress movements demanded political representation; in the 1950s, the Jordanian National Movement sought to radically curtail royal power in favor of elected government. In the 1990s, civil society groups like the professional syndicates and opposition forces like the Muslim Brotherhood claimed the mantle of democracy, pressing King Hussein to open up the political system while opposing controversial policies like the Israeli peace treaty.

Under King Abdullah, such dissidents have become more grizzled as they partake in activism and protest. As Chapter 6 showed, they rally around familiar issues, such as solidarity with Palestine, economic demands for more jobs, political outcry against corruption, and greater democracy. But even the youngest activists know how their regime and its coercive guardians tilt the playing field by biasing parliamentary elections, handicapping opposition parties, dominating the media, manipulating laws, and when all else fails punishing critics through outright repression. However, despite periodic crackdowns against prominent opposition forces such as Islamists, they have also learned to sidestep such constraining measures. As the Arab Spring and its subsequent years highlighted, frustrated Jordanians spearhead grassroots movements, coordinate spontaneous protests, defy edicts to stay home, pioneer creative forms of dissent, and claim new online spaces of expression in the name of democratic participation. They do not back down.

Jordan's royal autocracy and its restive society are locked in a mutually constitutive dance, sometimes swaying together but often deviating from one another as well. When they diverge, the voices of people—communities, classes, movements, parties, activists, and crowds—ring out with collective demands for greater opportunities and freedom. This social din comprises no less an important part of Jordanian politics than the institutions of the Hashemite state, and the political elites who operate it.

Bigger Forces Loom

Across international affairs, smallness has profound implications. Most small states can never become great powers. Some, like Jordan, have only middling control over their economic development and external security because they are buffeted by outside pressures and threats. Whereas much of domestic politics distills into a tug of war between state and society, in matters of economic development and foreign policy, the quintessential flashpoint revolves around how Jordan's government and people make the best of unfavorable conditions. Put another way: the kingdom faces regional dangers it cannot fight, as well as economic constraints it cannot flee.

Jordanians, for instance, never chose to have a small economy. As Chapter 7 reviewed, the limited wealth, high unemployment, and rising poverty that have punctuated the economic arena over the past several decades partly come from geographic misfortune. Regional conflicts and external competition within the Middle East hamper Jordan's precious energy imports and trade flows; its lack of water and shrinking agricultural footprint, thanks to an increasingly arid ecology, do not help. Against all odds, early state planners had success in lightly industrializing the economy after the 1950s. However, following the late 1980s financial crisis, a newer paradigm of neoliberal economic reforms advanced by the Hashemite regime subjected the kingdom to a different set of challenges. Here, Jordan's financial gambles and economic mismanagement come into sharper relief.

From the 1990s onward, royal technocrats prioritized the relentless quest for profit and modernization through market-based capitalism. However, few new productive industries and job-creating sectors have flourished. Instead, privatization, free trade, and austerity measures that have slashed social spending have not enriched the masses. Indeed, many Jordanians—including tribal communities traditionally protected by the monarchy—see their lot as having horrendously deteriorated in an era in which market competition has replaced state-led guidance as the overarching strategy for national economic development. The regime's own stubborn policy commitments borne out of its authoritarian qualities, such as military overspending, business cronyism, and bureaucratic wastage, have made things worse and further limited inclusive and sustainable growth. Massive foreign aid from Western allies like the United States and global lenders like the World Bank today keep this economic system afloat, but such dependency is not sustainable, not least because economic privations have become the leading catalyst for contentious demonstrations and opposition.

The same grind of navigating unforgiving headwinds also characterizes Jordan's foreign policy. In terms of military capabilities and external prestige, the kingdom has a weak and vulnerable profile. This is problematic in a fickle Middle East neighborhood, where rival states, terrorist attacks, and radical ideologies have frequently imperiled the Hashemite monarchy's perceived stability and peace. It makes do with a strategy of naked opportunism: the royal leadership entertains new alliances, strikes diplomatic deals, and flexibly shifts its position on geopolitical crises so long as this neutralizes whatever external threat seems to jeopardize its immediate security the most. It has few grand ambitions save keeping its reign stable and borders secure.

This coldly rational logic explains why the kingdom has become one of America's closest client states in the world. By defending Western interests and facilitating US strategic goals in the Middle East—which include hosting an armada of Western military forces—Jordan's monarchy reaps diplomatic backing, economic support, and security assistance. It makes sense to align with American hegemony, even if this brings accusations from Jordanian critics that the Hashemites have sold out their lot to the West. What makes even less sense to ordinary Jordanians is why their leadership ever made peace with Israel. The Israeli-Palestinian conflict has deteriorated tragically since the 1990s, raising fears in Amman that conservative Israeli governments will seize what remains of Palestine and displace a new wave of Palestinian refugees upon the East Bank. Despite having crafted peace with Israel in 1994, Jordan wields little leverage to prevent its neighbor from further dismantling the dream of Palestinian self-determination by unleashing new hailstorms of violence drowning the West Bank and Gaza Strip.

Economic turbulence and regional challenges have political manifestations in Jordan. A sluggish economy, where a third of the populace lives in poverty and nearly one in two young people cannot find a job, makes few households happy.

Meanwhile, a flailing foreign policy that puts the kingdom on the losing side of the Israeli-Palestinian crisis ratchets up domestic pressure on the Hashemite palace. There are no easy answers to these dilemmas, but that is the point: these dilemmas are formidable, and yet Jordan muddles through.

A Better Measuring Stick

Jordan has plentiful political challenges, economic hardships, and regional crises ahead. Its people will not stop mobilizing for greater rights or voicing their grievances through protest. High unemployment, worsening poverty, and steep living costs borne out of the false hope of neoliberal fortune will not solve themselves. The calamitous events that have shaken the Middle East beyond the Hashemite Kingdom's borders—revolution, war, terrorism—will not disappear. Given this foreboding road, it is tempting to use the lowest common denominator in forecasting the future. So long as Jordan looks better off than, say, a broken Lebanon, a war-torn Syria, or a sectarianized Iraq, then all is well. It might last for yet another century still.

This is the wrong take because it uses the wrong measuring stick. Both Jordan's leadership and its people want not merely to avoid something bad, but rather to accomplish something distinctively good and, therefore, worthy of being called an overachievement. As this book has considered, their competing imaginations give rise to lucid possibilities—of democracy and prosperity, dignity and inclusion, stability and strength, poise and pride. These visions can propel the intrepid outlook of this critical country, but only on terms that Jordanians themselves choose through shared struggle and bold inspiration. It is up to everyone else, including the West, to catch up to this audacity.

NOTES

Chapter 1

1. The most comprehensive English-language histories include Philip Robins, *A History of Jordan*, 2nd ed. (Cambridge University Press, 2020); and Kamal Salibi, *The Modern History of Jordan* (IB Tauris, 1998). In Arabic, the most well-known, if aging, chronology remains Sulayman Musa and Munib al-Madi, *Ta'rikh al-urdun fil-qarn al-'ashrin, 1900–1995* [The History of Jordan in the Twentieth Century, 1900–1995], 2 vols. (Maktabat Al-Muhtasib, 1995).
2. Myriam Ababsa, "Jordan's Land Cover: A Land of Contrasts," in *Atlas of Jordan: History, Territories, and Society*, ed. Myriam Ababsa (IFPO, 2014), 40–41.
3. Eugene Rogan, *Frontiers of the State in the Late Ottoman Empire: Transjordan, 1850–1921* (Cambridge University Press, 1999), 21.
4. Betty Anderson, "The Evolution of Jordanian Studies," *Critique: Critical Middle Eastern Studies* 12, no. 2 (2003): 197, https://doi.org/10.1080/1066992032000130648.
5. Take, for instance, the late Robert Fisk's ode to Beirut: "[The Lebanese] are a fine, educated, moral people whose generosity amazes every foreigner, whose gentleness puts any Westerner to shame, and whose suffering we almost always ignore. They look like us, the people of Beirut. They have light-coloured skin and speak beautiful English and French. They travel the world. Their women are gorgeous and their food exquisite." Western journalists have given no equivalent elegy for Jordan and its people. Robert Fisk, "Paradise Lost: Robert Fisk's Elegy for Beirut," *The Independent*, July 19, 2006.
6. Thomas Friedman, *From Beirut to Jerusalem*, Rev. ed. (Picador, 2012), 65.
7. I am indebted to Jordanian economist Riad Khouri, who, after decades of banter, reminded me of this droll term. Personal interview, Riad Khouri, Amman, Jordan, May 19, 2024.
8. Mohammed Ayoob, *Will the Middle East Implode?* (Polity, 2014), 162–163.
9. This counts research essays dedicated primarily to Jordan—that is, "single-country" case studies and articles.
10. Elena Corbett, *Competitive Archaeology in Jordan: Narrating Identity from the Ottomans to the Hashemites* (University of Texas Press, 2014), 195–207.
11. Many global consumers were first introduced to Petra in the 1989 Hollywood film *Indiana Jones and the Last Crusade*, which used its Nabatean ruins as the setting for a modern-day biblical tale.
12. Paula Froelich, "Ladies' Night in Amman, Jordan, Is Not as Tame as You Might Think," *New York Post*, May 6, 2015.
13. Robin Wright, "Beyond ISIS Turmoil, Jordan Is Flush with Problems," *Wall Street Journal*, February 4, 2015.
14. Fares Braizat, "Jordan on the Brink Again, Really?" *Jordan Times*, April 19, 2019.
15. Peter Mansfield, "Syria and Jordan: The Desert and the Sown," *Asian Affairs* 16, no. 1 (1985): 20–28, https://doi.org/10.1080/03068378508730169.

16. James Morris, *The Hashemite Kings* (Pantheon, 1959), 189.
17. Central Intelligence Agency, "Assessment of Situation in Jordan and Estimate of Outlook," National Intelligence Estimate ORE 23–49, March 10, 1959, declassified document.
18. Stephen Kaplan, "United States Aid and Regime Maintenance in Jordan, 1957–1973," *Public Policy* 23, no. 2 (1975): 189–217.
19. Lawrence Tal, "Is Jordan Doomed?" *Foreign Affairs* 72, no. 5 (1993): 45–58, https://doi.org/10.2307/20045813.
20. Stephen Glain, *Mullahs, Merchants, and Militants: The Economic Collapse of the Arab World* (Thomas Dunne, 2004), 135.
21. Borzou Daragahi, "Jordan's King Risks Shah's Fate, Critics Warn," *The Los Angeles Times*, October 1, 2006.
22. Kamran Bokhari, "Jordan: The Small Kingdom in the Middle," *Geopolitical Futures*, December 20, 2016, https://geopoliticalfutures.com/jordan-the-small-kingdom-in-the-middle/.
23. David Schenker, "Saving Jordan's King Abdullah Must Be a U.S. Priority," Policy Analysis of The Washington Institute for Near East Policy, March 21, 2013, https://www.washingtoninstitute.org/policy-analysis/saving-jordans-king-abdullah-must-be-us-priority.
24. Stephen D. Krasner, "Sharing Sovereignty: New Institutions for Collapsing and Failing States," *International Security* 29, no. 2 (2004): 85–120, https://doi.org/10.1162/0162288042879940.
25. See, for instance, "Surprisingly Stable at the Moment," *The Economist*, November 9, 2013; "The Uneasy Crown," *The Economist*, October 20, 2016; and "Unstable Neighbours and Bad Policy Are Just Two of Jordan's Problems," *The Economist*, April 28, 2018.
26. Hassan Bin Talal, "Return to Geneva," *Foreign Policy* 57 (1984/1985): 12–13, https://www.jstor.org/stable/1148324.
27. Alan George, *Jordan: Living in the Crossfire* (Zed, 2005).
28. Cameron Forbes, "Plucky Little Jordanians Cock a Snook at World," *Sydney Morning Herald*, September 6, 1990.
29. Asher Susser, *Jordan: Case Study of a Pivotal State* (The Washington Institute for Near East Policy, 2000), 13–36.
30. Yehuda Lukacs, *Israel, Jordan, and the Peace Process* (Syracuse University Press, 1997), 138–180.
31. Adam Garfinkle, "Jordan in World Politics," in *Jordan in the Middle East: The Making of a Pivotal State*, eds. Joseph Nevo and Ilan Pappé (Frank Cass, 1994), 286.
32. Bassam al-Badarin, "'Asaas al-istiqraar' . . . kalimat almaniyyah fi wasf al-urdun ['The Basis of Stability' . . . a German Word in Describing Jordan]," *Al-Quds Al-Arabi*, March 16, 2022.
33. Beverly Milton-Edwards and Peter Hinchcliffe, *Jordan: A Hashemite Legacy*, 2nd ed. (Routledge, 2009), 5.
34. Fawaz Gerges, "The Study of Middle East International Relations: A Critique," *British Journal of Middle Eastern Studies* 18, no. 2 (1991): 208–220.
35. See, for instance, Khalid Al-Subul, *Al-hashimiyyun: min hukm al-imarah al-'uthmaniyyah illa ta'sis al-mamaalik al-'arabiyyah* [The Hashemites: From Governance of the Ottoman Emirate to the Establishment of the Arab Kings] (Al-Ahliyyah Lil-Nashr Wal-Tawzi', 2011).
36. Andrew Shryock, "Dynastic Modernism and its Contradictions: Testing the Limits of Pluralism, Tribalism, and King Hussein's Example in Hashemite Jordan," *Arab Studies Quarterly* 22, no. 3 (2000): 57–79.
37. John Bagot Glubb, *A Soldier with the Arabs* (Harper, 1957), 438.
38. "Master of Survival," *The New York Times*, September 22, 1970.
39. Uncritical treatments of King Hussein span his entire lifetime. Samples include Peter Snow, *Hussein: A Biography* (Barrie and Jenkins, 1972), Uriel Dann, *King Hussein's Survival Strategy* (Washington Institute for Near East Policy, 1992), and Roland Dallas, *King Hussein: A Life on the Edge* (Fromm, 1999). Broadcast specials have also proliferated, most recently the two-part *King Hussein*, dir. Suhaib Abu Doulah (Al-Jazeera, 2017). The most balanced biographies are better rooted in academic documents but nonetheless retain a celebratory tone. These are Avi Shlaim, *Lion of Jordan: The Life of King Hussein in War and Peace* (Vintage, 2009); and Nigel Ashton, *King Hussein of Jordan: A Political Life* (Yale University Press, 2010).

40. Lee Smith, "The Arab World's Can-Do Guy," *Slate*, May 7, 2004, https://slate.com/news-and-politics/2004/05/the-arab-world-s-can-do-guy.html.
41. Jeffrey Goldberg, "The Modern King in the Arab Spring," *The Atlantic*, April 2013, 45–55.
42. Alia Awadallah, "Washington Needs to Get to Know Jordan's Next King," *Foreign Policy*, July 13, 2020, https://foreignpolicy.com/2020/07/13/crown-prince-hussein-the-next-king-of-jordan/.
43. These are the eight Arab kingdoms (Jordan, Morocco, Saudi Arabia, Bahrain, Kuwait, Qatar, Oman, and the United Arab Emirates), Eswatini, and Brunei.
44. Ahmad Majdoubeh, "Planning for the Coming 100 Years," *Jordan Times*, February 6, 2021.
45. Joel Migdal, *State in Society: Studying How States and Societies Transform and Constitute One Another* (Cambridge University Press, 2001), 58–94.
46. Tariq Tell, "The Resilience of Hashemite Rule: Studies in the History of Jordan, 1946–67," in *The Resilience of Hashemite Rule: Politics and the State in Jordan, 1946–67*, ed. Tariq Tell (CERMOC, 2001), 13.

Chapter 2

1. Rana F. Sweis, *Voices of Jordan* (Hurst, 2018), 3.
2. The classic exposition on this topic comes from Manuel Castells, *The Urban Question: A Marxist Approach* (MIT Press, 1979).
3. Luna Khirfan and Bessma Momani, "Tracing Participatory Planning in Amman," in *Order and Disorder: Urban Governance and the Making of Middle Eastern Cities*, ed. Luna Khirfan (McGill-Queens University Press, 2017), 95.
4. Mohamed Tarawneh and Abdel Hakim Al-Husban, "Rural Poverty in Jordan: Assessment and Characterisation," *Anthropology of the Middle East* 6, no. 2 (2011): 94–107, https://doi.org/10.3167/ame.2011.060208.
5. Philippe Droz-Vincent, "Cities, Urban Notables and the State in Jordan," in *Villes, Pratiques Urbaines et Construction Nationale en Jordanie*, eds. Myriam Ababsa and Rami Farouk Daher (IFPO, 2013), 103–126.
6. Jillian Schwedler, *Protesting Jordan: Geographies of Power and Dissent* (Stanford University Press, 2022), 63–96.
7. These and subsequent population data are drawn from Jordanian Department of Statistics, *Online Statistical Databank*, https://dosweb.dos.gov.jo/.
8. Jon Gorvett, "Westerners at Home in Amman," *The New York Times*, June 25, 2008.
9. Much has been written about these megaprojects. See, for instance, Christopher Parker, "Tunnel-Bypasses and Minarets of Capitalism: Amman as Neoliberal Assemblage," *Political Geography* 28, no. 2 (2009): 110–120, https://doi.org/10.1016/j.polgeo.2008.12.004; and Najib B. Hourani, "Urbanism and Neoliberal Order: The Development and Redevelopment of Amman," *Journal of Urban Affairs* 36, no. 2 (2014): 634–649, https://doi.org/10.1111/juaf.12092.
10. See, for instance, Bessma Momani, *Arab Dawn: Arab Youth and the Demographic Dividend They Will Bring* (University of Toronto Press, 2015).
11. Networks of Mediterranean Youth Project, *Jordan Youth Media Perception Survey, Ages 18–29* (NET-MED, 2020).
12. Daoud Kuttab, "How Jordan Censors Journalists," *Foreign Policy*, October 29, 2021, https://foreignpolicy.com/2021/10/29/jordan-abdullah-pandora-papers-journalism-censorship-press-freedom/.
13. I am grateful to Katrina Sammour, among Jordan's most renowned activists and political commentators, for hammering home this insight. Personal interview, Katrina Sammour, Amman, Jordan, June 18, 2019.
14. "Unemployment Rate Hit 21.9% in Q1 2023," *Jordan Times*, May 31, 2023.
15. Adam Almqvist, "Autocracy after the Welfare State: Youth Governance and Authoritarian Durability in the Hashemite Kingdom of Jordan," PhD diss., University of Chicago, 2023.
16. These, and subsequent Arab Barometer data in this chapter, are available on the Arab Barometer's website, https://www.arabbarometer.org/.
17. Sarah Tobin, *Everyday Piety: Islam and Economy in Jordan* (Cornell University Press, 2016).

18. Muhammad Abu Rumman and Neven Bondokji, *Al-hall al-islaami fil-urdun: al-islaamiyun wal-dawlah wa-rihaanaat al-dimuqraatiyyah wal-'amn* [The Islamic Solution in Jordan: Islamists, the State, and the Ventures of Democracy and Security] (Friedrich Ebert Stiftung, 2013).
19. Janine Clark, *Islam, Charity, and Activism: Middle-Class Networks and Social Welfare in Egypt, Jordan, and Yemen* (Indiana University Press, 2004), 82–114.
20. Dörthe Engelcke, *Reforming Family Law: Social and Political Change in Jordan and Morocco* (Cambridge University Press, 2019), 113–132.
21. Al-Quds Center for Political Studies, *Al-din wal-dawlah: al-urdun numudhajan* [Religion and the State: Jordan as a Case Study] (Dar Al-Nadwa Al-Dawliyyah, 2010).
22. Michael Robbins and Lawrence Rubin, "The Rise of Official Islam in Jordan," *Politics, Religion, and Ideology* 14 (2013): 59–74, https://doi.org/10.1080/21567689.2012.752359.
23. Philip Odeh Madanat, *Framing the Friday Sermon to Shape Opinion: The Case of Jordan* (Lexington Books, 2019), 83–113.
24. Stacey Gutkowski, "We Are the Very Model of a Moderate Muslim State: The Amman Messages and Jordan's Foreign Policy," *International Relations* 30, no. 2 (2016): 206–226, https://doi.org/10.1177/0047117815598352.
25. Kanchan Chandra, "What Is Ethnic Identity and Does It Matter?" *Annual Review of Political Science* 9 (2006): 397–424, https://doi.org/10.1146/annurev.polisci.9.062404.170715.
26. Géraldine Chatelard, "The Constitution of Christian Communal Boundaries and Spheres in Jordan," *Journal of Church and State* 52, no. 3 (2010): 476–502, https://doi.org/10.1093/jcs/csq079.
27. Seteney Shami, "Historical Processes of Identity Formation: Displacement, Settlement, and Self-Representations of the Circassians in Jordan," *Iran and the Caucasus* 13 (2009): 141–159, https://doi.org/10.1163/160984909X12476379008160.
28. Lillian Frost and Nathan Brown, "Constitutions and Citizenship: Rights in Law and Practice in Jordan and the Arab World," in *Routledge Handbook of Citizenship in the Middle East and North Africa*, eds. Roel Meijer, James Sater, and Zahra Babar (Routledge, 2020), 130–143.
29. Oroub El-Abed, "The Invisible Citizens of Jordan," in *Minorities and State-Building in the Middle East: The Case of Jordan*, eds. Paolo Maggiolini and Idir Ouahes (Palgrave Macmillan, 2021), 111–130.
30. Kirk Sowell, "Reforming Jordan's Labor Market," *Sada* Newsletter of the Carnegie Endowment for International Peace, November 21, 2017, https://carnegieendowment.org/sada/2017/11/reforming-jordans-labor-market?lang=en.
31. This is why the precise number of Jordanians of Palestinian origin is so obscure. Put another way, Palestinians in Jordan include both citizens and noncitizens, and some of those citizens are officially counted as refugees.
32. Rawan Arar and David Scott FitzGerald, *The Refugee System: A Sociological Approach* (Polity, 2023), 41.
33. Nicholas Seeley, "The Politics of Aid to Iraqi Refugees in Jordan," *Middle East Report* 256 (2010): 37–42, https://merip.org/2010/09/the-politics-of-aid-to-iraqi-refugees-in-jordan/.
34. Gerasimous Tsourapas, "The Syrian Refugee Crisis and Foreign Policy Decision-Making in Jordan, Lebanon, and Turkey," *Journal of Global Security Studies* 4, no. 4 (2019): 464–481, https://doi.org/10.1093/jogss/ogz016.
35. Ann Marie Baylouny, *When Blame Backfire: Syrian Refugees and Citizen Grievances in Jordan and Lebanon* (Cornell University Press, 2020).
36. Benedict Anderson, *Imagined Communities: Reflections on the Origins and Spread of Nationalism* (Verso, 1983).
37. See, for instance, Ibrahim Abdullah Nasser, Safaa Ni'ma Shweihat, and Muhammad Salim Al-Zaboon, *Al-Muwaatanah al-urduniyyah* [Jordanian Citizenship] (Dar Al-Fikr, 2009).
38. Stefanie Nanes, "Hashemitism, Jordanian National Identity, and the Abu Odeh Episode," *The Arab Studies Journal* 18, no. 1 (2010): 162–195.
39. Riad Nasser, *Palestinian Identity in Jordan and Israel: The Necessary "Other" in the Making of a Nation* (Routledge, 2005), 67–142.

40. Joseph Massad, *Colonial Effects: The Making of National Identity in Jordan* (Columbia University Press, 2001), 155–159.
41. Ghassan Charbel, "Al-malik: uhibb al-ahmar li-annahu lawn al-kuffiyyah al-urduniyyah [The King: I Love Red Because It Is the Color of the Jordanian Kuffiyeh]," *Amman News*, November 11, 2009.
42. Curtis Ryan, "'We Are All Jordan' . . . But Who Is We?" *Middle East Report Online*, June 13, 2010, https://merip.org/2010/07/we-are-all-jordan-but-who-is-we/.
43. The Palestinian Authority's Palestinian Central Bureau of Statistics does release periodic estimates for the global Palestinian diaspora, including those in Jordan. In 2019, the bureau projected that 4.4 million Palestinians resided in the kingdom, which at the time had around 7.2 million citizens. "'Al-Ihsaa' al-filistini: 4.4 milyun filistini fil-urdun [Palestinian Statistics: 4.4 Million Palestinians in Jordan]," *AllofJo.net*, September 6, 2019.
44. Andrew Shryock, *Nationalism and the Genealogical Imagination: Oral History and Textual Authority in Tribal Jordan* (University of California Press, 1997).
45. A useful catalogue that traces the history and origins of Jordan's tribes is Abdelraouf Rawabdeh, *Mu'jam al-'asha'ir al-urduniyyah* [Dictionary of Jordanian Tribes] (Dar Al-Shuruq Lil-Nashr Wal-Wawzi', 2010).
46. Raouf Sa'd Abujaber, *Pioneers over Jordan: The Frontier of Settlement in Transjordan, 1850–1914* (IB Tauris, 1989).
47. An excellent history is Hind Abu al-Sha'ar, *Diraasaat fi-ta'rikh al-urdun al-ijtima'i wal-iqtisaadi, 1894–1938* [Studies in the Social and Economic History of Jordan, 1894–1938] (Greater Amman Municipality, 2009).
48. Sean Yom and Katrina Sammour, "Why Jordan's Identity Can't Be Bought," *The Washington Post*, June 24, 2019, https://www.washingtonpost.com/politics/2019/06/24/why-jordans-identity-cant-be-bought/.
49. For a fiery critique of such ideas, see Ahmad al-Tall, *Al-urdun wa-mu'aamarat al-watan al-badil* [Jordan and the Conspiracy of the Alternative Homeland] (Al-Sayil Lil-Nashr Wal-Tawzi', 2013). Such Jordanian opposition also extends to the lesser version of the alternative homeland project—the "confederal" proposal, which would pair Israeli annexation over the largest and most fertile parts of the West Bank with returning smaller areas of the Palestinian territory to Jordan to administer. The Hashemite Kingdom would still host millions of new Palestinian refugees.
50. Linda Layne, *Home and Homeland: The Dialogics of Tribal and National Identities in Jordan* (Princeton University Press, 1994), 14–23.
51. Geoffrey Hughes, "Cutting the Face: Kinship, State and Social Media Conflict in Networked Jordan," *Journal of Legal Anthropology* 2, no. 1 (2018): 49–71, https://doi.org/10.3167/jla.2018.020104.
52. Haim Gerber, "Modernization in Nineteenth-Century Palestine: The Role of Foreign Trade," *Middle Eastern Studies* 18, no. 3 (1982): 250–264.
53. Shaul Mishal, *West Bank/East Bank: The Palestinians in Jordan, 1949–1967* (Yale University Press, 1978), 9–18. For an insightful study of how Palestinians reshaped Jordan's urbanization, see Marwan D. Hanania, "The Impact of the Palestinian Refugee Crisis on the Development of Amman, 1947–1958," *British Journal of Middle East Studies* 55, no. 1 (2014): 461–482, https://doi.org/10.1080/13530194.2014.942978.
54. Naseer H. Aruri, *Jordan: A Study in Political Development (1921–1965)* (Martinus Nijhoff, 1972), 7.
55. Joseph Nevo, "September 1970 in Jordan: A Civil War?" *Civil Wars* 10, no. 3 (2008): 217–230, https://doi.org/10.1080/13698240802168056.
56. Samuel Plapinger, "Insurgent Recruitment Practices and Combat Effectiveness in Civil War: The Black September Conflict in Jordan," *Security Studies* 31, no. 2 (2022): 251–290, https://doi.org/10.1080/09636412.2022.2072234.
57. Yezid Sayigh, *Armed Struggle and the Search for State: The Palestinian National Movement, 1949–1993* (Oxford University Press, 2000), 262–267.
58. For instance, see Jihad Hattar, *Dhikriyat 'an ma'rika aylul: al-urdun 1970* [Memories of the September Battle: Jordan 1970] (Ittihad Al-'Aam Lil-Kuttab Wal-Suhufiyin Al-Filistiniyyin, 1977).

59. Laurie A. Brand, "Palestinians and Jordanians: A Crisis of Identity," *Journal of Palestine Studies* 24, no. 4 (1995): 46–61, https://doi.org/10.2307/2537757.
60. Luigi Achilli, *Palestinian Refugees and Identity: Nationalism, Politics, and the Everyday* (IB Tauris, 2015).
61. Luisa Gandolfo, *Palestinians in Jordan: The Politics of Identity* (IB Tauris, 2012), 177–183.
62. "Film withaa'qi 'an filistiniyi al-urdun [Documentary Film about Jordan's Palestinians]," *Al-Jazeera*, June 29, 2011.

Chapter 3

1. "Masadir muttaliah: dawaa'ir san'a al-qiraar fil-urdun lan taqbal bi-ta'dilaat jawhariyyah fil-dustur [Informed Sources: The Jordanian Decision-Making Circles Will Not Accept Essential Amendments to the Constitution]," *AllofJo.Net*, 19 March 2011.
2. Philippe Schmitter and Terry L. Karl, "What Democracy Is . . . and Is Not," *Journal of Democracy* 2, no. 3 (1991): 67–73.
3. Adam Przeworski, *Why Bother with Elections?* (Polity, 2018), 4.
4. Michael Coppedge, Staffan Lindberg, Svend-Erik Skaaning, Jan Teorell, "Measuring High Level Democratic Principles Using the V-Dem Data," *International Political Science Review* 37, no. 5 (2016): 580–593, https://doi.org/10.1177/0192512115622046.
5. Larry Diamond, *Developing Democracy: Toward Consolidation* (The Johns Hopkins University Press, 1999), 2–19.
6. Juan J. Linz, *Totalitarian and Authoritarian Regimes* (Lynne Rienner, 2000), 159–165.
7. Paul Brooker, *Non-Democratic Regimes*, 3rd ed. (Red Globe Press, 2013).
8. Benjamin Smith, "Life of the Party: The Origins of Regime Breakdown and Persistence under Single-Party Rule," *World Politics* 57, no. 3 (2005): 421–451, https://doi.org/10.1353/wp.2006.0004.
9. Samuel Huntington, *Political Order in Changing Societies* (Yale University Press, 1968), 177–190.
10. Jason Brownlee, "Hereditary Succession in Modern Autocracies," *World Politics* 59, no. 4 (2007): 595–628, https://doi.org/10.1353/wp.2008.0002.
11. The pressures of balancing opposition and finding supporters is magnified in ruling monarchies, because for many scholars they qualify as a subtype of personalistic autocracy. See Barbara Geddes, Joseph Wright, and Erica Frantz, *How Dictatorships Work* (Cambridge University Press, 2018), 210–211.
12. Robins, *A History of Jordan*, 264.
13. Personal interview, Minister of Political Development Sabri Rbeihat, Amman, Jordan, June 14, 2006.
14. Aruri, *Jordan: A Study in Political Development*, 73.
15. Sufian Obeidat, *Qiraa' fil-ta'dilaat al-dusturiyyah al-urduniyyah 2016: mazid min al-isti'thaar bil-sultah* [Reading the 2016 Jordanian Constitutional Amendments: More Monopolization of Power] (Arab Center for Research and Policy Studies, 2016).
16. Sean Yom, "Jordan: Ten More Years of Autocracy," *Journal of Democracy* 20, no. 4 (2009): 151–166, https://doi.org/10.1353/jod.0.0125.
17. Personal interview, journalist Suleiman Al-Khalidi, Amman, Jordan, August 1, 2022.
18. A rare Middle East exception came from Qatar in 2013, when Emir Hamad abdicated in favor of his son, Tamim.
19. Michael Herb, *All in the Family: Absolutism, Revolution, and Democracy in the Middle Eastern Monarchies* (State University of New York Press, 1999).
20. Graham Jevon, *Glubb Pasha and the Arab Legion: Britain, Jordan and the End of Empire in the Middle East* (Cambridge University Press, 2017), 179–203.
21. One account of King Hussein and Prince Hassan's fallout is described in Randa Habib, *Hussein and Abdullah: Inside the Jordanian Royal Family* (Saqi, 2010), 136–165. Father-son nostalgia rings louder in Robert Satloff, "Why King Abdullah Is King," *The American Interest*, April 18, 2020, https://www.the-american-interest.com/2020/04/18/why-king-abdullah-is-king/.

22. US Embassy in Amman, "In Jordan, Crown Princes Come and Go," Wikileaks Cable: 04AMMAN9486_a, November 29, 2004, https://wikileaks.org/plusd/cables/04AMMAN9486_a.html.
23. Sean Yom, "Jordan Has Become a Banana Monarchy," *Foreign Policy*, 15 April 2021, https://foreignpolicy.com/2021/04/15/jordan-king-hamzah-crisis-hashemites-us-banana-monarchy/.
24. "Fareed Zakaria GPS: Interview with King Abdullah II of Jordan," *CNN*, July 25, 2021, https://www.cnn.com/videos/tv/2021/07/25/exp-gps-0725-king-abdullah-biden-middle-east.cnn.
25. Fuad Batayneh, *Al-mashhad al-urduni: min 'irth al-thaqaafah illa mafhum al-dawlah* [The Jordanian Landscape: From Cultural Heritage to Concept of the State] (Arab Foundation for Studies and Publishing, 2005), 184–188.
26. Habib, *Hussein and Abdullah*, 192.
27. The interior minister straddles a more imprecise line. He is a line minister hypothetically subordinate to the prime minister, but the job of overseeing civil policing and internal security endows him with considerable influence and usually puts him in direct contact with the monarchy.
28. Nawaf Tell, "Jordanian Security Sector Governance: Between Theory and Practice," Paper presented at the Workshop on Challenges of Security Sector Governance in the Middle East, Geneva Centre for the Democratic Control of Armed Forces, Geneva, Switzerland, July 12–13, 2004.
29. Raja Talab, "Al-razzaz wa-saqf al-tawaqu'aat [Razzaz and the Ceiling of Expectations]," *Al-Rai*, June 11, 2018.
30. Hussein Abu Rumman, "Al-wizaaraat al-siyaadah fil-urdun: dharuraat al-tahdith wa-fath al-tawaafuth al-mughliqah amaam al-islaah [The Sovereignty Portfolios of Jordan: The Necessities of Modernization and Opening Closed Windows for Reform]," *Al-Sijill* 37 (2008): 1, 8.
31. Mohammad al-Momani, "Jordan Seeks to Preempt Discontent with New Government," *Sada* Newsletter of the Carnegie Endowment for International Peace, February 11, 2011, https://carnegieendowment.org/sada/2011/02/jordan-seeks-to-preempt-discontent-with-new-government.
32. Fatema Alhashemi and Tony Goldner, "At the Apex: Reforming Cabinet Structures in Jordan," in *Public Sector Reform in the Middle East and North Africa: Lessons of Experience for a Region in Transition*, eds. Robert Beschel and Tarik Yousef (Brookings Institution Press), 17–44.
33. Confidential personal interview, former prime minister, Amman, Jordan, July 12, 2016.
34. Scott Williamson, *The King Can Do No Wrong: Blame Games and Power Sharing in Authoritarian Regimes* (Cambridge University Press, 2024), 146–172.
35. Khalid Issa Aladwan and Khaled Mufadi Aldabbas, "The Jordanian Parliamentary Institution: A Study in Political Representation," *Dirasat: Human and Social Sciences* 42, no. 1 (2015): 269–270, https://doi.org/10.12816/0019893.
36. "Minassaat al-urdun: majlis al-'ayaan am 'aa'ilaat? [Platforms of Jordan: Council of Notables or Families?]" *Al-Quds Al-Arabi*, September 28, 2020.
37. The lower house's website is located at https://representatives.jo/.
38. A useful guide to how parliamentary committees in Jordan operate is Fayez Mohammed Abu Shamala, *Dawr al-nizam al-daakhili fil-amal al-barlamani: diraasat tatbiqiyyah 'ala 'amaal majlis al-nuwaab al-urduni* [The Role of the Internal System in Parliamentary Work: An Applied Study in the Works of the Jordanian Lower House] (Dar Al-Khalij, 2019).
39. Marwa Shalaby and Scott Williamson, "Executive Compliance with Parliamentary Powers under Authoritarianism: Evidence from Jordan," *Governance* 37, no. 4 (2024): 1163–1182, https://doi.org/10.1111/gove.12830.
40. Personal interview, Member of Parliament Myassar Al-Sardiyyah, Amman, Jordan, June 14, 2012.
41. Ellen Lust, "Reinforcing Informal Institutions through Authoritarian Elections: Insights from Jordan," *Middle East Law and Governance* 1, no. 1 (2009): 3–37, https://doi.org/10.1163/187633708X339444.

42. Center for Strategic Studies, *Jordanian Indicator Poll Series 27: The Pulse of the Jordanian Street* (University of Jordan: CSS, 2021), https://jcss.org/en/993/jordanian-index-poll-series-jordanian-street-pulse-27/.
43. Sean Yom, "Jordan and Morocco: The Palace Gambit," *Journal of Democracy* 28, no. 2 (2017): 132–146, https://doi.org/10.1353/jod.2017.0030.
44. Benjamin Schuetze, "Marketing Parliament: The Constitutive Effects of External Attempts at Parliamentary Strengthening in Jordan," *Cooperation and Conflict* 53, no. 2 (2018): 237–258, https://doi.org/10.1177/0010836718768632.
45. Bassam al-Badarin, "Al-urdun: wuzaraa' min al-sin [Jordan: Ministers from China]," *Al-Quds Al-Arabi*, November 5, 2019.
46. Samuel Eisenstadt, *Traditional Patrimonialism and Modern Neopatrimonialism* (SAGE, 1973), 50–56. See also Herbert Kitschelt and Steven Wilkinson, eds., *Patrons, Clients, and Policies: Patterns of Democratic Accountability and Political Competition* (Cambridge University Press, 2009).
47. Sa'eda al-Kilani, *How to Become a Minister in Jordan: Wasta vs. Transparency in Senior Posts Appointments* (Lulu, 2016), 90–125.
48. William Najib Nassar, *Ma'ziq al-dimuqratiyyah fil-watan al-arabi: fil zill al-nizam "al-batrimuniliyyah al-jadida," al-urdun namudhajan* [The Democratic Predicament in the Arab World: In the Shadow of the New Neopatrimonial Regime, the Jordanian Model] (Center for Arab Unity Studies, 2016), 153–175.
49. Hassan Salih 'Uthman and Hamid Ahmad Al-Shubaki, *Rijalaat ma' al-malik 'abdullah: mu'assis al-mamlakah al-urduniyyah al-hashimiyyah* [Men with King Abdullah: The Founder of the Hashemite Kingdom of Jordan] (Ministry of Culture, 1995).
50. Personal interview, political expert Wael Al-Khatib, Amman, Jordan, June 18, 2011.
51. Mehran Kamrava, *Fragile Politics: Weak States in the Greater Middle East* (Hurst, 2016).
52. Muhammad Shihan, *Development Bureaucracy in Jordan* (Dar Al-Hamed, 1999), 139–143.
53. Rami Tbaishat, Ali Rawabdeh, Khaled Qassem Hailat, Shaker Aladwan, Samir Al-Balas, and Mohammed Iqbal Al-Ajlouny, "Reforming Policy Roles in the Jordanian Policy-Making Process," *Journal of Public Affairs* 19 (2019): e1886, 4–5, https://doi.org/10.1002/pa.1886.
54. Marwan Kardoosh, "The Aqaba Special Economic Zone, Jordan: A Case Study of Governance," Working Paper of the Center for Development Research, University of Bonn, January 2005.
55. Rifaat Al-Faouri, *Al-wasta fil-qitaa' al-hukumi al-urduni* [Wasta in the Jordanian Government Sector] (Department of Public Administration, 1997).
56. Laila Azzeh, "Wasta Seen as a Necessary Evil by Jordanians, Survey Finds," *Jordan Times*, February 13, 2017.
57. International Republican Institute, *Public Opinion Survey: Residents of Jordan* (IRI, 2018).
58. Agustina Giraudy, Eduardo Moncada, and Richard Snyder, eds., *Inside Countries: Subnational Research in Comparative Politics* (Cambridge University Press, 2019).
59. Janine A. Clark, *Local Politics in Jordan and Morocco: Strategies of Centralization and Decentralization* (Columbia University Press, 2018), 92–93.
60. Khalid Samaara al-Zu'bi, *Al-nizam al-idaari fil-urdun* [The Administrative System in Jordan] (Lajnat Ta'rikh Al-Urdun, 1994), 31–46.
61. E.J. Karmel, "Designing Decentralization in Jordan: Locating the Policy among the Politics," *Middle East Law and Governance* 14, no. 2 (2022): 155–184, https://doi.org/10.1163/18763375-13030001.

Chapter 4

1. Elliott Abrams, "Dictators Go, Monarchs Stay," *Commentary* 134 (2012): 26–31, https://www.commentary.org/articles/elliott-abrams/dictators-go-monarchs-stay/.
2. Robert Kaplan, "Order after Empire," *Foreign Affairs*, August 8, 2023, https://www.foreignaffairs.com/middle-east/order-after-empire.
3. Sean Yom and F. Gregory Gause, "Resilient Royals: How Arab Monarchies Hang On," *Journal of Democracy* 23, no. 4 (2012): 74–88, https://doi.org/10.1353/jod.2012.0062.
4. Milan Svolik, *The Politics of Authoritarian Rule* (Cambridge University Press, 2012), 3–12.

5. Johannes Gerschewski, "The Three Pillars of Stability: Legitimation, Repression, and Cooptation in Autocratic Regimes," *Democratization* 20, no. 1 (2013): 13–38, https://doi.org/10.1080/13510347.2013.738860. For an application to the Middle East, see André Bank, Eva Bellin, Michael Herb, Lisa Wedeen, Sean Yom, and Saloua Zerhouni, "Authoritarianism Reconfigured: Evolving Forms of Political Control," in *The Political Science of the Middle East: Theory and Research since the Arab Uprisings*, eds. Marc Lynch, Jillian Schwedler, and Sean Yom (Oxford University Press, 2022), 35–61.
6. Christian Davenport, "State Repression and Political Order," *Annual Review of Political Science* 10 (2007): 1–23, https://doi.org/10.1146/annurev.polisci.10.101405.143216.
7. Abel Escribà-Folch, "Repression, Political Threats, and Survival under Autocracy," *International Political Science Review* 34, no. 5 (2013): 543–560, https://doi.org/10.1177/0192512113488259.
8. Eva Bellin, "The Robustness of Authoritarianism in the Middle East: Exceptionalism in Comparative Perspective," *Comparative Politics* 36, no. 2 (2004): 139–157, https://doi.org/10.2307/4150140.
9. Sheena Chestnut Greitens, *Dictators and Their Secret Police: Coercive Institutions and State Violence* (Cambridge University Press, 2016).
10. Beatriz Magaloni, "Credible Power-Sharing and the Longevity of Authoritarian Rule," *Comparative Political Studies* 41, no. 4–5 (2008): 715–741, https://doi.org/10.1177/0010414007313124.
11. Bueno de Mesquita, Alastair Smith, Randolph Siverson, and James Morrow, *The Logic of Political Survival* (MIT Press, 2005), 51–55.
12. Jason Brownlee, *Authoritarianism in an Age of Democratization* (Cambridge University Press, 2007).
13. Michael Albertus, Sofia Fenner, and Dan Slater, *Coercive Distribution* (Cambridge University Press, 2018), 12–17.
14. Bruce Riedel, *Jordan and America: An Enduring Friendship* (The Brookings Institution, 2021), 183.
15. Sean Yom and Pete W. Moore, "The Fortress State: Extreme Militarization in Jordan," *Middle East Law and Governance* 16, no. 4 (2024): 371–386, https://doi.org/10.1163/18763375-20241498.
16. Figures from Jordanian Department of Statistics, *Labor Force Survey 2024* (DOS, 2025). Broken down, the JAF's official size amounts to nearly 115,000 active duty personnel. The PSD employs roughly 60,000 across its urban and rural divisions; the gendarmerie employs over 30,000 troops. The GID's budget and payroll are secret, but common estimates of its officers and agents number around 15,000.
17. In 2024, the Jordanian government tallied 1,281,431 male Jordanians registered as employed. Figure from Jordanian Department of Statistics, *Labor Force Survey 2024* (DOS, 2025).
18. James Quinlivan, "Coup-Proofing: Its Practice and Consequences in the Middle East," *International Security* 24, no. 2 (1999): 131–165, https://doi.org/10.1162/016228899560202.
19. Jordan Strategy Forum, *Social Capital in Jordan: What Is the Level of Trust in Our Institutions, and Why?* (JSF, 2018).
20. The distinction between high- and low-intensity repression comes from Steven Levitsky and Lucan Way, *Competitive Authoritarianism: Hybrid Regimes after the Cold War* (Cambridge University Press, 2010), 56–61.
21. Abd Al-Haleem M.A. Al-Adwaan, "Jordanian Popular Political Activity and National Security," *World Applies Sciences Journal* 32, no. 4 (2014): 704–717.
22. Marta Vidal, "Awash in U.S. Aid, Jordan Escalates Repression," *Foreign Policy*, November 13, 2022, https://foreignpolicy.com/2022/11/13/jordan-repression-crackdown-dissent-protests-democracy-monarchy-us-aid/.
23. Petter Nesser and Henrik Gråtrud, "When Conflicts Do Not Overspill: The Case of Jordan," *Perspectives on Politics* 19 (2021): 492–506, https://doi.org/10.1017/S15375927190 0389X.
24. P.J. Vatikiotis, *Politics and the Military in Jordan: A Study of the Arab Legion, 1921–1957* (Cass, 1967), 137.

25. For an overview of this and other conflicts involving the JAF, see Syed Ali El-Edroos, *The Hashemite Arab Army, 1908–1979: An Appreciation and Analysis of Military Operations* (Publishing Committee, 1980).
26. Data from World Bank, *World Development Indicators* (IBRD, various years).
27. ʿAbbas Murad, *Al-dawr al-siyaasi lil-jaysh al-urduni* [The Political Role of the Jordanian Army] (PLO Research Center, 1973), 132–136.
28. Massad, *Colonial Effects*, 163–221.
29. Curtis Ryan, "The Armed Forces and the Arab Uprisings: The Case of Jordan," *Middle East Law and Governance* 4, no. 1 (2012): 153–167, https://doi.org/10.1163/187633712X626062.
30. Personal interview, (retired) General Imad Saliba Ma'ayah, Amman, Jordan, June 16, 2012.
31. Anne Marie Baylouny, "Militarizing Welfare: Neo-liberalism and Jordanian Policy," *Middle East Journal* 62, no. 2 (2008): 277–303, https://doi.org/10.3751/62.2.15.
32. Vatikiotis, *Politics and the Military in Jordan*, 80.
33. Shana Marshall, "Jordan's Military-Industrial Sector: Maintaining Institutional Prestige in the Era of Neoliberalism," in *Businessmen in Arms: How the Military and Other Armed Groups Profit in the MENA Region*, eds. Elke Grawert and Zeinab Abul-Magd (Rowman & Littlefield, 2016), 119–134.
34. Pete W. Moore, "A Political-Economic History of Jordan's General Intelligence Directorate: Authoritarian State-Building and Fiscal Crisis," *Middle East Journal* 73, no. 2 (2019): 242–262, https://doi.org/10.3751/73.2.14.
35. Early GID directors insisted that they did not use torture or other extrajudicial methods, even against those suspected of outright crimes, such as assassination attempts against King Hussein, and that the intelligence directorate was little more than a specialized law enforcement agency. See, for instance, Mohammed Al-Rawashdeh, "Badran yatahaddath ʿan awwal ayaam ta'sis daa'irah al-mukhabaraat al-ʿaamah [Badran Discusses the First Days of the Establishment of the GID]," *Al-Ghad*, January 28, 2015. However, many older Jordanians attest that the GID regularly employed violent and abusive tactics during the martial law period of the 1970s and 1980s. Palestinians, in particular, saw such violence as another expression of Transjordanian nativism aimed at punishing them for the Black September civil war. See further *Nahw urdun watani dimuqrati* [Toward a National Democratic Jordan] (Palestine Liberation Front, 1980), 34–47.
36. Sufian Obeidat, "Al-islah al-amni fil-urdun: min ayna yabda' [Security Reform in Jordan: Where to Start]?" Working Paper of the Arab Reform Initiative, December 18, 2009.
37. Human Rights Watch, *Suspicious Sweeps: The General Intelligence Directorate and Jordan's Rule of Law Problem* (HRW, 2006).
38. Confidential personal interview, youth activist, Amman, Jordan, August 1, 2016.
39. Neil MacFarquhar, *The Media Relations Department of Hizbollah Wishes You a Happy Birthday* (PublicAffairs, 2009), 192–193.
40. Rana al-Sabbagh, "Al-urdun: maa ṣirr al-taghyiraat fi ʿal-daa'irah' alatti tahmi al-ʿarsh [What Is the Secret of the Changes in the Directorate that Protects the Throne]?" *Daraj*, May 17, 2019.
41. "CIA Arms for Syrian Rebels Supplied Black Market, Officials Say," *The New York Times*, June 26, 2016, https://www.nytimes.com/2016/06/27/world/middleeast/cia-arms-for-syrian-rebels-supplied-black-market-officials-say.html.
42. Fahd Al-Khitan, "Risaalat al-malik li-mudir al-mukhabarat al-ʿaamah [The King's Message to the GID Director]," *Arabi21*, February 21, 2021.
43. Tell, "Jordanian Security Sector Governance," 5.
44. Jessica Watkins, *Creating Consent in an Illiberal Order: Policing Disputes in Jordan* (Cambridge University Press, 2022).
45. Tariq Tell, "Early Spring in Jordan: The Revolt of the Military Veterans," Working Paper of the Carnegie Middle East Center, November 4, 2015, https://carnegieendowment.org/research/2015/11/early-spring-in-jordan-the-revolt-of-the-military-veterans?lang=en¢er=middle-east.
46. Jillian Schwedler, "Routines and Ruptures in Anti-Israeli Protests in Jordan," in *Microfoundations of the Arab Uprisings: Mapping Interactions between Regimes and*

Protesters, eds. Frédéric Volpi and James M. Jasper (Amsterdam University Press, 2018), 75–82.

47. Ziad Abu-Rish, "Protests, Regime Stability, and State Formation in Jordan," in *Beyond the Arab Spring: The Evolving Ruling Bargain in the Middle East*, ed. Mehran Kamrava (Oxford University Press, 2014), 305.
48. Muddather Abu-Karaki, Raed Faqir, and Majed Ahmad Marashdah, "Democracy and Judicial Controlling in Jordan: A Constitutional Study," *Journal of Politics and Law* 4, no. 2 (2011): 180–195, https://doi.org/10.5539/jpl.v4n2p180.
49. Dana Moss, "Repression, Response, and Contained Escalation under 'Liberalized' Authoritarianism in Jordan," *Mobilization* 19, no. 3 (2014): 261–286, https://doi.org/10.17813/maiq.19.3.q508v72264766u92.
50. Personal interview, political activist Amer Tubaishat, Amman, Jordan, July 5, 2018.
51. Sean Yom, *From Resilience to Revolution: How Foreign Interventions Destabilize the Middle East* (Columbia University Press, 2016), 154–208.
52. Uriel Dann, *King Hussein and the Challenge of Arab Radicalism, 1955–1967* (Oxford University Press, 1989), 13. Official Jordanian works have also reproduced these stereotypes of tribal Jordanians. See, for instance, Ghazi bin Muhammad, *The Tribes of Jordan at the Beginning of the Twenty-First Century* (Rutab, 1999).
53. Sulayman Musa, *Dirasaat fi ta'rikh al-urdun al-hadith* [*Studies in the History of Modern Jordan*] (Ministry of Culture, 1999), 132–189.
54. Yoav Alon, *The Shaykh of Shaykhs: Mithqal al-Fayiz and Tribal Leadership in Modern Jordan* (Stanford University Press, 2016), 50–58.
55. Tariq Tell, *The Social and Economic Origins of Monarchy in Jordan* (Palgrave Macmillan, 2013), 83–93.
56. Detailed accounts of this state-building process include Mary Wilson, *King Abdullah, Britain and the Making of Jordan* (Cambridge University Press, 1987); Michael Fischbach, *State, Society and Land in Jordan* (Brill, 2000); Muhammad Ahmad Muhafazah, *Imarah sharq al-urdun: nash'atuha wa-tatawwuruha rub' qarn, 1921–1946* [The Emirate of Transjordan: Its Establishment and Development in a Quarter-Century, 1921–1946] (Dar Al-Furqan Lil-Nashr Wal-Tawzi', 1990); and Maan Abu Nowar's three-volume chronicle, beginning with *The History of the Hashemite Kingdom of Jordan: The Creation and Development of Transjordan, 1920–1929* (Ithaca, 1989).
57. Yoav Alon, *The Making of Jordan: Tribes, Colonialism, and the Modern State* (IB Tauris, 2007), 117–119.
58. Abla Amawi, "The Consolidation of the Merchant Class in Transjordan during the Second World War," in *Village, Steppe and State: The Social Origins of Modern Jordan*, eds. Eugene Rogan and Tariq Tell (British Academic Press, 1994), 167–184.
59. Maan Abu Nowar, *The Struggle for Independence 1939–1947: A History of the Hashemite Kingdom of Jordan* (Ithaca, 2001), 221–257.
60. Shaul Mishal, "Jordanian and Israeli Policy on the West Bank," in *The Hashemite Kingdom of Jordan and the West Bank: A Handbook*, eds. Anne Sinai and Allen Pollack (American Academic Association for Peace in the Middle East, 1977), 212–213.
61. Joel Migdal, *Palestinian Society and Politics* (Princeton University Press, 1980), 39–43.
62. Clinton Bailey, *Jordan's Palestinian Challenge, 1948–1983: A Political History* (Westview, 1984), 7–26.
63. Kimberly Katz, *Jordanian Jerusalem: Holy Places and National Spaces* (University Press of Florida, 2005).
64. Lawrence Axelrod, "Tribesmen in Uniform: The Demise of the Fida'iyyun in Jordan, 1970–71," *The Muslim World* 68, no. 1 (1978): 25–45.
65. Asher Susser, *Jordan, Palestine, and the Politics of Collective Identity: A History* (Lynne Rienner, 2024), 131–141.
66. Adnan Abu Odeh, *Jordanians, Palestinians, and the Hashemite Kingdom in the Middle East Peace Process* (United States Institute for Peace 1999), 190–236.

67. Yitzhak Reiter, "Higher Education and Sociopolitical Transformation in Jordan," *British Journal of Middle Eastern Studies* 29, no. 2 (2002): 137–164, https://doi.org/10.1080/1353019022000012641.
68. Michael Mazur, *Economic Growth and Development in Jordan* (Croom Helm, 1979), 108–113.
69. Paul Jureidini and R. D. McLaurin, *Jordan: The Impact of Social Change on the Role of the Tribes* (Praeger, 1984), 39–40.
70. Ibrahim Al-Shraah, "Al-ittihad al-watani al-ʿarabi al-urduni bayna ʿaami 1971–1974: dirasa ta'rikhiyyah tahliliyyah [The Jordanian Arab National Union between the Years of 1971–1974: An Analytical Historical Study," *Al-Najah University Journal of Research in the Humane Sciences* 26, no. 3 (2012): 731–766.
71. Daria Zakharova, "Development of Social Protection Institutions," in *Jordan: Selected Issues and Statistical Appendix*, ed. Mohsin Khan (IMF, 2004), 101–103.
72. Jamal Al-Shalabi and Yahya Ali, "The Crisis of the Center with the Peripheries in Jordan," *Confluences Méditerranée* 2 (2013): 75–86, https://doi.org/10.3917/come.085.0075.
73. Sean Yom, "Bread, Fear, and Coalitional Politics in Jordan: From Tribal Origins to Neoliberal Narrowing," in *Economic Shocks and Authoritarian Stability: Duration, Financial Control, and Institutions*, ed. Victor Shih (University of Michigan Press, 2020), 210–235.
74. "Al-'aahil al-urduni yatawalla zimam attawaasul maʿa al-ʿashaa'ir khashyat infilaat al-awdhaaʿ [Jordanian King Takes Over Communication with Tribes Given Fear of Uncontrollable Situation]," *Al-Arab*, June 2, 2021.
75. Yazan Doughan, "The New Jordanian Patriotism after the Arab Spring," Policy Brief of the Crown Center for Middle East Studies at Brandeis University, March 2020, https://www.brandeis.edu/crown/publications/middle-east-briefs/pdfs/101-200/meb134.pdf.

Chapter 5

1. King Abdullah bin Hussein, "Jordan's Security Backbone: Pluralism and National Unity," *World Policy Journal* 30, no. 3 (2013): 40.
2. For more on how post–Cold War autocracies have combined superficial acceptance of pluralism with political abuses against opposition, see Daniel Brumberg, "Democratization in the Arab World? The Trap of Liberalized Autocracy," *Journal of Democracy* 13, no. 4 (2002): 56–68, https://doi.org/10.1353/jod.2002.0064; Arch Puddington, *Breaking Down Democracy: Goals, Strategies, and Methods of Modern Authoritarians* (Freedom House, 2017); and Andreas Schedler, ed., *Electoral Authoritarianism: The Dynamics of Unfree Competition* (Lynne Rienner, 2006).
3. Personal interview, political organizer Labib Kamhawi, Amman, Jordan, June 16, 2013.
4. International Crisis Group, *The Challenge of Political Reform: Jordanian Democratisation and Regional Instability* (ICG, 2003), 2.
5. Curtis Ryan, *Jordan and the Arab Uprisings: Regime Survival and Politics Beyond the State* (Columbia University Press, 2018), 15.
6. Yahya Sadowski, "The New Orientalism and the Democracy Debate," *Middle East Report* 183 (1993): 14–21, https://doi.org/10.2307/3012572. See also Elie Kedourie, *Democracy and Arab Political Culture* (Frank Cass, 1994).
7. Michael Lipka, "Muslims and Islam: Key Findings in the US and Around the World," *Pew Research Center*, August 9, 2017, https://www.pewresearch.org/short-reads/2017/08/09/muslims-and-islam-key-findings-in-the-u-s-and-around-the-world/.
8. Tancred Bradshaw, *The Glubb Reports: Glubb Pasha and Britain's Empire Project in the Middle East, 1920–1956* (Palgrave Macmillan, 2016), 46. The Howeitat (also transliterated as Huwaytat) are a large, traditionally Bedouin confederation in the southern expanse of Jordan.
9. Confidential personal interview, US diplomatic officer, Amman, Jordan, June 19, 2006.
10. Alfred Stepan, "Religion, Democracy, and the 'Twin Tolerations,'" *Journal of Democracy* 11, no. 4 (2000): 44, https://doi.org/10.1353/jod.2000.0088. Further, if democratic compatibility is measured by the sheer number of people from any culture or religion who practice it, then the most liberal tradition in the world is Hinduism: every time a growing Hindu-majority (and Muslim-minority) India holds elections, it is the largest numeric exercise of democracy in human history.

11. Kathryn Stoner and Michael McFaul, eds., *Transitions to Democracy: Comparative Perspectives* (The Johns Hopkins University Press, 2013).
12. See, for instance, Pew Research Center, "Most Muslims Want Democracy, Personal Freedoms, and Islam in Political Life," Report of the Pew Global Attitudes Project, July 2012, https://www.pewresearch.org/global/2012/07/10/most-muslims-want-democracy-personal-freedoms-and-islam-in-political-life/.
13. Eugene Rogan, *Frontiers of the State in the Late Ottoman Empire* (Cambridge University Press, 1999), 184–217.
14. Ahmad Shuqayrat, *Ta'rikh al-idaarah al-'uthmaniyyah fi sharq al-urdun: 1864–1918* [History of Ottoman Administration in Transjordan, 1864–1918] (Dar Min Al-Muhit Illa Al-Khalij Li-Nashr Wal-Tawzi', 1992).
15. Ronen Yitzhak, "The Role of Arab Nationalists in the Establishment of the Emirate of Trans-Jordan, 1921–1924," *The Journal of the Middle East and Africa* 13, no. 2 (2022): 125–143, https://doi.org/10.1080/21520844.2022.2064650.
16. Maysun ' Ubaydat, *Al-tatawwur al-siyaasi li-sharq al-urdun fi 'ahd al-imaarah, 1921–1946* [The Political Development of Transjordan in the Era of the Emirate, 1921–1946] (Lajnat Ta'rikh Bilad Al-Sham, 1993), 170–176.
17. Imad Haitham Nasir, *Al-'ashaa'ir wal-walaa' al-siyaasi fil-urdun, 1921–1946* [Tribes and Political Loyalty in Jordan, 1921–1946] (Al-Aan Publishers, 2018), 99–120.
18. Sulayman Musa and Munib al-Madi, *Ta'rikh al-urdun fil-qarn al-'ashrin, 1900–1959* [The History of Jordan in the Twentieth Century, 1900–1959] (Maktabat al-Muhtasib, 1988), 291–297.
19. Harrison B. Guthorn, *Capital Development: Mandate Era Amman and the Construction of the Hashemite State (1921–1946)* (Gingko, 2021), 121.
20. Despite his complicated politics, Mustafa al-Tal is celebrated today as one of Jordan's most renowned literatteurs given his wider contributions to modern Arab poetry. See, for instance, Mahmoud Obeidat, *Sirat al-shaa'ir al-munaadil mustafa wahbi al-tal ('arar)* [Biography of the Activist Poet Mustafa Wahbi Al-Tal ('Arar)] (Ministry of Culture, 1996).
21. Kamel Abu Jaber, "The Legislature of the Hashemite Kingdom of Jordan: A Study in Political Development," *The Muslim World* 59, nos. 3–4 (1969): 220-250, https://doi.org/10.1111/j.1478-1913.1969.tb02637.x.
22. Maan Abu Nowar, *The Development of Transjordan, 1929–1939* (IB Tauris, 2006), 184–185.
23. Esmond Wright, "Abdallah's Jordan: 1947–1951," *Middle East Journal* 5, no. 4 (1951): 439–460.
24. Hazem Zaki Nuseibeh, *Ta'rikh al-urdun al-siyaasi al-mu'aasir maa bayna 'aami 1952–1967* [The Modern History of Jordan between 1952–1967] (Lajnat Ta'rikh Al-Urdun, 1990), 59–75.
25. Amnon Cohen, *Political Parties in the West Bank under the Jordanian Regime, 1949–1967* (Cornell University Press, 1982).
26. Avi Plascov, *The Palestinian Refugees in Jordan, 1948–1957* (Frank Cass, 1981), 29–40.
27. These ideals come through in the personal memoirs of Free Officers. See, for instance, Shahir Abu Shahut, *Al-jaysh wal-siyaasah fil-urdun: dhikriyaat 'an harakat al-dhubaat al-urduniyyin al-ahrar* [The Army and Politics in Jordan: Memories of the Jordanian Free Officers Movement] (NP, 1989).
28. Betty Anderson, *Nationalist Voices in Jordan: The Street and the State* (University of Texas Press, 2005), 117–146.
29. The British leadership of the Arab Legion, embodied by Glubb Pasha's position as its commanding general, had become a flashpoint of controversy by the mid-1950s. See further Sa'ad Abudayeh, *The Lord of the Desert: A Study of the Papers of the British Officer John B. Glubb in Jordan and Iraq* (Westphalia Press, 2022), 225–278.
30. Hani Hourani, ed., *Hukumat sulayman al-nabulsi, 1956–1957* [The Government of Sulayman al-Nabulsi, 1956–1957] (Dar Sindibad, 1999), 169–187.
31. Bassam Btoush, "The Position of the Jordanian Parliament from the Internal Policies of the Government of Suleiman Al-Nabulsi (1956-1957)," *Dirasat: Human and Social Sciences* 49, no. 5 (2022): 238-251, https://doi.org/10.35516/hum.v49i5.2753.

32. Lawrence Tal, *Politics, the Military, and National Security in Jordan: 1955–1967* (Palgrave Macmillan, 2002), 44–49.
33. Robert Satloff, *From Abdullah to Hussein: Jordan in Transition* (Oxford University Press, 1994), 174.
34. Patrick Seale, "Abd Al-Hamid Sharaf," in *The Shaping of an Arab Statesman: Abd al-Hamid Sharaf and the Modern World*, ed. Patrick Seale (Quartet Books, 1983), 8.
35. Fahed Al-Khitan, "Fi dhikra hibbat nisaan . . . al-mataalib dhaatiha [On the Anniversary of the April Unrest . . . The Same Demands]," *Ammon News*, April 16, 2011.
36. King Hussein bin Abdullah, "Interview with Hillary Bowker," *CNN International*, October 30, 1995.
37. Kamel Abu Jaber and Schirin Fathi, "The 1989 Jordanian Parliamentary Elections," *Orient* 31, no. 1 (1990): 67–86.
38. Adam Jones, "From Vanguard to Vanquished? The Tabloid Press in Jordan," *Political Communication* 19, no. 2 (2002): 176–177, https://doi.org/10.1080/10584600252907434.
39. Curtis Ryan, *Jordan in Transition: From Hussein to Abdullah* (Lynne Rienner, 2002); and Hayil Wad'an Al-Da'jah, *Al-tahawwul al-dimuqrati fil-urdun: 1989–1997* [Democratic Transformation in Jordan: 1989–1997] (Ministry of Culture, 2005).
40. Personal interview, political writer Musa Kilani, Amman, Jordan, June 14, 2011.
41. Malik Mufti, "Elite Bargains and the Onset of Political Liberalization in Jordan," *Comparative Political Studies* 32, no. 1 (1999): 105–109, https://doi.org/10.1177/0010414099032001004.
42. Eleanor Gao and Kharis Templeman, "When Do Elections Help Autocrats? The Plight of Palestinians under SNTV in Jordan," *Electoral Studies* 86 (2023): 1–10, https://doi.org/10.1016/j.electstud.2023.102627.
43. Al-Quds Center for Political Studies, *Al-qawaanin al-naazimah lil-'amal al-hizbi fil-urdun* [*The Regulatory Laws for Party Work in Jordan*] (Al-Quds Center, 2010), 39–58.
44. Hadil Ghabbun, "Huquq al-insaan: 34 'alaaf muntasibu al-ahzaab [Human Rights: 34 Thousand Members of Parties]," *Al-Ghad*, November 8, 2019.
45. Sarah Bush, "Jordan: Quotas and Change in Women's Political Representation," in *The Palgrave Handbook of Women's Political Rights*, eds. Susan Franceschet, Mona Lena Krook, and Netina Tan (Palgrave Macmillan, 2019), 503–515.
46. Janine Clark, "Threats, Structures, and Resources: Cross-Ideological Coalition Building in Jordan," *Comparative Politics* 43, no. 1 (2010): 101–120, https://doi.org/10.5129/001041510X12911363510475.
47. Ali Muhafazah, *Al-dimuqratiyyah al-muqayyidah—haalat al-urdun: 1989–1999* [Restricted Democracy—The Case of Jordan: 1989–1999] (Center for Arab Unity Studies, 2001), 283–307.
48. "Man' al-kutub fil-urdun: wisayyat 'ala al-qiraa' wa-tajaahul lil-qanun [Banning Books in Jordan: Guardianship over Readers and Ignoring the Law]," *7iber.com*, February 6, 2014, https://www.7iber.com/2014/02/jo-book-censorship/.
49. See, for instance, Glenn Robinson, "Defensive Democratization in Jordan," *International Journal of Middle East Studies* 30, no. 3 (1998): 387–410, https://doi.org/10.1017/S002074380006623X; Russell Lucas, *Institutions and the Politics of Survival in Jordan: Domestic Responses to External Challenges, 1988–2001* (State University of New York Press, 2005); and Hussein Abu Rumman, ed., *'Aqd min al-dimuqratiyyah fil-urdun, 1989–1999* [A Decade of Democracy in Jordan, 1989–1999] (Al-Urdun Al-Jadid, 2001).
50. Jillian Schwedler, "Don't Blink," *Middle East Report Online*, July 3, 2002, https://merip.org/2002/07/dont-blink/.
51. Muhammad al-Qatatshah and Mustafa al-Adwan, eds., *Al-tanmiyyah al-siyaasiyyah fil-urdun* [Political Development in Jordan] (Jordanian Political Science Association, 2004).
52. Ryan, *Jordan and the Arab Uprisings*, 114–144. See also Nur Köprülü, "Jordan since the Uprisings: Between Change and Stability," *Middle East Policy* 21, no. 2 (2014): 111–126, https://doi.org/10.1111/mepo.12075.
53. In 2010, for instance, Jordan experimented with an obscure "virtual" subdistricting system that baffled voters and was never repeated again. Ellen Lust, Sami Hourani, and Mohammad

El-Momani, "Jordan Votes: Election or Selection?" *Journal of Democracy* 22, no. 2 (2011): 119–129, https://doi.org/10.1353/jod.2011.0032.

54. Mohammed Torki Bani Salameh, "Electoral Districts' Distribution in Jordan: Political Geographical Analysis," *Asian Journal of Comparative Politics* 9, no. 2 (2024): 179–200, https://doi.org/10.1177/20578911231173599.
55. E.J. Karmel and David Linfield, "Jordan's Election Law: Reinforcing Barriers to Democracy," *Middle East Law and Governance* 13, no. 3 (2021): 395-408, https://doi.org/10.1163/18763375-13031307.
56. Curtis Ryan, "Jordanian Islamists and the War on Gaza," *Mediterranean Politics* 30, no. 2 (2025): 406–415, https://doi.org/10.1080/13629395.2024.2439698.
57. Gail Buttorff, *Authoritarian Elections and Opposition Groups in the Arab World* (Palgrave Macmillan, 2019), 91–127.
58. José Ciro Martínez, "Jordan's Self-Fulfilling Prophecy: The Production of Feeble Political Parties and the Perceived Perils of Democracy," *British Journal of Middle Eastern Studies* 44, no. 3 (2017): 356–372, https://doi.org/10.1080/13530194.2016.1193805.
59. Personal interview, research director Ahmad Awad, Amman, Jordan, June 27, 2018.
60. Kristen Kao, "Electoral Institutions and Identity Based Clientelism in Jordan," *Political Research Quarterly* 76, no. 3 (2023): 1235–1248, https://doi.org/10.1177/10659129221128752.
61. Author's figures based upon aggregate electoral estimates from the United States Agency for International Development and Jordanian NGOs since 2007. It is telling that the Independent Election Commission does not always make turnout figures sorted by age available for public consumption, which is a standard feature of voting data in democracies.
62. "King Says Jordan Committed to Political, Media Pluralism," *Jordan Times*, August 15, 2023.
63. Center for Defending Freedom of Journalists, *Silence of the Media: State of Media Freedom in Jordan 2022* (CDFJ, 2022).
64. Reem Al Masri, "Online Public Engagement in Jordan," *Sur: International Journal of Human Rights* 15, no. 27 (2018): 117–126, https://sur.conectas.org/en/online-public-engagement-in-jordan/.
65. "Jordan Blocks Access to *Middle East Eye* after Investigation on Gaza Aid Drops," *Middle East Eye*, May 15, 2025, https://www.middleeasteye.net/news/jordan-blocks-access-middle-east-eye-days-after-investigation-gaza-aid-drops.
66. Ebtihal Mahadeen, "The Print and Online Media in Jordan—Between Liberalization and Control," in *Routledge Handbook on Arab Media*, eds. Noureddine Miladi and Noha Mellor (Routledge, 2020), 125–134.
67. Isam Uraiqat, "Wedding Jokes Are Not Funny to Jordan's Royals," *New Lines Magazine*, July 12, 2023, https://newlinesmag.com/spotlight/wedding-jokes-are-not-funny-to-the-jordanian-royals/.
68. Sean Yom, "Jordan: The Ruse of Reform," *Journal of Democracy* 24, no. 3 (2013): 127–139, https://doi.org/10.1353/jod.2013.0051.
69. Marwan Muasher, "A Decade of Struggling Reform Efforts in Jordan: The Resilience of the Rentier System," Working Paper of the Carnegie Endowment for International Peace, May 2011, p. 15, https://carnegieendowment.org/2011/05/11/decade-of-struggling-reform-efforts-in-jordan-resilience-of-rentier-system-pub-43939.
70. King Abdullah bin Hussein, "Discussion Papers," Official Website of King Abdullah II of Jordan, accessed June 2, 2020, https://kingabdullah.jo/en/vision/discussion-papers.
71. Shaker Jarrar, "Ijhaadh al-dimuqratiyyah al-urduniyyah: min hibbat nisaan illa hirak 2011 nahwa al-malakiyyah al-mutlaqah [Aborting Jordanian Democracy: From the April Unrest to the 2011 Hirak toward Absolute Monarchy]," *7iber.com*, April 17, 2017, https://www.7iber.com/politics-economics/obstructing-jordanian-democracy-absolute-monarchy/.
72. Sean Yom and Wael Al-Khatib, *Democratic Reform in Jordan: Breaking the Impasse* (Project on Middle East Democracy, 2022), https://mideastdc.org/publication/report-democratic-reform-in-jordan-breaking-the-impasse/.
73. Camille Abescat, "Elections in Jordan: The Parties' Return to Parliament," *Orient XXI*, October 2, 2024, https://orientxxi.info/magazine/elections-in-jordan-the-parties-return-to-parliament,7659.

Chapter 6

1. Ahmad Al-Zaʿatari, *Al-inhinaa' 'ala juthat 'amman* [Bending Over the Corpse of Amman] (Arab Cultural Center, 2014), 141.
2. Areej Abuqudairi, "Jordan: 'We Are Tired of Living Like the Dead,'" *Al-Jazeera*, July 30, 2016, https://www.aljazeera.com/news/2016/7/30/jordan-we-are-tired-of-living-like-the-dead.
3. Charles Tilly and Sidney Tarrow, *Contentious Politics* (Oxford University Press, 2007), 7–8.
4. "296 mushaajarattan jaamiʿiyyah shaaraka fiiha 4 alaaf taalibin bayna 2010–2013 [296 University Fights, in Which 4 Thousand Students Participated, between 2010–2013]," *Al-Rai*, February 17, 2014.
5. Stefanie Nanes, "Fighting Honor Crimes: Evidence of Civil Society in Jordan," in *Deconstructing Sexuality in the Middle East*, ed. Pinar İlkkaracan (Ashgate, 2008), 65–82.
6. James C. Scott, *Weapons of the Weak: Everyday Forms of Peasant Resistance* (Yale University Press, 1985).
7. "Al-hukumah al-urduniyyah tamdhi bi-ijraa' al-intikhaabaat li-taʿziz manaaʿah qati' al-naakhibin [The Jordanian Government Proceeds with Elections to Reinforce the Herd Immunity of the Voters]," *AlHudood*, November 3, 2020, https://alhudood.net/40944/.
8. Kurt Shock, *Civil Resistance Today* (Polity, 2015), 96–139.
9. Hani Hourani and Hussein Abu Rumman, *Tatawwur al-mujtama' al-madani fil-urdun wal-waaqi' al-raahin* [The Development of Civil Society in Jordan and Its Current Reality] (Dar Sindibad, 2004), 21–70.
10. See, for instance, Amr El-Shobaki, ed., *Harakat al-ihtijaajiyyah fil-watan al-arabi* [Protest Movements in the Arab World] (Center for Arab Unity Studies, 2014); Mark Haas and David Lesch, eds., *The Arab Spring: The Hope and Reality of the Uprisings* (Routledge, 2016); and Sean Yom, "Understanding the Arab Spring: One Region, Several Puzzles, and Many Explanations," *Government and Opposition* 50, no. 4 (2015): 682–704, https://doi.org/10.1017/gov.2015.19.
11. Schwedler, *Protesting Jordan*, 193–249.
12. For one stereotypical portrayal, see Zvi Bar'el, "Jordan's King at Critical Juncture as Public Unrest Boils Over into Mass Protests," *Haaretz*, March 7, 2018, https://www.haaretz.com/middle-east-news/2018-06-05/ty-article/.premium/jordan-king-abdullah-critical-juncture-roiled-mass-protests/0000017f-e7ba-dc7e-adff-f7bf70dd0000.
13. Pénélope Larzillière, *Activism in Jordan* (Zed, 2016), 73–95.
14. Sean Yom, "Jordan's Protests Are a Ritual, Not a Revolution," *Foreign Policy*, June 11, 2018, https://foreignpolicy.com/2018/06/11/jordans-protests-are-a-ritual-not-a-revolution/.
15. John Helliwell, Richard Layard, Jeffrey Sachs, Lara Aknin, Jan-Emmanuel De Neve, and Shun Wang, eds., *World Happiness Report 2023* (Sustainable Development Solutions Network, 2023). The *World Happiness Report* utilizes survey data from the Gallup World Poll that measure how respondents evaluate their lives.
16. David Pollock, "Jordan's Public Internally Focused, but Shares US View on Iran and Regional Peace," Policy Analysis of the Washington Institute for Near East Peace, February 26, 2019, https://www.washingtoninstitute.org/policy-analysis/jordans-public-internally-focused-shares-us-view-iran-and-regional-peace.
17. Russell Lucas, "Public Attitudes on Peace with Israel in Jordanian Politics," *Middle Eastern Studies* 57, no. 3 (2021): 469–484, https://doi.org/10.1080/00263206.2021.1898380.
18. Jillian Schwedler, "Palestine and the Limits of Permissible Protest in Jordan," *Middle East Report* 309 (2023), https://merip.org/2024/01/jordan-palestine-and-permissible-protest/.
19. Personal interview, journalist Mohammad Ersan, Amman, Jordan, August 1, 2016, italics mine.
20. Jamal Altahat, "Jordan's Week of Protests Signals Key Change in Power Balance," *Arab Reform Initiative*, July 8, 2018, https://www.arab-reform.net/publication/jordans-week-of-protests-signals-key-change-in-power-balance/.
21. Confidential personal interview, deputy director of civil society organization, Amman, Jordan, May 19, 2024.

22. Raed Faqir, Muddather Abu-Karaki, and Majed Ahmad Marashdah, "The Impact of Corruption on Human Rights and the Legal Mechanisms for Its Compacting: Case of Jordan," *Mediterranean Journal of Social Sciences* 2, no. 3 (2011): 460–461.
23. Anan Abuhummour, "Summative Evaluation of Implementation of Jordan's National Anti-Corruption Strategy, 2013-2017, in the Perspective of Public Choice Theory," *Poverty and Public Policy* 15, no. 4 (2023): 402–430, https://doi.org/10.1002/pop4.384.
24. Despite government regulations, information about many domestic corruption scandals have leaked out to independent journalists and outside media. Al-Jazeera, for instance, helped uncover the Casinogate affair. See further *Al-Jazeera Investigations,* "Jordan: Casinogate," https://transparency.aljazeera.net/en/projects/jordancasinogate/.
25. Lachlan Markay and Zachary Basu, "The Pandora Papers PR War," *Axios,* October 5, 2021.
26. Various guides to Jordanian CSOs exist. For a classic manual, see Al-Urdun Al-Jadid Research Center, *The Contemporary Jordanian Civil Society: Characteristics, Challenges, and Tasks* (CIVICUS, 2010). For an online index, see Phenix Center, "Guide to Civil Society Organizations in Jordan," http://www.civilsociety-jo.net/ar/home.
27. Personal interview, civil society director Amer Bani Amer, Amman, Jordan, June 19, 2011.
28. In early 2025 during President Trump's second term, the American government dismantled most of USAID's civil society assistance programs around the world, including in Jordan. While it remains unclear whether USAID's technical and financial funding for Jordanian CSOs will return, its accumulated effects are still considerable.
29. Alena Sander, "Rethinking Shrinking Civic Space in the Global Souths—How Development Donors Contribute to the Restriction of Civil Society in Jordan," *Democratization* 30, no. 1 (2023): 22–39, https://doi.org/10.1080/13510347.2022.2096595.
30. Anne Marie Baylouny, *Privatizing Welfare in the Middle East: Kin Mutual Aid Associations in Jordan and Lebanon* (Indiana University Press, 2010), 92–116.
31. Mounah Abdel-Samad, "Legislative Advocacy under Competitive Authoritarian Regimes: The Case of Civil Society in Jordan," *Voluntas* 28 (2017): 1035–1053, https://doi.org/10.1007/s11266-015-9592-0.
32. Rana Husseini, *Years of Struggle: The Women's Movement in Jordan* (Friedrich Ebert Stiftung, 2021).
33. For excellent studies of this difficult situation, see Ebtihal Mahadeen, *Women and the Media in Jordan: Gender, Power, Resistance* (Palgrave Macmillan, 2022); Fida Adely, *Gendered Paradoxes: Educating Jordanian Women in Nation, Faith, and Progress* (University of Chicago Press, 2012).
34. Laurie Brand, "Development in Wadi Rum? State Bureaucracy, External Funders, and Civil Society," *International Journal of Middle East Studies* 33, no. 4 (2001): 571–590, https://doi.org/10.1017/S0020743801004056.
35. Musa Shtweiwi, *The Role of Civil Society Organizations in the Political Reform of Jordan* (Center for Strategic Studies, 2014), 38–44.
36. Joseph Nevo, "Professional Associations in Jordan: The Backbone of An Emerging Civil Society," *Asian Studies Review* 25 (2001): 169–184, https://doi.org/10.1080/10357820108713303.
37. *AccessNow*, "Between a Hack and a Hard Place: How Pegasus Spyware Crushes Civic Space in Jordan," February 1, 2024, https://www.accessnow.org/publication/between-a-hack-and-a-hard-place-how-pegasus-spyware-crushes-civic-space-in-jordan/.
38. Pete W. Moore and Bassel Salloukh, "Struggles under Authoritarianism: Regimes, States, and Professional Associations in the Arab World," *International Journal of Middle East Studies* 39, no. 1 (2007): 53–76, https://doi.org/10.1017/S0020743807222536.
39. Hani Hourani, *The Jordanian Labour Movement: History, Structure, and Challenges* (Friedrich Ebert Stiftung, 2001), 15–16.
40. Fida Adely, "The Emergence of a New Labor Movement in Jordan," *Middle East Report* 264 (2012): 34–37, https://merip.org/2012/08/the-emergence-of-a-new-labor-movement-in-jordan/.

41. Jordan Labor Watch, *Jordan's Paradoxical Approach to Trade Unions* (Phenix Center, 2019), 5–6.
42. For more on the rise of Islamism as political opposition across the MENA, see Shadi Hamid and Williams McCants, eds., *Rethinking Political Islam* (Oxford University Press, 2017).
43. Egbert Harmsen, *Islam, Civil Society, and Social Work: Muslim Voluntary Welfare Associations in Jordan between Patronage and Empowerment* (Amsterdam University Press, 2008), 173–288.
44. Joas Wagemakers, *Salafism in Jordan: Political Islam in a Quietist Community* (Cambridge University Press, 2016), 95–176.
45. Sean Yom and Katrina Sammour, "Counterterrorism and Youth Radicalization in Jordan: Social and Political Dimensions," *CTC Sentinel* 10, no. 4 (2017): 25–30.
46. Incisive overviews of Jordan's Muslim Brotherhood include Joas Wagemakers, *The Muslim Brotherhood in Jordan* (Cambridge University Press, 2020); and Ibrahim Gharaibeh, *Min al-da'wah illa al-siyaasah: al-ikhwan al-muslimun fil-urdun* [From Outreach to Politics: The Muslim Brothers in Jordan] (Dar Sirin Lil-Nashr Wal-Tawzi', 2017).
47. Marion Boulby, *The Muslim Brotherhood and the Kings of Jordan* (Scholars Press, 1999), 73–114.
48. Bakr Muhammad Al-Badur, *Tajribah al-niyaabiyyah lil-harakat al-islaamiyyah fil-urdun, 1989–2007* [The Parliamentary Experience of the Islamic Movement in Jordan, 1989–2007] (Markaz Al-Ma'mun Lil-Nashr Wal-Tawzi', 2011).
49. Jillian Schwedler, *Faith in Moderation: Islamist Parties in Jordan and Yemen* (Cambridge University Press, 2006), 149–191.
50. Lamis El Muhtaseb, "Preaching and Ruling: The Jordanian Muslim Brotherhood Post-Arab Uprisings," *Mediterranean Politics* 27, no. 1 (2020): 79–100, https://doi.org/10.1080/13629395.2020.1748471.
51. Mohammad Abu Rumman and Neven Bondokji, *From Caliphate to Civil State: The Young Face of Political Islam in Jordan after the Arab Spring* (Friedrich Ebert Stiftung, 2018), 77–105.
52. Mahmoud Farag and Muath Abudalu, "Electoral Reform in Authoritarian Regimes: Veto Player Uncertainty in Jordan," *Zeitschrift für Vergleichende Politikwissenschaft* 16 (2022): 463–481, https://doi.org/10.1007/s12286-022-00534-8.
53. "Watha'iq al-ikhwaan wa-milyaaraatihim fi qabdhat al-dawlah al-urduniyyah [The Brotherhood's Documents and Billions Are in the Grasp of the Jordanian State]," *Raseef22*, April 23, 2025.
54. Confidential personal interview, student member of Nashama movement at Jordan University, Amman, Jordan, July 3, 2018, emphasis mine.
55. Jamal Al-Shalabi, *Al-urdun: thuwwaar bi-la thawra* [Jordan: Revolutionaries without Revolution] (Arab Foundation for Studies and Publishing, 2018).
56. Sean Yom, "Mobilization without Movement: Opposition and Youth Activism in Jordan," in *Struggles for Political Change in the Arab World: Regimes, Oppositions, and External Actors after the Spring*, eds. Lisa Blaydes, Amr Hamzawy, and Hesham Sallam (University of Michigan Press, 2022), 148–174.
57. Sara Ababneh, "The Time to Question, Rethink and Popularize the Notion of 'Women's Issues': Lessons from Jordan's Popular and Labor Movements from 2006 to Now," *Journal of International Women's Studies* 21, no. 1 (2020): 271–288.
58. Asef Bayat, *Revolution without Revolutionaries: Making Sense of the Arab Spring* (Stanford University Press, 2017).
59. Abu-Rish, "Protests, Regime Stability, and State Formation in Jordan," 299–302.
60. Sean Yom, "The New Landscape of Jordanian Politics: Social Opposition, Fiscal Crisis, and the Arab Spring," *British Journal of Middle Eastern Studies* 42, no. 3 (2015): 284–300, https://doi.org/10.1080/13530194.2014.932271.
61. For more on the Hashemite regime's approach to the Arab Spring, see Martin Beck and Simone Hüser, "Jordan and the 'Arab Spring': No Challenge, No Change?" *Middle East Critique* 24, no. 1 (2015): 83–97, https://doi.org/10.1080/19436149.2014.996996; and Maria Josua, "Co-optation Reconsidered: Authoritarian Regime Legitimation Strategies in the Jordanian 'Arab Spring,'" *Middle East Law and Governance* 8, no. 1 (2016): 32–56, https://doi.org/10.1163/18763375-00801001.

62. Jacob Amis, "Hirak! Civil Resistance and the Jordan Spring," in *Civil Resistance in the Arab Spring: Triumphs and Disasters*, eds. Adam Roberts, Michael Willis, Rory McCarthy, and Timothy Garton Ash (Oxford University Press, 2016), 169–193.
63. Colfax Phillips, "Dhiban as Barometer of Jordan's Rural Discontent," *Middle East Report* 292/293 (2019): 15–19, https://merip.org/2019/12/dhiban-as-barometer-of-jordans-rural-discontent/.
64. Mohammed Yaghi and Janine Clark, "Jordan: Evolving Activism in a Divided Society," in *Taking to the Streets: The Transformation of Arab Activism*, eds. Lina Khatib and Ellen Lust (The Johns Hopkins University Press, 2014), 236–267.
65. Sean Yom, "Tribal Politics in Contemporary Jordan: The Case of the Hirak Movement," *Middle East Journal* 68, no. 2 (2014): 229–247, https://doi.org/10.3751/68.2.13.
66. E. J. Karmel and Sara Kuburic, "The Impact of Moral Injury on Social Movements: The Demobilization of Jordan's 'Arab Spring' Protestors," *Globalizations*, October (2021): 1–18, https://doi.org/10.1080/14747731.2021.1992571.
67. See, for instance, Muath Abudalu, "A Jordanian Protest Group: The Free Assembly, A Failure to Launch," *Canadian Journal for Middle East Studies* 2, no. 1 (2017): 46–62.
68. Curtis Ryan, "Resurgent Protests Confront New and Old Red Lines in Jordan," *Middle East Report* 292/293 (2019): 30–34, https://merip.org/2019/12/resurgent-protests-confront-new-and-old-red-lines-in-jordan/.
69. Sara Ababneh, "Do You Know Who Governs Us? The Damned Monetary Fund," *Middle East Report Online*, June 30, 2018, https://merip.org/2018/06/do-you-know-who-governs-us-the-damned-monetary-fund/.
70. Sean Yom and Wael Al-Khatib, "Youth Revolts and Political Opposition in Jordan," *The Washington Post*, December 20, 2018, https://www.washingtonpost.com/news/monkey-cage/wp/2018/12/20/youth-revolts-and-political-opposition-in-jordan/.
71. "Niraan ghaza tamtadd illa al-urdun [Fires of Gaza Spread to Jordan]," *Al-Quds al-Arabi*, March 31, 2024.
72. Matt Lacouture, "Privatizing the Commons: Protest and the Moral Economy of National Resources in Jordan," *International Review of Social History* 66 (2021): 113–137, https://doi.org/10.1017/S002085902100016X.
73. Lamis Andoni, "Risaalat al-sha'b al-urduni lam tassil [The Message of the Jordanian People Was Not Delivered]," *Al-Araby Al-Jadid*, December18, 2022.

Chapter 7

1. International Republican Institute, *State of the State: Nationwide Survey of Jordan, Wave 4* (IRI, 2024), https://www.iri.org/resources/state-of-the-state-nationwide-survey-of-jordan-wave4/.
2. Magdi Amin et al., eds., *After the Spring: Economic Transitions in the Arab World* (Oxford University Press, 2012); and Ferdinand Eibl, Shimaa Hatab, and Steffen Hertog, "Political Economy and Development," in *The Political Science of the Middle East*, 132–156.
3. See, for instance, Robert Springborg, *Political Economies of the Middle East and North Africa* (Polity, 2020); and Steffen Hertog, *Locked Out of Development: Insiders and Outsiders in Arab Capitalism* (Cambridge University Press, 2022).
4. Another useful comparator is GDP per capita adjusted by purchasing power parity (PPP), which adjusts the raw figure by taking into account that living costs differ across countries due to exchange rates and other factors. When recalibrated for PPP, Jordan's 2024 per capita GDP jumps to about $12,400—but is still one of the lowest five in the MENA.
5. Taher Kanaan and Marwan Kardoosh, "The Story of Economic Growth in Jordan: 1950–2003," Working Paper of the Economic Research Forum, Amman, Jordan, 2005.
6. Linda Glawe and Helmut Wagner, "The Middle-Income Trap: Definitions, Theories and Countries Concerned—A Literature Survey," *Comparative Economic Studies* 58 (2016): 507–538, https://doi.org/10.1057/s41294-016-0014-0.

7. Mohammad Ersan, "Jordan: Dire Economic Prospects Force Youth to Chase American Dream, Despite Risks," *Middle East Eye*, August 28, 2024, https://www.middleeasteye.net/news/dire-economy-forces-youth-american-dream-risky-migration-routes.
8. Many Jordanian websites ended their reproduction of Hajjaj's comics due to the government enacting strict cybercrimes laws after the Arab Spring. However, this particular cartoon has been widely reproduced by outside blogs. See, for instance, "Emad Hajjaj Cartoons," *East by Mideast* (blog), June 30, 2011, https://eastbymideast.wordpress.com/2011/01/30/emad-hajjaj-cartoons/.
9. William Christou, "Mansaf on 'Layaway' Sparks Outrage in Struggling Jordan," *The New Arab*, March 30, 2023, https://www.newarab.com/news/mansaf-layaway-sparks-outrage-struggling-jordan.
10. Unemployment means the proportion of the active labor force seeking a job but unable to obtain one.
11. Data from Jordanian Department of Statistics, *Online Statistical Databank*, https://dosweb.dos.gov.jo/.
12. Phenix Center, *'Athar 'azma "Kuruna" 'ala al-awdhaa' al-iqtisaadiyyah lil-'usar fil-urdun* [The Impact of the Corona Crisis on Economic Conditions for Families in Jordan] (Phenix Center, 2020).
13. Mona Amer, "The School-To-Work Transition of Jordanian Youth," in *The Jordanian Labour Market in the New Millennium*, ed. Ragui Assaad (Oxford University Press, 2014), 64–104.
14. Data from World Bank, *World Development Indicators* (IBRD, various years).
15. Jordan Strategy Forum, *Jordan's Informal Economy: A Potential Opportunity for Higher Productivity and Economic Growth* (JSF, 2023).
16. "More Than One-Third of Jordanians Live Below Poverty Line, Report Finds," *Jordan News*, July 12, 2023.
17. International Republican Institute, *Public Opinion Survey: Residents of Jordan, November 14–22, 2019* (IRI, 2019), https://www.iri.org/wp-content/uploads/2020/03/jordan_scrubbed_slides_3.27.20_1.pdf.
18. Myriam Ababsa, Olga Koukoui, and Irène Salenson, "The Crisis of Affordable Housing in Jordan," Policy Brief of the Agence Française de Développement, May 2021, https://www.afd.fr/en/ressources/crisis-affordable-housing-jordan.
19. Human Rights Watch, *"We Lost Everything:" Debt Imprisonment in Jordan* (HRW, 2021), https://www.hrw.org/report/2021/03/16/we-lost-everything/debt-imprisonment-jordan.
20. Data from World Inequality Database, https://wid.world/.
21. Katharina Lenner and Lewis Turner, "The Jordan Compact, Refugee Labour and the Limits of Indicator-oriented Formalization," *Development and Change* 55, no. 2 (2024): 302–330, https://doi.org/10.1111/dech.12824.
22. See, for example, Fida Adely, *Working Women in Jordan: Education, Migration, and Aspiration* (University of Chicago Press, 2024).
23. Data from World Bank, *World Development Indicators* (IBRD, various years).
24. Osama Sweidan, "Political Instability and Economic Growth: Evidence from Jordan," *Review of Middle East Economics and Finance* 12, no. 3 (2016): 279–300, https://doi.org/10.1515/rmeef-2015-0025.
25. I am indebted to Marwan Kardoosh, among the brightest of Jordanian economists, for this observation. Personal interview, Marwan Kardoosh, Amman, Jordan, August 2, 2016.
26. Jamal Husein, "Foreign Aid, Workers' Remittances, and Economic Growth in Jordan," *International Journal of Social Economics* 46, no. 4 (2019): 532–548, https://doi.org/10.1108/IJSE-06-2018-0293.
27. Elizabeth Whitman, "A Land without Water," *Nature* 573, no. 7772 (2019): 20–23, https://doi.org/10.1038/d41586-019-02600-w.
28. Ali 'Anbar, "Ishkaliyyah al-maa' wal-taghyirat al-manakhiyyah fil-badiyyah al-urduniyyah [The Problematique of Water and Climate Changes in the Jordanian Countryside]," in *Tanmiyyah al-aryaaf wal-bawadi fil-urdun* [The Development of Rural Areas and Deserts in Jordan], eds. Ibrahim Badran and Zahir Tawfiq (Al-Aan Publishers, 2017), 11–42.

29. For more on the Disi Water Conveyance system, see Sean Yom, "Water, Stateness, and Tribalism in Jordan: The Case of the Disi Water Conveyance Project," in *Making Sense of the Arab State*, eds. Steven Heydemann and Marc Lynch (University of Michigan Press, 2024), 247–273.
30. Jordanian Department of Statistics, *Food Balance Sheet* (DOS, 2023).
31. Food and Agricultural Organization, *Jordan Food Security Update: Implications of COVID-19* (FAO, 2020), 18.
32. José Ciro Martínez, *States of Subsistence: The Politics of Bread in Contemporary Jordan* (Stanford University Press, 2022), 79–133.
33. Data for this and other energy-related figures in this chapter from World Bank, *World Development Indicators* (IBRD, various years).
34. Ghaida Abu-Rumman, Adnan Khdair, and Sawsan Khdair, "Current Status and Future Investment Potential in Renewable Energy in Jordan: An Overview," *Heliyon* 6, no. 2 (2020): e03346, https://doi.org/10.1016/j.heliyon.2020.e03346.
35. The literature on oil-rentier states is cosmic. Two well-cited works include Hazem Beblawi, "The Rentier State in the Arab World," in *The Arab State*, ed. Giacomo Luciani (UC Press, 1990), 85–98; and Michael Ross, *The Oil Curse: How Petroleum Wealth Shapes the Development of Nations* (Princeton University Press, 2013).
36. Daron Acemoglu, Simon Johnson, and James A. Robinson, "Reversal of Fortune: Geography and Institutions in the Making of the Modern World Income Distribution," *Quarterly Journal of Economics* 117, no. 4 (2002): 1231–1294, https://doi.org/10.1162/003355302320935025.
37. The classic tract on late development is Alexander Gerschenkron, *Economic Backwardness in Historical Perspective* (Harvard University Press, 1962). See also Atul Kohli, *State-Directed Development: Political Power and Industrialization in the Global Periphery* (Cambridge University Press, 2004).
38. David Harvey, *A Brief History of Neoliberalism* (Oxford University Press, 2005).
39. Hani Hourani, *Al-tarkib al-iqtisaadi al-ijtima'i li-sharq al-urdun* [The Socioeconomic Structure of Transjordan] (PLO Research Center, 1978).
40. Tariq Tell, "Guns, Gold, and Grain: War and Food Supply in the Making of Transjordan," in *War, Institutions, and Social Change in the Middle East*, ed. Steven Heydemann (University of California Press, 2000), 33–58.
41. Pete W. Moore, *Doing Business in the Middle East: Politics and Economic Crisis in Jordan and Kuwait* (Cambridge University Press, 2009), 49–64.
42. International Bank for Reconstruction and Development, *The Economic Development of Jordan* (The Johns Hopkins University Press, 1957), 441–443.
43. Paul Kingston, "Rationalizing Patrimonialism," in *The Resilience of Hashemite Rule: Politics and the State in Jordan, 1946–67*, ed. Tariq Tell (CERMOC, 2001), 115–155.
44. Oliver Wils, "From Negotiation to Rent Seeking, and Bach? Patterns of State-Business Interaction and Fiscal Policy Reform in Jordan," in *Networks of Privilege in the Middle East*, ed. Steven Heydemann (Palgrave Macmillan, 2004), 142–145.
45. Zayd Sha'sha, "The Role of the Private Sector in Jordan's Economy," in *Politics and the Economy in Jordan*, ed. Rodney Wilson (Routledge, 1991), 79–89.
46. Mazur, *Economic Growth and Development in Jordan*, 95.
47. Eliyahu Kanovsky, "Jordan's Economy: From Prosperity to Crisis," in *Middle East Contemporary Survey, Vol. XII*, eds. Ami Ayalon and Haim Shaked (Routledge, 1991), 333–385.
48. Khalil Hammad, "The Role of Foreign Aid in the Jordanian Economy, 1959–1983" in *The Economic Development of Jordan*, eds. Bichara Khader and Adnan Badran (Croom Helm, 1987), 11–31.
49. Data from Central Bank of Jordan, *Annual Statistical Bulletin* (CBJ, various years).
50. Mohamad Amerah, *Unemployment in Jordan: Dimensions and Prospects* (Center for International Studies, 1993), 53–60.
51. Yann Le Troquer and Rozenn Hommery al-Oudat, "From Kuwait to Jordan: The Palestinians' Third Exodus," *Journal of Palestine Studies* 28, no. 3 (1999): 37–51, https://doi.org/10.2307/2538306.

52. Colin Power, "How Neoliberalism Comes to Town: Policy Convergence, (Under)Development, and Jordanian Economics under King Abdullah," *Middle East Law and Governance* 12, no. 2 (2020): 167–97, https://doi.org/10.1163/18763375-01202002.
53. Sufyan Alissa, "Rethinking Economic Reform in Jordan: Confronting Socioeconomic Realities," Working Paper of the Carnegie Endowment for International Peace, July 2007, pp. 12-13, https://carnegieendowment.org/research/2007/07/rethinking-economic-reform-in-jordan-confronting-socioeconomic-realities?lang=en.
54. Rami Farouk Daher, "Welfare Genocide: Rentierism, Neoliberalism, and the Corporatization of the Public Sector in Jordan," in *Neoliberal Governmentality and the Future of the State in the Middle East and North Africa*, ed. Emel Akçali (Palgrave Macmillan, 2016), 53–56.
55. Jane Harrigan, Hamed Al-Said, and Chengang Wang, "The IMF and the World Bank in Jordan: A Case of Over Optimism and Elusive Growth," *Review of International Organizations* 1, no. 3 (2006): 263–292, https://doi.org/10.1007/s11558-006-9490-8.
56. Anne Marie Baylouny, *Privatizing Welfare in the Middle East: Kin Mutual Aid Associations in Jordan and Lebanon* (Indiana University Press, 2010).
57. Luis Abugattas-Majluf, "Jordan: Modern Reformer without Upgrading?" *Studies in Comparative International Development* 47, no. 2 (2012): 231–253, https://doi.org/10.1007/s12116-012-9112-9.
58. Government of Jordan, *Jordan 2025: A National Vision and Strategy* (GOJ, 2015), 48.
59. Indeed, since the 2008–2009 global financial crisis, some Western economists have argued loudly against neoliberal economic policies, holding that the higher inequality and social problems wrought by capitalist excess could only nourish the right-wing populism endangering all global democracies. See, for instance, Joseph Stiglitz, *The Road to Freedom: Economics and the Good Society* (WW Norton, 2024).
60. Pete W. Moore, "The Fiscal Politics of Rebellious Jordan," *Middle East Report Online*, June 21, 2018, https://merip.org/2018/06/the-fiscal-politics-of-rebellious-jordan/.
61. Markus Loewe, Jonas Blume and Johanna Speer, "How Favoritism Affects the Business Climate: Empirical Evidence from Jordan," *Middle East Journal* 62, no. 2 (2008), 259–276, https://doi.org/10.3751/62.2.14.
62. Katherine Blue Carroll, *Business as Usual? Economic Reform in Jordan* (Lexington Books, 2003), 57–65.
63. Laith Alajlouni, "'Loyalty vs. Voice': What Explains the Divergent Attitudes of the Business Elite toward Democratization? The Case of Jordan," Master's Thesis, Central European University, 2020.
64. These newer patterns of state-business relations are helpfully explained by Steve Monroe, *Mirages of Reform: The Politics of Elite Protectionism in the Arab World* (Cornell University Press, 2025).
65. Ishac Diwan, Adeel Malik, and Izak Atiyas, eds., *Crony Capitalism in the Middle East: Business and Politics from Liberalization to the Arab Spring* (Oxford University Press, 2019).
66. Timothy Piro, *The Political Economy of Market Reform in Jordan* (Rowman and Littlefield, 1998), 79–93. For a broader overview of how authoritarian interests shaped neoliberal economic reforms, see Warwick Knowles, *Jordan since 1989: A Study in Political Economy* (IB Tauris, 2005).
67. Yitzhak Reiter, "The Palestinian-Transjordanian Rift: Economic Might and Political Power in Jordan," *Middle East Journal* 58, no. 1 (2004): 72–92, https://doi.org/10.3751/58.1.14.
68. Jamil Jreisat, "Public Administration Reform in Jordan: Concepts and Practices," *International Journal of Public Administration* 41, no. 10 (2018): 781–791, https://doi.org/10.1080/01900692.2017.1387991.
69. Data reported by the Jordanian government and obtained from World Bank, *World Development Indicators* (IBRD, various years).
70. Data from Jordanian Department of Statistics, *Online Statistical Databank*, https://dosweb.dos.gov.jo/.
71. Ragui Assaad, "The Structure and Evolution of Employment in Jordan," in *The Jordanian Labor Market*, 1–38.

72. "Around 388,000 Civil Service Bureau Applicants Await Postings," *Jordan Times*, January 27, 2021.
73. Fadi Alasfour, "Costs of Distrust: The Virtuous Cycle of Tax Compliance in Jordan," *Journal of Business Ethics* 155 (2019): 243–258, https://doi.org/10.1007/s10551-017-3473-y.
74. Data from Central Bank of Jordan, *Annual Statistical Bulletin* (CBJ, 2023).
75. Anne Mariel Peters and Pete W. Moore, "Beyond Boom and Bust: External Rents, Durable Authoritarianism, and Institutional Adaptation in the Hashemite Kingdom of Jordan," *Studies in Comparative International Development* 44, no. 3 (2009): 256–285, https://doi.org/10.1007/s12116-009-9053-0.

Chapter 8

1. Personal interview, Ambassador Hassan Abu Nimeh, Amman, Jordan, June 29, 2006.
2. Marianne Kneuer, "Autocratic Regimes and Foreign Policy," in *Oxford Encyclopedia of Foreign Policy Analysis*, ed. Cameron Thies (Oxford University Press, 2018), 96–115.
3. An excellent overview is the classic Sa'ad Abudayeh, *'Amaliyat ittikhaadh al-qiraar fi-siyaasat al-urdun al-khaarijiyyah* [The Decision-Making Process in Jordanian Foreign Policy] (Da'irat Al-Thaqaafah Wal-Funun, 1983).
4. Sometimes, royal emissaries sent abroad are personal confidantes of the ruler rather than state officials. For example, the late King Hussein often asked his brother Prince Hassan and cousin General Zayd bin Shaker—two of his closest advisers—to serve as his representative in Arab and Western capitals. King Abdullah has similarly rotated through an entourage of personal retainers in maintaining good relations with Jordan's allies.
5. This concept of regime security is best detailed in Raymond Hinnebusch and Anoushiravan Ehteshami, eds., *The Foreign Policies of Middle East States*, 2nd ed. (Lynne Rienner, 2014).
6. Robert Rothstein, *Alliances and Small Powers* (Columbia University Press, 1968); and Kenneth Waltz, *Theory of International Politics* (Addison-Wesley, 1979).
7. Samih Al-Ma'aytah, "Jighrafiyaa sharira [An Evil Geography]," *Al-Ghad*, August 30, 2023.
8. Christine Ingebritsen, Iver Neumann, and Sieglinde Gstöhl, eds., *Small States in International Relations* (University of Washington Press, 2006).
9. Bassel Salloukh, "Regime Autonomy and Regional Foreign Policy Choices in the Middle East: A Theoretical Explanation," in *Persistent Permeability? Regionalism, Localism, and Globalization in the Middle East*, eds. Bassel Salloukh and Rex Brynen (Ashgate, 2004), 81–104.
10. Hussein Majali, "Al-urdun bi-muwaajaha harb al-mukhaddiraat [Jordan Faces a Drug War]," *Al-Rai*, October 1, 2022.
11. Stephen Walt, *The Origins of Alliances* (Cornell University Press, 1987); and F. Gregory Gause, *The International Relations of the Persian Gulf* (Cambridge University Press, 2010).
12. "If Shaken, Jordan Will Burn Everyone Around," *Jordan Times*, May 22, 2019.
13. Steven David, *Choosing Sides: Alignment and Realignment in the Third World* (The Johns Hopkins University Press, 1991).
14. Lisa Anderson, "Democratization and Foreign Policy in the Arab World," in *Liberalization and Foreign Policy*, ed. Miles Kahler (Columbia University Press, 1997), 133.
15. Laurie Brand, *Jordan's Inter-Arab Relations: The Political Economy of Alliance-Making* (Columbia University Press, 1994).
16. Insightful works on how identity policies shapes foreign policy in the Middle East include Shibley Telhami and Michael Barnett, eds., *Identity and Foreign Policy in the Middle East* (Cornell University Press, 2002); and May Darwich, *Threats and Alliances in the Middle East: Saudi and Syrian Policies in a Turbulent Region* (Cambridge University Press, 2019).
17. Marc Lynch, *State Interests and Public Spheres: The International Politics of Jordan's Identity* (Columbia University Press, 1999).
18. Hassan Barari, *Jordan and Israel: A Troubled Relationship in a Volatile Region* (Friedrich Ebert Stiftung, 2014), 94–99.

19. Bahgat Korany and Ali E. Hillal Dessouki, "Foreign Policy as a Strategic National Asset: The Case of Jordan," in *The Foreign Policies of Arab States: The Challenge of Globalization*, eds. Bahgat Korany and Ali E. Hillal Dessouki (American University of Cairo Press, 2008), 253–282.
20. Adeed Dawisha, "Jordan in the Middle East: The Art of Survival," in *The Shaping of an Arab Statesman*, 61–74.
21. Curtis Ryan, *Inter-Arab Alliances: Regime Security and Jordanian Foreign Policy* (University Press of Florida, 2009), 204–207.
22. Malcolm Kerr, *The Arab Cold War: Gamel 'Abd Al-Nasir and His Rivals, 1958–70* (Oxford University Press, 1970).
23. Juan Romero, "Arab Nationalism and the Arab Union of 1958," *British Journal of Middle Eastern Studies* 42, no. 2 (2015): 179–199, https://doi.org/10.1080/13530194.2014.994317.
24. "Jordan: Death in Amman," *Time Magazine*, September 12, 1960.
25. Joseph Nevo, "Jordan and Saudi Arabia: The Last Royalists," in *Jordan in the Middle East: The Making of a Pivotal State, 1948–1988*, eds. Joseph Nevo and Ilan Pappé (Frank Cass, 1994), 103–106.
26. Samir Mutawi, *Jordan in the 1967 War* (Cambridge University Press, 1987), 85–121.
27. Amatzia Baram, "Baathi Iraq and Hashimite Jordan: From Hostility to Alignment," *Middle East Journal* 45, no. 1 (1991): 51–70.
28. Curtis Ryan, "'Jordan First': Jordan's Inter-Arab Relations and Foreign Policy under King Abdullah II," *Arab Studies Quarterly* 26, no. 3 (2004): 43–62.
29. Morten Valbjørn and André Bank, "The New Arab Cold War: Rediscovering the Arab Dimension of Middle East Regional Politics," *Review of International Studies* 38, no. 1 (2012): 3–24, https://doi.org/10.1017/S0260210511000283.
30. Jean-Loup Samaan, "Jordan's New Geopolitics," *Survival* 54, no. 2 (2012): 15–26, https://doi.org/10.1080/00396338.2012.672700.
31. Karam Shaar and Caroline Rose, "From 2015–2023: The Captagon Trade's Trends, Trajectory, and Policy Implications," Intelligence Briefing of the New Lines Institute for Strategy and Policy, May 2024, pp. 22–23, https://newlinesinstitute.org/wp-content/uploads/20240519-Intelligence-Briefing-Captagon-NLISAP-1.pdf.
32. The best-known work on this controversial fact is Avi Shlaim, *Collusion across the Jordan: King Abdullah, the Zionist Movement, and the Partition of Palestine* (Oxford University Press, 1988).
33. Madiha Rashid al-Madfai, *Jordan, the United States, and the Middle East Peace Process, 1974–1991* (Cambridge University Press, 1993), 46–61, 158–190.
34. Jeffrey K. Sosland, *Cooperating Rivals: The Riparian Politics of the Jordan River Basin* (State University of New York Press, 2008), 93–140.
35. Shaul Mishal, "Conflictual Pressures and Cooperative Interests: Observations on West Bank-Amman Political Relations, 1949–1967," in *Palestinian Society and Politics*, ed. Joel Migdal (Princeton University Press, 1980), 174.
36. W. Andrew Terrill, "The Political Mythology of the Battle of Karameh," *Middle East Journal* 55, no. 1 (2001): 91–111.
37. Marc Lynch, *State Interests and Public Spheres*, 89–99.
38. For a typical homage to the peace process, see Abdul Salam Majali, Jawad Anani, and Munther Haddadin, *Peacemaking: The Inside Story of the 1994 Jordanian-Israeli Treaty* (University of Oklahoma Press, 2006).
39. Fawaz Mawqif Dhunun, *Al-urdun wa-muhituhu al-iqlimi* [Jordan and Its Regional Environment] (Arab Scientific Publishers, 2016), 130–139.
40. Onn Winckler, "Missed Opportunity? Jordan's (Insufficient) Economic Dividends from the Peace Treaty with Israel," *Middle Eastern Studies* 57, no. 3 (2021): 429–442, https://doi.org/10.1080/00263206.2021.1898385.
41. See, for instance, Ian Lustick, *Paradigm Lost: From Two-State Solution to One-State Reality* (University of Pennsylvania Press, 2019).
42. Bassam al-Badarin, "I'aadat qiraa'at 13 ittifaaqiyyah ma'a israa'il [Re-reading 13 Agreements with Israel]," *Al-Quds Al-Arabi*, December 4, 2023.

43. Naser Tahboub, "The Impact of US President Trump's Middle East Peace Plan on Jordan and Palestinians," *Dirasat: Human and Social Sciences* 50, no. 5 (2023): 116–133, https://doi.org/10.35516/hum.v50i5.1165.
44. "Al-makhaawif 'ala al-istiqraar al-daakhili waraa' qalaq al-urduni min al-tas'id fi-ghaza [Fears over Internal Stability behind Jordan's Concern for Gaza Escalation]," *Al-Arab*, 20 October 2023.
45. "Al-urdun yuwaajih tahdidan wujudiyyan bi-sabab khuttat trump li-tahjir al-filistiniyyin [Jordan Faces an Existential Threat Because of Trump's Plan to Expel Palestinians]," *Al-Arab*, February 6, 2025.
46. US Department of State, "Memorandum of Conversation for Royal Diwan Meeting," 3 September 1975, declassified document.
47. The White House, "Remarks by President Biden and His Majesty King Abdullah II ibn Al Hussein, King of the Hashemite Kingdom of Jordan," July 19, 2021, https://www.whitehouse.gov/briefing-room/speeches-remarks/2021/07/19/remarks-by-president-biden-and-his-majesty-king-abdullah-ii-ibn-al-hussein-king-of-the-hashemite-kingdom-of-jordan-before-bilateral-meeting/.
48. Said K. Aburish, *A Brutal Friendship: The West and the Arab Elite* (St. Martin's, 1997), 216–232.
49. Confidential personal interview with Foreign Ministry official, Amman, Jordan, August 2, 2022.
50. Yom, *From Resilience to Revolution*, 41–43. See also David Lake, *Hierarchy in International Relations* (Cornell University Press, 2011).
51. Adam Casey, "The Durability of Client Regimes: Foreign Sponsorship and Military Loyalty, 1946–2010," *World Politics* 72, no. 3 (2020): 411–447, https://doi.org/10.1017/S0043887120000039.
52. Tancred Bradshaw, *Britain and Jordan: Imperial Strategy, King Abdullah I and the Zionist Movement* (IB Tauris, 2012), 67–101.
53. Ali Muhafazah, *Al-'alaqaat al-urduniyyah al-britaaniyyah: min ta'sis al-imarah hatta ilghaa' al-mu'aahadah (1921–1957)* [Jordanian-British Relations: From the Establishment of the Emirate until the Treaty Cancellation, 1921–1957] (Dar Al-Nahar Lil-Nashr, 1973), 209–267.
54. Irene Gendzier, *Notes from the Minefield: United States Intervention in Lebanon, 1945–1958* (Columbia University Press, 2006), 301.
55. Diplomatic histories of the US-Jordanian relationship make this clear. See, for instance, Miriam Joyce, *Anglo-American Support for Jordan: The Career of King Hussein* (Palgrave Macmillan, 2008), and Clea Lutz Hupp, *The United States and Jordan: Middle East Diplomacy during the Cold War* (IB Tauris, 2014).
56. Douglas Little, "A Puppet in Search of a Puppeteer? The United States, King Hussein, and Jordan, 1953–1970," *International History Review* 27, no. 3 (1995): 540–543, https://doi.org/10.1080/07075332.1995.9640719.
57. "Quick Condemnation of Jordan Attacks," *CNN*, November 10, 2005, https://www.cnn.com/2005/WORLD/meast/11/09/jordan.blasts.worldreax/.
58. Riedel, *Jordan and America*, 142–185.
59. William Arkin, "The Great Wall of Jordan: How the US Wants to Keep the Islamic State Out," *Vice News*, February 24, 2016, https://www.vice.com/en/article/the-great-wall-of-jordan-how-the-us-wants-to-keep-the-islamic-state-out/.
60. See, for instance, Khalil Harb, "From the 'Battle of Dignity' to the Shield of Shame: How Jordan Has Fallen," *The Cradle*, April 16, 2024, https://thecradle.co/articles/from-the-battle-of-dignity-to-the-shield-of-shame-how-jordan-has-fallen.
61. Benjamin Schuetze, *Promoting Democracy, Reinforcing Authoritarianism: US and European Policy in Jordan* (Cambridge University Press, 2019).
62. Dima Toukan, "Challenge of Localization under Restrictive Government Rule," *Global Studies Quarterly* 5, no. 1 (2025), https://doi.org/10.1093/isagsq/ksaf012.
63. Sean Yom and Mohammad al-Momani, "The International Dimensions of Authoritarian Regime Stability: Jordan in the Post–Cold War Era," *Arab Studies Quarterly* 30, no. 1 (2008): 39–60.
64. Anne Mariel Zimmerman, *US Assistance, Development, and Hierarchy in the Middle East: Aid for Allies* (Palgrave Macmillan, 2017), 125–162.

65. This pales in comparison to Israel, which historically is the most generously funded American client state. From 1948 through 2024, Israel received over $160 billion in US military and economic assistance.
66. Mohammad Ghazal, "No Strings Attached to $10.15b US Aid Package to Jordan," *Jordan Times*, October 5, 2022.
67. Imad El-Anis, *Jordan and the United States: The Political Economy of Trade and Economic Reform in the Middle East* (IB Tauris, 2011), 86–102.
68. The CIA's early operations in Jordan are outlined by the late Jack O'Connell, the American adviser and lawyer to King Hussein. See Jack O'Connell and Vernon Loeb, *King's Counsel: A Memoir of War, Espionage, and Diplomacy in the Middle East* (WW Norton, 2010), 130–141.
69. Ken Silverstein, "US, Jordan Forge Closer Ties in Covert War on Terrorism," *Los Angeles Times*, November 11, 2005.
70. Sean Yom, "US Security Assistance in Jordan: Militarized Politics and Elusive Metrics," in *Security Assistance in the Middle East: Challenges and the Need for Change*, eds. Robert Springborg and Hicham Alaoui (Lynne Rienner, 2023), 211–230.
71. Pete W. Moore, "Washington's Bahrain in the Levant," *Middle East Report Online*, May 23, 2012, https://merip.org/2012/05/washingtons-bahrain-in-the-levant/.

Chapter 9

1. Wahib al-Sha'ir, *Al-urdun . . . illa 'ayna? Huwiyyah al-wataniyyah wal-istihqaaqaat al-mustaqbaliyyah* [Jordan . . . To Where? National Identity and Future Entitlements] (Center for Arab Unity Studies, 2004).

INDEX

For the benefit of digital users, indexed terms that span two pages (e.g., 52–53) may, on occasion, appear on only one of those pages.

Page numbers followed by *f* and *t* indicate figures and tables, respectively.

S